T0312237

Lives of the Laureates

Lives of the Laureates

Thirty-Two Nobel Economists

seventh edition

Edited by Roger W. Spencer and David A. Macpherson

The MIT Press
Cambridge, Massachusetts
London, England

This book was set in Sabon by Toppan Best-set Premedia Limited.

Library of Congress Cataloging-in-Publication Data

Names: Spencer, Roger W., editor. | Macpherson, David A., 1960- editor.
Title: Lives of the laureates : thirty-two Nobel economists / edited by Roger W. Spencer and David A. Macpherson.
Description: Seventh edition. | Cambridge, Massachusetts : The MIT Press, [2020] | Includes bibliographical references.
Identifiers: LCCN 2019027552 | ISBN 9780262043779 (hardcover) | ISBN 9780262551946 (paperback)
Subjects: LCSH: Economists--Biography. | Nobel Prize winners--Biography. | Nobel Prizes.
Classification: LCC HB76 .L58 2020 | DDC 330.092/2--dc23
LC record available at https://lccn.loc.gov/2019027552

Contents

Introduction to the Seventh Edition

This book consists of autobiographical accounts of the careers of thirty-two people who have three qualities in common. First, they are all economists. Second, each of them has been awarded the Alfred Nobel Memorial Prize in Economic Science. Third, each traveled to San Antonio, Texas, to deliver his story in person at Trinity University.

The Nobel Prize in Economics was not created by Alfred Nobel himself. In 1901 his will established prizes in physics, chemistry, medicine or physiology, literature, and peace. He wished to reward specific achievements rather than outstanding persons. In the case of the natural sciences, the awards were to be given for "discoveries," "inventions," and "improvements." In 1968 the Central Bank of Sweden, in connection with its tercentenary celebration, initiated a new award, the Central Bank of Sweden Prize in Economic Science in Memory of Alfred Nobel. This prize was to be granted in conformity with the standards that governed the awarding of the original Nobel Prizes. According to the rules established by the Central Bank of Sweden, the "prize shall be awarded annually to a person who has carried out a work in economic science of the eminent significance expressed in the will of Alfred Nobel."[1]

The idea for a series of autobiographical lectures by Nobel laureates in economics was that of William Breit, who spent a good part of his academic career studying, teaching, and writing about the lives and ideas of leading contemporary U.S. economists.[2] His abiding interest in the relationship between biography and the creative process led naturally to the thought of providing a forum in which outstanding economists would express in their own words, in any way that seemed congenial, a personal memoir under the general rubric "my evolution as an economist." At the very least, such a forum would preserve part of the rich record of accomplishment that helped to shape the direction and character of economic science in the post–World War II era. But the larger purpose was to provide important source material for a theory of scientific discovery.

Little is known about the process by which original ideas germinate and are eventually accepted by one's peers. To what extent is the substance of scientific work in social science a reflection of the lives of those who produced it? What is the role of influential teachers and colleagues? To what degree are the problems to which these thinkers addressed themselves a result of their own backgrounds, and of the economic and social problems of their times? What forces were most responsible for leading them to their insights? In short, what is it that enables an individual to discover something that seizes and holds the attention of a large segment of a scientific community? To help answer such questions was the major rationale behind the series.

But whom should we invite? It was clear that budgetary and time constraints would limit the number of invitations, and so the roster was restricted in the following ways: only economists who served on the faculties of U.S. universities at the time the Nobel Prize was awarded would be included, and the roster would represent as many different facets of economics in terms of types of contributions, specific areas, methods of analysis, and ideological differences as possible. In 1983, when the program was being planned, there were twelve Nobel Prize winners who met the first criterion, though one was too ill to travel. A difficult winnowing process in accordance with the second criterion narrowed the final list to eight. Only one invitee declined to participate.

The autobiographical lectures that made up the first edition of this volume were presented at Trinity University during the 1984–85 year. The success of the project encouraged then Trinity University president Ronald Calgaard to allow the series to continue.

During the three years immediately following the end of the original series, a trio of Americans was honored with the Alfred Nobel Memorial Prize in Economic Science: Franco Modigliani of MIT in 1985, James M. Buchanan of George Mason University in 1986, and Robert M. Solow of MIT in 1987. Each of them accepted the request to present a lecture in which he would chart the route that had led him to the highest accolade a scholar can receive. These lectures were included in the second edition of *Lives of the Laureates,* published in 1990.

As more Nobel Prize winners accepted the invitation to speak at Trinity, a third edition was published in 1995, a fourth in 2004, a fifth in 2009, and a sixth in 2014. The seventh edition of *Lives of the Laureates* includes six new lectures, by Roger B. Myerson (co-recipient in 2007), Thomas J. Sargent (co-recipient in 2011), Amartya Sen (1998), A.

Michael Spence (co-recipient in 2001), Christopher A. Sims (co-recipient in 2011), and Alvin E. Roth (co-recipient in 2012).

To make room in a single volume for all participating Nobelists, the publisher developed a new concept that involved additional editing of most earlier contributions to permit the return of four lectures that had been dropped and the incorporation of six new chapters. The editing was accomplished with a view toward keeping the essential messages of the earlier Nobelists while maintaining their singular, unique voice. For many of the laureates, the assignment has been a difficult one. There is an understandable reluctance to give a public talk about one's own intellectual contributions. As one of the invitees put it, "I do not know that I could keep it between the Scylla of false modesty and the Charybdis of boastfulness, and I am afraid I would find the whole business rather stressful." Moreover, most of their work in its professional formulation was technical in nature, difficult to understand by those not trained as economists. Yet each was being asked to make his contribution accessible to a lay audience at a public lecture open to the whole community. This provided greater difficulties for some than for others. Paul A. Samuelson's and Kenneth J. Arrow's scientific contributions are largely in the domain of mathematical economics. Lawrence R. Klein, among others, made heavy use of statistical techniques and econometrics. All the Nobel economists express themselves in the technical vocabulary of their discipline.

Yet in each instance, as the reader of these pages will discover, the speaker managed to convey the nature and significance of his contributions. (The essays in this book are in the order in which they were presented in the Trinity lecture series.) It is hard to imagine a less painful way of grasping the essentials of Arrow's impossibility theorem than hearing it (or reading about it) in his own words. And is there anywhere a more clearly presented conception of what goes into econometric model building than is to be found in Klein's essay? George J. Stigler's masterful explanation of his information theory is lucid and accessible to almost everyone with an interest in this fruitful innovation. The recent Nobel laureates follow in this trend. Indeed, each participant achieved the goal of clarity without sacrificing inherently difficult content.

The visit of each of the Nobel laureates was an unqualified success. The audiences were large and appreciative. Some of the laureates traveled considerable distances to attend. Each economist met with students and faculty informally. At small receptions, at restaurants, over coffee, and at dinners in private homes, students and faculty were able to talk with some of the most highly regarded economists of the twentieth and twenty-first centuries. Notwithstanding their formidable reputations as scholars and, in some cases, strong personalities, their modesty impressed all who came into contact with them. An important side benefit of the lecture series was the lesson that some of the most illustrious figures of modern economics are human after all.

Looking back over these lectures, one is struck by the many currents in the stream of modern economics. The reader will find that paths cross in unexpected ways, that disparate thinkers were often influenced by the same teachers, and that serendipity, in addition to perseverance and hard work, plays a role in the successful creation of scientific knowledge. Equally significant, these autobiographical essays reveal psychological truths—perhaps hidden from the subjects themselves—that an especially perceptive reader may discern. Taken as a whole, they provide a comprehensive picture of the diversity, richness, and profundity that are the hallmarks of contemporary economic thought.

Apart from an afterword by the editors, this edition of *Lives of the Laureates* ends with Alvin Roth's lecture, delivered in March 2019. The Trinity University series, however, is an ongoing enterprise. Readers who would like to follow subsequent presentations in the series can visit our website at http://www.trinity.edu/nobel. The site offers a chronology of lectures in the series, plus selected quotations from each laureate's presentation at Trinity University.

Notes

1. For an authoritative discussion of the history, purpose, and qualifications for the Nobel Prize in Economics by one of the members of the Nobel Prize Committee, see Assar Lindbeck, "The Prize in Economics Science in Memory of Alfred Nobel," *Journal of Economic Literature* 23 (March 1985): 37–56.

2. See William Breit, "Biography and the Making of Economic Worlds," *Southern Economic Journal* 53 (April 1987): 823–833.

Acknowledgments

There are many people who have contributed to this series over the years. The first is Bill Breit, who not only conceived of the Nobel series at Trinity but also brought in the MIT Press to publish the book he titled *Lives of the Laureates*. Ronald Calgaard, president of Trinity University at the time, saw merit in the project and helped foster its development. Subsequent Trinity University presidents John Brazil, Dennis Ahlburg, and Danny Anderson have generously continued to support the Nobel series endeavor. The precedent initiated by President Calgaard in hosting a dinner at his campus home prior to each lecture has been graciously continued by his successors. The dinner is a perfect prologue to each Nobel economist's public lecture.

For this edition, as for the previous ones, we owe much to colleagues in the Department of Economics at Trinity University for their enthusiasm and cooperation. Special mention should be made of former colleague Barry T. Hirsch, co-editor of the fourth and fifth editions of this title. It is a pleasure to acknowledge a debt to our assistants, Rande Spector, Blanca Kirkman, Maria Alvarado, and especially Irma Escalante, for their skillful management of the many tasks and arrangements that accompany such an enterprise. We acknowledge the important contribution of Emily Taber at the MIT Press, who was the first to advance the potential of a special edit to permit the inclusion of nearly all speakers in the Trinity series. Other MIT Press staff members important to the completion of this seventh edition include Deborah Cantor-Adams, Laura Keeler, and Marjorie Pannell.

—Roger W. Spencer
—David A. Macpherson

W. Arthur Lewis

I had never meant to be an economist. My father had wanted me to be a lawyer, but as he died when I was seven he had no vote at the appropriate time. That came when I was awarded the St. Lucia government scholarship in 1932, tenable at any British university. I did not want to be a doctor either, nor a teacher. That put me into a hole, since law, medicine, preaching, and teaching were the only professions open to young blacks in my day. I wanted to be an engineer, but neither the colonial government nor the sugar plantations would hire a black engineer. What to do? My mother, without whom I could not have gone so far, would support whatever I might choose. As I leafed through the University of London prospectus, my eye was caught by something called the Bachelor of Commerce degree, which offered accounting, statistics, business law, business management, economics, a foreign language, and economic history. What was this economics? I had never heard of it before, and nobody in St. Lucia knew what it was—though my sample was small and unrepresentative. No matter. The rest of the degree was very practical and would give me a basis for a job in business or some kind of administrative work. So I settled for this and went off to London for the B.Com. degree in 1933, at the age of eighteen.

At the London School of Economics it turned out that I was good at economics, so when I graduated with a first in 1937 I was given an LSE scholarship to do a Ph.D. in economics. Next year I was appointed for one year as a teaching assistant and the year after that I became an assistant lecturer. Years of wondering how I would ever earn a living, and of smiling confidently when friends and relatives pushed the question at me, could now be forgotten. I was going to be an economist.

Though ignorant of economics, I knew what was meant by administration. I had left school in 1929 and had been a junior clerk in the government service for the intervening four years. There I had acquired the clerical skills—to type, make notes, write letters, and file—that helped me as an undergraduate. I became familiar as well with administrative and legal structures, knowledge that would also help me.

Fate had decided that I was to be an economist. What kind of economist I was to be was also settled: an applied economist. This did not mean just that I should apply economics to industrial or other structural problems. It meant that I would approach a problem from its institutional background, recognizing that the solution was as likely to be in the institutional setting as in the economic analysis.

What part of applied economics I would work in was also settled for me, since my assistant lectureship was in the commerce department, under Professor Sir Arnold Plant. He was my mentor, and without his word at crucial points I would have received neither the scholarship nor the assistant lectureship. (This was the school's first black appointment, and there was a little resistance.) He and I had intellectual difficulties, since he was a laissez-faire economist and I was not; but this did not stand in the way of our relationship.

Because Plant was a specialist in the organization of British industry, he put me to lecture in this field and suggested a Ph.D. thesis topic in the field; and so I became an "expert" on British industrial organization. I liked the subject, so it was no hardship to me.

I worked in industrial organization from 1937, when I was given a scholarship for the purpose, until 1948, when I went to Manchester and later published *Overhead Costs,* which was essentially an updated version of my Ph.D. thesis.

I dropped industrial economics in 1945 to teach another subject not of my own choosing, namely, a survey of the world economy between the two wars. This came about in the following way. The acting chairman of the economics department in 1945 was Friedrich Hayek. One day he said to me, "We fill up our students with trade cycle theory and explanations of the Great Depression, but the entering class was born in 1927, cannot remember the Depression, and has no idea what we are talking about. Why don't you give a course of lectures on what happened between the wars?" "The answer to your question," I said, "is very easy. It is that I myself have no idea what happened between the wars." "Well," said Hayek, "the best way to learn a subject is to teach it." So that was how I came some four years later to publish a small book entitled *Economic Survey 1919–1939*, summarizing what we then thought we knew about the world economy between 1919 and 1939.

My approach was to accept that industrial recessions had occurred from time to time over the preceding century with intervals of four to ten years, and that the problem was not why there was a recession in 1929, but why, having started, it had become so deep. What distinguished the outbreak of this particular sequence? One cannot give an account of the Great Depression in two paragraphs, but one can list the decisive elements. These are seven.

1. In the U.S. economy, prosperity coincided with a railway-construction-immigration-housing cycle. Congress having restricted immigration from 1924, the construction boom of the second half of the 1920s was weak, and the abnormal weakness of the first half of the thirties weakened the whole economy.
2. Both domestic and international agricultural prices had been falling since the mid-1920s, capacity having grown faster than demand. Rural consumption was low, and in the United States an abnormal number of rural banks failed.
3. Monetary and fiscal authorities believed that the best way to revive production was to reduce the flow of income and acted accordingly. This action presumably worsened the depression.
4. The industrial slump was as bad in Germany as in the United States. The weakness of the one compounded the weakness of the other.
5. Capitalists everywhere lost confidence and reduced their investment flows. This spiraled. Less investment meant less production, less income, more excess capacity, less investment, and so on.
6. The New York Stock Exchange, which had talked itself into overconfidence in the late twenties, now talked itself down and reflected all the unpleasantness occurring elsewhere.

7. One country after another left the gold standard, imposed exchange controls, and raised tariff levels. International trade fell by 30 percent in volume.

To the question of whether the Great Depression was unique, the answer was yes and no. No: the United States had a major recession about once every twenty years. Yes: the Great Depression of 1929 was much greater than any of its predecessors.

Let me come back to autobiography. My research career falls into three parts. First I studied industrial structure. Second I tackled the history of the world economy, from the middle of the nineteenth century. And third I worked on problems of economic development. I have told you about the first two and now come to economic development.

My interest in the subject was an offshoot of my anti-imperialism. I can remember my father taking me to a meeting of the local Marcus Garvey association when I was seven years old. So it is not surprising that the first thing I ever published was a Fabian Society pamphlet, called *Labour in the West Indies,* which gave an account of the emergence of the trade union movement in the 1920s and '30s and, more especially, of the violent confrontations between the unions and the government in the 1930s. This was not a propaganda pamphlet. It was based on newspaper research and on conversations with some of the union leaders.

In London, meeting fellow anti-imperialists from all over the world, I launched upon a systematic study of the British colonial empire and its practices—color bars, prohibiting Africans from growing coffee in Kenya so that they were forced into the labor market to work for cash to pay their taxes, and all the rest.

In 1946 LSE set up a special course for social workers from the colonies, who were brought over for a year, and I was asked to teach them elementary economics. I made it a course on economic policy. I remember stopping a student who was in the middle of a passionate attack on the British governor of his country for some particular policy and saying to him, "But what would you do if you were the minister? Within ten years your country will be independent, and you will be a minister or head of a department. Reciting the evils of the British government will not help you. You will need a positive program of your own. The year you spend at LSE is your opportunity to learn how to face up to difficult problems." My dating was a little premature; it took seventeen years instead of ten for his country to become independent—but otherwise I was right, even to the point of his becoming a department head.

I give you this background because it explains something of the emphasis of my writings. I have always taken it for granted that what matters most to growth is to make the best use of one's own resources, and that the exterior events are secondary. An expert on development should be able to give the minister practical advice. I do not adhere to this austerely. I am interested in historical processes and occasionally excite myself with the philosophy of the international economic order, but what I think about and write about most is domestic policy.

I began to teach development economics systematically when I went to Manchester in 1948 as a full professor. The emphasis was heavily on policy. One must therefore have a good idea of the sociological background and also of the political linkages. There are economists who put too much emphasis on prices, forgetting that it may be easier to solve a problem by changing the institutions wherein it is embedded than by changing prices. There are other, structural economists, who avoid the use of prices as a policy instrument because of adverse effects on the distribution and volatility of income. I am usually somewhere in between. One purpose of the book that I published in 1955, *The Theory of Economic Growth,* was to give shape to the discussion and to ensure that anyone interested in the economics of a problem would find it deployed with all its social ramifications.

My chief contribution to the subject was the two-sector model, advanced the year before. I arrived at this through looking at the distribution of income over a long period. I had read in the works of John and Barbara Hammond that the Industrial Revolution had not raised urban wages. If this was so, it would explain why the share of profits in the national income would rise, contrary to the expectation of the neoclassical economists that it would be constant. This constancy of real wages I felt to be bound up with another mystery. A number of developing countries had been developing for a long time: Ceylon, for example, for a hundred years. Why was the standard of living of the masses still so low? One could understand this for much-exploited South Africa, but how for fairly enlightened Ceylon?

The answer to both questions came by breaking an intellectual constraint. In all the general equilibrium models taught to me the elasticity of supply of labor was zero, so any increase in investment would increase the demand for labor and raises wages. Instead, make the elasticity of supply of labor infinite, and my problems are solved. In this model, growth raises profits because all the benefits of advancing technology accrue to employers and to a small class of well-paid workers that emerges in an urban sea of a low-wage proletariat. In the commodities market an unlimited supply of tropical produce also gives the benefit of advancing technology to the industrial buyers, by the process already described.

This model attracted the attention of economists all over the world because it applied in so many situations. One had to be careful that it did apply to the particular situation and use it only if it did. It was particularly useful in handling the problem of migration, which rose to significance after the war in most countries of the world, developed or developing, as people moved in vast numbers between the country and the town and from poor to rich countries. It is, for example, the way to approach the effects of mass migration of Mexicans to the United States or Turks to Germany. Add the population explosion, the element of technological unemployment, and the movement of women out of the household into the marketplace, and developing countries find themselves with a supply of urban labor too large for full employment. The wage level of unskilled workers then has upper and lower bounds that function much like an infinite elasticity of supply. Needless to say, absolute infinity is neither needed nor intended. The impact of the model is now greatly reduced. Undergraduates are no longer given models in which the elasticity of supply of labor is always zero, so the possibility that it may sometimes be nearly infinite is no big thing. Actually, several books and articles were written about it over the next few years, but the excitement has died down.

Development economists can be divided into two categories: the gloomy and the optimistic. The gloomy subgroups do not necessarily agree with each other. Some hold that participation in foreign trade weakens the developing economy by destroying its handicraft industries or by sponsoring the demand for foreign goods. Others are concerned about multinational corporations. Still others believe that the poorest economies cannot get off the ground without financial help, which will not flow in adequate amounts. I have always been in the optimistic category, at first because I took it for granted that anything the Europeans could do we could do, but with the passage of time also because the speed at which developing countries were moving in the 1950s, '60s, and '70s left no room for doubt that most of these economies, though not all, have what it takes.

I make the point to remind you, if reminder be necessary, that the study of economic growth is still in its infancy. Countries rise up and fall, and we are not in a position to predict which ones will do best or worst over the next twenty years. This is equally true of developed and developing countries. Economics is good at explaining what has happened over the past twenty years, but when we turn to predicting the future it tends to be an essay in ideology.

Between 1957 and 1973 I spent nine years out of the library and in an administrative office: at the United Nations in New York; as economic adviser to the prime minister of Ghana, Dr. Nkrumah; as head of the University of the West Indies; and as president of the Caribbean Development Bank. I learned very little of relevance to the theory of economic development (in contrast with earlier visits to India and to Ghana), but I did learn a lot about administration. I have published ten books and about eighty other pieces. I guess that if I had remained in the university I would have written one more book and a dozen more articles. Set this against what I was doing, which was to build up high-quality institutions, whose high standards would yield fruit of their own and also be an inspiration to others.

Looking back over my life, it has been a queer mixture. I have lived through a period of transition and therefore know what it is like at both ends, even though the transition is not yet complete. I have been subjected to all the usual disabilities—refusal of accommodations, denial of jobs for which I had been recommended, generalized discourtesy, and the rest of it. All the same, some doors that were supposed to be closed opened as I approached them. I have got used to being the first black to do this or that, which gets to be more difficult as the transition opens up new opportunities. Having to be a role model is a bit of a strain, but I try to remember that others are coming after me, and that whether the door will be shut in their faces as they approach will depend to some small extent on how I conduct myself. As I said at the beginning, I had never intended to be an economist. My mother taught us to make the best of what we have, and that is what I have tried to do.

W. Arthur Lewis

Awarded Nobel Prize in 1979. Lecture presented September 27, 1984.

Dates of Birth and Death

January 23, 1915; June 15, 1991

Academic Degrees

B.Com. University of London, 1937
Ph.D. University of London, 1940

Academic Affiliations

Lecturer, University of London, 1938–48
Stanley Jevons Professor of Political Economy, University of Manchester, 1948–58
Vice Chancellor, University of West Indies, 1959–63
James Madison Professor of Political Economy, Princeton University, 1963–91

Selected Books

Overhead Costs, 1949
Principles of Economic Planning, 1949, 1969
The Theory of Economic Growth, 1955
Some Aspects of Economic Development, 1969
The Evolution of the International Economic Order, 1978

Lawrence R. Klein

In studying the development of great economists and trying to understand why economic thinking takes particular directions, it has always seemed fruitful to me to look at the interaction, often one-way, between the prevailing situation of the economy and developing tendencies in economic thought. This has been most noticeable in macroeconomics but is also the case in the whole of economics. A primary example, which is closely tied up with my own development, is the emergence of Keynesian economics to deal with the problems of the 1920s and '30s, especially the Great Depression. Keynes was intensely interested in the problems of the day and tried to develop an economic theory that would deal with these problems. It was long in coming. His career got a large impetus from the Treaty of Versailles, then the problems of the gold standard in England, inflation after World War I, unemployment, and the world collapse after 1929.

For our university catalog, all professors are being asked to write a sentence or three about why they entered their respective fields. I entered economics because, as a youth during the Depression, I wanted intensely to have some understanding of what was going on around me. It was psychologically difficult to grow up during the Depression. It was easy to become discouraged about economic life and did not give one, at eighteen or twenty years, the feeling that there were boundless opportunities just waiting for exploitation. The young people of the past two or three decades have had nuclear war to worry about, but they have also had feelings of abundant opportunities if peace could be preserved.

But I was blessed with something else, that just happened. I was carrying around in my head the feeling that mathematics could be used in the analysis of economic problems. I spent most of my undergraduate time in either mathematics or economics classes. I was not a creative mathematician or any kind of a match for *wunderkinder*; I saw that readily enough in math competitions. But I was fascinated by university-level mathematics and had some hunches about applications of mathematics to economics, say, to the expression for demand curves and the estimation of revenues. It was a great surprise for me to go into the U.C. Berkeley library and find journals for a whole budding subject, carried out at an advanced level, handling problems that were far more complicated than anything that I had thought about.

My undergraduate advisers gave me no encouragement to study mathematics along with economics; I went my own way and took the best of Berkeley in the early 1940s—first-class departments in economics, mathematics, and mathematical statistics. Of course, one can go back to high school or, in my case, junior college and find roots; there are some indeed, but my professional beginnings were in the Berkeley that existed just before World War II and the scholarship I won to MIT. There I met the dazzling *wunderkind* Paul Samuelson. When I was browsing in the Berkeley library and came across early issues of *Econometrica*, Samuelson's contributions caught my eye. When I got an opportunity to go to MIT, it was the possibility of working with Samuelson that confirmed all my choices. I was attached to him as a graduate assistant from the outset, and I tried to maximize my contact with him, picking up insights that he scattered on every encounter.

Working with Samuelson, who was at the forefront of interpreting Keynesian theory for teaching and policy application, I was put immediately in the midst of two challenging contests—one to gain acceptance for a way of thinking about macroeconomics and another to gain acceptance for a methodology in economics, namely, the mathematical method. Later, both challenges were to be overcome, but for ten or twenty years opposition was fierce.

Once Samuelson's *Economics* became a widely used text in first courses in the subject, Keynesian economics was firmly embedded. There was no turning back from that achievement. The successive student generations turned more toward the mathematical approach in graduate school, and they taught or did research in this vein. That eventually established the mathematical method, first in the United States, then in Europe, Japan, India, and other centers. Much of the foundation was built in Europe, and many of the American masters at mathematical economics were immigrants, but Samuelson, Friedman, and others gave it a native-born American flavor, and the approach truly caught on in this country.

The MIT years were, for me, a start in the professional field of economics, and my first position after leaving graduate school was with the Cowles Commission at the University of Chicago. Being just twenty-four years old when I started work there, I was almost in the position of having another chance at graduate school. As in many scientific fields of study, I was essentially a postdoctoral fellow.

A truly exceptional group of people was assembled in Chicago during the late 1940s. I doubt that such a group could ever be put together again in economics. From our closely knit group, four Nobel laureates have emerged, and two others came from the next bunching of Cowles researchers—partly at Chicago and partly at Yale. We worked as a team and focused on a single problem—to put together an econometric model of the American economy (a second attempt after Tinbergen's of the 1930s)—using the best of statistical theory, economic theory, and available data. After about four or five years of intensive research built up around this theme, the team dispersed to new openings in academic life. The effort was kept alive through my own research, and many of the brilliant people of our group went on to do their work in quite different branches of economics—Koopmans in activity analysis, Arrow in general equilibrium theory, Simon in decision analysis, Anderson in statistics, Marschak in the theory of organizations, and so on.

In our attempts to bring together econometric methods and Keynesian analysis of the macroeconomy we felt quite confident. In the field of postwar planning we imagined that we had the well-being of the economy right in the palms of our hands. Over the coming decade we accomplished much more by way of model building and using than we ever thought possible in our wildest dreams of postwar America, but it was never good enough. We built systems that evolved from our teamwork at the Cowles Commission, and they have become part of the standard tool kit of economists. They play a very big role, but they do not dominate the policy process. They take a leadership role in forecasting, but they are not the sole survivors in the forecasting derby.

Scientists at Chicago were, secretively, carrying out more significant team research than we economists at the Cowles Commission. Because the director of the Cowles Commission was an old friend (from Europe of the two previous decades) of Leo Szilard, a leader among the scientists, we had a great deal of interaction. Szilard, one of the cleverest people of this century, dabbled in amateur economics. He constructed parlor games of the macroeconomy to demonstrate a scheme of monetary control that he thought would lead the world to a cycle-free existence. He taught us a lot about the strategy of intellectual research and the blending of politics and science. Many of us interacted with him and also with the amazing John von Neumann, who frequently visited Chicago on his way to Los Alamos. In those days, a trip across country involved changing trains in Chicago. Another visitor who had a profound influence on everyone at Cowles was Abraham Wald, the mathematical statistician from Columbia University.

The next phase of my career was to become more internationally minded. These days, some of us travel all over the world every month; European trips are almost routine. But when I left the Cowles Commission in 1947, I set out on an ocean voyage to Europe, after a summer's research activity in Ottawa putting together the first model of the Canadian economy. That project has survived many generations and gave birth to an active professional community in Canada that still functions on an expanded level.

Visits to centers of economic and econometric research throughout Europe were part of my education. I learned a great deal about the world, but was more attracted by the liveliness of the development of our subject in America. Seeing Europe dig out from the postwar rubble was a learning experience, and it opened many professional relationships that remain active. It certainly had a major impact on my own career development. Before the war Cambridge, England, and London were the centers of economic thinking that shaped the world. Traveling fellows gravitated there for study. America had begun to compete, but from 1946 onward the magnet was the United States. Students came from all over to do their work in America. This was true in many fields and has not changed appreciably in the last forty years.

In that seasoning year abroad I made contact with the true Keynesians, the Cambridge group who worked directly with Keynes. I never met Keynes himself, but I got good insight into the group's thinking from Kahn, Joan Robinson, and Sraffa. I also met Kaldor and Stone on that trip. The interesting thing to me was that my teacher, Paul Samuelson, had inferred all that there was to know about this group without ever having been there. People in Cambridge remarked about this to me.

I had come to Europe for the first time only months ahead of Paul Samuelson and met him on his first stop—Norway—where I was spending most of the year abroad, learning from Frisch. Samuelson had just published *Economics* and was enjoying an early enthusiastic acceptance. He toured Western Europe just as I was completing my year there.

A problem with the interpretation of the Keynesian system was the influence of wealth on savings. In the literature of macroeconomics this became known as the Pigou effect, although Pigou had written about it more in terms of liquid assets rather than total wealth. People had emerged from the war with large holdings of liquid assets (especially government savings bonds), so it was a popular and important subject to investigate.

I had returned from Europe to join the National Bureau of Economic Research under the leadership of Arthur Burns. There I worked on production function estimation, focusing on the railroad sector, but after one year I worked jointly on a project with the Survey Research Center of the University of Michigan and the National Bureau of Economic Research to use the Surveys of Consumer Finance to throw more light on saving behavior, especially with respect to the Pigou effect.

One line of economic research that emerged after World War II was the one I was following in econometrics, particularly macroeconometrics. But survey research flourished during the war, as a tool to help government plan civilian activity in a way that would aid the military effort. One of the primary groups, located in the Department of Agriculture during the war, set up academic ties and formed the Institute for Social Research at the University of Michigan, Ann Arbor. I felt comfortable working with this statistical team. Also the cross-disciplinary attitude intrigued me. I learned a great deal about the interfaces between economics on the one hand and psychology, sociology, and other disciplines on the other.

At the Survey Research Center I learned a great deal about household behavior and techniques for measuring it. The work was based on samples of human populations consisting of a few thousand cases for each study. This initiated me into the realm of large-scale data processing, done by punched cards and electromechanical machines. Electronic computers were in existence but were not yet being used for most economic or social problems.

After I came to Michigan, where I was teaching econometrics on a small scale but was mainly concerned with survey research, I received some money from the Ford Foundation, which suddenly had found it necessary for tax purposes to make large grants of money available to several universities. Few people in the economics department had any ideas about how to spend the sum that was to be allocated to them. I then established the Research Seminar in Quantitative Economics, assembled some research students, and went back to econometric model building—restarting the research begun at the Cowles Commission.

One of those research students was Arthur Goldberger. He and I put together a new model of the U.S. economy called the Klein–Goldberger model. It streamlined the models built at the Cowles Commission, used some of the survey findings, and set about forecasting the economy on a regular basis.

Colin Clark, the intrepid Australian statistical economist, set us up for a great success. In the pages of the influential *Manchester Guardian*, which came my way in the weekly world edition, he observed that the winding down of the Korean War would possibly cause a large-scale recession. He frightened people about the most fearsome economic event of our time—a 1929-style collapse as a result of a cumulative downward spiral.

I looked at our model results for forecasts for 1953–54 and concluded that it did not look like 1929 again. I wrote a paper with Arthur Goldberger for the *Guardian* and was delighted to find that they would publish it, in large display accompanied by an intriguing Low cartoon.

In a piecemeal fashion the statistical work on the Klein–Goldberger model made use of the computer for parts of the computations connected with model estimation. For solution of the model we set aside a day or two of laborious hand calculation with a desktop machine. A large-scale digital computer was installed at Michigan, and we started a project for automatic model solution—simulation, if you like—but it was not quite brought to fruition before I was to leave Ann Arbor.

In the McCarthy era I left Michigan for the peace and academic freedom of Oxford, where I joined the Institute of Statistics and worked on the British Savings Surveys, patterned after the Michigan Surveys. While at Oxford I went back to model building, this time for Great Britain. My friend of twenty-five subsequent years, Professor Sir James Ball, attended my lectures on econometrics at Oxford and worked with me on the Oxford model. Some progress was made in using the computer at Oxford for more of the numerical work, but again it was not for model solution.

In 1958 I returned to America and took up a professorship at Pennsylvania, where I admired the position of the president, provost, and deans on the serious matter of academic freedom. From the beginning of my tenure at Pennsylvania and the Wharton School, I set out again to build a model of the American economy. This time I turned to quarterly data and, encouraged by my survey experience in England and Michigan, I used some *expectations* magnitudes. I started the first generation of a series of Wharton models.

The Wharton models shifted to a quarterly time frame, to emphasize interest in short-run business cycle movements, used more data on survey anticipations, and stated all the accounting identities in current prices. This last change corrected a defect in the specification of the Klein–Goldberger model. The first version of this new model was used for forecasting the American economy, and projections were sent round to economist members of the Kennedy administration, who voiced disbelief in the optimistic forecasts—recovery from the 1960–61 recession. Within a few years I was to turn my attention to a new approach, and I abandoned further work on this first version, but I turned over complete files, consisting of data listings and equations, together with a trained assistant to the Department of Commerce. They had asked me for help in starting a model-building project there. This evolved, with the help of other Pennsylvania Ph.D. products, into what is now the OBE model (Office of Business Economics, Department of Commerce). This model has taken on a life of its own and is a distinguished member of the American family of models, but its roots are the first Wharton model.

At this stage I went in two research directions, each of which had a fundamental impact on my own professional development. The Committee on Economic Stability of the Social Science Research Council planned, in 1959, the creation of a new, enlarged, short-run forecasting model. I was one of the principal investigators of that project and played a role in designing a cooperative approach to model building, namely, assignment of a specialist to each sector of the economy. I undertook, together with other members of the steering committee, to fashion it into a consistent whole. In general, we had a model that was composed of the best practice in each department, and it functioned as a whole. But the real advances that emerged from this joint effort were (1) a detailed monetary sector that drew on Federal Reserve talent and was the forerunner of important monetary sectors in many subsequent models, thus repairing a defect of the Klein–Goldberger model; (2) an explicit input-output sector of inter-industry flows that was tied consistently to the traditional macro models of final demand and income determination; (3) the preparation of a *data-bank* for the systematic accounting of all the data used in the system;

and (4) automation of the computing for the project, with a remarkable breakthrough in the ability to solve large systems of nonlinear dynamic equations. Other features of the research on this joint project have been outstanding and are documented in three project volumes, especially the final one.[1]

After the Social Science Research Council started the cooperative project, it was transferred to the Brookings Institution and became known as the Brookings model. In its cooperative setup, we consulted many participants on its progress, development, and use. This was particularly striking in the case of computation. We struggled hard with the computer aspects among a group at the University of Pennsylvania (helped a great deal by our innovative young Ph.D. candidates, who prepared many of the first-generation computer programs for econometrics), a group at Brookings, and a group at MIT. I devised a clumsy algorithm at Pennsylvania; a suggestion by E. Kuh at MIT to G. Fromm at Brookings provided the essential link. When they communicated their findings about Gauss iteration methods, we tested them in Philadelphia and immediately switched to what has become a worldwide standard for solving large dynamic systems in economics. From the early days of computer application at Michigan, model simulation had been an obstacle to efficient model application, but once we saw the key principle, we were able to harness the computer for generations to come.

The SSRC–Brookings model was but one line of development, away from the first Wharton model. The second was to develop an entirely new model for a different kind of use—commercial forecasting. I secured a small sum from the Rockefeller Foundation for the construction of the first Wharton model. We then established a research unit at the Wharton School for general quantitative studies in economics, financed by the Ford Foundation and National Science Foundation. But I could see that these sources of support were temporary and would run out during the mid-1960s.

Meanwhile, several major corporations had independently approached me for help in their efforts at econometric model building to assist their economic research departments. I accordingly proposed to five core companies that we build one model for them at the Wharton School and provide forecasts in exchange for support of our research program in econometrics.

Michael Evans joined the Pennsylvania faculty in 1963 and participated in our new forecasting venture with the private sector. He brought with him a separate model that he had developed in his dissertation research at Brown University. At first we prepared two forecasts, one from his model and one from the original Wharton model. After a short period a combined model was built, fused from the two, and this was the first to be published in a series of Wharton volumes.

The Wharton Econometric Forecasting Unit thrived. From five supporting participants in 1963 it expanded into a separate nonprofit corporation in 1969 (wholly owned by the University of Pennsylvania). It was sold in 1980 to a publishing corporation and was acquired by a French computer company in 1983. Both Data Resources, Inc., and Chase Econometrics took up commercial forecasting after 1969, and an entire new industry was born. It now has many competing firms and does business in the hundreds of millions of dollars.

With the growth of new centers of activity with models and support systems, it was natural to phase out the old Brookings model project. It had served its purpose and was superseded by the expanded commercial modeling systems and some fresh academic ventures.

During the 1960s the computer was finally harnessed for the needs of econometrics; it had first been used for scientific, engineering, and large-scale data processing (such as censuses). During this decade all those complicated calculations that we had contemplated during the development years of econometrics at the Cowles Commission became possible. I spent a great deal of time with student collaborators and IBM researchers working on nonlinear problems associated with maximum likelihood and other methods of statistical estimation, but we also perfected the simulation techniques that grew out of Brookings model research activities. We pioneered two developments that took econometric methods one step further: the presentation of results in standard national accounting form that were readily understood by users of econometric analysis and the use of time sharing. Data banking and perfection of time-sharing were carried much further on a "user-friendly" basis for Data Resources, but the Wharton team had time-sharing facilities before DRI was founded. Computer developments were only started in the 1960s. They flowered in the next decade and became available to a large army of researchers and students throughout the world.

In addition to the standard uses of the computer for data management, statistical inference, applications (mainly simulation), and presentation of results in easy-to-read tables and graphs, many deep research techniques were developed, starting as early as the late 1950s. These were based on stochastic simulations, which involved the disturbance of dynamic model solution by properly drawn random errors. This research was pioneered by Irma Adelman in studying dynamic properties of the Klein–Goldberger model and by Harvey Wagner in constructing Monte Carlo experiments to test statistical techniques in econometrics.[2]

The Wharton team did not use these methods first, but we used them to good advantage to learn a great deal about the cyclical and inference properties of our family of models. Some large-scale stochastic simulations of the Brookings model had already advanced the use of computer-based experimental techniques, and we drew on this fund of information. In this extended research effort, we learned to understand the various response characteristics of large-scale models—multipliers, sensitivities to parameter shift, and long-term trends of the system. The total computer effort of mechanizing the operation of large-scale models meant that the Wharton team was able to respond quickly and informatively to such major events as President Nixon's new economic policy, the oil embargo, and the fall of the shah's government in Iran.

During my long stay at Pennsylvania, several related efforts were conceived and executed in addition to the build-up of the Wharton models and their various applications to forecasting and macroeconomic analysis. Soon after I arrived, I became involved in a venture with two colleagues in Japan, Professors Michio Morishima and Shinichi Ichimura, both of whom I had known in either England or the United States. We collaborated in the founding of a new scholarly journal, the *International Economic Review*. There were two principal objectives: to foster the development of modern (Anglo-American) economics in Japan and to take the burden off *Econometrica*, which had a large backlog of unpublished articles. In looking back at that venture, I would say that it made a contribution to the development of modern economics in Japan, although that might have happened anyway. We probably helped the transformation. We probably did not relieve the pressure on *Econometrica*, except temporarily, and we joined many other new journals in a virtual explosion of article preparation and the launch of new periodicals. At any rate, the *International Economic Review* still stands as a collegial collaboration between Osaka University and the University of Pennsylvania of almost twenty-five years' duration, and is now self-sustaining. In the founding years, inexpensive Japanese printing, beautiful rice paper, and support from the Kansai Economic Federation made publication of the review possible. Those features are gone, but the review has a healthy existence. The establishment of the review and other relationships took me to Japan in 1960 and on many subsequent occasions. In this connection, I prepared a model of the Japanese economy with Yoichi Shinkai and participated in a model project at Osaka University. Over the years, many Japanese models have rendered these efforts obsolete, but the research on Japan, together with the previous econometric research on the United Kingdom, directed my interest toward international model building.

In 1966 researchers at DuPont Company in Wilmington asked me to supply three models of developing countries where the company was involved in direct investment. Accordingly, I assembled a research team among the students of the economic research unit of Pennsylvania's economics department and prepared models for Argentina, Brazil, and Mexico. The company, as agreed, made their proprietary use of these models, but the system, complete with databases and equations, were, as agreed in advance, in the public domain. The research scholar for Mexico, Abel Beltrán del Rio, went with me to Monterrey in the summer of 1969. There we obtained a commitment from private companies for research support for elaboration and replicated use of the Mexican model in forecasting, policy, and scenario analysis of the economy. Within Wharton Econometrics we formed DIEMEX (Department de Investigaciónes Econométricos de México). From a base of a few private-sector supporters in Monterrey and Mexico City in 1969 this has evolved into a self-sustaining system with some 150 supporters—U.S. companies, Mexican government agencies, international organizations, and others. What interests me most in this success is that the same technologies for model preparation, computer use, presentation of model results, and contributions to decision-making in the private and public sectors could be fully transferred from our base in Philadelphia to a developing country. This is a prize case, but similar efforts have worked in many other parts of the world as well.

Starting with Latin America, I was able to foster model-building efforts in many developing countries. There are many models in the Far East, some in Africa, and some in the Middle East. Data deficiency has always been a problem, but that is gradually being overcome, and now practically the entire developing world is being modeled. Some of our best students had gone to various UN groups to work on problems of economic development among the emerging countries. I took on a consulting agreement in the mid-1960s with a group in UNCTAD to help them build models of LDCs in order to estimate capital needs for growth.

Parallel with model building for developing countries, a related effort directed at socialist or centrally planned economies was also initiated. The developing country models were deliberately structured to reveal some of the unique characteristics of these areas. They were not simply copies of models in the style of the neoclassical Keynesian synthesis that were being built for each of the industrial democracies (OECD countries); they had unique supply-side features, specialized foreign trade character-istics, distributional aspects, and demographic aspects plainly displayed. I had long been fascinated by the challenging problem of modeling the centrally planned economy, with its controlled markets and plan targets. In the summer of 1970, on the occasion of a lecture in Vienna at the Insti-tute for Advanced Studies, I discussed these problems with economists in Bratislava who had contacted me in the United States. I continued these discussions during that summer in Novosibirsk and Budapest.

Finally, in 1973 I collaborated with my colleagues in Sovietology on a project to model the USSR SOVMOD I, and succeeding generations grew from that effort. In discussions and formal presentations, this model was put before Soviet economists, and I believe that by now we have a better understanding of that country's economic system. Visiting scholars from Bratislava, Budapest, Łodz, Novosibirsk, Moscow, and Beijing have, over a period of more than ten years, contributed to our appreciation of the fundamental differences in structure between the Western market economy and the Eastern command economy.

The modeling of the pieces—different OECD countries, some LDCs and some CPEs—set the stage for the next step, namely, the modeling of the international system. In a meeting of the SSRC Committee on Eco-nomic Stability and Growth in 1967 I suggested that we approach the growing international problem through a cooperative project designed, to some extent, along the lines of the SSRC–Brookings model project. Country representatives would take the place of sector representatives, and we could put together a consistent system of the leading economic centers of the world economy. The SSRC committee had earlier hoped to see such an effort undertaken by the OECD. We held a meeting in London in 1967 under the intriguing title "Is the Business Cycle Obso-lete?" We, fortunately, recognized the continuing presence of the cycle, but were not successful in starting research on model building for anal-ysis of the international problem at that conference. We did, however, establish some lasting contacts at that meeting that served us well for later developments.

With a small grant from the Ford Foundation, Bert Hickman, Aaron Gordon, and I assembled a group of international model builders from leading OECD countries in summer 1968 at Stanford, where I was giving some class lectures. We decided to launch a new project to model the international transmission mechanism. Initial support came from the International Monetary Fund, with active participation of Rudolf Rhomberg, and from the National Science Foundation.

This was truly a group endeavor. Many individual model builders from different countries and many specialists in international economics convened at formative meetings, realizing that there was a researchable project but not knowing exactly how to go about it. Through the dynamics of group discussion and person-to-person analysis, we finally decided on some procedures and goals. Out of that effort we spawned project LINK—The International Linkage of National Economic Models.[3] More than fifteen years later the project is still functioning and trying to break new ground.

At an early stage we recognized that the developing countries and the socialist countries would play an increasingly important role in the world economy. Although the IMF was mainly interested in the analysis of OECD countries, the UN supporters of the project continuously pressed for attention to the role of the LDC and CPE areas. The project has grown from a system of thirteen OECD countries, four regions of developing countries, and one region of socialist countries to an enlarged system of seventy-two country/area groups comprising each of the OECD countries, most large developing countries individually, and most large socialist countries individually. That is the most ambitious coordinating task for model building that has ever been undertaken, and we are in the midst of putting all the pieces together now in Philadelphia. Each separate piece exists.

During the fifteen-year period of development we have succeeded in allowing for floating exchange rates, coping with oil price changes, adding country detail, introducing primary commodities, streamlining the enormous computational program, and tackling many policy problems through scenario analysis. Analysis of capital flows, coordination of policies among countries, and methods of optimal control are high on the present research agenda.

The computer, as one can easily see, has played a large role in my involvement with econometric research and application, but that part of the story is not yet finished. Interesting new developments are on the horizon. I am now involved in three research directions: (1) Use of the microcomputer for conventional econometrics. This involves collapsing the size of systems to fit limited, tabletop capacities, but these limitations are steadily disappearing. Some studies, especially of developing countries, are necessarily compact, small enough to fit the present generation of microcomputers. (2) Cooperative computing, whereby conventional computers are linked in a network for simultaneous computation; the LINK system is an ideal trial case. (3) Use of the supercomputer to accommodate the ever-increasing demands of the expanding LINK system, now consisting of more than 15,000 dynamic nonlinear equations.

Just as the Brookings model gave way to improved versions at the various commercial econometric centers, official agencies and some individual university centers, there is a possibility that project LINK could be eclipsed. The Federal Reserve System has its own multicountry model, as does the OECD, Japan's Economic Planning Agency, the Common Market, and Wharton Econometrics. What seemed chancy and questionable in 1968 has become an often duplicated reality for analysis of the world economy.

When I went to Eastern Europe and the USSR in 1970, embryonic groups were starting up activity in econometric model building. I helped, where possible, and had many trainees at either the University of Pennsylvania or Wharton Econometrics. The same thing was true of activities in the developing countries. The case of the People's Republic of China is somewhat different. After the renormalization of relationships in 1978, I led a team of economists sponsored by the National Academy of Sciences, in fall 1979, to try to establish scholarly contacts. As a follow-up to that visit I organized, privately, with the Chinese Academy of Social Sciences, a summer workshop in econometrics in 1980. Also, visiting scholars from China have come to Philadelphia. Progress is limited but promising toward the preparation of a China model, maintained in the PRC, for LINK. We already have our own version of a China model built by Laurence Lau of Stanford University. A repeat visit in 1984 continued in the vein of teaching econometric method and trying to encourage participation in Project LINK. Similar workshops and efforts for LINK-compatible model building were undertaken in Taiwan during 1982 and 1983. Meetings with economists in Manila (Asian Development Bank and Philippine Institute for Development Studies), Bangkok (UN Economic and Social Commission for Asia and the Pacific), and New Delhi (Delhi University) are furthering the effort to have good LINK models for the whole Far East.

This account of forty years' research activity in economics and econometrics has avoided the political or the popular side. In 1976 I served as Jimmy Carter's coordinator of his economic task force. During his administration I tried to be helpful in various White House economic matters. I gave similar assistance to Milton Shapp, the governor of Pennsylvania, and W. Wilson Goode, the mayor of Philadelphia. All these private ventures contributed enormously to my own education. They taught me a bit about handling the media, about public appearances, and about the trade-offs between economic and political considerations. That experience was very interesting and I am glad that I did it, but I feel most comfortable in academia, doing the things I have described in this essay.

As for popularizing, I continue to write a periodic column for the Los Angeles *Times* and have had my stints at *Newsweek, Business Week,* and *Le Nouvel Observateur.* The *Manchester Guardian* in 1954 took my every word and table and published it as is. The same is true in my continuing relationship with the Los Angeles *Times,* but I feel the same way about other popular excursions into the media as I feel about politics. The trade-offs with what I believe to be good economics are not acceptable, and I feel more comfortable writing in the scholarly domain.

Notes

1. *The Brookings Quarterly Econometric Model of the United States,* ed. J. Duesenberry, G. Fromm, L. Klein, and E. Kuh (Chicago: Rand McNally, 1965); *The Brookings Model: Some Further Results,* ed. J. Duesenberry, G. Fromm, L. Klein, and E. Kuh (Chicago: Rand McNally, 1969); *The Brookings Model: Perspectives and Recent Developments,* ed. G. Fromm and L. Klein (Amsterdam: North-Holland, 1975).

2. Irma and Frank Adelman, "The Dynamic Properties of the Klein-Goldberger Model," *Econometrica* 27 (October 1959): 596–625; H. Wagner, "A Monte Carlo Study of Estimates of Simultaneous Linear Structural Equations," *Econometrica* 26 (January 1958): 117–133.

3. The evolution of project LINK is spelled out in three volumes and updated by some descriptive articles. See R. J. Ball, *The International Linkage of National Economic Models,* J. Waelbroeck, *The Models of Project LINK,* J. Sawyer, *Modeling the International Transmission Mechanism* (Amsterdam: North-Holland, 1973, 1976, 1979); B. G. Hickman and L. R. Klein, "A Decade of Research by Project LINK," *ITEMS,* Social Science Research Council, NY (December 1979), 49–56; L. R. Klein, Peter Pauly, and Pascal Voisin, "The World Economy: A Global Model," *Perspectives in Computing* 2 (May 1982): 4–17.

Lawrence R. Klein

Awarded Nobel Prize in 1980. Lecture presented October 25, 1984.

Dates of Birth and Death

September 14, 1920; October 20, 2013

Academic Degrees

B.A., University of California, Berkeley, 1942
Ph.D., Massachusetts Institute of Technology, 1944

Academic Affiliations

Lecturer in Economics, University of Michigan, 1950–54
Senior Research Officer, Oxford University Institute of Statistics, 1954–55
Reader in Econometrics, Oxford University Institute of Statistics, 1956–58
Professor of Economics, University of Pennsylvania, 1958–64
Visiting Professor, Osaka University, summer 1960
University Professor of Economics, University of Pennsylvania, 1964–67
Benjamin Franklin Professor, University of Pennsylvania, 1968–85
Benjamin Franklin Professor, Emeritus, University of Pennsylvania, 1985–2013
Distinguished Visiting Professor, City University of New York, 1962–63, 1982
Visiting Professor, The Hebrew University of Jerusalem, 1964
Visiting Professor, Princeton University, spring 1966
Ford Visiting Professor, University of California, Berkeley, 1968
Visiting Professor, Stanford University, summer 1968
Visiting Professor, Institute for Advanced Studies, Vienna, summer 1970, winter 1974
Visiting Professor, University of Copenhagen, spring 1974

Selected Books

The Keynesian Revolution, 1947, 1966
A Textbook of Econometrics, 1953, 1974
An Econometric Model of the United States, 1929–1952, 1955
(with A. S. Goldberger)
The Brookings Quarterly Econometric Model of the United States, 1965
(with J. Duesenberry, G. Fromm, and E. Kuh)
Econometric Models as Guides for Decision Making, 1981

Kenneth J. Arrow

Studying oneself is not the most comfortable of enterprises. One is caught between the desire to show oneself in the best possible light and the fear of claiming more than one's due. I shall endeavor to follow the precept of that eminent seeker after truth, Sherlock Holmes, on perhaps the only occasion on which he was accused of excessive modesty. "'My dear Watson,' said he, 'I cannot agree with those who rank modesty among the virtues. To the logician all things should be seen exactly as they are, and to underestimate one's self is as much a departure from truth as to exaggerate one's own powers'" ("The Greek Interpreter").

An individual examining himself cannot claim omniscience. I cannot really claim to know all the forces impinging on my life, personal or intellectual. Indeed, as will be seen, there are some elements in the development of my ideas and interests that I cannot now reconstruct. On occasion, on rereading an old scholarly paper of mine, I have realized that my mental recollection was in some degree in error. In effect, the speakers in this series are asked to be historians and biographers of themselves; and, like all historians and biographers, they can occasionally make mistakes. Recollection can be taken as reliable when it can be checked against the documentary record. Otherwise, it is imperfectly reliable evidence, though of a kind to which the speaker, such as myself, has unique access.

I will be brief in sketching my biography. My family, on both sides, were immigrants who arrived in this country about 1900 and settled in New York. My parents were born abroad but came here as infants, so they were effectively first-generation Americans. My father's family was very poor, my mother's hardworking and moderately successful shop-keepers. Both were very intelligent. My mother completed high school, my father college. My father was unusually successful in business when young, and the first ten years of my life were spent in a household that was comfortable and, more important for me, had many good books. Later, my father lost everything in the Great Depression, and we were very poor for about ten years.

I was early regarded as having unusual intellectual capacity. I was an omnivorous reader, and I added to that a desire to systematize my under-standing. As a result, history, for example, was not merely a set of dates and colorful stories; I could understand it as a sequence in which one event flowed out of another. This sense of order crystallized during my high school and college years into a predominant interest in mathematics and mathematical logic.

By following obscure references in footnotes, I learned about the then rapidly developing field of mathematical statistics, which gave a theo-retical foundation to statistical practice and led to profound changes in it. When at college graduation, in 1940, I found there were still no jobs available in high school teaching, I decided to enter graduate studies in statistics. There were then no separate departments of statistics and few places where mathematical statistics was taught. I enrolled at Columbia University to study with a great statistician, Harold Hotelling. Hotelling had his official position in the department of economics and had written a small number of important papers in economic theory. When I took his course in mathematical economics, I realized I had found my niche.

I received strong moral support from Hotelling and indeed from the whole economics department, somewhat surprisingly, as apart from Hotelling, economic theory was not well regarded by them. The emphasis was almost entirely on empirical and institutional analyses. The depart-ment's support was expressed in the most tangible and necessary way—good scholarships. As a result I learned economic theory as I had learned so much else, by reading. In my case at least, I believe this self-education was much better than any lectures I could have attended anywhere. The use of mathematics in economics had had a long history, but it was then still confined to a small group. By reading selectively, I could choose my teachers, and I chose them well.

I was an excellent student, but I was doubtful that I was capable of genuine originality. This concern was concentrated on the choice of topic for a Ph.D. dissertation. There were many possibilities for an acceptable dissertation, but I felt that I had to justify the expectations of my teachers and for that matter of myself by doing something out of the ordinary. This responsibility was crushing rather than inspiring. Four years of military service, though interesting in itself, served further to delay my coming to grips with my aspirations. Finally, a series of abortive research ideas, each of which seemed to be more of a distraction than a help, culminated in my first major accomplishment, known as the theory of social choice.

I will go into some detail about the genesis of this contribution of mine because it displays the interaction between the state of economic thinking in general and my own special talents and background. It differs in one significant way from the other areas of my research, which I will discuss later. The question was essentially a new one, on which there had been virtually no previous analysis. The others had been discussed to some extent in the literature, and my role was to bring new analytical methods or new insights. In social choice theory, I was almost completely the creator of the questions as well as some answers.

It had been argued by the more advanced economic theorists that economic behavior in all contexts was essentially rational choice among a limited set of alternatives. The household chooses among collections of different kinds of goods. The collections available to it are those that it can afford to buy at the prevailing prices and with the income available to it. A firm chooses among alternative ways of producing a given output and also chooses among different output levels. To say that choice is rational was interpreted by these theorists, such as Hotelling, John Hicks, and Paul Samuelson, as meaning that the alternatives can be ranked or ordered by the chooser. From any given range of alternatives, say, the technically feasible production processes or the collections of commodities available to a household within its budget limits, the choosing agent selects the highest-ranking alternative available.

To say that alternatives are ordered in preference has a very definite meaning. First, it means that any two alternatives can be compared. The chooser prefers one or the other or possibly is indifferent between them. Second, and this is somewhat more subtle, there is a consistency in the ordering of alternatives. Let us imagine three alternatives labeled A, B, and C. If A is preferred to B and B to C, we would want to insist that A is preferred to C. This property is referred to as *transitivity*.

Though this formulation of choice had been originated for use in economic analysis, it was clearly applicable to choice in other domains. Hotelling, John von Neumann, Oskar Morgenstern, and Joseph Schumpeter had already suggested some applications to political choice, the choice of candidates for election or of legislative proposals. Voting could be regarded as a method by which individuals' preferences for candidates or legislative proposals could be combined or aggregated to make a social choice.

The question first came to me in an economic context. I had observed that large corporations were not individuals but were supposed (in theory, at least) to reflect the will of their many stockholders. To be sure, they all had a common aim, to maximize profits. But profits depend on the future, and the stockholders might well have different expectations as to future conditions. Suppose the corporation has to choose among alternative directions for investment. Each stockholder orders the different investment policies by the profit he or she expects. But because different stockholders have different expectations, they may well have different orderings of investment policies. My first thought was the obvious one suggested by the formal rules of corporate voting. If there are two investment policies, call them A and B, that one chosen is the one that commands a majority of the shares.

But in almost any real case, there are many more than two possible investment policies. For simplicity, suppose there are three, A, B, and C. The idea that seemed natural to me was to choose the one that would get a majority over each of the other two. To put it another way, since the policy is that of the corporation, we might want to say that the corporation can order all investment policies and choose the best. But since the corporation merely reflects its stockholders, the ordering by the corporation should be constructed from the orderings of the individual stockholders. We might say that the corporation prefers one policy to another if a majority of the shares are voted for the first as against the second.

But now I found an unpleasant surprise. It was perfectly possible that A has a majority against B, and B against C, but that C has a majority against A, not A against C. In other words, majority voting does not always have the property that I have just called transitivity.

To see how this can happen, let me take an election example. Suppose there are three candidates, Adams, Black, and Clark, and three voters. Voter 1 prefers Adams to Black and Black to Clark. We will suppose that each voter has a transitive ordering, so voter 1 will prefer Adams to Clark.

Suppose voter 2 prefers Black to Clark and Clark to Adams, and therefore Black to Adams, while voter 3 prefers Clark to Adams and Adams to Black. Then voters 1 and 3 prefer Adams to Black, so that Adams is chosen over Black by the group. Similarly, Black receives a majority over Clark through voters 1 and 2. Transitivity would require that Adams be chosen over Clark in the election. But in fact voters 2 and 3 prefer Clark to Adams. This intransitivity is sometimes called the paradox of voting. Of course, the intransitivity need not arise; it depends on what the voters' preferences are. The point is that the system of pairwise majority voting cannot be guaranteed to produce an ordering by society as a whole.

The observation struck me as one that must have been made by others, and indeed I wondered if I had heard it somewhere. I still don't know whether I did or not. In any case the effect was rather to cause me to drop the whole matter and study something else.

About a year later my thoughts recurred to the question of voting, without any intention on my part. I realized that under certain special but not totally unnatural conditions on the voters' preferences, the paradox I had found earlier could not occur. This I thought worth writing about. But when I started to do so, I picked up a journal and found the same idea in an article by an English economist, Duncan Black. The result that Black and I had found could have been thought of any time in the last one hundred fifty years. That two of us came to it at virtually the same time is an occurrence for which I have no explanation.

Priority in discovery is the spur to science, and being anticipated was correspondingly frustrating. I again dropped the study of voting for what I took to be less fascinating but more significant topics, on which I made little progress. But a few months later I was asked a chance question that gave the problem sufficient significance to justify a reawakened interest. The then new theory of games was being applied to military and diplomatic conflict. In this application, nations were being regarded as rational actors. How could this be justified when nations are aggregated of individuals with different preference orderings? My earlier results, I realized, taught me that one could not always derive a preference ordering for a nation from the preference orderings of its citizens by using majority voting to compare one alternative with another.

This left open the possibility that there were other ways of aggregating individual preference orderings to form a social ordering, that is, a way of choosing among alternatives that has the property of transitivity. A few weeks of intensive thought made the answer clear.

Given any method of aggregating individual preference orderings to yield a social choice that satisfies a few very natural conditions, there will always be some individual preference orderings that will cause the social choice to be intransitive, as in the example given.

My studies in logic helped to formulate the question in a clear way, which stripped it of unnecessary complications. But I did not use the concepts of mathematical logic in any deep way.

This result quickly attracted attention. One by-product was that I learned from several correspondents of what previous literature there was. The paradox of majority voting had indeed been discovered before—in fact, by the French author the Marquis du Condorcet in 1785! But there was not a continuous literature. There were some ingenious unpublished proposals for conducting certain elections at Oxford about 1860, based on the possibility of paradox. They were circulated by a mathematician named Charles L. Dodgson. Dodgson also wrote an adventure tale for the daughter of one of his colleagues, Alice Lidell, which he published under a pseudonym, Lewis Carroll. The only significant published paper on social choice had appeared in 1882 in an Australian journal, hardly everyday reading matter. I know few if any interesting research topics that have had such a spotty and intermittent history.

The subsequent record is very different. The literature has exploded. A recent survey, not intended to be complete, listed more than six hundred references. A journal devoted entirely to social choice theory and related issues has been started.

Social choice is a topic in which there was little direct relation to past work, although the connection with parallel developments in the theory of economic choice was important. I would like to discuss two further contributions of mine, which illustrate different relations to current economic theory and to the world of economic reality.

The first of the two is the study of what is known as general equilibrium theory. This is an elaboration of the simple but not easily understood point that in an economic system everything affects everything else. Let me illustrate. The price of oil became very low in the 1930s because of discoveries in Texas and the Persian Gulf area. Homeowners shifted in great numbers from coal to oil for home heating, thereby decreasing the demand for coal and employment in the coal mines. Refineries expanded, so more workers were employed there. There was as well a demand for refinery equipment, a complicated example of chemical processes. This in turn induced demands for skilled chemical engineers and for more steel. Gasoline was cheaper, so that more automobiles were bought and used. Tourist areas accessible by road but not by railroad began to flourish, while railroads decayed. Each of these changes in turn induced other changes, and some of these in turn reacted on the demand for and supply of oil.

The economic lesson of this story is that the demand for any one product depends on the prices of all products, including the prices of labor and capital services, which we usually call wages and profits. Similarly, the supply of any product or of labor or capital depends on the prices of all commodities. What determines what prices will prevail? The usual hypothesis in economics is that of equilibrium. The prices are those that cause supply to equal demand in every market. This hypothesis, like many others in economics and indeed in the natural sciences, is certainly not precisely true. But it is a useful approximation, and those who disregard it completely are much further from the truth than are those who exaggerate the prevalence of equilibrium.

The general equilibrium theory, or perhaps vision, of the economy was first stated in full-fledged form by a French economist, Leon Walras, in 1874. But it was hard to use as a tool of analysis and too difficult for economists with little mathematical training to understand. Only in the 1930s did interest revive, especially through the masterful exposition and development by John Hicks, with whom I had the honor of sharing the Nobel Prize in 1972.

But there was an unresolved analytical issue, recognized by at least some. General equilibrium theory asserts that the prices of all commodities are determined as the solution of a large number of equations, those that state the equality of supply and demand on each market. Did these equations necessarily have a solution at all? If not, the general equilibrium theory could not always be true. Indeed, some work by German economists about 1932 suggested the possibility that the equations need not have a meaningful solution. A Viennese banker named Karl Schlesinger, who had studied economics in the university and continued to follow developments in the subject, recognized that the apparent difficulties rested on a subtle misunderstanding and felt that the existence of general equilibrium could be demonstrated. He hired a young mathematician, Abraham Wald, to work on the problem. Wald came up with a proof of existence under certain conditions not easy to interpret; indeed, in light of later work, they were much too stringent. Even so, the proof was difficult.

The heavy tread of history breaks in on the story. Schlesinger would not believe that Austria could fall to Hitler; when it did, he committed suicide. Wald did succeed in leaving and came to the United States, where he shifted his interests to mathematical statistics. He was one of my teachers at Columbia. I came to learn, I do not know how, of the unsolved or only partially solved problem of the existence of general equilibrium. But when I asked Wald about his work on the question, he merely said that it was a very difficult problem. Coming from him, whose mathematical powers were certainly greater than mine, the statement was discouraging.

As frequently happens in the history of science, however, help came from developments in other fields. The theory of games was in a process of rapid development. One theorem, proved by a mathematician named John Nash, struck me as being parallel in many ways to the existence problem for competitive equilibrium. By borrowing and adapting the mathematical tools used by Nash, I was able to state very generally the conditions under which the equations defining general equilibrium had a solution.

There was more than mathematics involved, though. It was necessary to state the general equilibrium system much more explicitly. As Schlesinger had already shown in part, the exact assumptions that were made needed clarification, and much was learned in the process.

As you may see from this account, the existence proof was based on general theoretical progress in economics and in mathematics, and I was certainly not the only one with access to it. Indeed, while writing up my results, I learned that Gerard Debreu, the Nobel laureate in economic sciences for 1983, had independently come to essentially the same results. We decided to publish the results jointly. Just before our paper appeared, there was one by a third economist, Lionel McKenzie, along similar though not identical lines.

Multiple discoveries are in fact very common in science and for much the same reason. Developments in related fields with different motivation help one to understand a difficult problem better. Since these developments are public knowledge, many scholars can take advantage of them. It is pleasant to the ego to be first or among the first with a new discovery. However, in this case at least, the evidence is clear that the development of general equilibrium theory would have gone on quite as it did without me.

The third contribution I would like to discuss is drawing the economic implications of differences in information among economic agents. My sustained interest arose from considering a practical problem, the organization of medical care, but the ground had been prepared by my studies in mathematical statistics, some of my earlier theoretical work on the economics of risk bearing, and some developments by others of these topics. My contribution here, unlike the first two examples, has been not so much a specific and well-defined technical accomplishment as a point of view that has served to reorient economic theory.

The general equilibrium theory, like most economic theory up to about 1950, assumed that the economic agents operated under certainty. That is, the households, firms, investors, and so forth knew correctly the consequences of their actions or, in some versions, at least acted as if they did. Thus, producers were assumed to know what outputs they would get for given inputs. Investors would know what prices would prevail in the future for the goods they were planning to sell.

I don't mean to imply that economists were so foolish as not to recognize that the economic world was uncertain or that economic agents didn't realize that this was the case. Indeed, some literature clearly showed that much economic behavior could only be explained by assuming that economic agents were well aware of uncertainty; for example, investors held diversified portfolios and bought insurance. However, a general formulation that would permit integration with standard economic theory and in particular with general equilibrium theory was lacking. I was able to work out such a formulation, which introduced the concept of contingent contracts, contracts for delivery of goods or money contingent on the occurrence of any possible state of affairs. In effect, I postulated the existence of insurance against all conceivable risks. My rather sketchy paper was greatly enriched and extended by Gerard Debreu. The idea was simplicity itself and yet novel.

It has become a standard tool of analysis, in this case rather more than I intended. I considered the theory of contingent contracts as a sketch of an ideal system to which the methods of risk bearing and risk shifting in the real world were to be compared. It was clear enough empirically that the world did not have nearly as many possibilities for trading risks as my model would have predicted. I did not, however, have at first a particularly good explanation for the discrepancy.

A considerable insight came a few years later. I was asked by the Ford Foundation to take a theorist's view of the economics of medical care. I first surveyed the empirical literature on the subject. My theoretical perspective suggested that there was inadequate insurance against the very large financial risks. Indeed, insurance coverage, both governmental and private, has expanded greatly since then. But I soon realized that there were obstacles to the achievement of full insurance. Insurance against health expenditures creates an incentive to spend more freely than is desirable.

Was there a general theoretical principle behind this? The concept of insurance against uncertainties did not fully reflect the actual situation, namely, that different individuals may have different uncertainties. The person insured knows more about his or her state of health than the insurer. The fact that individuals have informational differences is a key element in any economic system, not just in health insurance.

The theme may be stated without elaboration. Informational differences pervade the economy and have given rise to both inefficiencies and contractual arrangements and informal understandings to protect the less informed. My own contributions here were conceptual rather than technical, and the present theory is the result of many hands.

I have tried to present, as clearly as I can, the genesis of some of my researches. They have all been related to the present state of thinking by others. The field of science, indeed, the whole world of human society, is a cooperative one. At each moment, we are competing, whether for academic honors or business success. But the background, and what makes society an engine of progress, is a whole set of successes and even failures from which we all have learned.

Kenneth J. Arrow

Awarded Nobel Prize in 1972. Lecture presented November 5, 1984.

Dates of Birth and Death

August 23, 1921; February 21, 2017

Academic Degrees

B.S., City College, New York, 1940
M.A., Columbia University, 1941
Ph.D., Columbia University, 1951

Academic Affiliations

Assistant Professor of Economics, University of Chicago, 1948–49
Acting Assistant Professor of Economics and Statistics, Stanford University, 1949–50
Associate Professor of Economics and Statistics, Stanford University, 1950–53
Executive Head, Department of Economics, Stanford University, 1953–56
Professor of Economics, Statistics, and Operations Research, Stanford University, 1953–68
Visiting Professor of Economics, Massachusetts Institute of Technology, fall 1966
Fellow, Churchill College (Cambridge), 1963–64, 1970, 1973
Professor of Economics, Harvard University, 1968–74
James Bryant Conant University Professor, Harvard University, 1974–1979
Joan Kenney Professor of Economics and Professor of Operations Research, Stanford University, 1979–91
Joan Kenney Professor of Economics and Professor of Operations Research, Emeritus, Stanford University, 1991–2017

Selected Books

Social Choice and Individual Values, 1951, 1963
Studies in the Mathematical Theory of Inventory and Production, 1958 (with S. Karlin and H. Scarf)
Public Investment, the Rate of Return, and Optimal Fiscal Policy, 1970 (with M. Kurz)
Essays in the Theory of Risk-Bearing, 1971
The Limits of Organization, 1974
Collected Papers of Kenneth J. Arrow, Vols. 1–6, 1983–1985

Paul A. Samuelson

Economics in My Time

The last five or six decades have seen American economics come of age and then become the dominant center of world political economy. When I began the study of economics back in 1932 on the University of Chicago Midway, economics was literary economics. A few original spirits—such as Harold Hotelling, Ragnar Frisch, and R. G. D. Allen—used mathematical symbols; but, if their experiences were like my early ones, learned journals rationed pretty severely acceptance of anything involving the calculus. Such esoteric animals as matrices were never seen in the social science zoos. At most a few chaste determinants were admitted to our Augean stables.

Do I seem to be describing Eden, a paradise to which many would like to return in revulsion against the symbolic pus-pimples that disfigure not only the pages of *Econometrica* but also the *Economic Journal* and the *American Economic Review*?

Don't believe it. Like Tobacco Road, the old economics was strewn with rusty monstrosities of logic inherited from the past, its soil generated few stalks of vigorous new science, and the correspondence between the terrain of the real world and the maps of the economics textbook and treatises was neither smooth nor even one-to-one.

The Great Takeoff

Yes, 1932 was a great time to be born as an economist. The Sleeping Beauty of political economy was waiting for the enlivening kiss of new methods, new paradigms, new hired hands, and new problems. Science is a parasite: the greater the patient population, the better the advance in physiology and pathology; and out of pathology arises therapy. The year 1932 was the trough of the Great Depression, and from its rotten soil was belatedly begot the new subject that today we call macroeconomics.

Do I refer to the Keynesian revolution? Of course I do. But people are wrong to associate with that name the particular policies and ideologies found fifty years ago in the writings of John Maynard Keynes, Alvin Hansen, Joan Robinson, Abba Lerner, and Michael Kalecki. The New Classical School, through the quills of Robert Lucas, Tom Sargent, and Robert Barro, reversed those Keynesian doctrines 180 degrees. Nevertheless, the present-day equations found in monetarism, eclectic mainstream Keynesianism, or rational expectationism are a galaxy removed from what were in Walras and Marshall—or in Frank Knight and Jacob Viner, my great neoclassical teachers in Chicago. The macromethodology innovated by Keynes's 1936 *General Theory* constitutes both the 1985 swords that slash at Keynesianism and the shields that defend mainstream macroeconomics.

So far I have been talking about the internal logic and development of economics as a science. It has been an inside-the-seminar-room survey of the subject, where of course the observations of the economic world have been brought into that seminar room. As a result of outside influences the period from 1932 to 1975 was a favorable one for economists like me, in that it was an epoch of tremendous university expansion and job opportunity. If one can borrow from the vulgar terminology of economic science fiction, my generation of economic activity was buoyed by the great wave of a Kondratieff expansion.

The New Deal and the welfare state created a vast new market for economists in government. Then came the war, which was carried on by armaments, cannon fodder, and economists: when the business cycle was put into hibernation by the wartime command economy, whenever problems of quantitative resource allocation ran out, economists could chance their arm on the new science of operations research, a game at which only the rare brilliant physicist could beat the run-of-the-mill economists.

Then came the postwar boom in education. Where there had been in 1935 only a few strong centers for economic research—Harvard,

Chicago, Columbia, and a few others—now everywhere in the land there grew up excellent graduate departments. No longer did one wait to be made a full professor at forty-five; the typical new Shangri-La in the firmament of postwar economics was created by an activist department chairman, given the go-ahead signal by his administration to go out and hire hotshot stars at twice his own salary. Like beardless colonels in the wartime air corps, thirty-year-old full professors deigned to grace prestigious academic chairs.

Life at the Top

I have seen economists grow in public esteem and in pecuniary demand. Surveys have shown that the highest-paid scientists, physical and biological scientists as well as economists, are not to be found in private industry but rather in the university—perhaps in-and-out of the universities would put it more accurately. I don't know scholars who have agents. But some do have lecture bureaus. And being a public member on corporate boards has become a new way of life.

It is a heady experience to advise the Prince on a sabbatical tour of duty in Washington. Newspaper columnists from academia, serendipitously, acquire the omniscience they need for the job.

"And gladly teach" used to refer to the lecture hall and seminar table, but now includes telling congressional committees there is no free lunch and telling TV audiences to buy cheap and sell dear.

Trees do not grow to the sky. Every Kondratieff wave has its inflection point. The 1932–1965 expansion in economists' prestige and self-esteem has been followed by some leaner years. We have become more humble and, as Churchill said, we have much to be humble about. Economists have not been able to agree on a good cure for stagflation. That disillusions noneconomists. And, to tell the truth, it punctures our own self-complacency. We shop around for new paradigms the way alchemists prospect for new philosophers' stone. Just because a National Bureau paper is silly does not mean it is uninteresting. Just because it is profound does not mean that it is admired.

Mea Culpa

So far I have been talking about economics. The title of this series, "My Evolution as an Economist," suggests that I should be talking about *me*. Mr. Dooley said that Theodore Roosevelt was going to write a book about the Spanish-American War called *Me and Cuba*. It would begin with Teddy's tribute, "My black sergeant was the bravest man I ever knew. He followed me up San Juan Hill."

I can claim that in talking about modern economics I am talking about me. My finger has been in every pie. I once claimed to be the last generalist in economics, writing about and teaching such diverse subjects as international trade and econometrics, economic theory and business cycles, demography and labor economics, finance and monopolistic competition, history of doctrines and locational economics. Kilroy, having been there, must share the guilt. (Goethe wrote that there was no crime he'd ever heard of that he didn't feel capable of committing. Bob Solow's reaction was that Goethe flattered himself. And perhaps what I called "crime" is a mistranslation of what Goethe meant only as "error.")

Here is my worst error. Do you remember the infamous wrong prediction by economists that after World War II there would be mass unemployment? I was not part of the multi-agency team that produced the official 1945 forecast of doomsday. But, if you look at the yellowing files of the *New Republic,* you will find a well-written article by this humble servant that involves a large squared forecasting error on the downward side. My friend and mentor, Alvin Hansen, who believed in a postwar restocking boom, could have taught me better. And so could Sumner Slichter and a host of Keynesians and non-Keynesians.

I reproach myself for a gross error. But I would reproach myself more if I had persisted in an error after observations revealed it clearly to be that. I made a deal of money in the late 1940s on the bull side, ignoring Satchel Paige's advice to Lot's wife, "Never look back." Rather I would advocate Samuelson's law: "Always look back. You may learn something from your residuals. Usually one's forecasts are not so good as one remembers them; the difference may be instructive." The dictum "If you must forecast, forecast often" is neither a joke nor a confession of impotence. It is a recognition of the primacy of brute fact over pretty theory. That part of the future that cannot be related to the present's past is precisely what science cannot hope to capture. Fortunately, there is plenty of work for science to do, plenty of scientific tasks not yet done.

Other Testimonies

I shall not shirk talking more specifically about my own development as a scholar and scientist. But, as I do not believe in the kind of elegant variation that follows "he said" with "he averred," and then with "vouchsafed the speaker," I shall not try to duplicate some earlier autobiographical writings. Peppered through many of the technical articles in the four volumes of my *Collected Scientific Papers* are various personal reminiscences. But the richest vein of this kind of ore will be found in, first, my 1968 presidential address before the World Congress of the International Economic Association. It is cunningly titled "The Way of an Economist," ambivalent words denoting both the economic road traveled and the personal style of the Siegfried traversing that road. Similarly, today in speaking of "economics in my time," I also mean economics in my own peculiar rhythms and style.

A second source is my "Economics in a Golden Age: A Personal Memoir," which appeared in the Daedalus book Gerald Holton edited, *The Twentieth Century Sciences: Studies in the Biography of Ideas* (New York: W. W. Norton, 1972).

A third source, one whose title was imposed on me, is *My Lifetime Philosophy*. This appeared in the series for students in the *American Economist* 27 (1983): 5–12, and in the fifth volume of *Collected Scientific Papers of Paul A. Samuelson* (2000).

The Scientist Delineated

Here briefly, in the third person for objectivity, is the superficial outline of my scientific career.

PAS has already been incredibly lucky throughout his lifetime, overpaid and underworked. A bright youngster, favored by admiring parents, he shone at school until the high school years, when he became an underachiever. The calendar lies in naming May 15, 1915, as his time of birth. Truly he was born on the morning of January 2, 1932, at the University of Chicago.

He was made for academic life. An A student at Chicago and an A+ one at Harvard, PAS wandered by chance into economics. Economics turned out to be made for him as the Darwinian genes from generations of commercial ancestors encountered their teleological destiny.

Every honor he aspired to came his way, and came early. He got the undergraduate social science medal his undergraduate year. Just when commencement loomed near, the Social Science Research Council created a new experimental fellowship program in economics, whose first award supported him handsomely at Harvard. Having drawn from Chicago giants like Knight, Viner, Henry Schultz, Henry Simons, Paul Douglas, John U. Nef, and Lloyd Mints, he levitated to Harvard Yard to learn from Joseph Schumpeter, Wassily Leontief, Edwin Bidwell Wilson, Gottfried Haberler, Edward Chamberlin, and Alvin Hansen. Before his SSRC fellowship gave out, he overcame the opposition of the Society of Fellows to economics and rode on the shoulders of Vilfredo Pareto into the sacred circle of Junior Fellows. The philosopher Willard van Orman Quine, the mathematician Garrett Birkhoff, the double-Nobel physicist John Bardeen, the chemists Bright Wilson and Robert Woodward, the polymath Harry T. Levine were his companions in arms in the Society of Fellows. There he hit his stride and began to turn out articles faster than the journals could absorb such quasi-mathematical stuff.

It is not true that PAS began life as a physicist or mathematician. Well into his undergraduate course he discerned that mathematics was to revolutionize modern economics. Proceeding to learn mathematics, PAS still remembers how a Lagrange multiplier first swam into his ken and how, with a wild surmise, it gave him independent discovery of the Edgeworth–Stackelberg asymmetric solution for duopoly—an insight that has kept him immune to the false charms of Nash–Cournot purported solutions.

His *Foundations of Economic Analysis,* written mostly as a Junior Fellow but usable later for the Ph.D. union card, won the David A. Wells Prize at Harvard. Later, in 1947, it helped him receive the first John Bates Clark Medal of the American Economic Association, awarded for scholarly promise before the age of forty. Its quality was thrice blessed: later still it contributed to his 1970 Nobel Prize in Economics, the second time that fabricated (or "forged") honor was awarded and the first time to an American.

Hegira down the River

If PAS was born as a child his freshman year at Chicago, he was born a second time as a man that October 1940 day he succumbed to a call from MIT. MIT's force met no detectable Harvard resistance, so the movable object moved. It was the best thing that could have happened to PAS. A boy must always remain a boy in his father's house. On his own acres a man can build his own mansion, and after 1941 PAS, along with magnificent colleagues, was able to help build up what became recognized as a leading world center for economics. Living well is the best revenge, Hemingway's crowd used to say; but, in sober truth, the example of MIT's Norbert Wiener, who in his days of fame still brooded over his ejection from Harvard Yard, led PAS ever to cherish his Harvard connections and labor for the greater glory of Cambridge and Middlesex County.

Peer recognition came early and often: from the American Academy of Arts and Sciences, the National Academy, the American Philosophical Society, and the British Academy. Just as it is the first million that is the hardest, one honor leads to another. After the first dozen honorary degrees, all it takes is longevity to double the number. The first such degree—from Chicago, alma mater and basilica of a church he no longer believed in—PAS found most touching. When Harvard honored a prophet in his own country, he also liked that.

Vice-presidencies and presidencies in professional societies came his way: the Econometric Society, the American Economic Association, the International Economic Association. As yet there is no Galaxy Political Economy Club.

A scholar at a new place for economic study like MIT receives plenty of offers from all over the world. PAS revealed a preference to be an immovable object, and, when made an institute professor in 1966, with magnificent research opportunities and optional teaching duties, he in effect returned to the womb of a perpetual junior fellowship. Having arrived in Paradise, he stayed there.

But not without excursions to the outside. Many a tutorial he gave to congressional committees. Often when he became a consultant to a federal agency, that precipitated its demise. The U.S. Treasury and the Federal Reserve Board did, however, survive his academic counsels. Murmuring that the United States was too precious to be turned over exclusively to big-picture thinkers like John Kenneth Galbraith and Walt Whitman Rostow, PAS gave economic tutorials to Adlai Stevenson and Averell Harriman; and worked his way as adviser to Senator J. F. Kennedy, candidate Kennedy, and president-elect Kennedy. Moses-like, PAS did not pass into the promised land beyond the Potomac, but as an *éminence grise* he had the fun of backing the poker hands of such magnificent Joshuas as Walter Heller, James Tobin, and Kermit Gordon at the Kennedy Council of Economic Advisers.

What can the good fairies give the man who has everything? George Stigler, referring to Samuelson's 1947 *Foundations* and his newly published 1948 best-selling textbook, *Economics,* introduced him with the words, "Samuelson, having achieved fame, now seeks fortune." Soon the smoke of burning mortgage could be sniffed in Belmont, Massachusetts. More than this, J. K. Galbraith's prophesy in a *Fortune* review, that a new generation would receive its economics from *Economics,* turned out to be right on the mark. PAS was heard to mutter complacently, "Let those who will write the nation's laws if I can write its textbooks." Being denounced by William Buckley for blaspheming God and man at Yale, the textbook took on a new aura of respectability and sales soared all over the world.

A quarter of a century ago the author of *Economics* commented on the new layer of fame that accrues to a scholar who writes a best-seller, stating modestly,

> Writing a beginning textbook is hard work. But its rewards have been tremendous—and I do not mean simply pecuniary rewards. Contact with hundreds of thousands of minds of a whole generation is an experience like no other that a scholar will ever meet. And writing down what we economists know about economics has been truly an exciting experience. I can only hope that some of this excitement will rub off on the reader.

By Joy Possessed

Stop! Enough is enough. Of such *Who's Who* boilerplate, enough is too much. What has been described above could be said of many a successful go-getter. A West Pointer who hated soldiering might settle for a Faustian bargain in which promotions and blue ribbons compensated for a wasted life.

The reward that has counted for me in scholarship and science is the marvelous hunt through enchanted forests. I began to write articles for publication before I was twenty-one. I have never stopped. I hope never to stop. When Harry Johnson died, he had eighteen papers in proof. That is dying with your boots on! (Even for Harry, who never did things by halves or held down to the golden mean, eighteen was overdoing it.)

My mind is ever toying with economic ideas and relationships. Great novelists and poets have reported occasional abandonment by their muse. The well runs dry, permanently or on occasion. Mine has been a better luck. As I have written elsewhere, there is a vast inventory of topics and problems floating in the back of my mind. More perhaps than I shall ever have occasion to write up for publication. A result that I notice in statistical mechanics may someday help resolve a problem in finance.

Like a gravid spouse, I achieve the release of publication. Have I published too much? Others must form their judgment on this. Speaking for myself, in my heart of hearts I have regretted almost no chapter, article, note, or footnote my quill has penned. And I have rued many an excision forced on me by editors of only finite patience or self-imposed for reasons of space and aesthetic measure.

Perhaps this betrays the lack of taste that marks the gourmand and not the gourmet? I hope not. I certainly sympathize with the view expressed in the following conversation of the classicist-poet A. E. Housman. A friend asked him why he was not including in a collection of his writings on Latin a certain item: "Don't you think it good?" "I think it good," Housman replied, "but not good enough for me." And not infrequently when I read some scholar's latest work, I have asked of Robert Solow what G. H. Hardy asked of J. E. Littlewood: "Why would a man who could write such an article do so?"

The able scholar with writer's block elevates by the mere passage of time the standards each future work must hurdle. It is easy to write a letter every day, but when you have not done so for five years, there is really nothing to report.

Repeatedly I have denied the great-man or great-work notion of science. Every drop helps, the old farmer said, as he spat into the pond. One does the best one can on the most pressing problem that presents. And, if after you have done so, your next moves are down a trajectory of diminishing returns, then still it is optimal to follow the rule of doing the best that there is to do. Besides, at any time a Schumpeterian innovation or Darwinian mutation may occur to you, plucking the violin string of increasing return.

Between Mozart and Brahms, I'm for Mozart. I am thankful for the precious gold pieces Pierro Sraffa left us. But economics would be the better if he had also blessed us all with some dozens of rubies and pearls. And, as I remember his eloquent but sad eyes, one wonders whether he would not have been the happier man if—as William James puts it—he had been born with a bottle of champagne to his credit. Maynard Keynes, who suffered from no writer's cramp, when asked at the end of his life what he'd have done different if he had it all over to do, replied, "I'd have drunk more champagne."

Earlier I confessed to having always been overpaid and underworked. Even good friends might agree with the first of these adjectives, but several will protest at the second, perhaps protesting, "Come off it, you work all the time, weekends and during vacations and, if legend holds, often during the reveries of the midnight hours." True enough. It is precisely my point though that working out economic analysis is play, not work. I am notorious for shirking tasks I hate to do. I minimize administrative duties, displaying an incompetence in their performance that chokes off additional assignments. Like Dennis Robertson, I always wash the forks last in the realization that should an atomic holocaust be imminent there may never be a need to do them.

If I am required to fill out an elaborate questionnaire, that liability is likely to stimulate me to write a new model in the theory of trade or in population genetics. Anything to put off the evil day of duty.

Remembered Kisses

Novels about painters, musicians, poets, or scientists notoriously fail to convey what they do in the working hours of the week. Come to think of it, novels about allegedly great business tycoons similarly fail to capture what it is precisely that they do.

Therefore, speaking to an audience of economists, I should be more specific and describe some particular acts of scientific gestation. How did I first notice the problem? When did a breakthrough occur? What were the steps of development? And how, in retrospect, was the pattern of knowledge affected by the research?

But where to begin? I toyed with the experiment of describing the big ledger that, for a year like 1983, served as a partial diary of research doodlings. Thus the January 1 entry might be jottings on how to devise a numerical example of a linear programming system that violates a crude version of the Le Chatelier principle in economics. This never got published. Yet. It refers back to work done in 1949, and indeed in1937, when I was a student at E. B. Wilson's knee—or perhaps shoulder. One might then trace in the daybook a return on January 2 and 3 to the problem, and perhaps discern how it modulates into a related problem.

Suffice it to say that, in the course of a year, there will be a half a hundred such finger exercises. But it would be misleading to believe that my 1983 research is well described, or even sampled, by the chance items that happen to get jotted down in one bedside journal. Therefore, I had better reserve for another and longer day detailed discussion of how some familiar result was conceived and came into being. (The impatient reader can be referred for a sample to my 1982 contribution to the Jørgen Gelting Festschrift, which I titled "A Chapter in the History of Ramsey's Optimal Feasible Taxation and Optimal Public Utility Prices.")

Chasing the Bitch Goddess of Success

Let me close with a few remarks on the motivations and rewards of scientists. Scientists are as avaricious and competitive as Smithian businessmen.

The coin they seek is not apples, nuts, and yachts; nor is it the coin itself, or power as that term is ordinarily used. Scholars seek fame. The fame they seek, as I noted in my 1961 American Economic Association presidential address, is fame with their peers—the other scientists whom they respect and whose respect they strive for. The sociologist Robert K. Merton has documented what I call this dirty little secret in his book *The Sociology of Science*.

I am no exception. Abraham Lincoln's law partner and biographer William Herndon observed that there was always a little clock of ambition ticking in the bosom of honest and whimsical Abe. No celebrity as a *Newsweek* columnist, no millions of clever-begotten speculative gains, no power as the Svengali or Rasputin to the prince or president could count as a pennyweight in my balance of worth against the prospect of recognition for having contributed to the empire of science.

Once I asked my friend the statistician Harold Freeman, "Harold, if the Devil came to you with the bargain that, in exchange for your immortal soul, he'd give you a brilliant theorem, would you do it?" "No," he replied, "but I would for an inequality." I like that answer. The day I proved that no one could be more than 60,000 standard deviations dumber than the mean, that Samuelson inequality made my day. The fact that subsequent writers have both generalized beyond it and discovered antecedents of it in earlier writings has not altered my pleasure in it. For that is the way of science, and sufficient to the day is the increment to the house of science that day brings.

Being precocious, I got an early start. Unconsciously and consciously, I was a young man in a hurry because I felt that the limited life span of my male ancestors tolled the knell for me. My father died young when I was twenty-three. I was supposed to resemble him, and the effect on me was especially traumatic. What I was to do I would have to do early, is what I thought. Actually, modern science granted me respite. Heredity, always, is modifiable by environment. Whatever the reason, I have been granted bouncing good health, a factor given too little weight in allocating merit to scientists and in explaining their achievements. A respected friend of mine, sometimes unfairly marked down as an underachiever, has been subject all his life to debilitating migraines. I say he is the meritorious one for having, as the Bible says, used his pound so judiciously.

There is another aspect to early, full (even overfull) recognition. It relaxes you. Why fret about priorities when, in the time you might spend in recriminations and turf claiming, you can dip your hook into the waters and be pulling out other pretty fish?

I long ago enunciated the doctrine that scholars work for their self-esteem, in the sense of what they all agree to judge meritorious. However, once your need for glory in the eyes of others has been somewhat appeased, you become free to work for your own approval. The job you will think well done is the one that brings true bliss. Perhaps part of this involves the faith that what one craftsman will like, so will eventually the rest.

There was never a time when I didn't strive to please myself. There have been those who thought that my fooling around with thermodynamics was an attempt to inflate the scientific validity of economics; even perhaps to snow the hoi polloi of economists who naturally can't judge intricacies of physics. Actually, such methodological excursions, if anything, put a tax on reputation rather than enhancing it. So what? Taxes are the price we pay for civilization. Such work is fun. And I perceive it adds to the depth and breadth of human knowledge.

At a deeper level one works not just to gain fame and esteem with colleagues. Not just to please oneself and enjoy the fun of the chase. At a deeper level the antagonist of Dr. A. B. Physiologist is not some rival physician at Göttingen or Oxford. The opponent is cancer. So at bottom is it with the economist. There is an objective reality out there that we are trying to understand, hard as that task may be. If ever a person becomes sick to death of faculty intrigue and professional infighting, if ever one sees democracy and civilization crumbling around one, always one can retreat to that objective study of reality. The complex numbers do not dissemble, and even for toothache there is no better anodyne than five fast rounds with the puzzler of the business cycle or the intricacies of the theory of control.

I mean this literally and can illustrate what I mean by a true story. The late Voss Neisser, a refugee economist who graced the New School for Social Research, once told me what a relief it was in those grim days of Hitler's march toward power to grapple with the problem of the determining of Walrasian competitive equilibrium. I understood perfectly and agreed completely.

Someone asked me whether I enjoyed getting the Nobel Prize. I thought before answering. "Yes," I replied. "Few things in life bring undiluted pleasure, but this one actually did." The honor was a pleasant surprise and came early, but not so early as to worry even me. Friends whose opinions I valued were pleased. If there were contrary opinions, I was too obtuse to be aware of them. My family enjoyed the Stockholm hoopla. Some colleagues in science have looked back with pain at the public interviews and turmoil that took them out of their laboratories. I bore up well and discovered that it takes only a few days of dependence on one's own chauffeur to develop an addiction.

Indian Summer

Sociologists of science study how the Nobel award affects a scholar. Do the laureates go into an era of depressed fertility? Do they write fewer or more joint papers, and more often list their names first or list them last? Does citing of them accelerate? What is the propensity to change fields—for a physicist to tackle the problem of the brain, for a chemist to become an expert on peace or the minimum wage?

To me it was a case where my cup runneth over—almost. The last vestiges of guilt disappeared when I chose to go off the main turnpike of my discipline of economics: to explore R. A. Fisher's notion of survival value, or Clerk Maxwell's image of a Demon who cheats the second law of thermodynamics of its certainty. I still monitor business trends and the latest fads like a hawk. I still write articles in the many different provinces of political economy. But the last generalist no longer feels it necessary to keep on top of—I mean try to keep on top of—all the literatures of economics.

As I veer toward the traditional three score and ten, how do I feel about it? Goethe, who, like Wagner and Verdi, had a great long run, wrote that the difference between age and youth was that in youth, when you called on it, it was always there in response. By contrast, only on the best good days could the octogenarian attain the peak performance. To myself, I am sixty-nine going on twenty-five. All the days seem as good as ever. But, as the lyricist says and reason insists, the stock of what's left of the good times must shrink as you reach September.

Paul A. Samuelson

Awarded Nobel Prize in 1970. Lecture presented February 6, 1985.

Dates of Birth and Death

May 15, 1915; December 13, 2009

Academic Degrees

B.A., University of Chicago, 1935
M.A., Harvard University, 1936
Ph.D., Harvard University, 1941

Academic Affiliations

Assistant Professor of Economics, Massachusetts Institute of Technology, 1940
Associate Professor of Economics, Massachusetts Institute of Technology, 1944
Professor of International Economic Relations, Fletcher School of Law and Diplomacy, Tufts University, 1945
Professor of Economics, Massachusetts Institute of Technology, 1947
Institute Professor, Massachusetts Institute of Technology, 1966–86
Institute Professor, Emeritus, Massachusetts Institute of Technology, 1986–2009
Vernon F. Taylor Visiting Distinguished Professor, Trinity University, 1989

Selected Books

Foundations of Economic Analysis, 1947, 1983
Economics, 1948, 2001 (17th edition, with W. Nordhaus)
Linear Programming and Economic Analysis, 1958, 1987
(with R. Dorfman and R. M. Solow)
The Collected Scientific Papers of Paul A. Samuelson, Vols. 1–5, 1966–2000

Milton Friedman

The topic assigned to me was "My Evolution as an Economist." I am
sure, however, that some questions about the Nobel Prize hold greater
interest for at least some of you than my evolution as an economist—in
particular, how to get a Nobel Prize in Economics. So, as an empirical
scientist, I decided to investigate statistically what an economist has to
do to get a Nobel Prize.

As most of you may know, the economics award is relatively recent. It
was established by the Central Bank of Sweden in 1968 to commemorate
its three-hundredth anniversary. So far, twenty-two people have received
the Nobel award in economics. Not one of them has been female—so,
to judge only from the past, the most important thing to do if you want
to be a Nobel laureate is to be male. I hasten to add that the absence of
females is not, I believe, attributable to male chauvinist bias on the part
of the Swedish Nobel Committee. I believe that the economics profession
as a whole would have been nearly unanimous that, during the period
in question, only one female candidate met the relevant standards—the
English economist Joan Robinson, who has since died. The failure of
the Nobel Committee to award her a prize may well have reflected bias
but not sex bias. The economists here will understand what I am talking
about.

A second requirement is to be a U.S. citizen. Twelve of the twenty-two recipients of the Nobel Prize were from the United States, four from the United Kingdom, two from Sweden, and one each from four other countries. This generalization is less clear-cut than the first because the population of the United States is more than three times as large as Britain, but the number of Nobel recipients only three times as large. So on a per-capita basis, Britain has a better record than we have.

A third generalization is, at least to me, the most interesting statistical result. Of the twelve Americans who have won the Nobel Prize in Economics, nine either studied or taught at the University of Chicago. So the next lesson is to go to the University of Chicago. And I may say, in addition to those nine, one other, Friedrich Hayek, also taught at the University of Chicago for ten years. However, I have classified him as an Austrian rather than an American in my compilation. Beyond that, the statistics won't go, and that's all the advice I can give to potential Nobel laureates.

The most memorable feature of receiving a Nobel award is the week in Sweden in early December during which the formal ceremonies are held. It seemed to my wife and me when we were there that all of Sweden spends that week doing nothing but paying attention to the Nobel ceremonies. One party or affair succeeds another. The week culminates in a feast and a dance at which each laureate is required to give a toast lasting not more than three minutes to an already tipsy audience.

To turn to the suggested autobiographical subject matter, as I have thought back over my own life experience and that of others, I have been enormously impressed by the role that pure chance plays in determining our life history. I was reminded of some famous lines of Robert Frost:

Two roads diverged in a yellow wood,
And sorry I could not travel both
I took the one less traveled by,
And that has made all the difference.

As I recalled my own experience and development, I was impressed by the series of lucky accidents that determined the road I traveled. The first, and surely the most important, was the lucky accident that I was born in the United States. Both my parents were born in Carpatho-Ruthenia, which when they emigrated to the United States was part of Austro-Hungary, later, part of Czechoslovakia, currently, part of the Soviet Union. Both came to the United States as teenagers; they met and married in this country. If they had stayed at home, had nonetheless married one another, and had the same children, I would today be a citizen of the Soviet Union and not of the United States. That was surely pure accident, as it is for most residents of the United States, who like myself are the descendants of people who came to this country as immigrants one or two or three generations ago. As with my parents, most of them brought little with them except their hands and their mouths.

The second major lucky accident was a high school teacher I had as a sophomore. His field was political science—or civics, as it was called then—but he had a great love for geometry. The course I took from him in Euclidean geometry instilled in me a love and respect for and interest in mathematics that has remained with me ever since. I shall never forget his using the proof of the Pythagorean theorem (the theorem that the sum of the squares of the two sides of a right triangle equals the square of the hypotenuse) as an occasion to quote the last lines of Keats's *Ode on a Grecian Urn,* "Beauty is truth, truth beauty—that is all / Ye know on earth, / and all ye need to know."

A third event, or rather series of chance events, occurred during my college career. As Bill Breit told you, I went to Rutgers University, which today is a mega-university, a mammoth state university. In 1928, when I entered Rutgers, it was a small private college, though the process of converting it to a state university was already in its early stages, in the form of a system of competitive scholarships, tenable at Rutgers and funded by the state of New Jersey. I managed to win one of those scholarships, which relieved me of having to pay tuition to go to college.

My parents, like so many immigrants of that time, were very poor. We never had a family income that by today's standards would have put us above the poverty level. In addition, my father died when I was a senior in high school. However, thanks to the state scholarship plus the usual combination of such jobs as waiting on tables, clerking in stores, and working in the summer, I was well able to pay my own way through college—and indeed ended up with a small nest egg that helped meet the expenses of my first year of graduate study.

Because of my interest in math, I planned to major in mathematics. I was very innocent and the only occupation I knew of that used mathematics was being an insurance actuary, so that was my intended career. The actuarial profession is a highly specialized profession, which has an association that conducts a series of examinations that a budding actuary must pass to become a fellow and to become established in the profession. As an undergraduate, I took some of those exams. I passed a couple and failed a couple—the only exams I can remember ever failing.

By accident, I also took some courses in economics, and that is where
the Goddess of Chance entered the picture, because the Rutgers economics faculty included two extraordinary teachers who had a major impact
on my life. One was Arthur F. Burns, who many years later became chairman of the Federal Reserve System and is currently our ambassador to
West Germany. When I first studied under him, more than fifty years ago,
Arthur was in the process of writing his doctoral dissertation. Then, and
in my later contacts with him, he instilled a passion for scientific integrity
and for accuracy and care that has had a major effect on my scientific
work. The other teacher who changed my life was Homer Jones, who was
teaching at Rutgers to earn a living while working on a doctoral degree
at the University of Chicago. Both are still among my closest friends a
half-century later.

Homer later went on to become a vice-president in charge of research
at the Federal Reserve Bank of St. Louis. In that capacity he has had a
major influence on the spread of interest and knowledge about money
in the United States. The publications of the Federal Reserve Bank of St.
Louis are unquestionably cited more frequently in the scientific literature than those of any of the other eleven Federal Reserve banks; that is
entirely attributable to Homer.

If not for my good fortune in encountering those two extraordinary
people, my life would have been radically different, which brings me to
the fourth accident. When I finished college I still didn't know whether
I wanted to continue in mathematics or economics. Like all youngsters
who need financial assistance, I applied to a number of universities for
fellowships or scholarships. In the 1930s the kind of assistance a student
could get was much less generous than it is these days—it was a different world altogether. I was lucky enough to receive two offers of tuition
scholarships, one in applied mathematics from Brown University and one
in economics from the University of Chicago. The offer from Chicago
undoubtedly came because Homer Jones intervened on my behalf with
Frank Knight, who was his teacher at Chicago.

It was close to a toss of a coin that determined which offer I accepted.
If I had gone to Brown, I would have become an applied mathematician.
Having chosen Chicago, I became an economist. As Frost said, "Two
roads diverged in a yellow wood." I cannot say I took the less traveled
one, but the one I took determined the whole course of my life.

The reason I chose as I did was not only, perhaps not even primarily, the intellectual appeal of economics. Neither was it simply the influence of Homer and Arthur, though that was important. It was at least

as much the times. I graduated from college in 1932, when the United States was at the bottom of the deepest depression in its history before or since. The dominant problem of the time was economics. How to get out of the Depression? How to reduce unemployment? What explained the paradox of great need on the one hand and unused resources on the other? Under the circumstances, becoming an economist seemed more relevant to the burning issues of the day than becoming an applied mathematician or an actuary.

The first quarter I was at Chicago, the fall of 1932, one course, with Jacob Viner, who was a great teacher, had a major effect on both my professional and personal life. Professionally, Viner's course in theory opened up a new world. He made me realize that economic theory was a coherent, logical whole that held together, that it didn't consist simply of a set of disjointed propositions. That course was unquestionably the greatest intellectual experience of my life.

In addition, it so happened that a fellow classmate was a beautiful young lady by the name of Rose Director. Because Viner seated people alphabetically, she sat next to me, and that too has shaped my whole life. We were married some years later and some forty-seven years later are still in that happy state. Again, consider the role of pure chance. Rose grew up in Portland, Oregon. I grew up in a small town in New Jersey. We met in an economics classroom in Chicago. Hardly something that could have been planned by anybody.

Other faculty members at Chicago included Frank Knight, Henry Simons, Lloyd Mints, Paul Douglas, and Henry Schultz. Economists will recognize their names; the rest of you will not. They were an extraordinarily talented and varied group of eminent economists. The graduate students were equally outstanding there—indeed one of them in addition to Rose is in this audience, Kenneth Boulding. I formed the view at that time, and have never seen reason to alter it since, that students don't learn from professors but from fellow students. The real function of a professor is to provide topics for bull sessions.

To continue with my own experience, Henry Schultz, who taught statistics and mathematical economics at Chicago, was a close friend of Harold Hotelling, a mathematical economist and statistician at Columbia, and recommended me to him. As a result, I was awarded a fellowship to Columbia. So after spending one year at Chicago I went to Columbia the next year.

Harold Hotelling gave me the same kind of feeling for mathematical statistics that Viner had for economic theory. In addition, Wesley C.

Mitchell introduced me to both the institutional approach to economic theory and the various attempts to explain the business cycle, and John Maurice Clark, to his own inimitable combination of pure theory and social and institutional detail. At Columbia, too, the graduate students were a remarkably able group, some of whom have remained lifelong friends.

As a result of my experience, I concluded that, at least in the mid-thirties, the ideal combination for a budding economist was a year of study at Chicago, which emphasized theory, and a year of study at Columbia, which emphasized institutional influences and empirical work.

The following year I returned to Chicago as a research assistant for Henry Schultz, and once again chance was good to me. Two fellow graduate students happened to be George Stigler and W. Allen Wallis.

George Stigler is also a Nobel laureate and a fellow lecturer in this series. He still teaches at the University of Chicago. George was and is a delight and a treasure as a friend and an intellectual influence. No economist has either a more lively and original mind or a better writing style. His writings are almost unique in the economic literature for their combination of economic content, humor, and literary quality. Few economists have germinated so many new ideas and so profoundly influenced the course of economic research. Allen Wallis went on to be dean of the business school at the University of Chicago, then chancellor of the University of Rochester, and is currently under secretary of state for economic affairs. Allen and George remain among Rose's and my closest friends and both have had a continuing influence on my own professional work.

The combination of influences stemming from Chicago and Columbia—the one heavy on theory, the other heavy on statistical and empirical evidence—has shaped my scientific work, essentially all of which has been characterized by a mixture of theory and fact—of theory and attempts to test the implications of the theory. I refer to "scientific work" to distinguish it from Rose's and my writings for the general public: *Capitalism and Freedom, Free to Choose,* and *Tyranny of the Status Quo.*

My doctoral dissertation grew out of a study I worked on under Simon Kuznets, another American Nobel laureate. Simon was then at the National Bureau of Economic Research. He hired me to work with him on a project growing out of data on professional incomes that he had collected in the course of constructing the initial Department of Commerce estimates of national income. The end result was a book Simon and I collaborated on titled *Income from Independent Professional Practice.*

The core of the book is the use of the economic theory of distribution to explain and interpret the data on the incomes of various professions. The book was finished just before World War II, but was not published until after the war because of a controversy about one of its findings. That finding had to do with the effect of the monopolistic position of the American Medical Association on the incomes of physicians—not exactly a topic that has lost interest over the subsequent forty-odd years. Similarly, a later book, *The Theory of the Consumption Function,* had the same characteristics of combining theory and empirical evidence, and that is also true of the various books I've written alone or in collaboration with Anna J. Schwartz on money.

Another major influence on my scientific work was the experience during World War II. The first two years of that war, 1941 to 1943, I spent at the U.S. Treasury as an economist in the division dealing with taxes. Indeed, Rose has never forgiven me for the part I played in devising and developing withholding at source for the income tax. There is no doubt that it would not have been possible to collect the amount of taxes imposed during World War II without withholding taxes at source. But it is also true that the existence of withholding has made it possible for taxes to be higher after the war than they otherwise could have been. So I have a good deal of sympathy with the view that, however necessary withholding may have been for wartime purposes, its existence has had some negative effects in the postwar period. Those two years in Washington gave me a liberal education in how policy is and is not made in Washington—a most valuable experience. Fortunately, I escaped before I caught Potomac Fever, a deadly disease for someone whose primary interest is scientific.

The second two years of the war, 1943 to 1945, I spent as a mathematical statistician at the Statistical Research Group of the Division of War Research of Columbia University. It had been set up to provide statistical assistance to the military services and to other groups engaged in war research. It was a subsidiary of the wartime-created Office of Scientific Research and Development. Harold Hotelling was its intellectual sponsor and Allen Wallis its executive director. That experience exposed me to physical scientists from a wide range of fields with whom I would otherwise never have had much contact. It also required me to apply statistical techniques to noneconomic data. Surprisingly, perhaps, it turned out that social scientists were often more useful than physical scientists in doing operational research that involved interpreting the results of battlefield experience. The reason is simple: social scientists are used to working with bad data and the wartime data were all very bad. Physical scientists are used to working with accurate data generated by controlled experiments. Many of them were at a loss as how to handle the data generated by experience in the field.

One episode from that period has contributed greatly to my long-term skepticism about economic forecasts and especially about econometric forecasts based on complex multiple regressions. One project for which we provided statistical assistance was the development of high-temperature alloys for use as the lining of jet engines and as blades of turbo superchargers—alloys mostly made of chrome, nickel, and other metals. The efficiency of jet engines and of gas turbines depends critically on the temperature at which they can operate. Raising the temperature a bit increases substantially the efficiency of the turbine, turbo supercharger, or jet engine. Experimentation was being carried on at MIT, Battelle Laboratory in Pittsburgh, and elsewhere. Our group advised on the statistical design of experiments and analyzed much of the resulting data. At one point in the course of doing so, I computed a multiple regression from a substantial body of data relating the strength of an alloy at various temperatures to its composition. My hope was that I could use the equations that I fitted to the data to determine the composition that would give the best result. On paper, my results were splendid. The equations fitted very well and they suggested that a hitherto untried alloy would be far stronger than any existing alloy. The crucial test was to hang a heavy weight on a specimen of the alloy, put it in an oven heated to a high and stable temperature, and measure how long it took for it to break. The best of the alloys at that time were breaking at about ten or twenty hours; my equations predicted that the new alloys would last some two hundred hours. Really astounding results!

A great advantage of the physical sciences over economics is that is possible to test such a prediction promptly. It is not necessary to wait ten years until experience generates new evidence, as is necessary with economic forecasts. So I phoned the metallurgist we were working with at MIT and asked him to cook up a couple of alloys according to my specifications and test them. In order to keep track of them, we had to name them. I had enough confidence in my equations to call them F1 and F2 but not enough to tell the metallurgist what breaking time the equations predicted. That caution proved wise, because the first one of those alloys broke in about two hours and the second one in about three. Ever since, I've been very skeptical of the economic forecasts that people like myself and others make by using multiple regression equations.

In my final comments, let me shift to a different aspect of the Nobel Prize in Economics. As some of you may know, the establishment of a Nobel Prize in Economics has been criticized on the grounds that economics is not a science. One of the severest critics has been Gunnar Myrdal, the Swedish economist who was awarded the Nobel Prize jointly with Friedrich Hayek. That was an alloy of a very peculiar kind—left and right. Myrdal accepted the prize, but subsequently he had second thoughts and wrote a series of articles condemning the prize and expressing regret that he had accepted it. Economics, he said, is not a science in the same sense as physics or chemistry or biology.

I believe that Myrdal is wrong. It is important to distinguish between the scientific work that economists do and the other things that economists do. Economists are members of a community as well as scientists. We do not spend 100 percent of our lives on our purely scientific work, and neither, of course, do physicists or chemists. In principle, I believe that economics has a scientific component no different in character from the scientific component of physics or chemistry or any of the other physical sciences. True, as those who believe otherwise often stress, the physicist can conduct controlled experiments and the economist cannot. But that is hardly sufficient ground to deny the scientific character of economics. Meteorology is a recognized science in which controlled experiments are seldom possible, and there are many other scientific fields that are equally limited. Economists may seldom be able to conduct controlled experiments—although some are possible and have been done—but uncontrolled experience often throws up data that are the equivalent of a controlled experiment. To give you a simple example, it would be hard to devise a better controlled experiment for comparing different economic systems than the experience provided by East Germany and West Germany: two nations that formerly were one, occupied by people of the same background, the same culture, and the same genetic inheritance, torn apart by the accident of war. On one side of the Berlin Wall is a relatively free economic system; on the other side, a collectivist society. Similar controlled experiments are provided by Red China and Taiwan or Hong Kong, and by North and South Korea.

No so-called controlled experiment is truly completely controlled. Two situations can differ in an infinite number of ways. It is impossible to control for all of them. Hence I do not believe that there is any difference in principle between so-called controlled experiments and so-called uncontrolled experience or between the possibility of doing scientific work in economics and in physics. In physics no less than in economics, it is important to distinguish between what people do in their scientific capacity and what they do as citizens. Consider the argument that is now raging about Star Wars, the strategic defense initiative. Some physicists issue manifestos opposing Star Wars; other physicists issue manifestos supporting Star Wars. Clearly, those manifestos do not reflect simply agreed scientific knowledge, but in large measure reflect the personal values, judgments about political events, and so on of the physicists. Their scientific competence or contribution should not be judged by such statements. It should be judged by their scientific work. The same thing, I believe, is true of economists.

To return to my own experience, I have been active in public policy. I have tried to influence public policy. I have spoken and written about issues of policy. In doing so, however, I have not been acting in my scientific capacity but in my capacity as a citizen, an informed one, I hope. I believe that what I know as an economist helps me to form better judgments about some issues than I could without that knowledge. But fundamentally, my scientific work should not be judged by my activities in public policy.

In introducing me, Bill Breit referred to my wanting to be judged by my peers. The episode he referred to occurred in a parking lot in Detroit. The morning on which it was announced that I had been awarded the Nobel Prize, I had agreed to go to Michigan to barnstorm on behalf of a proposed amendment to the state constitution requiring a balanced budget and limiting spending. I had to leave Chicago very early. In Detroit I was picked up at the airport by some of the people running the Michigan campaign and taken to the Detroit Press Club, for a press conference before we started our day of barnstorming. When we got to the parking lot of the press club, we were astonished to see how many reporters and TV people were there, and I remarked that I was amazed that the attempt to get an amendment was receiving so much attention. As I stepped out of the car, a reporter stuck a microphone in my face and said, "What do you think about getting the prize?" I said, "What prize?" He said, "The Nobel Prize." Naturally, I expressed my pleasure at the information. The reporter then said, "Do you regard this as the pinnacle of your career?" or something to that effect, and I said no. I said I was more interested in what my fellow economists would say about my work fifty years from now than about what seven Swedes might say about my work now.

When I was barnstorming that state, I wasn't doing it as a scientist; I was doing it as a citizen deeply concerned about a public issue. Similarly, when I engage in activities to promote a federal constitutional amendment to balance the budget and limit spending, I'm doing so as a citizen. The public has the impression that economists never agree. They have the impression that if three economists are in a room they will get at least four opinions. That is false. If scientific issues are separated from policy and value issues, there is widespread agreement among economists whatever their political views. Over and over again I have been in a group that includes both economists and practitioners of other disciplines. Let a discussion start about almost anything and, in ten minutes or so, you will find all the economists on the same side against all the rest—whether the economists are on the left or on the right or in the middle.

I have great doubts about whether Nobel Prizes as a whole do any good, but I believe that such doubts apply equally to Nobel Prizes in Physics as to Nobel Prizes in Economics.

I have wandered over much terrain and I am not sure that I have explained my evolution as an economist. Let me only say in closing that my life as an economist has been the source of much pleasure and satisfaction. It's a fascinating discipline. What makes it most fascinating is that its fundamental principles are so simple that they can be written on one page, that anybody can understand them, and yet that very few do.

Milton Friedman

Awarded Nobel Prize in 1976. Lecture presented March 21, 1985.

Dates of Birth and Death

July 31, 1912; November 16, 2006

Academic Degrees

B.A., Rutgers University, 1932
M.A., University of Chicago, 1933
Ph.D., Columbia University, 1946

Academic Affiliations

Part-time Lecturer, Columbia University, 1937–40
Visiting Professor of Economics, University of Wisconsin, 1940–41
Associate Professor of Economics and Business Administration, University of Minnesota, 1945–46
Associate Professor of Economics, 1946–48, Professor of Economics, 1948–63, Paul Snowden Russell Distinguished Service Professor of Economics, 1963–82, University of Chicago
Visiting Fulbright Lecturer, Cambridge University, 1953–54
Wesley Clair Mitchell Visiting Research Professor, Columbia University, 1964–65
Visiting Professor, UCLA, winter quarter, 67
Visiting Professor, University of Hawaii, winter quarter, 1972
Senior Research Fellow, Hoover Institute (Stanford), 1977–2006

Selected Books

Essays in Positive Economics, 1953
A Theory of the Consumption Function, 1957
Capitalism and Freedom, 1962, 2002
Price Theory: A Provisional Text, 1962, 1976
A Monetary History of the United States, 1867–1960, 1963
(with Anna J. Schwartz)

George J. Stigler

It is a good rule that a scientist has only one chance to become successful in influencing his science, and that is when he influences his contemporaries. If he is not heeded by his contemporaries, he has lost his chance: brilliant work that is exhumed by a later generation may make the neglected scientist famous, but it will not have made him important. Gossen was a genius, but nothing in the development of utility theory is different for his having lived. Cournot was a genius, and perhaps a bit of his work rubbed off on Edgeworth and later writers on oligopoly, but the theory of the subject dates from the 1880s, not from when he published it in 1838.

Contemporary fame does not ensure lasting fame—the leaders of what prove to be scientific fads recede from even the histories of the science. Today a young economist will not know that a stagnation thesis concerning the American economy was widely discussed in the late 1930s, and Alvin Hansen's name will never regain its onetime prominence. Even Edward Chamberlin's theory of monopolistic competition, it is now clear, failed to initiate a fundamentally new direction of economic theorizing.

So scientific creativity—successful, lasting creativity—must be recognized at the time or it becomes a personal rather than a social achievement. This series of lectures is presented by economists who have met at least the requirement that their work has been recognized by contemporaries. A later age will separate the fundamental from the faddish contributions.

The conditions for creativity in economics have changed in one absolutely basic respect in the last hundred years or so. Until as late as the 1870s or 1880s it was possible for an amateur to become an influential economist; today it is almost inconceivable that major contributions could come from a noneconomist. The knowledge of economics possessed by Adam Smith, or David Ricardo, or even Leon Walras and Francis Edgeworth was self-taught: they had not received formal training in the subject. In more or less modern times the only influential noneconomists I can name are Ramsey, Hotelling, and von Neumann; of course, each was a highly trained mathematician, and all date back forty or more years.

So to understand the conditions under which modern work in economics has emerged, one must look at the conditions of training and work of the modern scholar. Those conditions are no substitute for creativity, but they have become an indispensable condition for creativity to be exercised. I turn, therefore, to a semi-autobiographical sketch of my own life in economics, with primary attention to how the conditions of training and work influence the problems and methods of economic research.

Some Autobiography

I grew up in Seattle, attended schools there through a BBA degree at the University of Washington, proceeded to an MBA on the downtown Chicago campus of Northwestern University, spent one more year dodging unemployment at the University of Washington, and then went to the University of Chicago to get a Ph.D. That breathless sentence covers twenty-two years, on which I shall elaborate a bit. My father and mother migrated to the United States from Bavaria and Hungary, respectively. My father, whose skills as a brewer were devalued by Prohibition, went into the business of buying, repairing, and reselling residential property in Seattle during its depressed 1920s as well as the 1930s. I was a fully relaxed student before college days, a voracious and promiscuous reader but not a strong scholar.

At the University of Washington I did very well in classes, but usually chose the wrong classes. Lacking good judgment as well as guidance from my parents, whose formal education had been modest, I took innumerable "applied" business courses and a good deal of political science, but nothing in mathematics or the physical sciences. I was unknowingly providing proof of a proposition I have come to believe: that undergraduate training is to graduate training perhaps as 1 is to 8 in the acquisition of a research-level mastery of a field. Washington had some respectable economists but none who was at the first level.

Northwestern University began to open my eyes. I took, again, too many applied courses, this time chiefly in urban land economics. I studied with one able and stimulating economist, Coleman Woodbury, and he did as much as anyone to arouse my interest in scholarship as a career. But the University of Chicago was receiving pretty close to a tabula rasa in 1933, when I enrolled. Not that I knew it: twenty-two is not an age of humility.

There I met and got to know three economists I still consider to be outstanding: Frank Knight and Henry Simons, and a year later, on his return from the U.S. Treasury, Jacob Viner.

Knight was both a great and an absurd teacher. The absurdity was documented by his utterly disorganized teaching, with constant change of subject and yet insistent repetition of arguments. In the course on the history of economics he was interested mostly in the seamy side of religious history, but got great relish out of emphasizing the perversities and blunders of Ricardo and other historic figures in economics. His greatness is attested best by the fact that almost all of the students were much influenced by him. He communicated beyond any possible confusion the message that intellectual inquiry was a sacred calling, excruciatingly difficult for even the best of scholars to pursue with complete fidelity to truth and evidence.

Henry Simons was Frank Knight's disciple, but his example was enough to teach us that a disciple may have an independent mind, an ambivalent attitude toward some of his master's beliefs, and a wholly different goal in life. Simons believed that in the 1930s the world was at a crisis of historic magnitude: the survival of freedom and the economic viability of the Western world were at stake. With a wider perspective, Knight believed that the history of man was a history of social folly; the then-current crises were grave, but had equally grave precedents and would be handled as badly as they had been previously. Simons believed with all his heart that the crisis of the 1930s had to be handled well or the basic values of civilization would be lost, and he dedicated his life to that task.

One thing that Knight and Simons both succeeded in teaching me, and in fact overtaught, was that great reputation and high office deserve little respect in scientific work. We were told to listen to the argument and look at the evidence, but ignore the position, degrees, and age of the speaker. This studied irreverence toward authority had a special slant: contemporary ideas were to be treated even more skeptically than those of earlier periods. I didn't realize this distinction at the time because it was implicit rather than explicit. We were taught by example that Ricardo's errors and Marshall's foibles deserved more careful and thorough attention than the nonsense or froth of the day. One can make a case for the greater respect for earlier economists on the basis of the fact that their work had stood the test of time, but that case was not made explicitly.

When Viner returned to Chicago the next year we met a very different type of scholar: immensely erudite, rigorous and systematic in his instruction. Viner was the founder of the Chicago tradition of detailed training in neoclassical microeconomics, including training in its application to real problems. Viner filled the class of Economics 301 with a respect bordering on terror. I still recall the time when he asked a student to list the factors determining the elasticity of demand for a commodity. The student began well enough but soon put the conditions of supply in the list of determinants of demand elasticity. Viner calmly said, "Mr. X, you do not belong in this class." This remark produced a suitable tension in the rest of us. Yet outside the classroom he was kind and helpful, and my appreciation of him has risen steadily over time.

Among the very able people I met in Chicago were several students, and of course we knew each other in a way one could not know the professors. My special friends were Milton Friedman and Allen Wallis. It did not take long to recognize Milton's talents: he was logical, perceptive, quick to understand one's arguments—and quick to find their weaknesses. Friedman has surely exercised one of the major intellectual influences on me throughout my life.

Allen Wallis was so competent and systematic that we soon predicted, to his annoyance, that he would become a university president. A year later Paul Samuelson appeared as a senior in some of our graduate classes, and we had no difficulty in recognizing his quality. The give-and-take among us students (a group that included Kenneth Boulding and Sune Carlson) was the first experience I had of constant exchanges in a circle of first-class minds, and I acquired a lifelong taste for it.

I wrote my dissertation in the history of economic thought under Knight. He was the soul of kindness and generosity in dealing with me, then and forever after, but in retrospect there was a fly in the ointment. He was so strong-minded and so critical a student of the literature that it was a good many years before I could read the economic classics through my eyes instead of his. I have never brought myself to read through my doctoral dissertation, "Production and Distribution Theories: The Formative Period," because I knew I would be embarrassed by both its Knightian excesses and its immaturity.

So when I left Chicago in 1936 to begin teaching at Iowa State College, I had acquired a light smattering of mathematics, a partial command of price theory, a fondness for intellectual history, and an irreverence toward prevailing ideas bordering on congenital skepticism. In retrospect a most modest intellectual arsenal.

Iowa and Minnesota and Later

At times I found myself in the midst of a group of vigorous young economists, who were being brought together by Theodore W. Schultz. I still remember my first class, in economic principles. I had prepared the first few weeks of the course in outline, so I entered the class with confidence. Forty minutes later I had covered all the material in my outline, and there remained ten minutes, not to mention ten and a half weeks, still to go! I wish I could state that eventually I encountered the problem so often reported by colleagues, of never being able to cover all the material, but I never reached this utopia of knowledge or loquacity.

I spent most of my spare time at Ames finishing my doctoral thesis, and I received my Ph.D. in the spring of the second year. I had a number of excellent colleagues and students at Ames, but before I was well settled in, Frederic Garver invited me to come to Minnesota, and I accepted.

My closest colleagues at Minnesota were Garver, Francis Boddy, and Arthur Marget. Alvin Hansen had just gone to Harvard, and indeed it was largely his classes, but not his rank or salary, that I had inherited. It was rumored that my main rival had been Oskar Morgenstern; if that was true, I have fantasized that if he had been chosen I might have become the junior author of the theory of games!

By 1942 the outbreak of war led to a general retrenchment of academic life, and I took a sustained leave of absence from Minnesota, first to the National Bureau of Economic Research. I was hired to study the service industries as part of a program of studies of the trend of the output, employment, and productivity in the American economy. I and my associates collected an awful lot of numbers and published some monographs in such exotic fields as domestic science, education, trade, and (later) scientific personnel. These works were mostly quantitative, with mildly analytical skeletons, as when I made the first productivity measures relating output to an index of *all* inputs.

At the bureau I got to know Arthur Burns, Solomon Fabricant, and Geoffrey Moore. From them, and even more from Milton Friedman, I became persuaded of the importance of empirical evidence in the appraisal of economic theories; that is a theme to which I will return later. From the bureau I went to the Statistical Research Group at Columbia University, where statistical analysis was being used on military problems. The director was Allen Wallis, and the senior figures included Harold Hotelling, Milton Friedman, Jacob Wolfowitz, and, among other statisticians, L. J. Savage and Abraham Wald. I learned a little statistics there, and I did not seriously delay our nation's victory.

Near the end of the war I returned to Minnesota, and a year later Milton Friedman joined us. The reunion, alas, was brief, for a year later Friedman went to Chicago and I to Brown. (I may mention that in 1946 I was offered a Chicago professorship but managed to alienate the president, Ernest Colwell, in an interview and was vetoed. Thereby I probably hastened Friedman's return to Chicago by a year, and can claim some credit for helping found the new Chicago school.) And a year after that, I went to Columbia University, where Albert Hart, William Vickrey, and I taught the graduate theory course. I also assumed the teaching of industrial organization and the history of economics. Columbia then, as now, had a strong department, which included Arthur F. Burns, Carl Shoup, Ragnar Nurkse, and others. And that speedy journey brings me back to Chicago in 1958.

Back to Chicago

I was returning to an economics community in a stage of high prosperity. Friedman was an ascendant figure in world economics: his Consumption Function had revolutionized the statistical analysis of economic data, and his work on monetarism constituted the major attack on the ruling Keynesian doctrine. Modern labor economics was being fashioned by Gregg Lewis and by a recent Chicago Ph.D. already at Columbia, Gary Becker, and his colleague Jacob Mincer. Theodore Schultz was well into his work on the economics of education as well as continuing his influential work on economic growth. Arnold Harberger was making fundamental studies in public finance and developing a major role through both his work and his students in economic development.

My main work was to be in industrial organization. I already had Reuben Kessel and Lester Telser as colleagues, and to my great delight Ronald Coase joined us three years later. The main influence on me, however, was Aaron Director, with whom I had formed a close friendship at the first meeting of the Mt. Pelerin Society in 1947. Aaron was and is a paragon of all collegial virtues. He has a strong, independent mind and he has thought deeply on many questions, dissecting widely accepted and comfortable ideas to reveal their essential superficiality and frequent inconsistencies. He was in the law school, teaching primarily the antitrust course with Edward H. Levi, so his primary work was in antitrust economics.

I cannot recount the number of times in which Director's always courteous questioning led me either to change my views or to seek evidence to reinforce their relevance and weight. If we had been in Greece, I'm sure I would have called him Socrates. His questioning of McGee had already led to John's famous article on predatory pricing, his questioning of Telser soon contributed to Lester's famous article on resale price maintenance, and his questioning of Ward Bowman and Meyer Burstein and George Hilton led to their articles on price discrimination and the metering of demand. Concluding that Director would never write, later I was provoked to present one of his ideas with the title, "Director's Law of Income Redistribution."

My Work

Much the most important contribution I have made to economics is information theory. It could have originated in the attempt to generalize economic theories that usually assumed that economic actors had complete knowledge of their markets and technology. But it did not: my discomfort was with a theory that did not account for the fact that almost every product or service will have a distribution of prices, not a unique price, at a given time.

My own observations, partly of price data in antitrust areas, confirmed the existence of a variety of prices of a reasonably homogeneous good. The most obvious available explanation, product differentiation of Chamberlin's sort, seemed inappropriate to markets in automobiles of a given model at retail, bituminous coal, and the like. The apparent near-homogeneity of the products aside, there appeared to be no interesting empirical predictions derivable from monopolistic competition theory as to the extent of price dispersion, its changes over time, and the factors that led to the dispersion.

It occurred to me that it was the expensiveness of knowledge that sustained price differences. Search is never free and often expensive. To visit eight or ten automobile dealers in my search for a given automobile could cost a day plus transportation costs. To visit a second supermarket could require twenty minutes, and the average value of twenty minutes to an American adult is perhaps three dollars.

From the theory of search for the lowest price by a buyer or the highest price by a seller, we can deduce many corollaries. Clearly, the price dispersion relative to the average price will be less the more the buyer spends on it, because the costs of search do not go up as fast as the value of the commodity purchased. The dispersion of prices of automobiles relative to their average price will be lower than that of prices of microwave ovens. Again, knowledge decays gradually with the passage of time, so we expect goods bought frequently to have less price dispersion than infrequently purchased goods of equal value. The amount of search varies with the length of time one lives in a community, so tourists on average pay more for things than natives do.

I applied the theory to the labor markets and it shed light on a variety of the observed wage patterns. Information has other dimensions besides price, so I made a wholly different application of information to the problem of colluding oligopolists, where the central problem is to detect departures from the collusive agreement. Here I invoked observable quantities, not unobservable genuine transaction prices, to detect surreptitious competitive behavior. I also made an attempt to view the functions of advertising in this light, in contrast to the tradition of economists' hostility to advertising.

I must confess that I did not imagine the variety of informational problems in economics that would emerge in the next two decades. For a time it seemed essential to have the phrase "asymmetrical information" in the title of every journal article. Yet the subject is far from exhausted, and I have recently returned to the problem of political information.

I was not led to the economics of information by the previous literature; indeed that previous literature was virtually nonexistent. Only later did I realize that a suggestive treatment resided in Charles Babbage's discussion of what he called the verification of prices.

My work in the theory of economic regulation has a different but related intellectual history. Starting in the early 1960s, I made a series of studies of the actual effects of several public regulatory policies: state utility commission regulation of electric utility rates; SEC regulation of new stock issues; and the antitrust laws. I made these studies because I was skeptical of the prevailing practice in economics of treating the prescriptions of law as actual practice. My findings were often surprising: the regulation of electric utilities did not help residential users; the regulation of new stock issues did not help the widows and orphans who bought these issues.

Only slowly, I should say inexcusably slowly, did I come to the most obvious of questions: why do we get public regulation? I attempted to answer the question by looking at costs and benefits to the various parties. This approach was highly incompatible with the ruling approach in political science. There the introduction of a regulatory policy simply represented the response of the legislature to an aroused public demand for protection of the public interest. The demand of the public, in turn, was due to the existence and growth of some social evil, perhaps called to public attention by vigorous reformers. This "public interest" theory did very poorly in explaining protective tariffs or the farm program and had nothing to say about the dates at which policies were initiated: why was the social security system begun in the 1930s rather than the 1890s or the 1950s?

My work on regulation was much more closely related to that of others than was my work on information. Anthony Downs, James Buchanan, and Gordon Tullock had made large beginnings in the application of economic logic to politics, and my style of approach differed primarily in its strong empirical orientation.

These are examples of my theoretical work directed to the explanation of observed phenomena, with little or no relationship to the work of other economists. It is instructive to look also at a problem I worked on that emerged directly from the literature.

The determination of the efficient sizes of business enterprises is an interesting example. Economists sought to establish the most efficient size of enterprise in any industry by one of three methods: (1) a direct comparison of observed costs of enterprises of different sizes, (2) a direct comparison of rates of return on investment of enterprises of different sizes, and (3) an estimation of cost functions on the basis of technological information. Each of these methods encounters severe problems, always of data and often of logic.

I sought an answer by resorting to a sort of Darwinian approach, which had already been employed in a related manner by Alchian. My argument was essentially this: if I wish to know whether a tiger or a panther is the stronger animal, I put them in the same cage and return after a few hours. Similarly, by seeing the sizes to which firms competing in an industry were tending, I could deduce the efficient sizes—a method called the survivor technique.

The method seems obvious and, I later found, had antecedents as illustrious as John Stuart Mill, but for a considerable time the method encountered substantial opposition. The National Bureau of Economic Research, where it was written, did not wish to publish it, perhaps because it was too controversial.

There is no reliable way to discover something new: if there were, it would infallibly be discovered. It seems evident to me that Friedman's splendid theory of consumption function arose out of puzzles displayed by observable data, and Arrow's splendid impossibility theorem arose out of profound thought about the process of social decision-making.

Conclusion

I should warn you, although I confess I should have done so at the outset rather than at the conclusion of this lecture, that I am a strong supporter of the view that a knowledge of the life of a scholar is more often a source of misunderstanding than of enlightenment about his work. Obviously, my arguments for this view have not been convincing, or Professor Breit would not have organized this lecture series.

The reason that this biographical approach—it bears the oppressive name of prosopography—is misleading is that its devotees usually pick out of a scholar's life some circumstance or event that they find explains a given theory. To give you real and absurd examples, one historian said life on a small island led Malthus to fear overpopulation; another said John Stuart Mill could not be original because he wrote his *Principles* in less than two years.

I am not prepared to say that one's work is independent of one's life. Possibly if I had gone to Harvard instead of Chicago, I would have been a believer in monopolistic competition, a student of input-output tables, or a member of the Mason school of industrial organization. But I do not attach high probabilities to these possibilities. I am no longer a faithful follower, although I am still an admirer, of Frank Knight and Henry Simons: each person has a mind-style of his own, and eventually it asserts itself. This does not mean that we are immune to our environment, but it does argue for me that environmental influences will be subtle.

I not only believe this to be true but also I hope that it is true: the prospects for scientific progress would be bleak if we could train our students to become truly faithful disciples. If you understand my scientific work better for having heard me, I shall be both pleased and envious.

George J. Stigler

Awarded Nobel Prize in 1982. Lecture presented April 17, 1985.

Dates of Birth and Death

January 17, 1911; December 1, 1991

Academic Degrees

B.B.A., University of Washington, 1931
M.B.A., Northwestern University, 1932
Ph.D., University of Chicago, 1938

Academic Affiliations

Assistant Professor, Iowa State University, 1936–38
Assistant, Associate, and Full Professor, University of Minnesota, 1938–46
Professor, Brown University, 1946–47
Professor, Columbia University, 1947–58
Charles R. Walgreen Distinguished Service Professor of American Institutions, University of Chicago, 1958–81
Director, Center for the Study of the Economy and the State, University of Chicago, 1981–91

Selected Books

Production and Distribution Theories, 1941, 1994
The Theory of Price, 1946, 1987
Essays in the History of Economics, 1965
The Organization of Industry, 1968, 1983
The Citizen and the State: Essays on Regulation, 1975

James Tobin

Beginning with Keynes at Harvard

Rare is the child, I suspect, who wants to grow up to be an economist, or a professor. I grew up in a university town and went to a university-run high school, where most of my friends were faculty kids. I was so unfailing an A student that it was boring even to me. But I don't recall thinking of an academic career. I liked journalism, my father's occupation; I had put out "newspapers" of my own from age six. I thought of law; I loved to argue, and beginning in my teens I was fascinated by politics. I guess I knew that there was economics at the university, but I didn't know what the subject really was. Of course, economic issues were always coming up in classes on history and government—civics, in those days. I expected economics to be among the social science courses I would someday take in college, probably part of the pre-law curriculum.

I grew up happily assuming I would go to college in my hometown, to the University of Illinois. One month before I was scheduled to enroll as a freshman, I was offered and accepted a Conant Prize Fellowship at Harvard. I should explain how this happened. My father, a learned man, a voracious reader, the biggest customer of the Champaign Public Library, discovered in the *New York Times* that Harvard was offering two of these new fellowships in each of five midwestern states. President Conant wanted to broaden the geographic and social base of Harvard College. Having nothing to lose, I accepted my father's suggestion that I apply. University High School, it turned out, had without even trying prepared me superbly for the obligatory College Board exams. Uni High graduates only thirty to thirty-five persons a year, but it has three Nobels to its credit and, once I had broken the ice, many national scholarships.

Thus James Bryant Conant, Louis Michael Tobin, and University High School changed my life and career. Illinois was and is a great university. But I doubt that it would have led me into economics. For several reasons, Harvard did.

Harvard was the leading academic center of economics in North America at the time; only Columbia and Chicago were close competitors. Both its senior and junior faculty were outstanding. Two previous Nobel laureates in economics were active and influential members of the community when I was a student, Wassily Leontief on the faculty and Paul Samuelson as a Junior Fellow, a graduate student free of formal academic requirements. Of the senior faculty of the 1930s, Joseph Schumpeter would have been a sure bet for a Nobel, Alvin Hansen, Edward Chamberlin, and Gottfried Haberler likely choices. Haberler, still active, remains a possibility. Naturally, Harvard attracted remarkably talented graduate students. That able undergraduates might go on to scholarly careers was taken for granted.

Like many other economists of my vintage, I was attracted to the field for two reasons. One was that economic theory is a fascinating intellectual challenge, on the order of mathematics or chess. I liked analytics and logical argument. I thought algebra was the most eye-opening school experience between the three R's and college.

The other reason was the obvious relevance of economics to understanding and perhaps overcoming the Great Depression and all the frightening political developments associated with it throughout the world. I did not personally suffer deprivations during the Depression. But my parents made me very conscious of the political and economic problems of the times. My father was a well-informed and thoughtful political liberal. My mother was a social worker, recalled to her career by the emergency; she was dealing with cases of unemployment and poverty every day.

The second motivation, I observe, gave our generation of economists different interests and priorities from subsequent cohorts dominated by those attracted to the subject more exclusively by the appeal of its puzzles to their quantitative aptitudes and interests.

Thanks to Keynes, economics offered me the best of both worlds. I was fascinated by his theoretical duel with the orthodox classical economists. Keynes's uprising against encrusted error was an appealing crusade for youth. The truth would make us free, and fully employed too. I was already an ardent and uncritical New Dealer, much concerned about the depression, unemployment, and poverty. According to Keynesian theory, Roosevelt's devaluation of the dollar and deficit spending were sound economics after all.

Harvard was becoming the beachhead for the Keynesian invasion of the new world. The senior faculty was mostly hostile. A group of them had not long before published a book quite critical of Roosevelt's recovery program. Seymour Harris, an early convert to Keynes, was an exception, especially important to undergraduates like myself, in whom he took a paternal interest. Harris was an academic entrepreneur. He opened the pages of the *Review of Economics and Statistics,* of which he was editor, and the halls of Dunster House, of which he was senior tutor, to lively debates on economic theory and policy.

The younger faculty and the graduate student teaching fellows were enthusiastic about Keynes's book. Their reasons were similar to my own but better informed. A popular tract by seven of them, *An Economic Program for American Democracy,* preached the new gospel with a left-wing slant.

Most important of all was the arrival of Alvin Hansen to fill the new Littauer chair in political economy. Hansen, aged fifty, came to Harvard from the University of Minnesota the same year I was beginning economics. He had previously been critical of Keynes and had indeed published a lukewarm review of the *General Theory.* He changed his mind 180 degrees, a rare event for scholars of any age, especially if their previous views are in print. Hansen became the leading apostle of Keynesian theory and policy in America. His fiscal policy seminar was the focus of research, theoretical and applied, in Keynesian economics. Visitors from the Washington firing lines mixed with local students and faculty; I had the feeling that history was being made in that room. For undergraduates the immediate payoff was that Hansen taught us macroeconomics, though under the course rubric Money and Banking. Hansen was a true hero to me, and in later years he was to be a real friend also.

My honors thesis found fault with Keynes's logic. That may seem surprising. But I didn't think Keynes needed to insist on so sweeping a theoretical victory on his opponents' home court. His practical message was just as important whether unemployment was an incident of prolonged disequilibrium or of equilibrium. My first professional publication (1941) was an article in the *Quarterly Journal of Economics* based on my senior thesis; the *QJE* is, of course, edited and published at Harvard. The issue is very much alive today. It has also remained an interest of mine, a subject on which I have published several other papers, including my 1971 presidential address to the American Economic Association (1972).

Tools of the Trade, Theoretical and Statistical

By graduation time in 1939 I had forgotten about law and drifted into the natural decision, to become a professional economist. Harvard has a way of keeping its own: my fellowship was extended and I went on to graduate school. The transition was easy; I had taken courses with graduate students while I was a senior. Now I needed to pick up some tools of the trade. One was formal mathematical economic theory, and another was statistics and econometrics. Harvard was just beginning to catch up to the state of these two arts.

The professors who taught economic statistics were idiosyncratic in the methods they used and quite suspicious of methods based in mathematical statistical theory. Until the 1950s Harvard was pretty much untouched by the developments in Europe led by Ragnar Frisch and Jan Tinbergen or those in the United States at the Cowles Commission. Students like me, who were interested in formal statistical theory, took refuge in the mathematics department. For econometrics we squeezed as much as possible from a seminar on statistical demand functions offered by a European visitor, Hans Staehle. We also discovered that regressions, though scorned by Professors Crum and Frickey, were alive and well under the aegis of Professor John D. Black's program in agricultural economics. In the basement of Littauer Center we could use his electromechanical or manual Marchands and Monroes.

I did just that for my second published paper (1942), originally written for Edward S. Mason's seminar in the spring 1941 semester, on how to use statistical forecasts in defense planning; my example was estimation of civilian demands for steel. The paper was one reason Mason recommended me for a job in Washington with the civilian supply division of the nascent Office of Price Administration and Civilian Supply. So I left Harvard in May 1941, having completed all the requirements for the Ph.D. except the dissertation. I would not return until February

1946. After nine months of helping to ration scarce materials, I went in the Navy and served as a line officer on a destroyer until Christmas 1945.

Statistics and econometrics were important in my research after the war. In my doctoral dissertation (1947) on the determinants of household consumption and saving, I tried to marry "cross-section" data from family budget surveys with aggregate time series, the better to estimate effects of income, wealth, and other variables. In a later study of food demand (1950), I refined the method. This, along with my empirical and theoretical work on rationing, took place in England in 1949–50, at Richard Stone's Department of Applied Economics in Cambridge. I hoped that cross-section observations could resolve the ambiguities of statistical inference based on time series alone. Later, my interest in cross-section and panel data led me to the work of the Michigan Survey Research Center, where I spent a fruitful semester with George Katona, James Morgan, and Lawrence Klein in 1953.

My work on data of this type led me to propose a new statistical method, which became known as Tobit analysis (1958). Probit analysis, which originated in biology, estimates how the probabilities of positive or negative responses to treatment depend on observed characteristics of the organism and the treatment. In economic applications, yes responses often vary in intensity; for example, most families in a sample would report no when asked if they bought a car last year, while those who answer yes spent varying amounts of money on a car. My technique would use both yes-no and quantitative information in seeking the determinants of car purchases.

The label Tobit was perhaps more appropriate than Arthur Goldberger thought when he introduced it in his textbook. Perhaps not. My main claim to fame, a discovery enjoyed by generations of my students, is that, thinly disguised as a midshipman named Tobit, I make a fleeting appearance in Herman Wouk's novel *The Caine Mutiny*. Wouk and I attended the same quick Naval Reserve officers' training school at Columbia in the spring of 1942, and so did Willy, the hero of the novel.

Cowles Foundation Discussion Paper 1 (1955) was a precursor of the Tobit analysis mentioned above. The coming of Cowles was an important factor in the rise of economics at Yale to front-rank stature. I broadened the scope of the foundation's research to include macroeconomics. I was particularly eager to make room for the interests and talents of a young Yale assistant professor, Arthur Okun, who was working on macroeconomic forecasting and policy analysis.

Developing Keynesian Macroeconomics; Synthesizing It with the Neoclassical Tradition

My main program of research and writing after the war continued my early interests in Keynes and macroeconomics. I sought to improve the theoretical foundations of macro models, to fit them into the main corpus of neoclassical economics, and to clarify the roles of monetary and fiscal policies. In this endeavor I shared the objectives of many other economists, notably Abba Lerner, Paul Samuelson, Franco Modigliani, Robert Solow, J. R. Hicks, and James Meade. A new mainstream, synthesizing the Keynesian revolution and the classical economics against which it was revolting, was in the making. I am proud that Paul Samuelson called me a "partner in [this] crime."

The building blocks of the Keynesian structure were four in number: the relation of wages and employment; the propensity to consume; liquidity preference and the demand for money; the inducement to invest. I have already referred to my work on the first. I turn now to the other three.

Keynes's "psychological law" of consumption and saving stated that saving would be an ever-larger proportion of income as per capita real incomes became greater. National income data between the two world wars appeared to confirm his law. Statistical equations, fit to those data, extrapolated to much higher incomes, foretold trouble after the Second World War. Investment would have to be a much larger fraction of national income than ever before to absorb the high saving and avoid recession and unemployment. The extrapolation was wrong. Incomes rose as expected, but consumption was no smaller a proportion than before. This forecasting error triggered an agonizing reappraisal of the consumption function, with fruitful results.

My doctoral dissertation (1947) was on this subject. I thought Keynes's law should be interpreted to refer to the relation of lifetime consumption to lifetime income, not to a relation between those variables year by year. The same considerations implied that wealth, not just current income, determines consumption in the short run. As so often happens, this idea was in the air. Milton Friedman's permanent income theory and Franco Modigliani's life-cycle model were elegant explanations of saving behavior in this spirit. They showed how cyclical data could look "Keynesian" even though saving would be roughly proportional to income in the long run. I have written a number of papers on this subject over the years.

The episode is, I believe, an example of how economic knowledge advances when striking real-world events and issues pose puzzles we have to try to understand and resolve. The most important decisions a scholar makes are what problems to work on. Choosing them just by looking for gaps in the literature is often not very productive and at worst divorces the literature itself from problems that provide more important and productive lines of inquiry. The best economists have taken their subjects from the world around them.

The bulk of my work in the 1950s and 1960s was on the monetary side of macroeconomics. I had several objectives.

First, I wanted to establish a firm foundation for the sensitivity of money demand or money velocity to interest rates. Why was this important? The quantity theory of money, later called monetarism, asserted that there was no such sensitivity, that the velocity of money was constant except for random shocks and for slow, secular changes in public habits, banking institutions, and financial technology. The implication was that fiscal stimulus, such as government spending or tax reduction, could not affect aggregate spending on goods and services unless accompanied by money creation. The same implication applied to autonomous changes in private investment. In this sense Milton Friedman and other monetarists were saying not just that money matters, with which I agreed, but also that money is all that matters, with which I disagreed.

In an empirical paper in 1947 I let the data speak for themselves, loudly in favor of Keynes's liquidity preference curve. But I was not satisfied with Keynes's explanation of liquidity preference. He said people preferred liquid cash because they expected interest rates to rise to "normal" prosperity levels of the past, causing capital losses on holdings of bonds. As William Fellner, later to be my colleague at Yale, pointed out in a friendly debate with me in journal pages, Keynes could hardly call "equilibrium" a situation in which interest rates are persistently lower than investors' expectations of them. Fellner was espousing a principle of model building later called "rational expectations," and I agreed with him.

I found and offered two more tenable sources of the interest sensitivity of demand for money. One (1956) was based on an inventory theory of the management of transactions balances. As I learned too late, I had been mostly anticipated by William Baumol, but the model is commonly cited with both names. The second paper (1958) gave a new rationalization of Keynes's "speculative motive": simply, aversion to risk. People may prefer liquidity, and prefer it more the lower the interest rate on noncash assets, not because they expect capital losses on average but because they fear them more than they value the equally probable capital gains.

I had been working for some time on portfolio choices balancing such risks against expected returns, and the liquidity preference paper was an exposition and application of that work. Harry Markowitz had already set forth a similar model of portfolio choice, and our paths also converged geographically when he spent a year at Yale in 1955–56. My interest was in macroeconomic implications, his more in advising rational investors.

When my prize was announced in Stockholm in 1981, the first reports that reached this country mentioned portfolio theory. This caught the interest of the reporters who faced me at a hastily arranged press conference at Yale. They wanted to know what it was, so I did my best to explain it in lay language, after which they said "Oh no, please explain it in lay language." That's when I referred to the benefits of diversification: "You know, don't put all your eggs in one basket." And that is why headlines throughout the world said "Yale economist wins Nobel for 'Don't put all your eggs, …'" and why a friend of mine sent me a cartoon he had clipped, which followed that headline with a sketch of next year's winner in medicine explaining how his award was for "An apple a day keeps the doctor away."

The fact that one of the available assets in the model of my paper was riskless turned out to have interesting consequences. I felt somewhat uneasy and apologetic that I was pairing the safe asset with just one risky asset to represent everything else. This aggregation followed Keynes, who also used "*the* interest rate" to refer to the common yield on all non-money assets and debts. I proved that my results would apply even if any number of risky assets were available, each with different return and risk. The choice of a risky portfolio, the relative weights of the various risky assets within it, would be independent of the decision how much to put into risky assets relative to the safe asset, money. This "separation theorem" was the key to the capital asset pricing model developed by Lintner and Sharpe, beloved by finance teachers and students, and exploited by the investment managers and counselors who compute and report the "betas" of various securities.

The debate about fiscal and monetary policy, as related to the interest-sensitivity of demand for money, went on for a long time, too much of it a duel between Milton Friedman and me. In a Vermont ski line a young attendant checking season passes read mine and said in a French Canadian accent, "Tobeen, James Tobeen, not ze économiste! Not ze enemy of Professeur Friedman!" He was an economics student in Quebec; it made his day. He let me pass to the lift. This debate, I would say, ended for practical purposes when Friedman shifted ground, saying that no important issue of monetary policy or theory depended on interest sensitivity of money demand. The ground he shifted to was the basic issue between Keynes and the classics, the contention that the economy is always in a supply-constrained equilibrium wherein neither monetary nor fiscal policy can enhance real output.

Second, I proposed to put money into the theory of long-run growth. In the 1950s one phase of the synthesis of Keynesian and neoclassical economics was the development of a growth theory along neoclassical lines. Some, not all, Keynesians were ready to agree that in the long run employment is full, saving limits investment, and "supply creates its own demand." The short run was the Keynesian domain, where labor and capital may be underemployed, investment governs saving, and demand induces its own supply. Roy Harrod had started modern growth theory in 1939, followed by Evsey Domar in the 1940s and Trevor Swan, Robert Solow, Edmund Phelps, and many others in the 1950s and 1960s.

I was involved too. My 1955 piece, "A Dynamic Aggregative Model," may be my favorite; it was the most fun to write. It differed from the other growth literature by explicitly introducing monetary government debt as a store of value, a vehicle of saving alternative to real capital, and by generating a business cycle that interrupted the growth process. In three subsequent papers (1965, 1968, and 1985) I showed that the stock of capital in a growing economy is positively related to the rates of monetary growth and inflation.

Third, in a long series of papers I developed, together with William Brainard and other colleagues at Yale, a general model of asset markets and integrated it into a full macroeconomic model. In a sense we generalized Hicks's famous IS-LM formalization of Keynes by allowing for a richer menu of assets. As I already indicated, I had been uncomfortable with that unique "*the* interest rate" in Keynes and with the simple dichotomy of money versus everything else, usually described as money versus bonds. I thought nominal assets versus real capital was at least as important a way of splitting wealth, if it must be split in only two parts, and this is what I did in the growth models cited above.

Portfolio theory suggested that assets should be regarded as imperfect substitutes for each other, with their differences in expected yields reflecting their marginal risks. Our approach also suggested that there is no sharp dividing line between assets that are money and those that are not. The "Yale approach" to monetary and financial theory has been widely used in empirical flow-of-funds studies and in modeling international capital movements.

Our approach also explicitly recognizes the stock-flow dynamics of saving, investment, and asset accumulation, as in my 1981 Nobel lecture. These dynamics were explicitly ignored in Keynes, who defined the short run as a period in which the change in the stock of capital due to the flow of new investment is insignificant. Stock-flow dynamics are also ignored in IS-LM models. But flows do add to stocks. Investment builds the capital stock, government deficits enlarge the stocks of government bonds and possibly of money, trade surpluses increase the net assets of the nation vis-à-vis the rest of the world, and so on. Without these effects, macro stories about policies and other events are incomplete.

The bottom line of monetary policy is its effect on capital investment, in business plant and equipment, residences, inventories, and consumer durable goods. The effect is not well represented by the market interest rates usually cited, or by quantities of money or credit. Our approach to monetary economics and macroeconomics led us naturally to a different measure, closer to investment decisions. This has become known as "Tobin's q." It is the ratio of the market valuations of capital assets to their replacement costs, for example, the prices of existing houses relative to the costs of building comparable new ones. For corporate businesses, the market valuations are made in the securities markets. It is common sense that the incentive to make new capital investments is high when the securities giving title to their future earnings can be sold for more than the investments cost, that is, when q exceeds one. We see the reverse in takeovers of companies whose q's are less than one; it is cheaper to buy their productive assets by acquiring their shares than to construct comparable facilities from scratch. That is why in our models q is the link from the central bank and the financial markets to the real economy.

Policy and Public Service

As must be clear from my narrative, I have always been intensely interested in economic policy. Much of my theoretical and empirical research has been devoted to analyzing and discerning the effects of monetary and fiscal policies. In the 1950s I began writing occasional articles on current economic issues for general readership, some of them in the *New Republic*, the *Yale Review*, *Challenge*, and the *New York Times*.

Some of my friends in Massachusetts were advising Senator Kennedy. They told him and his staff about me. In the summer of 1960 Ted

Sorenson came to see me and arranged for the Kennedy campaign to employ me to write some memoranda and position papers on economic growth. Sorenson signed me up, even though I felt it necessary to tell him I favored Stevenson for the nomination. I didn't notice any effects of my memos during the campaign, but I was told that they were used by the Kennedy team at the party platform deliberations, mainly to oppose the exaggerated "spend to grow" views of Leon Keyserling and some union economists.

My message at the time was that we needed a tight budget, one that would yield a surplus at full employment, and a very easy monetary policy, one that would get interest rates low enough to channel the government's surplus into productive capital investment. The point was to have full employment, but by a mix of policies that promoted growth in the economy's capacity to produce. Incidentally, my message is similar today. After the 1960 election I served on a transition task force on the domestic economy chaired by Paul Samuelson. One day in early January 1961 I was summoned from lunch at the faculty club to take a phone call from the president-elect. He asked me to serve as a member of his Council of Economic Advisers. JT: "I'm afraid you've got the wrong guy, Mr. President. I'm an ivory-tower economist." JFK: "That's the best kind. I'll be an ivory-tower president." JT: "That's the best kind." I took a day or two to talk to Betty and to my colleagues and then said Yes. I served for twenty months.

Walter Heller was the chairman of the council, and Kermit Gordon was the other member. We had a fantastic staff, including Art Okun, Bob Solow, Ken Arrow, and a younger generation whose names would also be recognized as leaders in our profession today. We were all congenial, intellectually and personally, and we functioned by consensus without hierarchy or bureaucracy. We were optimistic, confident that our economics could improve policy and do good in the world. It was the opportunity that had motivated me to embrace economics a quarter century before.

The January 1962 *Economic Report* is the manifesto of our economics, applied to the United States and world economic conditions of the day. The press called it "the new economics," but it was essentially the blend of Keynesian and neoclassical economics we had been developing and elaborating for the previous ten years. The report was a collective effort, written mainly by Heller, Gordon, Solow, Okun, and Tobin. It doesn't appear on my personal bibliography, but I am proud of it as a work of professional economics as well as a public document. The January

1982 *Report* is the comparable document of Reaganomics, likewise the effort of professional economists to articulate a radically new approach to federal economic policy. It is interesting to compare the two; we have nothing to fear.

The Kennedy council was effective and influential because the president and his immediate White House staff took academics seriously, took ideas seriously, took us seriously. JFK was innocent of economics on inauguration day. But he was an interested, curious, keen, and able student. He read what we wrote, listened to what we said, and learned a lot.

Our central macroeconomic objective was to lower unemployment, 7 percent in January 1961, to 4 percent, our tentative estimate of the inflation-safe unemployment rate. That goal was achieved by the end of 1965, with negligible increase in the rate of inflation and with a big increase in capital investment. The sweet success turned sour in the late 1960s, when contrary to the advice of his council and other Keynesian advisers President Johnson failed to raise taxes to pay for the escalating costs of the war in Vietnam. Critics looking back on the 1960s accuse the Kennedy–Johnson economists of naive belief in a Phillips trade-off and of policies explicitly designed to purchase lower unemployment with higher inflation. The criticism is not justified. The council did not propose to push unemployment below what came to be known as the "natural rate." Moreover, beginning in 1961 the council and the administration adopted wage and price policies designed to achieve an inflation-free recovery; "guideposts for noninflationary price and wage behavior" were espoused in the report.

I returned to Yale in September 1962. I loved the job at the council, but I knew my principal vocation was university teaching and research. Fifteen-hour days and seven-day weeks were a hardship for me, my wife, and our four young children. I remained active as a consultant to the council, particularly on international monetary issues that had concerned me as a member. Moreover, I was now more visible outside my profession, so I wrote and spoke more frequently on issues and controversies of the day. But I knew that alumni of Washington often have difficulty getting back into mainline professional scholarship. I determined to accomplish that reentry, and I believe I did.

Kennedy and Johnson added the war on poverty to their agenda. Walter Heller and the council were very much involved. I became quite interested in the economic disadvantages of blacks and in the inadequacies, inefficiencies, and perverse incentives—penalties for work and marriage—of federal and state welfare programs. I wrote major papers on these matters in 1965 and 1968. This was not macroeconomics, but one implication of the Keynesian-neoclassical synthesis was that welfare and redistributional policies could be, within broad limits, chosen independently of macroeconomic goals. Nothing in our view of the functioning of capitalist democracies says either that prosperity requires hard-hearted welfare policies and small governments or that it requires redistribution in favor of workers and the poor.

I favored a negative income tax. So did Milton Friedman—although his version seemed to me too small to fill much of the poverty gap, and he refused to join a national nonpartisan statement of economists favoring the approach. I helped to design a negative income tax plan for George McGovern in 1972. Unfortunately, he and his staff botched its presentation in the heat of the California primary; I am sure most people to this day think McGovern was advocating a kooky budget-breaking handout. After the election Nixon proposed a family assistance plan pretty much the same as the McGovern scheme he had ridiculed during the campaign.

I have lived long enough to see the revolution to which I was an eager recruit fifty years ago become in its turn a mainstream orthodoxy and then the target of counterrevolutionary attack. The tides of political opinion and professional fashion have turned against me. Many of my young colleagues in the profession are as enthusiastic exponents of the new classical macroeconomics as I and my contemporaries were crusaders against old classical macroeconomics in the 1930s. Many of the issues are the same, but the environment is quite different from the Great Depression. The contesting factions are better equipped—our profession has certainly improved its mathematical, analytical, and statistical tools. I do not despair over the present divisions of opinion in economics. Our subject has always thrived and advanced through controversy, and I expect a new synthesis will evolve, maybe even in my lifetime. I haven't abandoned the field of battle myself. I hope I learn from the new, but I still think and say that Keynesian ideas about how the economy works and what policies can make it work better are relevant today—not just as Keynes wrote them, of course, but as they have been modified, developed, and refined over the last half-century.

James Tobin

Awarded Nobel Prize in 1981. Lecture presented April 30, 1985.

Dates of Birth and Death

March 5, 1918; March 11, 2002

Academic Degrees

A.B., Harvard University, 1939
M.A., Harvard University, 1940
Ph.D., Harvard University, 1947

Academic Affiliations

Junior Fellow, Harvard University, 1946–50
Associate Professor of Economics, Yale University, 1950–55
Professor of Economics, Yale University, 1955–57
Sterling Professor of Economics, Yale University, 1957–88
Sterling Professor of Economics, Emeritus, Yale University, 1988–2002

Selected Books

The American Business Creed, 1956 (with S. E. Harris et al.)
National Economic Policy, 1966
Essays in Economics, Vols. 1–4, 1971–1982
The New Economics One Decade Older, 1974

Franco Modigliani

Ruminations on My Professional Life

It's been a lot of fun for me to prepare this talk because it has forced me to go over my history and pick up a number of things I had forgotten and see connections I did not see before. I was somewhat taken aback and overawed by the title, "My Evolution as an Economist." It sounded as if I had to start from my invertebrate state and then move up to higher states. I then suddenly realized or remembered a very important thing: economics is a very old profession. In fact I think it is the oldest profession in the world. I know this claim is disputed by others. There is a story, I think authentic, of an argument about this among an engineer, an economist, and a surgeon. The problem was that each claimed that his profession was the oldest. The surgeon spoke first and said, "Remember at the beginning when God took a rib out of Adam and made Eve? Who do you think did that? Obviously, a surgeon." The engineer, however, was undaunted by all this and said, "Just a moment. You remember that God made the world before that. He separated the land from the sea. Who do you think did that except an engineer?" "Just a moment," protested the economist, "Before God made the world, what was there? Chaos. Who do you think was responsible for that?"

So tonight I am going to tell you about my contribution to chaos. One thing I want to stress, because I want you to consider it as I move through my story, is the very important question regarding an award like the Nobel Prize: How much is deserved and how much is luck? After I received the award many people wrote to me asking for a prescription for getting a Nobel Prize. How many books do you need and how many hours do you work? I have always answered that you need many books and you must work many hours, but most important: manage to have lots of luck. I have had a lot of luck. And as you may have already gathered, perhaps the first piece of luck in my life was to marry my wife, Serena. It was luck in the sense that I was a fresh, brash kid at that time—very, very, young. It was hard to recognize what could come out of this, but she helped me come through. I am sure that she decided to prove that the brash kid she married really was a good investment, and I hope that she feels she has succeeded.

Serena and I left our home in Italy, stayed in France for a while, and arrived in the United States in September 1939, just as war broke out. So when we landed, we knew we were to be here for a long time. I then cast around for something to do. It was now a matter of finding a job in order to live, and I began to work selling Italian and other foreign books. But I also looked around to see what I could do to continue an earlier interest in economics. And here again I was lucky and obtained a scholarship at the New School for Social Research, a great center for European scholars. There were many notable names in various disciplines, but a man who was particularly important to me was Jacob Marschak, recently arrived from England. Jacob Marschak was at once a great economist, a magnificent teacher, and an exceptional and warm human being. He took me in hand and persuaded me first of all that if I wanted to get anywhere as an economist, I had to study mathematics. I had had no training at all in math and in fact had a certain aversion to it. He persuaded me to carry out a certain amount of study of mathematics and statistics, which played a very important role as I tried to develop my own papers. The time was 1939. The *General Theory* of Keynes was the center of discussion, together with the work of Schumpeter on business cycles. We had seminars devoted to them and they were very exciting. Of course at that time we were coming out of the depression. Keynes gave you the feeling that the mysterious disease that produced the depression was something that could be understood and avoided in the future. So there was a lot of excitement associated with that study. In addition, Marschak invited me to participate in a seminar that was held in New York, organized by Oskar Lange, the famous economist from Poland. The participants included, in addition to Lange and Marschak, such powerful economists as Tjalling Koopmans and Abraham Wald. It was a very exciting experience. Unfortunately, in 1941 Marschak left the New School to go to the University of Chicago at the invitation of Oskar Lange, who was there permanently. But by that time I was well on my way, and furthermore, as Marschak left, another outstanding economist, Abba Lerner, came to the New School. I began to have some serious discussions with Abba Lerner, because although I respected him, I thought that he was oversimplifying the message of the *General Theory*. He accepted one aspect of the Keynesian theory that I think is not its essence, namely, the notion that rigid wages and a special feature of the demand for money—the so-called liquidity preference—could result in a "liquidity trap," where the economy is fundamentally an unstable system that will get buffeted by all shocks. There is no stable equilibrium to which it returns. I think Abba Lerner held very strongly to this view, and this led him to the idea that the only way to stabilize the economy is through fiscal policy. Running surpluses and deficits is the only way to compensate for shocks. I thought this was a much too simple view of Keynes. From my perspective this represented a limiting case of Keynes but not the normal run of things, and I began to work on the article that was to appear in 1944 under the title, "Liquidity Preference and the Theory of Interest and Money."

While I was working on the article, I began my first teaching job at the New Jersey College for Women, an institution within commuting distance of New York. I was able to get this offer because Pearl Harbor had been attacked and people were moving from colleges to Washington. As a result, an opening arose there for a term. I have fun these days telling our younger faculty what my teaching load was at that time: four courses per term, including two sections of economics, one section of statistics, and one section of economic history. On top of that I was teaching a course at the New School for Social Research. From the New Jersey College for Women I went to Bard College, which was then part of Columbia University. It is there that I completed my 1944 article on liquidity preference, which was to attract a good deal of attention.

It turned out that the referee for my 1944 article was Leonid Hurwicz, a very young economist with a great future who was to become a close friend when we were together at the University of Illinois. Its publication, while I was still relatively young, contributed greatly to my recognition as an economist and to my unexpected election to fellow of the Econometric Society in 1949. The main theme of the paper was that, except for the questionable assumption of absolute wage rigidity, the Keynesian system did allow in general for a self-restoring full employment equilibrium along classical lines. But there were some special circumstances under which this mechanism breaks down, and perhaps that is what happened in the Great Depression. These special circumstances should not have been regarded as the rule but as a limiting case. In particular the main stabilization device should be monetary policy, not fiscal policy. That was the theme of this paper.

My career at Bard College ended when I was called up for service in the armed forces. I had been left out for a while because I had a pre-Pearl Harbor child—a very valuable item at that time! However, on the verge of my induction the draft board told me that they were able to find other nonfathers, and I was released. Not long afterward the war ended, and I was offered the opportunity of returning to the New School.

I was there in two capacities: as a researcher at the Institute of World Affairs and as a teacher of mathematical economics at the New School itself. My research project at the institute was to build, together with Hans Neisser, a large-scale (for the time) econometric model of the world economy showing the linkages between countries. At a time when the most powerful computational device was an electric calculator, this was a rather ambitious scheme. But at least we succeeded in putting together a structure that was later used as a guide and a source of ideas for similar projects.

The other thing that happened during this period was that I began to be very much concerned with the study of saving, which was to be a central theme throughout my life. Why was I concerned? Because there was an idea that had its origin in some of the Keynesian writings that people were saving too much. If people save too much, the consequence might be a serious depression. The Keynesian followers argued that saving depends on income and that the proportion of income saved grows with income: if you are richer you save a larger fraction of your income. Because income was expected to rise in the postwar period, there was the implication that the saving rate would get larger and larger, and there were great doubts as to whether there would be enough investment opportunities to absorb the saving.

I didn't believe that the saving rate would tend to grow and grow. It just didn't sound right to me. I thought that this was one of the fads of the time, and I began to work on this problem and pursue the idea that the saving rate has a cyclical characteristic but not a rising trend. My findings suggested that saving is determined more by a person's income relative to his accustomed level than by his absolute income in a given period. This idea happened to be pursued at the same time by James Duesenberry at Harvard. The resulting theory is now known as the Duesenberry–Modigliani hypothesis.

Soon, I was offered the Political Economy Fellowship at the University of Chicago. This was a fairly prestigious and high-paying scholarship, something like $3,000 a year—a big salary at that time and enough to live on with the family. So I accepted the offer, took leave, and went there. But I had hardly arrived when I was approached by Howard Bowen, the dean of the College of Commerce at the University of Illinois, and asked to join the University of Illinois on a project titled "Expectations and Business Fluctuations." The salary was excellent, and the university was prestigious and had some very good people. I accepted. Earlier, I had rejected an offer from Harvard. I had a much faster career at Illinois and a much higher salary than my colleagues at Harvard. Also I had a chance to get to know the Midwest, which was very important for me, having been born in Europe.

At Illinois, I ran into a brilliant and delightful young man by the name of Richard Brumberg, a first-year graduate student. He became a very close friend of the entire family. I had been asked by Kenneth Kurihara to write a paper for a book to be called *Post-Keynesian Economics,* and I invited Brumberg to work with me on the paper. We hadn't decided on a topic until we went to a conference on saving at the University of Minnesota and were both very unhappy with the papers given. On the trip back by car to the University of Illinois we hatched an idea that looked like a possible improvement: the hypothesis that came to be called the life-cycle theory of saving.

While still at Illinois, I was invited to become an associate of the Cowles Commission, a Chicago-based organization connected with the Econometric Society. This connection put me in contact with another group of outstanding people that included Tjalling Koopmans, Jacob Marschak, Kenneth Arrow, Carl Christ, Herman Charnoff, and Herbert Simon.

The University of Illinois experience terminated with a dramatic fight in which essentially the McCarthy forces were trying to push out the dean, Howard Bowen, as well as the people he had brought in. He had attracted an excellent cast of people, but they were not from the "black earth" of Illinois. They came from the East Coast, they came from the West Coast, they were Keynesians—they had to be eliminated, particularly because they bothered the old guard, who felt passé, inferior to this new group. So the old guard was able to orchestrate a very famous fight in which the main figure was a trustee, Red Grange; I think some of you have heard of this name. To me he was completely unknown, but everybody knew the great football player Red Grange (the Galloping Ghost), and Red Grange led the fight against Bowen. Bowen resigned, as did most of the people who came with him. I still had to complete the project, so I stayed on for a year, but I began to look around. When I received an invitation from the Carnegie Institute of Technology, now Carnegie Mellon, I wisely accepted and spent eight precious years there, from 1952 to 1960.

During my stay at Carnegie Mellon I matured into the economist I am today. How did that happen? Well, Carnegie at that time was a very exciting place. The key figure of course was Herbert Simon, a genius and a great colleague. But around him there were some other fine scholars like Charles Holt, Merton Miller, William Cooper, Richard Cyert, and James March—all outstanding people. We also had great students, such as Jack Muth. He has become one of the heroes of the present time as the man who laid the foundations for the so-called rational expectations hypothesis, which is what young economists live by. All this provided an exciting atmosphere.

In addition, together with Richard Brumberg, I was able to complete a first contribution on the life-cycle hypothesis that dealt with individual behavior and a second part that dealt with aggregate behavior. This hypothesis explained saving patterns in much the same way as I had earlier explained the production pattern of firms: People consume at a relatively constant rate determined by their lifetime earnings. Therefore when their income is highest, they save a great deal, but when it is low, such as during their youth and in their later retirement years, they actually "dissave." This is similar to Milton Friedman's permanent income hypothesis but differs in that Friedman assumes an infinite time horizon for consumption and saving decisions, whereas my hypothesis depends on life being finite and differentiated—dependency, maturity, retirement. In essence a person's lifetime pattern of wealth accumulation can be described as a hump. Wealth is low during one's youth but grows as one begins to earn. It reaches a peak during one's middle years before retirement and declines after retirement. There may be some bequest element. That is, we allowed for the fact that some portion of wealth may be bequeathed. Our estimates now suggest that maybe one-fifth of wealth is the result of bequest, but the remaining four-fifths—or something between 75 percent and 80 percent—is of this hump type.

Hump wealth has one important implication that Richard and I discovered to our great delight. When you aggregate, that is, when you look not at the individual family but at the economy as a whole, it turns out that the aggregate wealth of a country (the aggregate saving) can be different in different countries in which each individual behaves identically over his life cycle. That is, imagine that in every country each person over his life cycle has identical behavior. Yet one country can have no saving and another country can save a lot. Why? Because, if you think of the implication of hump wealth, you will see that the main determinant of national saving is not income—which should not affect the path of wealth relative to income—but growth: the faster the country grows, the higher the saving income. The less you grow, the less you save. If you don't grow at all, aggregate ratio saving is zero. This macro implication and a number of corollaries that follow from it are significant because they give an entirely different view of the saving process. People tend to say that the Japanese save a lot because they are thrifty and we save little because we aren't thrifty. If my model is correct, it says that's nonsense. We are equally thrifty. They are growing at 8 percent per year and we are growing at 3 percent per year, and that is why we normally save 12 percent and they save well over 20 percent of their income.

It turns out that there is a lot of evidence to support the life-cycle hypothesis (or LCH) point of view. LCH does not imply that individual thriftiness is entirely immaterial. Rather it suggests that one can reduce the rate of saving to two elements: the shape of the path of wealth over life and how fast the economy grows. For a given path saving depends only on growth. However, the shape of the path has an influence. So it could be that the Japanese are inclined to postpone their consumption. If that were the case, they would have a bigger hump. Incidentally, there is some evidence that that is true. In Japan housing is enormously expensive, and there were until very recently very few facilities for the financing of housing—mortgages were very rare and extremely expensive. So people were forced to save a lot when they were young in order to be able to acquire a house. And that means they had to postpone higher consumption until after they had purchased a house.

There were several other contributions that were completed during this period at Carnegie Mellon. First, I took another crack at the working of the monetary mechanism in the economy, which I had handled in my 1944 article. I allowed for various developments that had happened in the meantime. This was 1963, and it represented a fairly definitive form of my view of how money works in the economy. In addition it was around 1957 that Merton Miller and I produced our two papers, the so-called Modigliani–Miller theorems, which have come to be known as Mo-Mi and Mi-Mo.

Mo-Mi is the proposition that the financial structure (debt-equity ratio) of a firm in a perfect capital market has no effect on its market valuation. This paper has since become quite well known, and it has been assigned to students in business and finance all over the world. And I regret that this is the case because students who read this paper usually come out hating me. They think it's a terrible paper, a very hard one to understand—and they are right. The reason is that this paper was never meant for students. The paper was meant to upset my colleagues in finance by arguing that the core issue that received most attention in corporation finance, namely finding out what exactly is the optimum capital structure, was not really an issue. It didn't make any difference. To be sure, it might make a difference if there were taxes. If so, you would have to approach the problem precisely in that way and ask, what is the effect of taxes and why do they make a difference?

Aside from the specific message about capital structure, the main methodological contribution—which I think is the reason the paper has become so important in the area of finance—was in changing the method of attack regarding the choice of financial structure and investment policy: The focus should be on the maximization of the market value of the firm debt plus equity rather than on the traditional, but not operational, maximization of profits. This contribution was much more general than the specific one about the fact that leverage doesn't count.

The second paper had to do with dividend policy. If you have a perfect capital market and no taxes, it makes no difference whether you pay a lot of dividends or very little; the market value of the firm would be unaffected. This once again went against the grain of the time. The profession spent a lot of time deciding whether you could fool the investors, seen as outsiders rather than owners of the firm, by giving them a little more of this or a little more of that. We essentially show that this is all irrelevant.

An important aspect of my life at this time is that I reestablished relations with Italy. Until 1945 we had considered going back to Italy. But as we watched what was going on there, we decided that we had had enough and were going to become U.S. citizens and make this our home. For a while I more or less cut off relations, but in the mid-1950s I reestablished contact and began to be interested in issues of economic policy in Italy.

In 1955 I spent a year as a Fulbright lecturer at the Universities of Rome and Palermo. I had completely forgotten how profoundly different the Italian and the American systems of higher education were. The Italian system was a three-caste structure, with the few, mostly old full professors occupying the upper caste, close to God; a group of hopeful, sometimes servile assistants constituted the second layer; and the students were at the bottom of the heap. I will always remember an episode that occurred during my stay at the University of Rome when Professor Papi, then rector of the university and a symbol of the system, invited me to speak at his faculty seminar but introduced me (then thirty-eight) as a promising young star! I thanked him but remarked that in the United States I was regarded as a bit passé!

In 1960 we left Carnegie Mellon and went to Northwestern for just a year. After this year we moved permanently to MIT. Let me divide the MIT period into two parts: the period up to 1974—corresponding to the first oil crisis—and the period since.

The decade from 1960 to 1970 was what you might call the golden era of Keynesianism. It should be understood, of course, that when I speak of Keynesianism I speak of wise Keynesians. I speak of Solow and Samuelson and Tobin and Heller and others of their ilk. I don't speak of the many aberrations that always exist. In the mid-1960s I was asked by the Federal Reserve Board to build a model of the American economy that could be used for forecasting and policy analysis. That model was built in collaboration with Albert Ando along basically Keynesian lines, but our type of Keynesian lines, in which money is very important. In fact we discovered that money was even more important than was thought because of the interaction between my consumption function and monetary policy. Because my consumption function shows that consumption depends on income and wealth, and because interest rates affect that wealth, here is one more channel through which monetary policy can have an effect on income. Furthermore we showed that in terms of our estimates this was faster than the traditional channel through investment, which involves considerable lags.

In terms of intellectual history I think it is important to acknowledge that there were two points on which we had to change our initial course. The first is that we started out with a model of the determinant of the price level that in the traditional Keynesian literature was referred to as the Phillips curve. This formulation allowed for the possibility of a long-run trade-off between inflation and unemployment. That mechanism was shown to be invalid by Ned Phelps and Milton Friedman, particularly in Friedman's presidential address to the American Economic Association during which he introduced the "vertical" Phillips curve. We readily accepted that, and by the late 1960s we had revised our model so that it included a vertical Phillips curve, for which we found plenty of support. The vertical Phillips curve essentially says that you cannot push unemployment below some critical level through inflation; if you try to have too much employment, you will get accelerating inflating, which will eventually have to be stopped by accepting a lot of unemployment.

As for the second change, when we started the model, inflation was not yet a problem. By the late 1960s, however, it had become serious. We had to allow for various effects of inflation on the economy, beginning with such a simple thing as the concept of the real interest rate, the rate of interest adjusted for the effect of inflation. The model is still used at the Federal Reserve together with other devices.

The other contributions of that period included, first of all, a fair amount of work pursuing the implications of the life cycle model. One that has become very important of late relates to the economic effects of deficit financing, or more broadly, the public debt. Using the life cycle framework, one can show that these deficits or debts have an effect on the well-being of future generations because they displace productive capital. When the government borrows, it absorbs a certain amount of saving, reducing what's available for investment, or equivalently, for increasing the stock of capital. That is the fundamental mechanism by which a deficit is deleterious. It was recognized that the deficit need not displace investment dollar per dollar because of the fact that life, though finite, extends beyond the time of the deficit. People therefore should recognize that if the deficit is increased now, they will have to pay additional taxes over the rest of their lives, and that should be reflected in their current behavior by some increase in saving. But still much of the deficit should displace private investment.

Then there were several attempts at testing the life cycle model empirically. One of these attempts consisted of gathering evidence that the debt displaces private productive capital. Another one was a comparative study across countries testing whether differential saving behavior could be explained in terms of rates of growth and population structure. These were found to be the main determinants of saving, accounting for a great deal of the observed differences. Finally with my colleague Jacques Drèze there was an extension of the life cycle to a world of uncertainty, which has since given rise to a substantial body of literature, including the combination of life cycle with the theory of portfolio.

An essay about which I am keenest in this period was my presidential address to the American Economic Association, of which I had become president in 1976. It was called "The Monetarist Controversy, or Should We Forsake Stabilization Policies?" This was essentially a head-on collision with the monetarists, who had become very powerful for a variety of reasons. The theme of this essay is that the differences between monetarists and nonmonetarists are not about the working of the economy or the potency of monetary versus fiscal policy; they are instead basically philosophical and political. The monetarists do not want to give the government the power to use discretion because they believe that the government is incapable of using it well. Due to their stupidity or bad faith the monetary authority could not be trusted with any discretionary power in deciding on the appropriate expansion of the money supply. It must be left instead to a mechanical rule. You can trust a computer to compute 3 percent but not the chairman and the board of the Federal Reserve to change that number as circumstances dictate. My argument was to show that this was the only important difference. In addition I pointed to evidence that a fixed rule is not adequate to stabilize the economy, that there is room for stabilization. Finally I showed that in fact stabilization policy tended to work. That was the fundamental message. This issue has reemerged lately, and I'll come back to it briefly.

Other things that happened during this period were further extensions of the life cycle hypothesis. In particular, one interesting application was a study of the effect of transitory tax cuts. In our history we have had a few cases in which taxes were reduced or increased with the announcement that the original tax rates would be reinstated within a year or two. That's what we call a transitory tax cut. The life cycle hypothesis implies that such tax cuts are rather powerless to affect consumption. Since people know that the tax cut is only for a short time, the difference that it makes to their life resources is small. So if they are rational, their consumption will not change much. But if you make a tax change that is "permanent," then of course you will know that you are going to be poorer hereafter, and that will affect consumption. There is evidence, especially from the 1969 temporary tax increase, that in fact transitory tax changes are not very effective in terms of affecting consumption.

Finally there was a series of tests on the then-fashionable idea that the national debt makes no difference to the economy. This idea is associated with the name of Robert Barro, who happens to be one of my students. But despite this circumstance I completely disagree with his theory even though it can be viewed as an extension of the life-cycle model. As I indicated before, the original life cycle model asserts the opposite. Mr. Barro's contrary result rests on the assumption of perfect rationality and infinite life. In this case, if the government cuts your taxes, incurring a corresponding deficit, and you are rational, you would save the additional after-tax income because you would realize that otherwise you would consume more now at the expense of less consumption thereafter, when additional taxes would be levied to service and retire the debt. Numerous tests carried out for the United States, Italy, and a cross section of other countries all decisively reject the Barro hypothesis.

Another new approach is the rational expectations paradigm, whose foundation happens to rest on my earlier analysis of the forecastability of social events. That is, they have in common the notion that a warranted forecast must be based on all relevant information available for the economy and must take fully into account the effect of the expectation on the event forecasted. This approach has led to the conclusion that policy is altogether powerless in systematically affecting the real economy. The economy goes its own way no matter what you do. However, I happen to disagree wholly with their formulations, not in principle but in every application I have seen. In particular, the ineffectiveness of policy is derived from two highly questionable assumptions: (1) that the economy is unaffected by policy even in the shortest run, as long as agents believe it, and (2) that the agents believe it.

I reject both hypotheses, the first because of slow adjustments in the economy that can be offset by policy, and the second because in my view agents can be expected to use a variety of models, including extrapolation of past experience, and in any event few could be expected to believe that policy is instantly neutral, because it is not. Empirical evidence fully supports my rejection of monetarists' attempts to build their models on their assumptions. Indeed such models have produced much poorer forecasts than those obtained by models like the MPS.

As I contemplate my contributions, I find one unifying thread: a propensity to swim against the current by challenging the self-evident orthodoxies of the moment, be it that the classics are altogether outdated, or that the rich must save a larger fraction of their income than the poor, or that debt financing is cheaper because the interest rate on high-quality debt is lower than the return on equity.

I would love to be able to continue to play that role. But I don't want to think too much about where I am going. I just like to let things come and be ready to jump in where there is excitement.

Franco Modigliani

Awarded Nobel Prize in 1985. Lecture presented March 24, 1987.

Dates of Birth and Death

June 18, 1918; September 25, 2003

Academic Degrees

D (Jurisprudence) University of Rome, 1939
D (Social Science) New School for Social Research, 1944

Academic Affiliations

Instructor, Bard College, 1942–44
Assistant Professor of Economics, New School for Social Research, 1943–44, 1946–48
Associate Professor of Economics, University of Illinois, 1949–50
Professor of Economics, University of Illinois, 1950–52
Professor of Economics and Industrial Administration, Carnegie Institute of Technology, 1952–60
Professor of Economics, Northwestern University, 1960–62
Professor of Economics and Finance, Massachusetts Institute of Technology, 1962–70
Institute Professor, Massachusetts Institute of Technology, 1970–88
Institute Professor, Emeritus, Massachusetts Institute of Technology, 1988–2003

Selected Books

National Incomes and International Trade, 1953 (with H. Neisser)
Planning Production, Inventories and Work Forces, 1960 (with others)
The Collected Papers of Franco Modigliani, Voumes 1–5, 1980–1989

James M. Buchanan

Born-Again Economist

I have been tempted to expand my title to "Born-Again Economist, with a Prophet but No God." Both parts of this expanded title are descriptive. I was specifically asked to discuss my evolution as an economist, an assignment that I cannot fulfill. I am not a "natural economist" as some of my colleagues are, and I did not "evolve" into an economist.[1] Instead I sprang full blown upon intellectual conversion, after I "saw the light." I shall review this experience below, and I shall defend the implied definition and classification of who qualifies as an economist.

The second part of my expanded title is related to the first. It is my own play on the University of Chicago saying of the 1940s that "there is no god, but Frank Knight is his prophet." I was indeed converted by Frank Knight, but he almost single-mindedly conveyed the message that there exists no god whose pronouncements deserve elevation to the sacrosanct, whether god within or god without the scientific academy. Everything, everyone, anywhere, anytime—all is open to challenge and criticism. There is a moral obligation to reach one's own conclusions, even if this sometimes means exposing the prophet whom you have elevated to intellectual guruship.

In an earlier autobiographical essay, "Better Than Plowing,"[2] I identified two persons who were dominant intellectual influences on my own methodology, selection of subject matter, attitude toward scholarship, positive analysis, and normative position. One of these, Knut Wicksell, influenced me exclusively through his ideas. I used the occasion of my Nobel Prize lecture to trace the relationship between Wicksell's precursory foundations and later developments in the theory of public choice, notably its constitutional economics component with which I have been most closely associated. By comparison and contrast this paper offers me the opportunity, even if indirectly, to explore more fully the influence of the second person identified, Frank H. Knight, an influence that was exerted both through his ideas and through a personal friendship that extended over a full quarter century.

The paper is organized as follows. In the following section I try as best I can to describe my state of mind, intellectually and emotionally, before I enrolled in the University of Chicago in 1946. Then I offer a retrospective description of my Chicago experience, with an emphasis on my exposure to the teachings of Frank Knight along with a subconscious conversion to a catallactic methodological perspective on the discipline. The next section briefly traces the catallactic roots of my contributions to public choice theory. After that I discuss the remembered events and persons who were important in giving me the self-confidence that was surely necessary for any career success. Frank Knight was important but by no means unique in this evolution (and in this respect the word "evolution" can be properly applied). I then discuss the influence of Knight's principle of the "relatively absolute absolute" upon my own stance, as moral philosopher, as constitutionalist, and as economic analyst. Finally, I defend my use of the title of my earlier autobiographical essay, "Better Than Plowing," which has been questioned by colleagues and critics. Here I try to examine the motivations that, consciously or unconsciously, may have driven me throughout the course of a long academic career. Why did I do what I did? It may be helpful to explore, even if briefly, this most subjective of questions.

Chicago, 1946

I enrolled in the University of Chicago for the winter quarter, 1946. I had chosen the University of Chicago without much knowledge about its faculty in economics. I was influenced almost exclusively by an undergraduate teacher in political science, C. C. Sims, who had earned a doctorate at Chicago in the late 1930s. Sims impressed on me the intellectual ferment of the university, the importance of ideas, and the genuine life of the mind that was present at the institution. His near-idyllic sketch appealed to me, and I made the plunge into serious study for the first time in my life. In retrospect I could not have made a better selection. Sims was precisely on target in conveying the intellectual excitement of the University of Chicago, an excitement that remains, to this day, unmatched anywhere else in the world.

During the first quarter I took courses with Frank Knight, T. W. Schultz, and Simeon Leland. I was among the very first group of graduate students to return to the academy after discharge from military service during World War II. We swelled the ranks of the graduate classes at Chicago and elsewhere.

Within a few short weeks, perhaps by mid-February 1946, I had undergone a conversion in my understanding of how an economy operates. For the first time I was able to think in terms of the ordering principle of a market economy. The stylized model for the working of the competitive structure gave me the benchmark for constructive criticism of the economy to be observed. For the first time I was indeed an economist.

I attribute this conversion directly to Frank Knight's teachings, which perhaps raises more new questions than it answers. Knight was not a systematic instructor. More important, he remained ambiguous in his own interpretation of what economics is all about. He was never able to shed the allocating-maximizing paradigm, which tends to distract attention from the coordination paradigm that I have long deemed central to the discipline.[3] But Knight's economics was a curious amalgam of these partially conflicting visions. And for me the organizational emphasis was sufficient to relegate the allocative thrust to a place of secondary relevance. In this respect I was fortunate in my ignorance. Had I received "better" pre-Chicago training in economics, as widely interpreted, I would have scarcely been able to elevate the coordination principle to the central place it has occupied in my thinking throughout my research career. Like so many of my peers, aside from the few who were exposed early to Austrian theory, I might have remained basically an allocationist.

There are subtle but important differences between the allocationist-maximization and the catallactic-coordination paradigm in terms of the implications for normative evaluation of institutions. In particular the evaluation of the market order may depend critically on which of these partially conflicting paradigms remains dominant in one's stylized vision.

To the allocationist the market is efficient *if it works*. His test of the market becomes the comparison with the abstract ideal defined in his logic. To the catallactist the market coordinates the separate activities of self-seeking persons *without the necessity of detailed political direction*. The test of the market is the comparison with its institutional alternative, politicized decision-making.

There is of course no necessary implication of the differing paradigms for identifying the normative stance of practicing economists. Many modern economists remain firm supporters of the market order while at the same time remaining within the maximizing paradigm. I submit here, however, that there are relatively few economists whose vision is dominated by the catallactic perspective on market order who are predominantly critics of such an order. Once the relevant comparison becomes that between the workings of the market, however imperfect this may seem, and the workings of its political alternative, there must indeed be very strong offsetting sources of evaluation present.

The apparent digression of the preceding paragraphs is important for my narrative and for an understanding of how my conversion by Frank Knight influenced my research career after Chicago. Those of us who entered graduate school in the immediate postwar years were all socialists of one sort or another. Some of us were what I have elsewhere called "libertarian socialists," who placed a high residual value on individual liberty but simply did not understand the principle of market coordination. We were always libertarians first, socialists second. And we tended to be grossly naive in our thinking about political alternatives. To us, the idealized attractions of populist democracy seemed preferable to those of the establishment-controlled economy. It was this sort of young socialist in particular who was especially ready for immediate conversion upon exposure to teachings that transmitted the principle of market coordination.[4]

An understanding of this principle enabled us to concentrate our long-held anti-establishment evaluative norms on politics and governance and open up the prospect that economic interaction, at least in the limit, need not embody the exercise of man's power over man. By our libertarian standards, politics had always been deemed to fail. Now by these same standards market may, just may, not involve exploitation.

An important element in Knight's economics was his emphasis on the organizational structure of markets, and it was this emphasis that elevated the coordination principle to center stage despite his continued obeisance to economizing-maximizing. Once attention is drawn to a structure, to process, and away from resources, goods, and services, many of the technical trappings of orthodox economic theory fall away. Here Knight's approach became institutional, in the proper meaning of this term.

It is useful at this point to recall that Frank Knight's career shared a temporal dimensionality with the seminal American institutionalists Clarence Ayres, John R. Commons, and Thorstein Veblen. He treated their technical economics with derision, but he shared with them an interest in the structure of social and economic interaction. Knight did not extend his institutional inquiry much beyond the seminal work on human wants that exposed some of the shallow presuppositions of economic orthodoxy. He did not, save in a few passing references, examine the structure of politics, considered the only alternative to markets.

Public Choice and the Catallactic Paradigm

Public choice is the inclusive term that describes the extension of analysis to the political alternatives to markets. It seems highly unlikely that this extension could have been effectively made by economists who viewed the market merely as an allocative mechanism, quite independently of its political role in reducing the range and scope of politicized activity. I can of course speak here only of my own experience, but it seems doubtful if I could have even recognized the Wicksellian message had not Knight's preparatory teachings of the coordination principle paved the way.

The point may be illustrated by the related, but yet quite distinct, strands of modern inquiry summarized under the two rubrics "social choice" and "public choice." I have elsewhere identified the two central elements in public choice theory as (1) the conceptualization of politics as exchange, and (2) the model of *Homo economicus*.[5] The second of these elements is shared with social choice theory, which seeks to ground social choices on the values of utility-maximizing individuals. Where social choice theory and public choice theory differ—and dramatically— lies in the first element noted. Social choice theory does not conceptualize politics as complex exchange; rather politics is implicitly or explicitly modeled in the age-old conception that there must exist some unique and hence discoverable "best" result. This element in social choice theory, from Arrow on, stems directly for the allocative paradigm in orthodox economics, and the maximization of the social welfare function becomes little more than the extension of the standard efficiency calculus to the aggregate economy.

By contrast, the extension of the catallactic paradigm—the emphasis on the theory of exchange rather than allocation—to politics immediately calls attention to the institutional structure of political decision-making. Without Frank Knight as teacher and as role model, would Knut Wicksell's great work have been discovered by the fledgling economist that I was in 1948? I have strong reasons for doubt on this score.

My own understanding, appreciation, and admiration for Frank Knight were aided and abetted by the development, early on, of a close personal relationship. Some three or four weeks after enrollment in his course I visited Knight's jumbled office. What was expected to be a five-minute talk stretched over two hours, to be matched several times during my two and a half years at Chicago, and beyond. He took an interest in me because we shared several dimensions of experience. Both of us were country boys, reared in agricultural poverty, well aware of the basic drudgery of rural existence but also appreciative of the independence of a life on the land. Knight left his native Illinois in his teens for rudimentary college instruction in my home state of Tennessee, and he enrolled in graduate studies at the University of Tennessee where I too had first commenced graduate work. These common threads of experience established for me a relationship that I shared with no other professor. We shared other interests, including an appreciation of the gloomy poetry of Thomas Hardy and the fun of the clever off-color joke.

Of course I was a one-way beneficiary of this relationship. Knight was the adviser who told me not to waste my time taking formal courses in philosophy, who corrected my dissertation grammar in great detail, and who became the role model that has never been replaced or even slightly dislodged over a long academic career. In trying to assess my own development, I find it impossible to imagine what I might have been and become without exposure to Frank Knight.

I was never a formal student of Earl Hamilton. I did not enroll in his economic history courses at Chicago. Nonetheless during my last year at Chicago, 1948, Hamilton sought me out and took a direct personal interest in my prospects. As with Knight, the sharing of common experience in rural poverty created a personal bond, supplemented in this case by a passion for baseball, reflected by trips to both Cubs and White Sox home games. Hamilton enjoyed giving advice to those he singled out for possible achievement, and with me two separate imperatives stand out in recall: the potential payoff to hard work and the value of mastery of foreign languages.

Perhaps Earl J. Hamilton's most important influence on my career came after 1948, during his tenure as editor of the *Journal of Political Economy*. First of all he forced me to follow up on his recommendation about language skills by sending me French, German, and Italian books for review. Second, he handled my early article submissions with tolerance, understanding, and encouragement rather than with brutal or carping rejections that might have proved fatal to further effort. Hamilton was indeed a tough editor, and every article that I finally published during his tenure was laboriously transformed and dramatically pared down through a process of multiple revisions and resubmissions. Without Hamilton as an editor who cared, my writing style would never have attained the economy it possesses, and my willingness to venture into subject matter beyond the boundaries of the orthodox might have been squelched early. With Earl J. Hamilton as editor, by the mid-1950s I had several solid papers on the record—a number sufficient to enable me to accept the occasional rejection slip with equanimity rather than despair.

The Relatively Absolute Absolute

I have already discussed how Frank Knight's willingness to challenge all authority—intellectual, moral, or scientific—indirectly established confidence in those for whom he served as role model. Any account of such an influence would be seriously incomplete, and indeed erroneous, if the philosophical stance suggested is one of relativism-cum-nihilism against the claim of any and all authority. It is at precisely this point that Frank Knight directly taught me the philosophical principle that has served me so well over so many years and in so many applications. This principle is that of the *relatively absolute absolute*, which allows for a philosophical way station between the extremes of absolutism on the one hand and relativism on the other, both of which are to be rejected.

Acceptance of this principle necessarily requires that there exist a continuing tension between the forces that dictate adherence to and acceptance of authority and those very qualities that define freedom of thought and inquiry. Knight's expressed willingness to challenge all authority was embedded within a wisdom that also recognized the relevance of tradition in ideas, manners, and institutions. This wisdom dictates that for most purposes and most of the time prudent behavior consists of acting as if the authority that exists does indeed possess legitimacy. The principle of the relatively absolute absolute requires that we adhere to and accept the standards of established or conventional authority in our ordinary behavior, whether this be personal, scientific, or political, while at the same time and at still another (and "higher") level of consciousness we call all such standards into question, even to the extent of proposing change.

In relation to my own work this principle of the relatively absolute absolute is perhaps best exemplified in the critically important distinction between the post-constitutional and the constitutional levels of political interaction. More generally, the distinction is that between choosing among strategies of play in a game that is defined by a set of rules and choosing among alternative sets of rules. To the chooser of strategies under defined rules, the rules themselves are to be treated as relatively absolute absolutes, as constraints that are a part of the existential reality but at the same time may be subject to evaluation, modification, and change. In this extension and application of the Knightian principle to the political constitution—and particularly by way of analogy with the choices of strategies and rules of ordinary games—I was stimulated and encouraged by my colleague at the University of Virginia, Rutledge Vining, who had also been strongly influenced by the teachings of Frank Knight.

Why "Better Than Plowing"?

As noted, in 1986 I wrote an autobiographical essay called "Better Than Plowing," a title I borrowed directly from Frank Knight, who used it to describe his own attitude toward a career in the academy. To me the title seemed also descriptive, and it does, I think, convey my sense of comparative evaluation between "employment" in the academy and in the economy beyond. This title also suggests, even if somewhat vaguely, the sheer luck of those of us who served in the academy during the years of the baby-boom educational explosion, luck that was translated into rents of magnitudes beyond imaginable dreams.

To my surprise constructive critics have challenged the appropriateness of the "Better Than Plowing" title for my more general autobiographical essay. To these critics this title seems too casual, too much a throwaway phrase, too flippant a description of a research career that, objectively and externally considered, seems to have embodied central purpose or intent. This unexpected invitation to write a second autobiographical essay provides me with an opportunity to respond to these critics and at the same time to offer additional insights into my development as an economist.

The many books and papers that I have written and published between 1949 and 1987 make up an objective reality that is "there" for all to read and to interpret as they choose. These words and pages exist in some space analogous to the Popperian third world. There is a surprising coherence in this record that I can recognize as well or better than any interpretative critical biographer. As Robert Tollison and I have suggested in our analysis of autobiography,[6] the autobiographer possesses a record over and beyond that which is potentially available to any biographer. The person whose acts created the objective record lives with the subject record itself. And such a person, as autobiographer, would be immoral if he relied on the objective record to impute to his life's work a purpose-oriented coherence that had never emerged into consciousness.

I recognize, of course, that my own research-publication record may be interpreted as the output of a methodological and normative individualist whose underlying purpose has always been to further philosophical support for individual liberty. In subjective recall, however, this motivational thrust has never informed my conscious work effort. I have throughout my career and with only a few exceptions sought to clarify ambiguities and confusions and clear up neglected pockets of analysis in the received arguments of fellow economists, social scientists, and philosophers. To the extent that conscious motivation has entered these efforts, it has always been the sheer enjoyment of working out ideas, of creating the reality that is reflected finally in the finished manuscript. Proof of my normative disinterest lies in my failure to be interested in what happens once a manuscript is a finished draft—a failure that accounts for my sometimes inattention to choice of publisher, to promotional details, and to the potential for either earnings or influence.

I look on myself as being much closer in spirit to the artist who creates on canvas or stone than to the scientist who discovers only that which he accepts to exist independently of his actions. And I should reject, and categorically, any affinity with the preacher who writes or speaks for the express and only purpose of persuading others to accept his prechosen set of values.

In all of this, once again, Frank Knight has served as my role model. His famous criticism of Pigou's road case is exemplary.[7] By introducing property rights, Knight enabled others to see the whole Pigovian analysis in a new light. Something was indeed created in the process. I like to think that perhaps some of my own works on public debt, opportunity cost, earmarked taxes, clubs, ordinary politics, and constitutional rules may have effected comparable shifts in perspective. The fact that these efforts have been commonly characterized by a reductionist thrust embodying an individualist methodology is explained, very simply, by my inability to look at the world through other than an individualist window.

It is as if the artist who has only red paints produces pictures that are only red of hue. Such an artist does not choose to paint red pictures and then, instrumentally, purchase red paints. Instead the artist uses the instruments at hand to do what he can and must do, while enjoying himself immensely in the process. The fact that others are able to secure new insights with the aid of his creations and that this in turn provides artist with a bit of bread—this gratuitous result enables the artist, too, to entitle his autobiographical essay "Better Than Plowing."

Notes

1. James M. Buchanan, "The Qualities of a Natural Economist," in *Democracy and Public Choice*, ed. Charles Rowley (New York: Blackwell, 1987): 9–19.

2. James M. Buchanan, "Better Than Plowing," *Banca Nazionale del Lavoro Quarterly Review* 159 (December 1986): 359–375.

3. For an extended discussion of Knight's ambiguity in this respect, see my paper "The Economizing Element in Knight's Ethical Critique of Capitalist Order," *Ethics* 98 (October 1987): 61–75.

4. For a discussion of two kinds of socialism in this setting, see the title essay in my book, *Liberty, Market, and State: Political Economy in the 1980s* (New York: New York University Press, 1985).

5. James M. Buchanan, "The Public Choice Perspective," *Economia delle scelte publiche* 1 (January 1983): 7–15.

6. James M. Buchanan and Robert D. Tollison, "A Theory of Truth in Autobiography," *Kyklos* 39, no. 4 (1986): 507–517.

7. Frank H. Knight, "Fallacies in the Interpretation of Social Cost," *Quarterly Journal of Economics* 38 (1924): 582–606. Reprinted in *The Ethics of Competition* (London: Allen and Unwin, 1935), 217–236.

James M. Buchanan

Awarded Nobel Prize in 1986. Lecture presented October 28, 1987.

Dates of Birth and Death

October 3, 1919; January 9, 2013

Academic Degrees

B.A., Middle Tennessee State College, 1940
M.S., University of Tennessee, 1941
Ph.D., University of Chicago, 1948

Academic Affiliations

Associate Professor, University of Tennessee, 1948–50
Professor, University of Tennessee, 1950–51
Professor, Department of Economics, Florida State University, 1954–56
Professor, James Wilson Department of Economics, University of Virginia, 1956–62
Paul G. McIntire Professor of Economics, University of Virginia, 1962–68
Professor of Economics, University of California, Los Angeles, 1968–69
University Distinguished Professor, Virginia Polytechnic Institute and State University, 1969–83
Holbert L. Harris University Professor, George Mason University, 1983–2007; Emeritus, 2007–13

Selected Books

Fiscal Theory and Political Economy, 1960
The Calculus of Consent, 1962 (with G. Tullock)
The Limits of Liberty, 1975
The Power to Tax, 1980 (with G. Brennan)
The Reason of Rules, 1985 (with G. Brennan)
Liberty, Market, and State, 1985
Economics: Between Predictive Science and Moral Philosophy, 1987
Explorations into Constitutional Economics, 1989
The Collected Works of James M. Buchanan, Vols. 1–20, 1999–2002

Robert M. Solow

To be honest, I should warn you that I am going to tell you as little about myself as I can get away with in a lecture about "My Evolution as an Economist." My reason is not that I have anything to hide. I wish I had more to hide; that would at least suggest an exciting life. My problem is that I think the "cult of personality" is slowly swamping our culture. You can see it at its most dangerous in presidential elections, where eyebrows seem to be more important than ideas. I tend to blame that on television, which is a better medium for eyebrows than for economic theory. But that sort of technological determinism won't quite do: it leaves us with the task of explaining the psychologization of almost everything, the success of pop books on character, the fact that seven out of ten nonfiction best sellers are biographies, the importance attached to the "personal relationship" between Mr. Reagan and Mrs. Thatcher. Something pretty deep is going on there. (I don't mean between Mr. Reagan and Mrs. Thatcher!) Fortunately, academic economists seem to have a big comparative disadvantage when it comes to personal interest. I wouldn't have anything to say to Barbara Walters even if she had anything to say to me.

Anyway, what I have called the cult of personality has to be a sign of cultural decay. ("Just lie back and tell us when you first had that feeling, Professor Solow.") I don't mean to twist and turn in order to avoid biographical details, but I would rather concentrate on social and intellectual currents of slightly broader significance.

Shortly after the death of John von Neumann some thirty-odd years ago Robert Strotz, who was then editor of *Econometrica,* asked me to write a memorial article about him. Von Neumann and Frank Ramsey must be the two noneconomists who have, in their spare moments, had the greatest influence on what professional economists actually do. (On the merits, Harold Hotelling certainly belongs in their class; but he is much closer to having been, or having become, a part-time professional economist.) I never wrote the article, but I did think about it for a while. A puzzle presented itself: How did von Neumann become interested in economics anyway? I asked a number of people who might have known, but none could give me a useful answer. Then I sent a note to Karl Menger (the grandson of the Menger who was a cofounder of the Austrian school of economics) because he had run a mathematical seminar in Vienna that was attended occasionally by von Neumann, Abraham Wald, and some economists. Menger gave me a wonderful answer to my question. He said that everyone in Austria-Hungary was interested in economics.

Well, I grew up in the 1930s—graduated from high school in January 1940, in fact. I can certainly say that everyone in Brooklyn in the 1930s was interested in economics. And not only in economics: intelligent high school students of my day were conscious not only of the Great Depression but also of the rise of Fascism and Nazism, events that were certainly not independent of the worldwide depression. It was an obvious fact of life to us that our society was malfunctioning politically and economically and that nobody really knew how to explain it or what to do about it.

This is important for the subject at hand. I think it throws some light on the current state and recent evolution of economics. I said that I graduated from high school in 1940. I was a couple of years younger than my classmates; but anyone who was eighteen in 1940 is sixty-six now. Soon there will be no more active economists who remember the 1930s clearly. The generation of economists that was moved to study economics by the feeling that we desperately needed to understand the Great Depression will soon have retired. Most of today's younger and middle-aged macroeconomists think of "the business cycle" as a low-variance, moderately autocorrelated, stationary, stochastic process taking place around a generally satisfactory trend. That is an altogether different frame of mind from the one with which I grew up in the profession.

Now maybe they have the right idea. I don't want to sound like an old codger who goes around all the time bundled up in fear that the Blizzard of '88 may happen again tomorrow. The underlying intellectual problem is more complicated than that. I don't think for a minute that a major depression is a probabilistically frequent event. But I am not sure that it is useful to model it as a probabilistically rare event either. I rather doubt that the probabilistic way of thinking about major depressions sends the right signals—or receives them—in the first place. I think that a lot of my contemporaries regard the possibility of deep recession mainly as an indicator that there are mechanisms latent in an industrial capitalist economy that can cause it to stall for an uncomfortably long time away from any satisfactory equilibrium. The trigger may be a mixture of endogenous and exogenous events. One of the jobs of macroeconomics, perhaps its main job, is to understand what those mechanisms are and what defensive policies they call for. That is surely not the only way of sizing up or thinking about macroeconomics. But it strikes me as a mistake for contemporary macroeconomics to assume away any such possibility.

I arrived at Harvard College in September 1940. Economics A was one of my four freshman courses. I had no idea then of becoming an economist; I probably didn't know there was such a thing as a professional economist, or what one did. My recollection is that I had some notion of studying biology; I certainly took a two-semester course in biology that first year and got an A, but it was pretty clear that biology was not for me. So I opted for a sort of general social science major, and for the next year or two I took courses in sociology, anthropology, and psychology as well as economics.

Undergraduate students of economics at Harvard College in 1940–1942 did not learn any coherent way of thinking about the Depression from which the United States was just emerging. The fact that real GNP rose by 8 percent between 1939 and 1940 and another 18 percent between 1940 and 1941 and that the unemployment rate fell by 7.3 percentage points between 1939 and 1941 under the stimulus of war production, both for export and for use at home, might have offered some hint. (We didn't know what the real GNP was, you realize; the data came later. But industrial production, which was measured, rose by 15 and 18 percent in 1940 and 1941, respectively.) Our textbooks and courses offered us no sense of a systematic understanding of the dramatic events taking place all around us. The memoirs of political figures of the time make it clear that they had no clue either.

It wasn't all dull, of course. I heard Sumner Slichter and John Dunlop lecture about labor economics, and Paul Sweezy about Marxian economics, and I learned things from all of them that I still remember.

Two of the three books that really formed my generation of economists after the war had already been published: *The General Theory of Employment, Interest and Money* in 1936 and Hicks's *Value and Capital* in 1939. (The third, Samuelson's *Foundations of Economic Analysis,* appeared in 1947.) The galaxy of star graduate students of the time—Samuelson, Metzler, Musgrave, Tobin, Alexander, et al.—were no doubt clued in to these ideas that would come to dominate economics for a while. None of it percolated to undergraduates so soon. The ideas were too new and Harvard economics was too sclerotic at the time. The point is that I had no feeling that economic analysis could penetrate to the heart of what was going on in the world. I certainly hadn't made up my mind to major in economics or to become an economist. What I did instead was to volunteer for the army. It seemed more constructive than what I was doing.

Three years later I came back and, almost without thinking about it, signed up to finish my undergraduate degree as an economics major. The timing was such that I had to make a decision in a hurry. No doubt I acted as if I were maximizing an infinite discounted sum of one-period utilities, but you couldn't prove it by me. To me it felt as if I were saying to myself: "What the hell."

At that time, September 1945, Harvard still had an effective "tutorial system." Every junior and senior—I was still a junior—was assigned a member of the faculty as a "tutor" to be seen for an hour once a week. The tutor would assign things to read, occasionally ask the tutee to write a short paper, and then the two would discuss the week's work. My tutor was Wassily Leontief. Maybe it was just dumb luck. Maybe the powers that be took note of the fact that I had been an A student. Maybe it was just the opposite; maybe being tutored by a foreigner—and a theorist at that—was like being stuck in a ghetto. In any case it was a turning point for me. From Leontief I learned that economics was not a hodgepodge but a subject with a disciplined theoretical and empirical structure. Over the next few years he taught me the details of some of that structure. I would have to say that it was Leontief who turned me into an economist.

He did one other thing for me that will now seem quaint, but it is worth mentioning for just that reason. In those days you could do an undergraduate degree in economics at Harvard, and probably a Ph.D. as well, without knowing or using a bit of calculus. (Everyone had to read the text of *Value and Capital* [or at least part I] but not the mathematical appendix, elementary as that is by today's standards.) I had been a good math student in high school; it might have been my best subject. But it never occurred to me to do any more at the college level, certainly not in connection with economics. It was probably forbidden for Professor Leontief to recruit students to the study of mathematics and mathematical economic theory, nor did he do so. What he did do was to begin some of our weekly sessions by saying: "You should read thus and such an article ... but no, you can't. You don't know any mathematics. Well, try this one instead." I may be slow-witted, but I'm not *stupid*. I wanted to read the good stuff. So pretty soon I signed up for the calculus sequence and went on in mathematics until I had learned a little more than I needed to know for everyday work. That is probably less than any good graduate student with an interest in theory knows today. It is amazing that it was such a big deal in those days. People got hot under the collar about it.

What I did not learn from Professor Leontief—and in fact did not learn at all during the years 1945 to 1949 while finishing my undergraduate degree and taking courses and examinations for the Ph.D.—was macroeconomics. That is an anachronistic turn of phrase anyway. There were no courses in macroeconomics in the catalog. There were courses on "business cycles"; mine was taught by Gottfried Haberler, and a very good course it was. *Prosperity and Depression* sticks to the ribs. I recommend it to anyone. When I began to teach at MIT in 1950, one of the first economics courses I taught was called "Business Cycles." It first acquired the label "Macroeconomics" a decade later, I would guess.

By macroeconomics I mean the study of complete aggregative models of the economy. Back then it was almost a code word for Keynesian economics, what he called "the theory of output as a whole." Trivial historical accident was at work in shaping my education. My contemporaries, some of them, learned about macroeconomics from Alvin Hansen. The locus was the graduate course in money and banking that he taught jointly with John H. Williams. As luck would have it, I enrolled in "Money and Banking" right after the war, probably in 1945 or 1946. Hansen was on leave; the entire two-semester course was taught by Williams. Moreover, because of the flood of returning veterans the graduate and undergraduate versions of "Money and Banking" were combined. (We used to say that the only difference was that the undergraduates were graded to a higher standard.) So I was never called upon to take the specifically graduate-level course.

John Williams was a famous skeptic about Keynes, about macroeconomics, in fact about everything. Skepticism is a very good thing in an economist, and perhaps his lesson stuck with me. In the particular case of macroeconomic theory, however, I never really learned what it was I was supposed to be skeptical *of*. Caught up as I was in learning economic theory in the Leontief manner, I never had as much contact with Alvin Hansen as I should have. I was never formally enrolled in the famous fiscal policy seminar, though I occasionally attended a session and my wife was a regular member.

There is a temptation to exaggerate this picture. I learned something about macroeconomics from slightly older and more advanced colleagues like James Duesenberry and Thomas Schelling. From Richard Goodwin, then an assistant professor, I learned not only the technique of building dynamic macroeconomic models but a whole attitude toward them that still strikes me as right. It emphasizes keeping them simple and focused, answering a simple question with a strong model. The art is in concentrating the subtlety in the right place.

And of course I could read. But graduate students then—and now?—had time to read only what they were expected to read. It is probably fair to say that I finished my coursework at Harvard in 1949 and passed my exam, still not having acquired what I thought economics was supposed to provide: a working understanding, not exactly of the business cycle but of the moving level of economic activity, its equilibrium or self-perpetuating properties, and its disequilibrium properties. It is hard to describe because the vocabulary that later came to seem suitable—that of Keynesian economics, not necessarily the "economics of Keynes"—is now unfashionable, and the vocabulary that is now fashionable seems designed to suppress the very curiosity that I am trying to describe.

I spent all of 1949–50 and part of 1950–51, when I started teaching at MIT, producing a Ph.D. thesis that tried to model the dynamics of the size distribution of incomes, mostly wage and salary incomes, as the outcome of a random process into and out of employment with accompanying transitions from one wage level to another. It was entirely my own idea.

I was an assistant professor of statistics in the Department of Economics and Social Science. Along with statistics and econometrics courses, I taught the graduate course on business cycles. Then of course I had to figure out for myself what it was that I wanted students to know. We often say among ourselves that the best way to learn a subject is to teach it. There is some truth in that, but one wants to be clear about what the kernel of truth is. You don't have to teach a subject to master its mechanical and technical details. Books will do quite nicely for that. The experience of teaching does, if you take it seriously, require you to figure out how to explain the subject at hand clearly; and that is already a higher level of understanding than the first. But there is a higher level yet. The second or third time you teach a course you may realize that you have a feeling for the topic's shape, its organizing principles, its message, its relation to the rest of economics and to real economic life. So it was; I began by teaching about business cycle theories—Pigou, Robertson, Haberler, Kalecki, Metzler, Hansen, Samuelson, Hicks, that sort of thing—and I ended up teaching macroeconomics (and growth).

It would be satisfying to say that I educated myself. But that would be at most half true. My new colleagues at MIT—Paul Samuelson, of course, but also Robert Bishop and Cary Brown—had been part of the transitional generation. They had been among the first to feel the shock waves when J. M. Keynes invented macroeconomics. (Make no mistake: that is what he did. I have elsewhere quoted A. C. Pigou, who must have known, on this subject. "Nobody before [Keynes], so far as I know, had brought all the relevant factors, real and monetary at once, together in a single formal scheme, through which their interplay could be coherently investigated." That is exactly what I am talking about.)

Macroeconomics in that spirit is what I had been missing. I found it in the conversation of my colleagues in the MIT department and pretty quickly and easily made it part of my own mental furniture. Strangely enough, for an American, I was at that time more familiar with the writings of the Swedish economists than with Keynes or the immediate English Keynesians. Somewhere in graduate school I had read Lindahl, Myrdal, Ohlin, Lundberg, and most especially Wicksell. Those books are still on my shelves. It was probably Haberler who introduced me to the modern Stockholm school (and the GI Bill that paid for the books). Wicksell I found for myself, and he has always been a favorite for several reasons. The one that matters here is that he, among the great nineteenth-century economists, came closest to the spirit of macroeconomics. In *Interest and Prices* and again in the note on "Åkerman's problem" one gets the feeling that he is verging on Pigou's definition. If only Wicksell had been able to put the two together!

Elsewhere I have described how I came to work on the theory of economic growth in the 1950s, and I do not want to repeat that story now. What I did not sufficiently emphasize in my Nobel lecture—it became clear to me only in the course of thinking through what I have just been saying—is the extent to which involvement in growth theory can be seen as (and really was) an integral part of my education in macroeconomics. Harrod–Domar theory was addressed to serious issues about the path of a capitalist economy. I was led to modify the model just to make it yield a path that could more plausibly claim to look like what one actually saw in historical time series. But this is just part of the general macroeconomic problem of representing a complete, closed, aggregative model. That my version of growth theory had capital-theoretic overtones was probably a residue from Wicksell.

The next evolutionary step was probably my stint at the Council of Economic Advisers during the Kennedy administration. Day-to-day economic policy had never been my specialty. I had been shocked to hear Paul Samuelson say at lunch one day that he thought the fundamental function of economic theory was to permit the writing of good financial journalism. I had to mature a little before I realized how close to true that was. But I was an onlooker during the campaign of 1960; no one asked me to serve on one of Kennedy's task forces or transition teams. So I was taken by surprise to get a late-night call from the three members of the council—Walter Heller, James Tobin, and Kermit Gordon—asking me to take leave and join the staff. The bait held out to me, the boy growth-theorist, was that I could be the council's ivory-tower economist and spend my time thinking about longer-term policy rather than the daily hurly-burly.

I believed it and I am sure they believed it. But it took me about two days in the old Executive Office Building to realize that all the action, and I mean intellectual action, was in meeting each day's excitement as it arose. It arose right away. The outgoing council had of course prepared the January 1961 *Economic Report*. The new council had to prepare a "mini-report" as the basis for its testimony before the Joint Economic Committee on March 6. Everyone pitched in of course, but the main authors of that statement were the three council members, Arthur Okun, and I (and Joseph Pechman, who was not on the staff but, as a longtime friend of Heller's, served as our old Washington hand). It was a six-week crash course in practical macroeconomics. I do not mean that phrase as a euphemism for sloppy macroeconomics. What I cherish about that experience was the conscious effort to use macroeconomic theory to interpret the world and, in a small way, to change it.

Tobin and I (alas, Gordon, Okun, and Heller are all dead) have just republished the 1961 statement and the January 1962 *Economic Report*, which was clearly intended as a kind of declaration of principle. (The volume also contains the January 1982 *Report*, introduced by the members of the first Reagan council. They can speak for themselves.) To many contemporary readers the 1962 *Report* will seem like a compendium of everything that was wrong with (Keynesian) macroeconomics before the "new classical" counterrevolution, a kind of "before" picture in a before-and-after advertisement. It goes without saying that neither Tobin nor I (nor Okun, if only he were still with us) would wish to write exactly the same things if we were writing the *Report* now, knowing what we have learned in the past quarter century. In fact it is not my purpose to defend the viewpoint of the *Report* even where I think it deserves defense. It is offered as a fair example of what people like me believed in 1961.

First of all—and perhaps here I am being defensive—there is no way we can be said to have neglected the supply side of the economy. There is a whole chapter on the importance of supply factors and supply-side incentives. We were, after all, the people who gave you the investment tax credit in the Revenue Act of 1962. How could the boy growth-theorist have neglected the supply side? What we did do was to give a reasoned argument that the U.S. economy was then, and had been for some time, operating with excess supply, involuntary unemployment, and underutilized capacity. We insisted on a sharp distinction between increases in real output that could be had just by stimulation of demand—what we called "closing the gap between actual and potential output"—and further increases in real output, which would require movement on the supply side. (It is worth remarking, especially now, that way back then Tobin and I were proposing that the right fiscal policy target was a federal budget surplus at full employment, maintained by monetary ease. Our goal was a higher rate of domestic investment and national saving, and we doubted that enough private saving was achievable. So much for the notion that "Keynesians" had some allergic fear of saving.)

A certain sort of contemporary economist would simply dismiss the very possibility of persistent excess aggregate supply. Is it not the hallmark of the well-trained economist to *know* that "markets clear"? Is there any coherent alternative? I have to admit that the 1962 *Economic Report* offers no sustained rebuttal of that view. It was, after all, written for the general public, not for other economists. So I have to reconstruct what we would have said had anybody put the question.

There are two possible answers. One is in a way Keynes's own: An economy can be in aggregative "equilibrium" with widespread involuntary unemployment and underutilized capacity. The equilibrium cannot be Walrasian, with all markets clearing, but it can be equilibrium all the same, in the relevant sense that there is no internal pressure for the situation to change. Keynes was not so precise, nor did he ever make good his claim to have demonstrated the theoretical soundness of this idea; but that is what he claimed. I think we would not have taken that line. The alternative answer could have gone something like this. There are dozens of nitty-gritty reasons why nominally quoted prices and wages should be imperfectly flexible. A list of them would be just a list, not a theory. It hardly needs to be added that miscellaneous nominal rigidities imply that real quantities and relative prices will often be in the wrong place and perhaps moving in the wrong direction. In consequence the economy's approach to market-clearing equilibrium after any disturbance may be intolerably slow and costly. Even if there were but One Equilibrium and It were Pareto-efficient, there would still be a large payoff to corrective policy, whether automatic or discretionary.

In the 1960s we would have taken that second line. It is the one that true believers have labeled "American Keynesianism," thus presumably classifying it with Wonder Bread and "Wheel of Fortune." Of course it had quintessential early expression in the famous articles by John Hicks and Franco Modigliani, not exactly backwoods Americans, but never mind that. The 1962 *Report* did not make such arguments, for the reason I have already stated, but I am sure that it is what was in Tobin's mind, and Okun's, and mine. The usual shorthand presumption was that the nominal wage is the sticky price; and that is enough to get the standard American-Keynesian results. But that was just a formality, an up-front way of establishing the model's credentials. If pressed, we would cheerfully have produced a variety of rigidities and imperfections and noted that they only strengthened the case.

A few years later I wrote a paper with Joseph Stiglitz, then just out of graduate school, that formalized the view of the world I have just been ascribing to "the old folks." We took it for granted that nominal wages and prices both adjusted slowly to excess demand or supply. Thus neither market had to clear in the short run, and the "short-side principle" applied in both. We were able to show how such an economy might have quite perverse dynamics and might even get itself trapped in situations a little like unemployment equilibrium, though not quite. Our model was quite clearly a precursor of the Bénassy–Drèze–Malinvaud "fixed-price temporary equilibrium" models that came to light five or ten years later (and have received less attention in the United States than they deserve). Our paper fell with a dull thud. This fate may have come about because we did not even discuss the "spillovers" from quantity-rationed markets to others that form much of the stuff of the French fixed-price models and give them their claim to be modeling "effective demand." We were not much interested in such microeconomic underpinnings; we were trying to show how a model economy could sometimes be demand limited and sometimes supply-limited. Our intended goal was a contribution to the "neoclassical synthesis" or, more picturesquely, "Bastard Keynesianism."

The funny thing is that I now think that Keynes had the right instinct. It is a better move to look for alternative, non-Walrasian equilibrium concepts as a foundation for macroeconomic analysis of modern industrial capitalism. It is better partly because of the hold that equilibrium analysis has on economists; and more significantly it is better because it corresponds at least as well to our intuitions and observations of economic life. Keynes could not make good on his claim to have produced a consistent notion of "unemployment equilibrium" because he lacked the analytical tools to do the job. Those came into economics only much later.

Nowadays there is a body of macroeconomic theory that goes under the name "New Keynesian Economics" and pursues the task of showing how information asymmetries, transactions costs, and similar facts of life can lead to the possibility of equilibria—self-sustaining situations—with "wrong" levels of employment and output. Usually, then, it can be shown that simple fiscal and monetary policies can improve the situation. (It is true, but hardly news, that inappropriate policies can make things worse. That is why baseball teams fire their managers.)

To my eye the New Keynesian Economics is a mixed bag. Its aims are right and its techniques are nice. But sometimes the particular facts of life it chooses to emphasize seem too farfetched or insignificant to bear the weight that is placed on them. It comes, maybe, from a kind of yearning for respectability and the well-founded belief that respectability comes from staying close to the traditional simplifying assumptions of economics. That is not wholly bad. It is certainly better than wholesale "new paradigm"-mongering. But there are times when common sense leads away from the tradition, and then I would choose common sense every time. If I am right that the main question in macroeconomics is why, after the inevitable real shocks, the economy can stay so far from full employment for so long, then transactions costs and information asymmetries seem too tangential to be the main answer.

In those days the Phillips curve was the particular way we coped with the idea of imperfectly flexible wages. Paul Samuelson and I wrote a paper in 1960 that may have coined the phrase "Phillips curve" and certainly helped to domesticate it in the United States. That is one of the things I would do differently now, but I want to say explicitly how.

About six months ago at a conference in Helsinki, Michael Parkin described that paper as "unfortunate." He didn't mean that it was unlucky in love; he meant that it had misled many people into the untrue belief that there was a stable trade-off between inflation and unemployment, along which policy could move and place the economy. I reacted defensively and pointed out that a careful reading of the paper would disclose that we had stated just about every qualification that one would now wish to attach to the Phillips curve idea. In particular we had remarked explicitly that any attempt to exploit the inflation-unemployment trade-off in policy terms, by buying low unemployment at the expense of permanently higher inflation, could easily have the effect of causing the Phillips curve to shift adversely, canceling the hoped-for gain. We even mentioned changing expectations as the route by which that could happen. It's true—we did.

After the conference, Assar Lindbeck observed to me that I had dodged the issue. Yes, the formal qualifications were there; but the tone of the paper was certainly optimistic about the possibility of choosing, by standard policy means, a point on the Phillips curve. I had to admit the justice of that observation. The eclectic American Keynesians of the 1960s were not sufficiently alert to the force of inflationary expectations. They expected more from the Phillips curve than it could deliver in practice.

That raises the question: What do I believe now? What I do not believe is the notion of a reasonably stable "natural rate of unemployment." That idea asserts the existence of a knowable, at worst slowly changing, unemployment rate (or rate of utilization more broadly defined) with the crucial property that maintaining a lower unemployment rate entails ever-accelerating inflation and maintaining a higher unemployment rate entails eventually ever-accelerating deflation. There was a time when I think I was the only respectable(?) economist who rejected this so-called long-run vertical Phillips curve, but I am glad to see that I am now acquiring some allies. From the very beginning I found both the theoretical and empirical foundations of the natural rate hypothesis to be flimsy.

On the theoretical side, Milton Friedman had defined the "natural rate" as the unemployment rate "ground out by the Walrasian equations of general equilibrium." But surely not very many of those who accepted the natural rate hypothesis realized that it made sense only if they took Walrasian general equilibrium to be a valid description of the real everyday economy. Other theoretical foundations were just as far-fetched. On the empirical side, econometric estimates of the natural rate were usually based on weak empirical relationships, any of which was susceptible to several interpretations. It is no great caricature to say that believers would assert, say, that the unemployment rate in Great Britain, some 9 to 10 percent, was below the natural rate. How do you know? Because inflation is accelerating. Why is inflation accelerating? Because unemployment is below the natural rate.

My preferred hypothesis is that there is no such thing as the natural rate, not in the sense of a well-defined number with the accelerationist property. Of course at any given time you can imagine puffing up aggregate demand so much that inflation accelerates. (Maybe, just maybe, you can imagine a level of demand so low that wages and prices fell faster and faster. I'd rather see than be one.) But what that critical level is depends on history, institutions, attitudes, and beliefs, including beliefs about the natural rate. If there are many equilibria for the economy, there are probably many possible "natural" rates.

I will just finish by telling you one or two things that I have learned about myself and about contemporary economics, more particularly things that I have learned or realized in the process of thinking about what to say in this lecture.

First of all, I have the feeling it is a mistake to think of economics as a Science, with a capital *S*. I also find it temperamentally uncongenial, and that may even be the source of my feeling. Theoretical physicists nowadays think they are on the verge of what they call, only partially self-mockingly, "The Theory of Everything." There is no Economic Theory of Everything, and attempts to construct one seem to merge toward a Theory of Nothing. If you think I am making a sly comment about some tendencies in contemporary macroeconomics, you are right.

That is perfectly consistent with a strong belief that economics should try very hard to be scientific with a small *s*. By that I mean only that we should think logically and respect fact. I will have more to say about "fact" in a minute.

I once heard Paul Streeten say that the world is divided into two kinds of people: those who think the world is divided into two kinds of people and those who do not. Economic theorists (and even some applied economists) seem to be divided into two classes of people, System Builders and Puzzle Solvers. What I have just been saying expresses a prejudice in favor of Puzzle Solvers. Puzzles are things that need explaining. They can arise from the pursuit of theory: paradoxes to be resolved, examples to be discovered (e.g., the optimal excise tax), questions in the form, "Is it possible that X?" Puzzles can just as well arise from observation: the corn-hog cycle, the "constancy" of distributive shares, the regularities that led to Okun's law. The closest I ever came to system building in the theory of economic growth was actually an attempt to solve a puzzle: How to reconcile the intrinsic instability in Harrod–Domar theory with the failure of economic history to look that way? We can certainly afford some true system builders, and they are certainly highly decorative; my hunch is that the system is too complex and too embedded in the noneconomic ever to be built by our methods.

Now I want to say something about fact. The austere view is that "facts" are just time series of prices and quantities. The rest is hypothesis testing. I have seen a lot of those tests. They are almost never convincing, primarily because one senses that they have very low power against lots of alternatives. There are too many ways to explain a bunch of time series. And sure enough, the next issue of the journal will contain an article exhibiting quite different functional forms, slightly different models. My hunch is that we can make progress only by enlarging the class of eligible facts to include, say, the opinions and casual generalizations of experts and market participants, attitudinal surveys, institutional regularities, even our own judgments of plausibility. My preferred image is the vacuum cleaner, not the microscope.

I am not, repeat not, saying that common sense or the opinion of the "practical man" is always right. The theories held by practical men are very often wrong or empty. What I am saying is that the economist cannot dispense with keeping his or her eyes open, looking around, and forming judgments about what makes sense and what is simply farfetched. Those cannot be uncritical judgments, but judgments to be defended by appeal to observation and to logic.

Enough of the Dismal Science. A friend of mine once presented me with a Columbia University Economics Department T-shirt. It shows a helicopter-drop of money—a favorite abstraction of monetary theorists—falling on an island—the favorite abstraction of economists—and the slogan is "Not half as dismal as you think." With that thought, I leave you.

Robert M. Solow

Awarded Nobel Prize in 1987. Lecture presented October 13, 1988.

Date of Birth

August 23, 1924

Academic Degrees

B.A., Harvard College, 1947
M.A., Harvard University, 1949
Ph.D., Harvard University, 1951

Academic Affiliations

Assistant Professor of Statistics, Massachusetts Institute of Technology, 1950–54
Associate Professor of Statistics, Massachusetts Institute of Technology, 1954–58
Professor of Economics, Massachusetts Institute of Technology, 1958–73
Institute Professor, Massachusetts Institute of Technology, 1973–95
Institute Professor, Emeritus, Massachusetts Institute of Technology, 1995–present

Selected Books

Linear Programming and Economic Analysis, 1958, 1987
(with R. Dorfman and P. A. Samuelson)
Capital Theory and the Rate of Return, 1963
Growth Theory: An Exposition, 1970, 2000
A Critical Essay on Modern Macroeconomic Theory, 1995 (with F. Hahn)
Monopolistic Competition and Macroeconomic Theory, 1998

William F. Sharpe

Introduction

What an honor. What an opportunity. What a challenge. What a temptation.

To speak about oneself before a captive audience is a rare opportunity indeed. The possibilities for self-aggrandizement boggle the mind. Why not abandon all pretense of false modesty? At the very least, seize the chance to propagandize for causes held dear—academic, political, personal.

Had I not read the contributions of my predecessors I might have succumbed to these temptations. However, not one of the others did. And I shall try very hard to resist any siren songs to the contrary.

The Invitation

When invited to give this lecture, I happily accepted. Surely speaking about one's evolution as an economist would be both easy and pleasant. But afterwards I read the written versions of the previous lectures. Not surprisingly, I found that my colleagues had been eloquent, erudite, sagacious, humorous, and both deep and broad in their coverage. How to follow in such footsteps? I considered feigning illness. The possibility of employing a ghost writer crossed my mind. But ultimately, I did neither. Here, for better or worse, are my comments on the subject at hand.

The Prize

First, the prize and the citation.

The Royal Swedish Academy awarded the 1990 Prize in Economic Sciences in Memory of Alfred Nobel to Harry Markowitz, Merton Miller, and myself "for their pioneering work in the theory of financial economics." I wish to emphasize the latter, for with this award, the field of *Financial Economics* completed *its* evolution to achieve the status of a field in both *Economics* and *Finance*.

A field of inquiry is much more important than anyone who practices it. Hence I will precede the personal chronology with some remarks on my field.

Financial Economics

One defines a subject at one's peril. This is especially true if the subject is one's own. But let me try.

In his speech at the prize ceremony Professor Assar Lindbeck of the Royal Swedish Academy of Sciences focused on financial markets, and the use thereof, by firms. Certainly the characteristics of financial instruments and their proper uses are central. From a more theoretical viewpoint, one can focus on the nexus between the *present* and the *future*. A financial instrument typically represents a property right to receive future cash flows. Such cash flows will, of course, come in the future—hence the *economics of time* must be understood. In many cases the flows are uncertain, hence the need for an approach to the *economics of uncertainty*. In addition, cash flows in the far future may depend on actions taken (or not taken) in the near future. This gives rise to the need for a theory of the *economics of options* (broadly construed). Finally, one needs information to estimate likely future outcomes, hence the requirement for an understanding of the *economics of information*.

I define financial economics so that it embraces all four of these important, difficult, and fascinating aspects of economics. While some may dispute the attempted appropriation of so much territory in the name of a group of *nouveax-arrivistes,* I believe that I am not alone in regarding this as appropriate.

Financial economics can be found in both economics departments and in finance departments of business schools. It also pervades practice. In economics departments, *positive* aspects tend to be emphasized; in the finance departments and in practice, *normative* applications. Positive theory attempts to describe the world; normative to offer prescriptions for action. The dichotomy is, however, far from complete. Positive theories assume various types of stylized normative behavior, and normative theories require a *gestalt*, which is usually based on positive theory.

The central question for positive financial economics is *valuation*—what is the value today of a set of future prospective cash flows? The central question for normative financial economics is the appropriate *use* of financial instruments in a world in which values are set wholly or partially in accord with the principles of positive financial economics.

Finance

Business school finance departments often break their offerings into three categories. The study of *investments* deals primarily with the *purchase* of financial instruments by individuals, pension funds, and the like. *Corporate finance,* to a major extent, deals with the *issue* of financial instruments by corporations. The third category, *financial institutions,* concerns organizations for which both the purchase and issuance of financial instruments are key.

To oversimplify, one can think of three different prototypical balance sheets. For investments, visualize financial instruments on the left and the net worth (or utility) of an individual or organization on the right. For corporate finance, visualize bricks and mortar, turret lathes, and the like on the left and financial instruments on the right. For financial institutions, visualize financial instruments on both sides.

Some business schools now begin their finance curriculum with a core course in financial economics, followed by required and/or elective courses in these three major areas of application. I had a small hand in bringing the Stanford curriculum to a rough approximation of this model. However, such a structure is still relatively unusual. In most business schools, financial economics is simply part of the first course in each of the applied areas. But it is inevitably an important part.

It was not always thus. Let me engage in some self-plagiarism by quoting from the 1978 edition of my textbook, *Investments:*

> In recent years the field of finance has truly undergone a revolution. Not too many years ago, investment textbooks were primarily devoted to ...

the mysteries of accounting, some of the details of the operations of major industries, and various rules of thumb for selecting "good" or "bad" securities. Institutional details ... were presented, along with historical data, but the reader was provided with no framework for understanding such phenomena. A theory of the formation of prices in capital markets was lacking.[1]

Needless to say, I went on to suggest that such a theory was at hand and that the student who used my book could use it to illuminate the dark corners of finance. I was even bold enough to say that "... empirical analysis has shown that it [the theory] describes the behavior of major capital markets quite well." This view now appears to have been somewhat too optimistic. Again I quote, this time from the 1985 edition of the book:

> Recent empirical work has cast some doubt on this comforting view of the world. Early statistical tests have been found to be relatively weak, suggesting that they may have been unable to identify important disparities between theory and reality. Moreover, systematic "anomalies" have been found, calling into question at least some aspects of the standard theories.[2]

This being said, however, theories of financial economics have not been discredited. Rather, they have become more comprehensive. In so doing they may have lost some of their simplicity and intuitiveness. But today only the foolhardy would venture into the world of finance without a solid understanding of financial economics. It is indeed here to stay.

Economics

Financial economics has had less impact on economics departments than on finance departments. Nonetheless, the synergy between the fields is great. And economists have had a profound influence on the development of financial economics. Again I beg indulgence for a quotation from my own writings. This from the preface to a 1982 book entitled, *Financial Economics, Essays in Honor of Paul Cootner.*

In 1950 the intersection of the fields of finance and economics was small indeed. Academic work in finance relied more often on rules of thumb and anecdotal evidence than on theory and adequate empirical studies.

Economists showed only fleeting interest in financial institutions, speculation, and the host of other aspects of uncertainty that comprise much of the domain of the field of finance.

Three decades later the situation is radically different. There is now a rich body of theory relevant to problems in finance; and extensive empirical tests have been conducted to see how well the theoretical constructs accord with reality. ...

Many of those who helped bring about the changes in finance were trained as economists. They approached finance problems with the attitudes and the standard tools of the economist. When they found the paradigms of traditional economics inadequate for the subject at hand, they invented new approaches. But, throughout, their style was that of the economist. As a result, we now have a domain increasingly referred to as *financial economics*.[3]

Paul Cootner, a close friend and colleague who died at far too young an age, was (as I said at the time) one of the first and one of the best financial economists. But there were, of course, many others. And almost all of those in the vanguard of the field were trained as economists, including Harry Markowitz, Merton Miller, and myself. Interestingly, five of those who contributed articles in honor of Paul Cootner are now laureates in Economics, and four (Paul Samuelson, Bob Solow, George Stigler, and myself) were participants in this lecture series.

In pronouncing the name of this field one should thus put equal emphasis on both the first and the second words.

Professional Practice

I suspect that no other field taught in business schools has had such an impact on its associated profession as has financial economics. Professional investors routinely speak of expected values; standard deviations; correlations; R-squared, beta, delta, and gamma values; convexity; binomial processes, and the like. Concepts that seemed abstract if not abstruse only a decade or two ago are now part of the everyday life of large numbers of traders throughout the world.

Financial economics has also influenced financial institutions. It spawned the index fund—a strategy designed to replicate the performance of a segment of the overall market with great precision and low cost. It provided the impetus for the huge market in derivative securities such as traded options, index futures, index options, swaps, and so on. Each of these formerly exotic instruments provides an efficient way for individuals and institutions to better control risk while pursuing specific objectives. Financial economics provides the structure for both the valuation and efficient use of such instruments.

A phrase of which I am particularly fond is this: *practical theory*. Financial economics contains an incredibly rich set of examples of such theories, and Wall Street, LaSalle Street, and Main Street have been quick to adopt them.

For a fascinating view of how this came about I strongly recommend Peter Bernstein's recently published *Capital Ideas: The Improbable Origins of Modern Wall Street*,[4] which documents the influence of a number of people, including six past Nobel Laureates, on investment practice.

Personal Evolution

I turn now to more personal reflections.

Whether one calls the development of financial economics a revolution (as I was wont to do in my youth) or evolution (in accordance with my charter here), it has been my great privilege to be both an observer of and a participant in the birth and maturation of this important field of inquiry. My own development was only a bit of a sideshow. But it may provide a better understanding of the larger canvas.

If there is a common thread in what follows it is the importance of luck. To be sure, good genes and hard work are necessary conditions for the attainment of this podium in this circumstance. But they are by no means sufficient. At many points in my decision tree, fortune decreed that I should take the branch on this path rather than another. To get here one must have the good luck to draw a great many favorable random numbers.

Undergraduate Work

My parents were both educators—my father a college president and my mother an elementary school principal. Due to disruptions caused by World War II, each had to return to graduate school in midlife. More than most, I learned at an early age to appreciate the joys of learning.

After completing my secondary education in the (then) excellent public schools in California, I enrolled at the University of California at Berkeley—intending to become the medical doctor that my mother wanted me to be. A lab course or two convinced me that such was not my métier. I then transferred to UCLA, determined to major in business administration. In the first semester of my sophomore year I took required courses in accounting and microeconomics. The former was, in reality, bookkeeping—and mindless bookkeeping at that. I loathed it. But microeconomics had everything: rigor, relevance, structure, and logic.

I found its allure irresistible. The next semester I changed my major to economics and never turned back.

Thus my first stroke of luck. I sometimes break out in a cold sweat thinking about what might have happened had I taken a modern accounting course and an institutional economics course.

I more or less supported myself while completing my education, through a succession of jobs including night work in a gas station, a swing shift posting transactions for a large company, grading papers for seven courses at once, various summer jobs, a teaching assistantship, and ultimately, a position as an economist.

As an undergraduate economics major I took an additional business course—one on investments. It was very traditional, very confusing, and very frustrating. Try as I might, I could find no unifying principle, no underlying structure. I was convinced that studying investments was not for me.

But again, luck was on my side. In my senior year I was able to work as a research assistant for J. Fred Weston, a professor in the business school and a major figure in the field of corporate finance. Fred introduced me to the early work in the then-nascent field of financial economics. I wasn't hooked yet, but I was certainly intrigued.

After graduation I interviewed for jobs in banking. Here my grades proved an impediment. The interviewer would typically look over my records, congratulate me, then ask why I hadn't considered graduate school. After a few such cases I tried grabbing the form, turning it over to the section on activities, offices held, fraternities, etc. then handing it back. Despite such attempts to show that I was a reasonably well-adjusted human being, nothing interesting came my way, and so I proceeded to a master's degree in economics at UCLA.

The Master's Degree

It was during this year that I irrevocably crossed the line to become an economist. Much of the credit (or blame) for this goes to Armen Alchian, who taught the graduate microeconomics sequence at UCLA. While personally gentle and traditional, Armen was (and is) clearly an eccentric economic theorist. He started the course by asserting that 95% of the material in economics journals was wrong or irrelevant—an assertion that I sometimes regard as not unduly pessimistic. He then proceeded to discuss the economics of the illegal market for buying babies. At one point he spent five of six lectures wrestling (somewhat unsuccessfully) with the meaning of *profit*. Indeed, most of his classes had the characteristics of a wrestling match. We witnessed a brilliant mind grappling (usually very successfully) with the most difficult concepts in economics in thoroughly creative and innovative ways. There could be no better training for a fledgling theorist and no higher standard. After two semesters with Armen Alchian, I was hooked. I wanted to be a microeconomist.

After obtaining the M.A., I fulfilled part of my ROTC obligation by serving as a Second Lieutenant in the Army Quartermaster Corps. I must admit that I rather enjoyed being outdoors much of the time and being (for once in my life) in reasonable physical condition.

The RAND Corporation

By indenturing myself to seven and a half years of reserve duty with two weeks of summer camp each year, I managed to limit my active duty to six months. Then through the good offices of Armen Alchian I was able to obtain a position at the RAND Corporation as a junior economist.

The RAND of 1956 was a unique organization. Funded almost entirely by the Air Force, it had contracted simply to do research that it considered worthwhile for its main client, along with a goodly dose of other work that would serve the public good. Employees were free to work any hours they chose, within wide limits. Office doors were open, intellectual discussions on the most wide-ranging topics were de rigueur, and everyone was expected to spend one day per week on research of strictly personal interest.

Those were heady days. Some of the key work in systems analysis, operations research, computer science, and applied economics was being done at RAND. One of our first computers was designed by John von Neumann. George Dantzig was working on linear programming. Some of the most illustrious academics served as consultants. Everyone was on a first-name basis. If ever there was a place for one interested in practical theory, the RAND Corporation in the 1950s was it.

Now, of course, the idea of working in a classified facility for the military establishment would prove an anathema for liberals (in the American political sense of the term), such as myself and most of the others at RAND. But those were simpler times. We truly believed that by improving the efficiency of the defense establishment we could help prevent war. There seemed to be no ambiguity and no moral dilemma.

At RAND I worked on problems involving optimization and trade-offs. We built many models, engaged in both data collection and empirical analysis, then brought all the pieces together using every bit of the then-available computer capacity at hand.

RAND pioneered in many aspects of computer science, leading me to become a "computer nerd" before the term came into common use. Time has in no way diminished my enthusiasm in this regard as my wife and my colleagues will attest.

Doctoral Work

Although RAND provided an extremely hospitable environment, I felt that ultimately I wanted to teach. Since personal economics precluded returning to full-time study, I thought my best choice would be to take the three education courses that, with my M.A. degree, would procure a credential for teaching in what were then termed junior colleges. I took only one of these—a night course on audio-visual education. It was, to be charitable, vacuous. The nadir came when the instructor showed a slide of a painstakingly constructed prize-winning bulletin board featuring the calendar for October. Another student pointed out that the bulletin board showed 30 days, not 31. The instructor was surprised but not embarrassed. While I would be the last to deny the importance of form, it seemed to me in this case it had totally triumphed over substance.

Rather than take the risk of having to endure another course of this caliber, I arranged to take the courses in the Economics Ph.D. program at UCLA while still working full-time at RAND. In addition to fields in microeconomics, monetary economics, economic history, and the development of economic thought, I managed to exploit a little-known provision in the department rules that allowed me to take a field in finance under Fred Weston. It was in this connection that I learned of the pioneering work of Harry Markowitz, which in large part began the development of financial economics.

After completing my courses and examinations, I set out to write what I hoped to be the definitive dissertation on transfer prices—the internal "shadow prices" that large firms sometimes use to provide incentives for divisions to operate efficiently. My interest in the subject had been piqued by some of the problems under investigation at RAND and by key work on the subject by Jack Hirshleifer, then at the University of Chicago. As it turned out, Jack moved to UCLA when I was approximately three months into the project. At Armen Alchian's suggestion, Jack read my work to date. To put it simply, he didn't consider it promising and strongly suggested that I find another topic.

To this day, I consider Jack one of my greatest benefactors.

Bent but not broken, I talked with Fred Weston. He suggested I talk with Harry Markowitz (who had recently joined RAND) about possible ideas for a dissertation. I did, and he suggested some. Armen Alchian was more than happy to have me work under Harry, even though Harry could not even appear as a member of my committee.

In 1952 Markowitz had shown that the investor's choice of a portfolio could be treated as a problem subject to mathematical and statistical formulation. Two key aspects of an investment strategy are its *expected return* and its *risk*. The former can be represented by the *mean* of a probability distribution of future return and the latter by the *variance* (or its square root, the *standard deviation*) of the distribution. An *efficient strategy* is one that provides the maximum expected return for given risk. Harry showed how to formulate the problem of finding all efficient strategies, given estimates of security expected returns, risks and correlations, and how to solve such problems using a quadratic programming algorithm that he had developed. His focus was strictly normative—he was concerned with the proper use of forecasts, not their properties.

My dissertation dealt with three related subjects. First, I explored the implications of a suggestion in Harry's 1958 book that one might characterize the "return-generating process" with what is today termed a *one-factor model*. In general, factor models identify one or more key influences, attempt to measure the sensitivity of each security to each of the specified factors, and assume that all other sources of risk are idiosyncratic—that is, unrelated across securities. In the dissertation I derived and experimented with computational schemes that would be efficient if only one such factor were posited. In later work I extended this to cover more realistic cases involving multiple factors.

Second, I worked with a practicing investment manager to attempt to apply the theory and the one-factor model using subjective judgments about future returns. This set of experiments was only partially successful. Curiously, the optimal portfolios kept producing large holdings of a relatively unknown company then called Haloid Xerox. Its price soon doubled several times over, perhaps justifying combining the manager's foresight with the discipline of the procedure. But I took from this experience the lesson that econometric methods are best suited to risk estimation, with judgment applied, if at all, to return estimation.

Third, and most important (as it has turned out), I asked the question that microeconomists are trained to ask. If everyone were to behave optimally (here, follow the prescriptions of Markowitz's portfolio theory), what prices will securities command once the capital market has reached *equilibrium*? To make the problem tractable I assumed that all investors made the same predictions and that returns were generated by the one-factor model. The conclusion was both startling and provocative. Security prices will adjust until there is a simple linear relationship between expected return and sensitivity to changes in the factor in question. Following the conventions of regression analysis, I used the symbol *beta* for the latter. Thus the result could be succinctly stated: securities with higher betas will have higher expected returns. Only the portion of risk due to the influence of the common factor will be rewarded in the long run. No compensation is needed nor available for the remainder (which I termed "nonsystematic risk"), since it can be reduced to a small amount by sensible diversification.

Thus was the capital asset pricing model born.

The University of Washington

Before completing my dissertation I had the opportunity to spend a day in Seattle. Uncharacteristically, the sun was shining and the waters were filled with sailboats. Since sailing was and is one of my passions, I applied for a position at the University of Washington. One was forthcoming, and I moved to Seattle.

At the time, the U.W. Business School was in the early stages of its transition from a traditional, nonrigorous, institutionally oriented program to the rigorous discipline-based academic school that it is now. This led to some frustrations but provided great opportunities. Teaching loads were heavy but those willing to try new courses were encouraged to do so. Continuing in the eclectic tradition of RAND, I taught courses in statistics, operations research, computer science and microeconomics, in addition to offerings in corporate finance and investments. It is certainly true that the best way to learn something is to attempt to teach it to others. At Washington I (at least) learned a great deal.

I also managed to complete a substantial amount of research. Most importantly, I derived the remaining essential elements of the capital asset pricing model in my first year there.

While the equilibrium results I had obtained in the dissertation were satisfying, they appeared to rely heavily on the strong assumption that only one factor was responsible for correlations among security returns. My instincts told me that it should be possible to generalize the model so that such an assumption would not be needed. After several false starts I found that in an efficient market of the type posited, the key relationship between expected returns and beta values would hold *no matter what the process generating security returns*. I proceeded to write the results, under the title "Capital Asset Prices: A Theory of Market Equilibrium under Conditions of Risk." Publication was delayed for over two years due to initial rejection by a referee and a change in the editorship of the *Journal of Finance*. In the meantime I presented my results and exchanged work with others in the rapidly developing field that we now call financial economics. One way or another we found each other and managed to convene at various conferences. The process of academic communication is somewhat mysterious, even to those who participate in it. But it is remarkably effective.

While at Washington but with funding from RAND, I combined two of my interests to produce a book called *The Economics of Computers*. I also took a year's leave to return to RAND to work on several nonmilitary projects, including one investigating the possible use of time-varying fees to better allocate landing rights and air space at the three major New York airports.

Stanford

In 1970 I moved to my current home—the Stanford Graduate School of Business. At the time Stanford was already prominent in finance and eager to incorporate more of the recent economics-based work in both the curriculum and the research program. Accordingly, Alan Kraus, Bob Litzenberger, and I set up the first formal Ph.D. sequence in finance and taught it as a team. In the process, we began to see the outlines of what we now call financial economics. My knowledge of the area also grew phenomenally, thanks to Alan and Bob.

In the 1970s, the Stanford Business School was rushing to achieve the "balanced excellence" in both research and teaching that it had set as a goal. To build on a finance faculty that already included Alan Kraus, Bob Litzenberger, Alex Robicheck, Ezra Solomon, and Jim Van Horne, we hired Paul Cootner, John Cox, Sandy Grossman, and Myron Scholes. In the economics department, Joe Stiglitz was working in the area, and we were all using Ken Arrow's monumental contributions to the field. We also set up a joint seminar series with U.C.–Berkeley, which brought us into contact with the likes of Hayne Leland, Barr Rosenberg, and

Mark Rubenstein. There could have been no better place for one with my interests.

At Stanford I taught finance and microeconomics at both the M.B.A. and Ph.D. level. Paul Cootner and I set up the Ph.D. sequence in microeconomics, from which I learned a great deal. However, I soon realized that I would rather concentrate my energy on financial economics, per se.

My biggest undertaking in these years was the writing of the previously quoted *Investments* textbook. It seemed to me that there was a need for a text in this area based solidly on financial economic theory. I postponed the project for two or three years since I realized that I would have to learn much about institutional details and industry practice if the book were to be sufficient for the purpose. Eventually I succumbed. The task proved to be formidable, but was a remarkable learning experience (to use a cliché).

In writing the text I found it necessary to not only document current theory but also to provide substantial amounts of new theory. The book thus became both the motivating force for my research and, in many cases, the venue for its publication.

Two examples of this stand out in my mind. One was an intuitive yet practical algorithm for solving a restricted class of portfolio optimization problems. Although simply a variant of a general class of approaches to nonlinear optimization, its rules can be stated in familiar economic terms such as utility maximization, choices based on marginal utilities, etc. The technique has proven quite useful and enjoys rather wide commercial application.

The second example concerned the valuation of options. The basis for the important Black—Scholes option valuation formula was, for me, hard to understand and virtually impossible to explain, since it was grounded in the difficult mathematics of continuous processes. Surely, I thought, there must be a discrete-time, discrete-state counterpart. Happily, there was. Moreover, numeric experiments showed that values obtained with the resultant *binomial process* converged quite rapidly to those of the continuous form as the number of discrete steps increased. I presented this approach in 1978 in my textbook. John Cox, Steve Ross, and Mark Rubenstein built on this foundation and showed that a wide variety of valuation problems could best be formulated in analogous ways. Such models, which we now realize to be special cases of the Arrow–Debreu state-preference paradigm, are also widely used by practitioners.

Wells Fargo

In the 1970s and 1980s I worked closely with an extremely innovative group at the Wells Fargo Bank in San Francisco to bring some of the lessons of financial economics to the world of money management. Under the leadership of Bill Fouse and Jim Vertin, Wells Fargo pioneered in the creation of index funds, passive portfolios tailored to meet investor objectives, estimation of beta values and expected returns using forecasts of future cash flows, estimation of risk, and more. Today Wells Fargo and Bill Fouse's Mellon Capital Management group manage over $125 billion using procedures based on financial economics.

Commerce

In 1986 I ventured more directly into the world of commerce. My wife, Kathy (who served as administrator), and I established a firm devoted to research and consulting on problems faced by the administrators of large, multiply managed pension, endowment and foundation funds. Our goals were to apply existing theory, develop new theory, and conduct empirical analyses to deal with issues associated with the *asset allocation* decision, taking into account the objectives of each fund. In all our work we assumed that markets were efficient—that is, we wished to help *tailor* a fund's investments to meet its needs, rather than try to "beat the market."

Working with a talented group of colleagues and a highly sophisticated and supportive group of clients, we accomplished much in this connection. Of the several new techniques that we developed, the one that we termed *style analysis* has proven particularly useful.

By far the largest part of the month-to-month variation of the return provided by, say, a mutual fund is attributable to the *types* of securities held, rather than the specific securities chosen within each type. For example, using a set of twelve *asset classes* to represent security types, we found that 80 to 90% of the variance in monthly returns for a typical U.S. mutual fund was due to "asset allocation." Given this, it is crucial that one be able to determine a fund's allocation across such major asset classes, which we termed its *style*.

Rather remarkably, we found that in many cases this can be accomplished quite well by comparing the monthly returns provided by the fund over past years with those that could have been obtained from index funds representing each of the major asset classes. The required procedure (quadratic programming) is simple in concept, although somewhat complex in practice.

Style analysis allows an external analyst to estimate a manager's exposures to key sectors of the market. The investor can thus align his or her holdings of funds much more efficiently than would be possible without this information. A fund's *performance* can also be separated into that due to its *style* and the remainder, which may be considered due to *selection*. This type of *performance attribution* makes possible far more precise answers to questions concerning market efficiency, the extent to which past performance can predict future performance, etc.

The firm's clients were not alone in welcoming this type of analysis. Our papers and lectures on the subject have been warmly received and several other firms are preparing to offer similar services. If imitation is the sincerest form of flattery, we have been well-flattered.

Further Research

Throughout my career I have tried to keep one foot in the academic world and one in the world of affairs. There is much to learn from each, and each needs the other. This is, of course, a difficult balancing act. At Sharpe Associates, I placed substantial emphasis on practice. After several years it seemed appropriate to stand back somewhat to allow more reflection, deeper research, and preparation of the proverbial book or two. Hence a decision to concentrate more on research and teaching.

It seems to me that my comparative advantage lies in the development, application and communication of *practical theory*. I expect to continue to focus on financial economics, with special attention to investment applications, with somewhat greater emphasis on the integration of existing ideas than the development of new ones (as befits one my age).

Conclusion

Academic practice dictates that one should end a paper or lecture with a set of conclusions. I shall not do so. This is due in part to a belief that I lack the necessary perspective and unbiasedness. I also fear that the result might sound too much like an obituary—which I hope would prove premature.

I will, however, say this. It has been exciting and satisfying almost beyond belief to have played a role, however small, in the evolution of a field of inquiry as important and lasting as that of financial economics.

Happily, there is far more to come, so that many generations of financial economists can look forward to the same sorts of thrills that I have been fortunate to experience.

Notes

1. William F. Sharpe, *Investments* (Englewood Cliffs, NJ: Prentice-Hall, 1978).

2. William F. Sharpe, *Investments*, 3rd ed. (Englewood Cliffs, NJ: Prentice-Hall, 1985).

3. William F. Sharpe and Cathryn M. Cootner, eds., *Financial Economics: Essays in Honor of Paul Cootner* (Englewood Cliffs, NJ: Prentice-Hall, 1982).

4. Peter L. Bernstein, *Capital Ideas: The Improbable Origins of Modern Wall Street* (New York: Free Press, 1992).

William F. Sharpe

Awarded Nobel Prize in 1990. Lecture presented February 19, 1992.

Date of Birth

June 16, 1934

Academic Degrees

A.B., University of California, Los Angeles, 1955
M.A., University of California, Los Angeles, 1956
Ph.D., University of California, Los Angeles, 1961

Academic Affiliations

Assistant Professor, University of Washington, 1961–63
Associate Professor, University of Washington, 1963–67
Professor, University of Washington, 1967–68
Professor, University of California, Irvine, 1968–70
Professor, Stanford University, 1970–73
Timken Professor of Finance, Stanford University, 1973–89
Timken Professor Emeritus of Finance, Stanford University, 1989–92
Professor of Finance, Stanford University, 1993–99
Professor of Finance, Emeritus, Stanford University, 1999–present

Selected Books

Portfolio Theory and Capital Markets, 1970, 2000
Investments, 1978, 1999 (6th ed., with G. Alexander and J. Bailey)
Asset Allocation Tools, 1987
Fundamentals of Investments, 1989, 2001 (with G. Alexander and J. Bailey)

Ronald H. Coase

After accepting Professor Breit's invitation to give a lecture in the series, "Lives of the Laureates," I read the book containing the previous lectures and found that the subject of my lecture was to be "My Evolution as an Economist." This led me to consider in what ways my ideas can be said to have evolved. The notion of an evolution in someone's ideas suggests a move from the simpler and cruder to something more complicated and more refined, brought about by a thought process which gradually improves the analysis. Lars Werin, speaking for the Royal Swedish Academy of Sciences, in introducing me at the Nobel Prize award ceremony, after referring to my article, "The Nature of the Firm," published in 1937, in which I explained, as I thought, why firms exist, said that I "gradually added blocks to [my] theoretical construction and had eventually—in the early 1960s—set forth the principles for answering all the questions," that is, the *principles* for answering all the questions relating to the institutional structure of the economic system. His statement about the final result is, I believe, substantially correct. But if his words are interpreted to mean that I started with a relatively simple theory and gradually, purposefully added building blocks until I had accumulated all that were needed to construct a theory of the institutional structure, it would give a misleading view of the development of my ideas. I never had a clear goal until quite recently. I came to realize where I had been going only after I arrived. The emergence of my ideas at each stage was not part of some grand scheme. In the end I found myself with a collection of blocks which, by some miracle, fit together to form, not a complete theory, but, as Lars Werin indicated, the foundation for such a theory.

The development of my ideas seems to me to have been more like a biological evolution in which the changes are brought about by chance events. How all this happened will be the subject of this lecture. It will, I think, throw some light on what Professor Breit calls the major rationale for this lecture series, learning about "the process by which original ideas are germinated and eventually accepted by one's peers." But if the occasion for the emergence of my ideas was provided by chance events, my response to them was no doubt influenced by the spirit of the age. Virginia Woolf has asserted that "on or about December 1910 human character changed" leading to "a change in religion, conduct, politics and literature."[1] If it is true that this date marks a turning point in human affairs, one would hardly expect that my approach in economics would be exactly the same as that of those who preceded me.

As you will by now have guessed, I was born in December, 1910. To be precise, I was born on December 29th at 3:25 p.m. The place was Willesden, a suburb of London. I was to be the only child of my parents. Years later, in 1929, at the age of eighteen, I went to the London School of Economics (LSE) to continue my studies. I passed part I of the final examination in 1930. For part II, I decided to take the Industry Group, supposedly intended for those who wanted to be works managers, but what universities say about their courses is not always to be taken seriously. However, although I could not have known this, I had made a fateful decision, one that would change my whole life.

Arnold Plant was appointed Professor of Commerce (with special reference to business administration) at the London School of Economics in 1930, having held a similar position at the University of Cape Town in South Africa. He took charge of the Industry Group. I therefore studied for the Industry Group in the very year that Plant took it over. In 1931, some five months before I completed my studies, I attended Plant's seminar. It was a revelation. He introduced me to Adam Smith's "invisible hand." You should remember that I had not taken a course in economics at LSE although some of the courses had economic content. The result was that my notions on economics were extremely wooly. What Plant did was to make me aware that producers compete, with the result that they supply what consumers value most. He explained that the economic system was coordinated by the pricing system. I was a socialist at the time, and all this was news to me. I passed the B.Com., part II, final examination in 1931. However, as I had taken the first year of university work while still at the Kilburn Grammar School and three years of residence at LSE were required before a degree could be granted, I had to decide what to do during this third year. The course that I had found most interesting in my studies for part II was industrial law, and my tentative decision was to use this third year to study for the B.Sc. (economics) degree, specializing in industrial law. Had I done so, I would undoubtedly have ended up as a lawyer. But this was not to be. No doubt as a result of Plant's influence, I was awarded a Sir Ernest Cassel Traveling Scholarship by the University of London for the year 1931–32. I was to work under the direction of Plant, and the year would be counted as a year's residence at LSE. This is how it happened that I took the road that would lead to my becoming an economist and *not* a basket-weaver, a historian, a chemist, a works manager, or a lawyer. "There is a divinity that shapes our ends, rough hew them though we may."

When I had completed my studies for the B.Com. degree, I knew a little about accounting, statistics, and law. Although I had never taken a course in economics at LSE, I had also picked up a little economics. Acting on hints in Plant's seminar, I had discussed economic problems with my friend Ronald Fowler, who was also taking the Industry Group. And LSE was a relatively small institution at that time. I knew students who were economics specialists and had discussions with them, particularly with Vera Smith (later Vera Lutz), Abba Lerner, and Victor Edelberg. That I had come to economics without any formal training was to prove a great advantage. I had never been trained what to think and therefore what not to think, and this gave me a lot of freedom in dealing with economic questions.

I proposed to use my Cassel Traveling Scholarship to go to the United States and to study vertical and lateral integration in industry. Plant had discussed in his lectures the various ways in which industries were organized, but we seemed to lack any theory that would explain why there were these differences. I set out to find this theory. There were two other problems that seemed in my mind to be connected to my main project. Plant had spoken in his seminar about the economic system being coordinated by the pricing system and had been critical of government schemes for the rationalization of industry—particularly those for coordinating the various means of transport. And yet, in his lectures on business administration, Plant spoke of management as coordinating the factors of production used in a firm. How could these two views be reconciled? Why did we need management if all the coordination necessary was already provided by the market? What was essentially the same puzzle presented itself to me in another form. The Russian Revolution had taken place in 1917. But we knew very little about how a communist system would operate. How could we? The first five-year plan was not adopted until 1928. Lenin had said that under communism the economic system would be run as one big factory. Some western economists were arguing that this could not be done. Yet there were factories in the western world and some of them were very large. Why couldn't the Russian economy be run as one big factory?

These were the puzzles with which I went to the United States. I visited universities but in the main I carried out my project by visiting businesses and industrial plants. I talked with everyone I met and read trade periodicals and the reports of the Federal Trade Commission. At the end of the year there was much about the organization of industry that I felt I did not understand. But I believed that I had solved part of the puzzle. Economists talked about the economic system as being coordinated by the pricing mechanism (or the market) but had ignored the fact that using the market involved costs. From this it followed that means of coordination other than through use of the market could not be ruled out as inefficient—it all depended on what they cost as compared with the cost of using the market. I realized that this way of looking at things could affect one's views on centralized planning. But, and this was what really mattered to me, it also meant that we could understand why there were firms in which the employment of the factors of production was coordinated by the management of the firm while at the same time there was also coordination conducted through the market. Whether a transaction would be organized within a firm or whether it would be carried out on the market depended on a comparison of the costs of organizing such a transaction within the firm with the costs of a market transaction that would accomplish the same result. All this is very simple and obvious. But it took me a year to realize it—and many economists seem unaware of it (or its significance) to this day.

I was appointed an assistant lecturer at the Dundee School of Economics and Commerce in October, 1932. If the Dundee School had not been established in 1931, I don't know what I would have done. As it was, everything fell into place. I was to be an economist and could evolve.

My duties involved lecturing in three courses all of which started in October. How I did it I can't now imagine. Duncan Black, the other assistant lecturer, has described how I arrived in Dundee with my head full of my ideas on the firm. Fortunately, one of the courses was on "The Organization of the Business Unit." In a letter to my friend Ronald Fowler that has been preserved, I described the contents of my first lecture in that course. It was essentially the argument that was later to be published as "The Nature of the Firm" (one of the two articles cited by the Royal Swedish Academy of Sciences in 1991 as justification for the award of the Nobel Prize). I could never have imagined in 1932 that these ideas would come to be regarded as so significant. Of course, I liked the lecture. In my letter to Fowler, after describing the contents of the lecture, I expressed my great satisfaction with it: "As it was a new approach (I think) to this subject, I was quite pleased with myself. One thing I can say is that I made it all up myself." As I said in my Nobel Prize lecture, "I was then twenty-one and the sun never ceased to shine."

At Dundee I began to read the literature of economics—Adam Smith, Babbage, Jevons, Wicksteed, Knight. Writing of my days at Dundee, Duncan Black, in notes prepared for Kenneth Elzinga in connection with the article he was writing about me for the *International Encyclopedia of the Social Sciences,* commented that at this early date my attitude was "surprisingly definite." He wanted an Economics that would both deal with the real world and do so in an exact manner.

In 1934 I was appointed an assistant lecturer in the University of Liverpool with the duty of lecturing on banking and finance, subjects on which I knew next to nothing. More important was that in 1935 I was appointed an assistant lecturer in economics at LSE. Here my duties were to lecture on the theory of monopoly (taking over a course that had previously been given by John Hicks who had gone to Cambridge), to assist Plant in the Department of Business Administration (the DBA) and to give the course on the economics of public utilities (previously given by Batson, who had gone to South Africa). In 1934 while still at Dundee, I had written the draft of an article entitled "The Nature of the Firm," a systematic exposition of the ideas in my 1932 lecture. At LSE I revised this draft and submitted it to *Economica,* in which it was published in 1937. It created little interest. I have recounted how, on the day it was published, on the way to lunch the two professors of commerce congratulated me but never referred to the article again. Lionel Robbins, in whose department I was, never referred to the article ever. It was not an instant success.

In September, 1939, war was declared. What I have just described is the work on which I was engaged in the seven years from 1932 to 1939. In 1940 I was appointed head of the Statistical Division of the Forestry Commission (responsible at that time for timber production in the United Kingdom), and in 1941 I moved to the Central Statistical Office, one of the Offices of the War Cabinet. I ended up responsible for munitions statistics, those relating to guns, tanks, and ammunition. I did not return to LSE until 1946. My six years in government service played little part in my evolution as an economist, except perhaps to confirm my prejudices. On my return to LSE I became responsible for the course on the principles of economics, a conventional exposition of mainstream economics. In 1946 I published an article, "Monopoly Pricing with Interrelated Costs and Demands," based on material in my prewar monopoly course. Another article published the same year, "The Marginal Cost Controversy," should also be mentioned because it illustrates the way in which my approach to economic policy differed from that of most of my contemporaries. Towards the end of the war, the economists in the Economics Section of the Offices of the War Cabinet began to consider the problems of postwar Britain. James Meade and John Fleming, in the Economics Section, wrote a paper on the pricing policies of state enterprises in which they advocated marginal cost pricing. Keynes, who was an adviser to the Treasury, saw the paper, was enthusiastic about it, and reprinted it in the *Economic Journal,* of which he was editor. I also saw the paper as did Tom Wilson (also in the Economics Section), and we did not like it. I published a short critical note in the *Economic Journal,* and after the war I wrote "The Marginal Cost Controversy." My main research activity was the continuation of my historical studies of British public utilities. In 1950 I published a book, *British Broadcasting: A Study in Monopoly.*

In 1951 I migrated to the United States. What prompted me to take this step was a combination of a lack of faith in the future of socialist Britain, a liking for life in America (I had spent part of 1948 there studying the working of a commercial broadcasting system), and an admiration for American economics. Among the older economists it was Frank Knight that I most admired; among my contemporaries it was George Stigler. And I have already mentioned the influence of Henry Schultz. My first appointment in America was at the University of Buffalo, due to the presence there of John Sumner, a specialist on public utilities, who had visited LSE before the war. In 1958 I joined the faculty of the University of Virginia and in 1964 the faculty of the University of Chicago.

On coming to the United States I decided to make a study of the political economy of broadcasting, based on experience in Britain, Canada, and the United States. This was essentially a continuation of the kind of research I had been conducting at LSE. I collected a great deal of material for this project. I spent the year 1958–59 at the Center for Advanced Study in the Behavioral Sciences at Stanford. While there I wrote an article titled "The Federal Communications Commission," which was published in the *Journal of Law and Economics*. This was to have far-reaching consequences.

In that article I examined the work of the Federal Communications Commission (the FCC) in allocating the use of the radio frequency spectrum. I suggested that this should be done by selling the right to use a frequency. The use of pricing for the allocation of resources was hardly a novel idea for an economist (and in any case the suggestion had already been advanced for the radio frequency spectrum by Leo Herzel). What was unusual in my paper was that I went on to discuss the nature of the rights that would be acquired. The main problem in the case of the radio frequency spectrum concerned interference between signals transmitted on the same or adjacent frequencies. I argued that if rights were well-defined and transferable, it did not matter what the initial rights were—they would be transferred and combined so as to bring about the optimal result. As I put it: "The ultimate result (which maximizes the value of production) is independent of the legal [position]."[2] This simple and, as I thought, obvious proposition, was disputed by the economists at the University of Chicago with whom I was in touch. It was even suggested that I should delete this passage from the article. However, I held my ground and later, after the article was published, a meeting was held at the home of Aaron Director at which I was able to convince the Chicago economists that I was right. I was then asked to write up my ideas for publication in the *Journal of Law and Economics*.

I took on this task with enthusiasm. I was a great admirer of what the *Journal of Law and Economics,* under the editorship of Aaron Director, had been accomplishing. In it were being published articles that examined actual business practices, the effects of different property rights systems, and the working of regulatory systems. I considered it essential that, if economics (and particularly that part called industrial organization) was to make progress, articles such as these should be published, but they were articles that, at that time, would have found difficulty in being published in the normal economic journals. My article on the FCC was an example. However, I wanted to go beyond the passage in the FCC article to which objections had been made and to deal more generally with what may be termed the rationale of a property rights system. I had discussed the case of *Sturges v. Bridgman* in the FCC article, but I wanted to examine other nuisance cases (something I could do because of the familiarity I had acquired with the Law Reports in my student days at LSE). Also, I had long thought (again from my student days) that although Pigou's *Economics of Welfare* was a great book for the problems it tackled, Pigou was not very sure-footed in his economic analysis. I had made two passing references to Pigou in the FCC article but did not discuss his views since that article was wholly devoted to the problem of the allocation of the use of the radio frequency spectrum. However, my discussions at Chicago had made clear to me the strength of the hold that Pigou's approach had on the economics profession, and this led me to want to deal with it directly. I also wanted to discuss the influence of positive transaction costs on the analysis, something that I had only alluded to in a footnote in the FCC article. These were the various objectives or themes that I wanted to weave together and which I think I managed to do in "The Problem of Social Cost."

This article received considerable attention almost immediately. Articles were written attacking and defending it. It became one of the most cited articles in the economics literature. It contained ideas that I had long held at the back of my mind but had never articulated. It is a curious aspect of this story that had these Chicago economists not objected to the passage in the FCC article, "The Problem of Social Cost" would probably never have been written and these ideas would have remained in the back of my mind.

I wrote the article in the summer of 1960 at LSE, where I had access to the Law Reports. I argued that Pigou had been looking at the problem of what is termed "externality" in the wrong way. It is a reciprocal problem, and it was Pigou's failure to recognize this (or at any rate to incorporate it in the analysis) that had prevented him (and the economics profession which had followed him) from developing the appropriate analysis. It was also true that Pigou's policy recommendations were unnecessary in a regime of zero transaction costs (which was implicitly his assumption) since in this case negotiations between the parties would bring about the optimal result. However, transaction costs are not zero and real world situations cannot be studied without introducing positive transaction costs. Once this was done, it became impossible to say what the appropriate policy recommendation should be without knowing what the transaction costs were and the factual situation of each case under consideration.

What should be done could only be learned as a result of empirical studies. What I did in "The Problem of Social Cost" was to provide not a solution but an approach. As I said in that article: "Satisfactory views on policy can only come from a patient study of how, in practice, the market, firms, and governments handle the problem of harmful effects. ... It is my belief that economists and policymakers generally have tended to overestimate the advantages which come from governmental regulation. But this belief, even if justified, does not do more than suggest that governmental regulation should be curtailed. It does not tell us where the boundary line should be drawn. This, it seems to me, has to come from a detailed investigation of the actual results of handling the problem in different ways."[3]

A year or two after the appearance of "The Problem of Social Cost," I received an invitation to join the faculty of the University of Chicago. What attracted me to the position at Chicago was that part of my duties would be to edit the *Journal of Law and Economics*. I have already spoken of my admiration for the *Journal* and the articles it contained. I wanted to continue this work, and I went to Chicago to do it. I greatly enjoyed editing the *Journal*. Using the resources of the law and economics program at the University of Chicago Law School and the opportunity of publication in the *Journal,* I encouraged economists and lawyers (at Chicago and elsewhere) to undertake empirical studies of the kind advocated in "The Problem of Social Cost." As a result, many splendid articles were published. This was a very happy period for me. Every article was an event. In the 1970s and '80s, articles of a similar character began to appear in other journals, and there were many citations to the "Nature of the Firm" as well as to "The Problem of Social Cost." I felt the time had come to bring together my essays on the institutional structure of production and in 1988 published *The Firm, the Market and the Law,* which reprinted my chief articles on this topic. It included an introductory essay which explained my central message.

In 1991, I was awarded the Alfred Nobel Memorial Prize in Economics. The two articles cited as justification for the award were "The Nature of the Firm," published over fifty years before and "The Problem of Social Cost," published thirty years before. The first article had been received with indifference, the second provoked controversy. Neither had commanded the assent of the economics profession and if, of which I am not sure, there is now general recognition of the importance of my work, it must have come very recently. Lars Werin at the awards ceremony in Stockholm, after saying that I had "remarkably improved our understanding of the way the economic system functions," added "although it took some time for the rest of us to realize it."

This lecture clearly provides grist to Professor Breit's mill in his quest to understand "the process by which original ideas are germinated and eventually accepted by one's peers." But what has my tale to contribute? It has often been remarked that original ideas commonly come from those who are young and/or have newly entered a field. This certainly fits my case. In 1932, when, in a lecture in Dundee, I introduced the concept of transaction costs into economic analysis, I was twenty-one, and, if economics was my field, I had only just entered it. However, at first sight, it is not easy to understand why the inclusion of transaction costs in economic analysis was an "original" idea. The puzzle I took with me to America was there for all to see, and my solution was simple and obvious. The explanation for this failure to include transaction costs in the analysis is not that other economists were not smart enough but that, in their work, they did not concern themselves with the problems of the institutional structure of the economy and so never encountered my puzzle. This situation came about, as Demsetz has explained, because economists since Adam Smith have taken as a major task to formalize his view that an economic system could be coordinated by the pricing system. What has been produced is a theory of the working of an economic system of extreme decentralization. It has been a towering intellectual achievement and has enduring value, but it is an economics with blinkers and has had the unfortunate effect of diverting attention from some very important features of the economic system. This explains, among other things, why, when it first appeared, "The Nature of the Firm" excited so little interest.

But why did "The Problem of Social Cost" attract so much attention so soon? I have recounted the somewhat peculiar circumstances that led to its writing. This had the result that, when it appeared, it had the strong support of a powerful group of economists at the University of Chicago and especially of George Stigler. My argument that the allocation of resources in a regime of zero transaction costs would be independent of the legal position regarding liability was formalized by Stigler and named by him the "Coase theorem." This attracted attention to my article, and many papers were published attacking and defending the "theorem." The fact that the "Coase theorem" dealt with a regime of zero transaction costs was also helpful since this meant that economists felt quite at home discussing it, remote from the real world though it may have been. It does not seem to have been noticed that the "theorem" applies to a world of positive transaction costs for all exchanges that are actually made, providing that the transaction costs are not significantly affected by the change in the legal position regarding liability, which will commonly be the case. Strangely enough, I believe the fact that the discussion was not concerned with the real world of positive transaction costs did not diminish but actually increased the attention given to my article. Another circumstance that led to much discussion in the literature was that I criticized Pigou's analysis (accepted by most economists). As a result many articles were written by economists defending Pigou (and themselves). Another, and quite separate, circumstance was that this article, by discussing the rationale of a property rights system and the effect of the law on the working of the economic system, extended the economic analysis of the law beyond its previous connection with antitrust policy. The article greatly interested lawyers and economists in American law schools, spawned an immense literature, and led to the emergence of the new subject of law and economics. All these quite special circumstances combined to make this article an immediate success. But it would be wrong to conclude that for the thesis of an article to gain acceptance it is necessary to have the support of a prestigious group or the stir of controversy or involve some similar circumstance. After all, "The Nature of the Firm," received at first with indifference, has by now had a very considerable influence on the thinking of many economists. Without the kind of factor that affected the reception of "The Problem of Social Cost," it just takes longer for a good idea to secure acceptance. As Edwin Cannan, the teacher of my teacher, Arnold Plant, said: "However lucky Error may be for a time, Truth keeps the book, and wins in the long run."[4]

Given the broad acceptance of my analysis in "The Nature of the Firm" and "The Problem of Social Cost," what is the task ahead? The Nobel Committee said that I had provided the blocks for the construction of a theory of the institutional structure. We now have to discover how they fit together so that we can construct it. I hope to assist in this work. But, as is obvious, in a few years my evolution will come to an end. However, other able scholars will continue their work, and the outlines of a comprehensive theory should begin to emerge in the near future. No doubt some of these scholars will visit you to present a lecture in this series and to tell you about their evolution.

Notes

1. Virginia Woolf, *Mr. Bennett and Mrs. Brown* (London: Hogarth Press, 1928), 4–5.

2. R. H. Coase, "The Federal Communications Commission," *Journal of Law and Economics* 2 (October 1959): 27.

3. R. H. Coase, "The Problem of Social Cost," *Journal of Law and Economics* 3 (October 1960): 18–19; and *The Firm, the Market, and the Law* (Chicago: University of Chicago Press, 1988), 118–119.

4. Edwin Cannan, *A History of the Theories of Production and Distribution in English Political Economy from 1776 to 1848* (London: Staples Press, 1893), 392.

Ronald H. Coase

Awarded Nobel Prize in 1991. Lecture presented April 12, 1994.

Dates of Birth and Death

December 29, 1910; September 2, 2013

Academic Degrees

B.Com. University of London, 1932
D.Sc. (Economics) University of London, 1951

Academic Affiliations

Assistant Lecturer, Dundee School of Economics and Commerce, 1932–34
Assistant Lecturer, University of Liverpool, 1934–35
Assistant Lecturer, London School of Economics, 1935–38, Lecturer, London School of Economics, 1938–47
Reader, London School of Economics, 1947–51 Professor of Economics, University of Buffalo, 1951–58, Professor of Economics, University of Virginia, 1958–64
Professor of Economics, University of Chicago Law School, 1964–70, Clifton R. Musser Professor of Economics, University of Chicago Law School, 1964–81
Distinguished Professor (visiting) of Law and Economics, University of Kansas, 1991
Clifton R. Musser Professor Emeritus of Economics, and Senior Fellow in Law and Economics, University of Chicago Law School, 1982–2013

Selected Books

British Broadcasting: A Study in Monopoly, 1950
The Firm, the Market, and the Law, 1988
Essays on Economics and Economists, 1994

Douglass C. North

I knew where I was going from the day I decided to become an economist. I set out to understand what made economies rich or poor because I viewed that objective as being the essential prerequisite to improving their performance. The search for the Holy Grail of the ultimate source of economic performance has taken me on a long and certainly unanticipated journey, from Marxism to cognitive science, but it has been this persistent objective that has directed and shaped my scholarly career.

When it came time to go to college I had been accepted to Harvard when my father was offered the position of head of the Metropolitan Life Insurance Company office on the west coast, and we moved to San Francisco. Because I did not want to be that far from home, I decided to go instead to the University of California at Berkeley. While I was there my life was completely changed by my becoming a Marxist.

Marxism was attractive because it appeared to provide answers to the pressing questions of the time, including the Great Depression that we were in—answers missing from the pre-Keynesian economics that I was taught in 1939–40. I was opposed to World War II, and indeed on June 22, 1941, when Hitler invaded the Soviet Union, I suddenly found myself the lone supporter of peace since everybody else had, because of their communist beliefs, shifted over to become supporters of the war.

Because I was preoccupied with liberal student activities, my record at the University of California as an undergraduate was mediocre, to say the least. I had only slightly better than a C average, although I did have a triple major in political science, philosophy, and economics. I had hoped to go to law school, but the war started, and because of the strong feeling that I did not want to kill anybody, I joined the Merchant Marine when I graduated from Berkeley in May of 1942.

I went to graduate school at the University of California at Berkeley— the only graduate school that would take me with my poor undergraduate record. My objective as a graduate student was to find out what made economies work the way they did or fail to work. Economic history appeared to be the best field for that objective. I cannot say that I learned much formal economics as a graduate student in Berkeley. My most influential professors were all outside the mainstream of orthodox economics—Robert Brady; Leo Rogin, a very influential teacher of history of economic thought; and M. M. Knight (Frank Knight's brother), who certainly was agnostic, to say the least, about theory, but who had a wonderful knowledge of the facts and background in economic history. He became my mentor and my thesis adviser at Berkeley. But while I learned by rote most of the theory I was supposed to know, I did not acquire a real understanding of theory.

It was not until I got my first job, at the University of Washington in Seattle, and began playing chess with Don Gordon, a brilliant young theorist, that I learned economic theory. In the three years of playing chess every day from noon to two, I may have beaten Don at chess, but he taught me economics; more important, he taught me how to reason like an economist, and that skill is still perhaps the most important tool that I have acquired.

I had written my dissertation on the history of life insurance in the United States and had had a Social Science Research Council Fellowship to go to the east coast and do the spade work. That turned out to be a very productive year. I not only sat in on Robert Merton's seminars in sociology at Columbia but also became involved in the Entrepreneurial Center of Arthur Cole at Harvard. The result was that Joseph Schumpeter, who had been an intellectual source of the Entrepreneurial School, had a strong influence upon me. My early work and publications centered around expanding on the analysis of life insurance in my dissertation and its relationship to investment banking.

I next turned to developing an analytical framework to look at regional economic growth and this led to my first article in the *Journal of Political Economy,* titled "Location Theory and Regional Economic Growth." That work eventually led me to developing a staple theory of economic growth.

I was very fortunate that, at a meeting of the Economic History Association, I came to know Solomon Fabricant, who was then director of research at the National Bureau of Economic Research; and I was invited to spend 1956–57 at the bureau as a research associate. That was an enormously important year in my life. I not only became acquainted with most of the leading economists who passed through the bureau but also spent one day a week at Johns Hopkins University in Baltimore with Simon Kuznets, whose wise council had a lasting influence on me. During the year at the NBER I did the empirical work that led to my early major quantitative study of the balance of payments of the United States from 1790 to 1860.

Between my year at the National Bureau and 1966–67, when I went off to Geneva as a Ford Faculty Fellow, I did my major work in American economic history, which led to my first book, *The Economic Growth of the United States from 1790 to 1860.* It was a straightforward analysis of how markets work in the context of an export staple model of growth.

By this time (1960) there was a substantial stirring among young economic historians to try to transform the field from its descriptive, institutional character to make it an analytical, quantitative discipline. The year that I was at the NBER, that organization and the Economic History Association had the first joint quantitative program on the growth of the American economy, a conference that was held at Williamstown, Massachusetts, in the late spring of 1957. It was at this meeting that I presented my paper on the balance of payments of the United States from 1790 to 1860. This meeting was really the beginning of the new economic history, but the new approach to economic history really coalesced when Jon Hughes and Lance Davis, two former students of mine who had become faculty members at Purdue, called the first conference of economic historians interested in trying to develop and apply economic theory and quantitative methods to history. The first meeting was held at Purdue in February of 1960. This conference was highly successful and became an annual affair. The participants were a mixture of economic historians, theorists, and econometricians. They were no-holds-barred meetings in which the speaker frequently got mauled, but we knew we were reshaping the field of economic history, and that was exciting. The reception that we received among economists was certainly enthusiastic. Economics departments very quickly became interested in having new economic historians or, as we came to call ourselves, cliometricians (Clio being the muse of history). Therefore, as I developed a graduate program jointly with my colleague, Morris David Morris, at the University of Washington, we attracted some of the best students to do work in economic history, and during the 1960s and early 1970s the job market was very responsive, and our students were easily placed throughout the country.

In 1966–67 I decided that I should switch from American to European economic history, and therefore, when I received the above-mentioned grant to live in Geneva for a year, I decided to retool. Retooling turned out to change my scholarly life radically, since I quickly became convinced that the tools of neoclassical economic theory were not up to the task of explaining the kind of fundamental societal change that had characterized European economies from medieval times onward.

Neoclassical theory was concerned with the operation of markets and assumed the existence of the underlying conditions that were a prerequisite to the operation of markets. It had nothing to say about how markets evolved. Moreover it was a static theory, and we needed to have a theory that was dynamic and could explain the evolution of economies through time. We needed new tools, but they simply did not exist. It was in the long search for a framework that would provide new tools of analysis that my interest and concern with the new institutional economics evolved. As a graduate student I had read Thorstein Veblen and John R. Commons and had been impressed by the insights they provided into the workings of economies, but they did not provide a theoretical framework. What we needed was a theoretical structure that we could use to explain and analyze economic history. The old institutional economics, because it failed to provide such a theoretical framework, never posed a serious alternative to neoclassical theory. Marxism was explicitly concerned with institutions, asked good questions, and had an explanation of long-run change, but there were too many flaws in the model. Making classes the unit of analysis and failing to incorporate population change as a key source of change were major shortcomings. The strengths of neoclassical theory were its uncompromising focus on scarcity and, hence, competition as the key to economics, its use of the individual as the unit of analysis, and the power of the economic way of reasoning. There had to be a way of melding the strengths of these diverse approaches into a theoretical structure. That is what I and others have set out to do in the new institutional economics.

Why focus on institutions? In a world of uncertainty they have been used by human beings in an attempt to structure human interaction.

They are the rules of the game of a society and in consequence provide the framework of incentives that shape economic, political, and social organization. Institutions are composed of formal rules (laws, constitutions, rules), informal constraints (conventions, codes of conduct, norms of behavior), and the effectiveness of their enforcement. Enforcement is carried out by third parties (law enforcement, social ostracism), by second parties (retaliation), or by the first party (self-imposed codes of conduct). Institutions affect economic performance by determining, together with the technology employed, the transaction and transformation (production) costs that make up the total costs of production. Since there is an intimate connection between the institutions and technology employed, the efficiency of a market is directly shaped by the institutional framework.

My initial effort to incorporate institutions into historical economic analysis resulted in two books, one with Lance Davis, *Institutional Change and American Economic Growth,* published in 1971, and the other with Robert Thomas, *The Rise of the Western World: A New Economic History,* published in 1973. Both were early attempts to develop some tools of institutional analysis and apply them to economic history. In the study with Lance Davis on American economic growth we attempted to spell out the way new institutions and organizations evolved in the context of American economic growth. In the study of Europe we made the formation of property rights the key to economic performance and explored the contrasting way they evolved in the Netherlands and England on the one hand and France and Spain on the other.

Both studies were still predicated on the assumptions of neoclassical economic theory. But there were too many loose ends that did not make sense—such as the notion that institutions were efficient (however defined). Perhaps more serious, it was not possible to explain long-run poor economic performance in a neoclassical framework. So I began to explore what was wrong. Individual beliefs were obviously important to the choices people make, and only the extreme myopia of economists prevented them from understanding that ideas, ideologies, and prejudices mattered. Once you recognize that, you are forced to examine the rationality postulate critically. The long road toward a new analytical framework involved (1) developing a view of institutions that would account for why institutions produced results that in the long run did not manage to produce economic growth, and (2) developing a model of political economy o be able to explain the underlying source of institutions.

Finally, one had to come to grips with why people had the ideologies and ideas that determined the choices they made.

It was Ronald Coase who provided a critical link that began to structure the evolving framework. In "The Nature of the Firm," Coase forced us to think about the cost of economic organization. But whereas Coase was concerned with the transaction costs that determined the existence of firms, I was concerned with the transaction costs that determined overall economic performance. George Stigler had once remarked to me that he thought the efficiency of economic organization had probably been as important as technological change in historical development. I was convinced that he was right. Transaction costs provided the wedge to examine the costs of economic organization. Coase's other critical contribution, "The Problem of Social Cost," provided the link to connect neoclassical theory to institutional analysis. The message of that essay was that when transaction costs were positive, institutions mattered and shaped the resultant market structure. I was fortunate in having several colleagues at the University of Washington who early on took Coase's work seriously. Steven Cheung, a student of Armen Alchian at UCLA, came to Seattle after a postdoctoral fellowship at Chicago, where he became acquainted with Coase. Cheung made a number of important contributions to transaction cost theory—in particular his emphasis on the costs of measurement of the multiple dimensions of a good or service or of the performance of agents as a critical source of transaction costs (since imperfect measurement resulted in imperfectly specified property rights). Yoram Barzel continued work that Cheung began (after Cheung left to go to the University of Hong Kong). I have learned a great deal from both of them, and their influence is apparent in my next book.

In *Structure and Change in Economic History* (1981) I abandoned the notion that institutions were efficient and attempted to explain why "inefficient" rules would tend to exist and be perpetuated. In that study I began to explore the transaction costs underlying different forms of economic organization in history and also to explore the way ideologies altered free-riding to influence political and economic decision-making. The theoretical chapters were followed by eight historical chapters that outlined a fundamental reinterpretation of economic history from the origins of agriculture in the eighth millennium B.C. to the twentieth century.

I was still dissatisfied with our understanding of the political process, and indeed searched for colleagues who were interested in developing political—economic models. Margaret Levi, a Marxist political scientist, and I had developed a political economy program, but there was little interest in the subject among the faculty. This led me to leave the University of Washington in 1983 after thirty-three years and to move to Washington University in St. Louis, where there was an exciting group of young political scientists and economists who were attempting to develop new models of political economy. This proved to be a felicitous move. I created the Center in Political Economy, which continues to be a creative research center.

The development of a political economic framework to explore long-run institutional change occupied me during all of the 1980s and led to the publication of *Institutions, Institutional Change, and Economic Performance* in 1990. In that study I explicitly attempted to evolve a theory of institutional change. The first step was to separate institutions from organizations. The former are the rules of the game but the latter are the players. That is, organizations are made up of groups of individuals with some objective function. They are firms, trade unions, cooperatives (economic organizations); political parties, legislatures, regulatory agencies (political organizations); churches, athletic associations, clubs (social organizations). Organizations and their entrepreneurs in the pursuit of their objectives (whether the firm maximizing profits or the political party trying to win an election, etc.) are the agent of change. The organizations themselves have come into existence because of the opportunities resulting from the incentives of the institutional framework. In the world of scarcity and competition that characterizes economies, they are in competition to survive. That competition will lead them to try to modify the institutional framework to improve their competitive position. The intensity of competition will determine the rate of change of institutions, but the direction of change will reflect the perceptions of the actors—the mental models that they possess that interpret the external environment for them.

An understanding of how human learning occurs appears to be the most promising approach to the mental constructs that humans develop to explain and interpret the world around them. But the learning is not just a product of the experiences of the individual in his or her lifetime, it also includes the cumulative experiences of past generations embodied in culture. Collective learning, according to Hayek, consists of those experiences that have passed the slow test of time and are embodied in our language, institutions, technology, and ways of doing things. The accumulated stock of knowledge of past experiences is built into our learning and is the deep underlying source of path dependence—the powerful influence of the past on the present and future. Learning then is an incremental process filtered by the culture of a society that determines the perceived payoffs, but there is no guarantee that the cumulative past experiences of a society will necessarily fit them to solve new problems. The learning process then appears to be a function of (1) the way in which a given belief system filters the information derived from experiences and (2) the different experiences confronting individuals and societies at different times.

This cognitive science/institutional approach to history offers the promise of making sense out of the economic past and the diverse performance of economies in the present. There is nothing automatic about evolving the conditions that will result in low-cost transacting in the impersonal markets that are essential to productive economies. Game theory characterizes the issue. Individuals usually will find it worthwhile cooperating with others in exchange when the play is repeated, when there is complete information about the other player's past performance, and when there are small numbers of players—in short, the conditions that characterize small-scale societies with personalized exchange. Cooperation is difficult to sustain when the game is not repeated (or there is an end game), when information about the other players is lacking, and when there are large numbers of players—in short, the conditions that characterize the interdependent world of impersonal exchange of modern productive economies. Creating the institutions that will alter benefit-cost ratios in favor of cooperative solutions is the major issue of economic performance because it entails the creation of effective—that is, productive—economic and political institutions. And given the inherent inefficiency of political markets and the key role that political institutions play in economic performance it is not surprising that economic performance through time has been less than satisfactory.

We still have a long way to go, but I believe that an understanding of how people make choices, under what conditions the rationality postulate is a useful tool, and how individuals make choices under conditions of uncertainty and ambiguity are fundamental issues that we must address in order to make further progress in the social sciences.

Note

The author would like to thank Alexandra Benham and Elisabeth Case for editing this essay.

Douglass C. North

Awarded Nobel Prize in 1993. Lecture presented October 25, 1994.

Dates of Birth and Death

November 5, 1920; November 23, 2015

Academic Degrees

B.A., University of California, Berkeley, 1942
Ph.D., University of California, Berkeley, 1952

Academic Affiliations

Acting Assistant Professor, University of Washington, 1950–51
Assistant Professor, University of Washington, Seattle, 1951–56
Associate Professor, University of Washington, Seattle, 1956–60
Visiting Associate Professor, Stanford University, 1958
Professor of Economics, University of Washington, 1960–83
Pitt Professor of American Institutions, Cambridge University, 1981–82
Henry R. Luce Professor of Law and Liberty and Professor of Economics and of History, Washington University in St. Louis, 1983–2015

Selected Books

The Economic Growth of the United States, 1790–1860, 1961
Growth and Welfare in the American Past: A New Economic History, 1966, 1983
Institutional Change and American Economic Growth, 1971 (with L. Davis)
The Rise of the Western World: A New Economic History, 1973 (with R. Thomas)
Structure and Change in Economic History, 1981
Institutions, Institutional Change, and Economic Performance, 1990

John C. Harsanyi

An Unusual Journey[1]

I was born May 29, 1920, in Budapest, Hungary. I attended the Lutheran Gymnasium in Budapest, one of the best high schools in Hungary, with such distinguished alumni as John von Neumann and Eugene Wigner. I was very happy at this school and received a superb education. In 1937, the year I graduated, I won the First Prize in Mathematics at the Hungary-wide annual competition for high school students. These mathematics competitions were a very important part of Hungarian high school education.

My parents owned a pharmacy, which provided us with a comfortable living. As I was their only child they wanted me to become a pharmacist, but my own preference had been to study philosophy and mathematics. When I actually had to decide my field of study, in 1937, I ended up choosing pharmacy, in accordance with my parents' wishes. I did so because Hitler was in power in Germany and his influence was steadily increasing in Hungary. As a pharmacy student, I would obtain a military deferment. Because I was of Jewish origin, I would otherwise have had to serve in a forced labor unit of the Hungarian army.

As a result of my choice to study pharmacy, I received a military deferment. But after the German army occupied Hungary in March 1944, I had to serve in a labor unit, from May to November 1944, when the Nazi authorities decided to deport my labor unit from Budapest to an Austrian concentration camp. I was lucky to escape from the railway station in Budapest, just before our train left for Austria. Most of my comrades eventually perished. I was far more fortunate. A Jesuit priest I had known provided me with refuge in the cellar of his monastery.

In 1946, following the war, I re-enrolled at the University of Budapest in order to obtain a Ph.D. in philosophy, with minors in sociology and psychology. I received credit for my prior studies in pharmacy, enabling me to get my Ph.D. in June of 1947, after writing a philosophy dissertation. From November 1947 to June 1948, I served as a junior faculty member at the University Institute of Sociology. It was at the Institute that I met Anne Klauber, a psychology student who later became my wife. Anne attended one of my courses. She was once late and I told her, "Young lady, you do not know that this class starts at 9 o'clock; it's 9:15 now." She got very angry. But, as events unfolded, her anger eased and we became close.

Political pressure cut short my tenure at the Institute. It was not enough that I was an anti-Marxist. I also felt compelled to coin bad jokes at the expense of my Communist colleagues. They accepted this quite graciously at first, but over time they increasingly became annoyed with Anne and me. Eventually, the political situation no longer permitted them to employ an outspoken anti-Marxist, as I was, and in June of 1948 I had to resign from the Institute. Anne did get on with her studies, despite being continually harassed by her Communist classmates, who urged her to break up with me because of my political views. She did not do so. But the harassment made her realize, before I did, that Hungary was becoming a completely Stalinist country. The only sensible course of action was to leave Hungary.

We made our way to Australia. After receiving my M.A. degree in economics in late 1953, I applied for a position as Lecturer, not in Sydney, but at the University of Queensland in Brisbane, and I immediately got this position. The reason was twofold. First, I had an M.A. degree, while the other candidates had only B.A.s. The other reason was that British and American journals had accepted my papers and promised to publish them.

And so we did get to Brisbane. Living in Brisbane presented a couple of problems, although these were not serious. The first problem for us was that Anne's parents had come with us to Australia to live with us in the same city. Now we were living in another city. A second problem was that Brisbane, while a very nice city, has a hot and humid climate during the summer, and the summer lasts for seven months. But we managed. Anne learned how to design women's frocks and became a frock designer for a small factory. Indeed, we made a good living combining her earnings with my academic salary.

We were in Brisbane from early 1954 until the middle of 1956, at which time I was awarded a Rockefeller Fellowship. The fellowship enabled Anne and me to be Stanford students for two years. During that time I got a Ph.D. in economics, with Ken Arrow as my dissertation supervisor. Following his advice, I spent much of my time at Stanford studying mathematics and statistics. Anne earned an M.A. from Stanford in child psychology/child development. My student visa expired in 1958 and, whether we wanted to or not, we had to go back to Australia. Actually, we went back quite willingly because I knew that with a Stanford Ph.D., I would get a very good job in Australia, which I did. I became what I call a Senior Fellow at the Australian National University in Canberra. This was a very prestigious and high-paying job that involved only research, which I preferred to teaching routine courses.

Although there were some quite good economists at the Australian National University, they had no interest whatsoever in game theory. Some did not even know what it was. I felt rather isolated and wrote to two of my American friends, Ken Arrow and Jim Tobin, two subsequent Nobel Prize winners. I asked for their help in getting an American position. They recommended and helped me obtain an appointment at Wayne State University in Detroit, and we moved back to America in 1961. In 1964, I moved to a position at the University of California at Berkeley, where I spent most of my career.

A Life of Research—From Nash to Selten

Let me now discuss my research. I begin by describing my research in Australia between our first arrival in Sydney in 1950 and our departure from Brisbane for Stanford in 1956. It was during that period that I started working on two subjects that have occupied me ever since.

One topic was utilitarian ethics, which I will discuss first, and the other was game theory. I published two papers in the *Journal of Political Economy*, one in 1953 ("Cardinal Utility in Welfare Economics and in the Theory of Risk-taking") and the other in 1955 ("Cardinal Welfare,

Individualistic Ethics, and Interpersonal Comparisons of Utility"), where I argued that if you want to understand moral problems, you must distinguish between people's *personal preferences*, based on their personal interest, and their *moral preferences*, based on unbiased and impartial criteria (in other words, on moral criteria). Let me try to explain to you how personal preferences work. Suppose that you learn that a new mayor will take up duties in San Antonio. You tell your friend that you welcome the new mayor and think that it is a good thing that he has been elected. Now when your friend asks you why you prefer the new mayor to somebody else, you can give two different types of answers. One is that the new mayor is likely to introduce changes that will benefit you personally—for instance, your business situation will improve because of the changes the new mayor introduces. Well, in this case, you must say that your preferences are based on selfish or personal preferences, not on moral considerations.

The other answer you might give your friend is that you think the new mayor will do a lot of good for almost everyone in the city, independent of any direct impact his actions will have on you. Then you can say that your preferences are based on moral preferences or considerations. In my 1953 and 1955 papers, I argued that the main task of ethics is to understand the difference between people's personal preferences, which usually are not based on any altruistic considerations, and their moral preferences, which are based on moral or impartial criteria and not on self-interest.

In order to develop a logical, mathematically precise theory of ethics you need some specific definition of what it means to be partial or impartial. I proposed that your preferences are impartial if you satisfy certain mathematical criteria. One such mathematical criterion would be that you are not influenced by your own personal position but are influenced by impartial considerations. One way to explain this is to say that we are considering a society which has n members; you can imagine that you rank these n members as the first, second, third, fourth, and so on to the end. The first person is in the best or most-favorable position, the second person is in the second-best position, and so forth. If you are really impartially motivated, then you have to make the choice as if you had the same probability, whatever the end, of being in any one of the social positions. For instance, suppose somebody asks you to choose between capitalism and socialism. Then you should make a choice as if you did not know which particular position you would be in. You are impartial if you do not know in advance whether you will be in a more favorable position under capitalism or in a more favorable position under socialism. Stated more precisely, in making your choice, it is assumed that you have the same probability of being in any one of the possible social positions.

And so it was these ideas that I eventually developed into a utilitarian theory of ethics and, more particularly, a rule utilitarian theory of ethics. As I have explained, this means that you develop an ethical theory based on moral rules that best serve the interest of all individual members of society and do it in an impartial way, without giving more weight to any individual's interest than to any other individual's interest.

Another important interest of mine was game theory. My interest was aroused by three brilliant articles of John Nash, one of the other two people with whom I was awarded the Nobel Prize. Nash published these articles in the period between 1950 and 1953. These influential papers were: "The Bargaining Problem" (*Econometrica*, 1950), "Noncooperative Games" (*Annals of Mathematics*, 1951), and "Two-Person Cooperative Games" (*Econometrica*, 1953).

I remember that when I had studied economics at the University of Sydney, I had been very disappointed to learn that classical economists did not provide a unique rational solution for the bargaining problem. In other words, suppose that you own a particular house and would like to sell it at a good price. Now suppose that you will not sell it for below $100,000—that is the minimum selling price you would ask. On the other hand, the person who most wants to buy your house will not pay more for it than $200,000. One would like to have a theory that can predict whether the eventual price would be closer to $100,000 or to $200,000, or what conditions determine whether it would be close to the lower limit or upper limit. Much to my disappointment, classical economic theory could not answer this seemingly simple question about price determination. I was very impressed to find that John Nash had a very clear mathematical answer to the question, and this answer was based on certain axioms that looked to me to be very plausible.

I also studied Nash's papers on bargaining very closely. The result was a paper that I published in 1956 in *Econometrica* ("Approaches to the Bargaining Problem Before and After the Theory of Games: A Critical Discussion of Zeuthen's, Hicks's, and Nash's Theories"). In this paper, I first of all found clear mathematical criteria for what determines whether the threats of two bargaining parties are really the best possible threats from their own points of view, thus providing a clear definition of optimal threat. I also showed that Nash's bargaining theory happened to be mathematically equivalent to a much earlier bargaining theory by the Danish economist Zeuthen, who published his theory in a 1930 book (*Problems of Monopoly and Economic Warfare*).

Another paper of mine ("A Bargaining Model for the Cooperative *n*-Person Game," 1959), also due to my study of Nash's work, addressed the so-called Shapley value, an important concept in game theory. This concept tells you how people are likely to divide a certain pie depending on how much each can make. But instead of having just two people to divide the pie, I looked at the more difficult question of how the shares of multiple parties, let's say ten people, might be determined. How the pie will be divided depends on how much money each coalition or possible combination of people can separately make. Thus, you want to know how much each player can make by himself, and how much players one and two together make, or five and six together make, how much each three person coalition can make, and so on. This is an interesting mathematical problem and Shapley found a good solution for it. But his theory was restricted to games in which people can transfer utility from one person to the other. He assumed that you could give five dollars to somebody else and he will be better off by five utility points, and if you give him ten dollars he will get ten units of utility. In other words, total utility does not increase or decrease when you transfer money from one to the other.

This was a very restrictive condition, but it was a great thing that he could devise a solution for the problem under these simplified conditions. I extended the Shapley value to games in which this simple condition does not hold, that is, without transferable utility. I also showed that the new generalized Shapley value was a generalization both of the original Shapley value and of Nash's bargaining solution for games in which threats, or so-called variable threats, play an important role. My paper united the two branches of game theory—the two-person "maximize the product of gains" solution of Zeuthen–Nash and the Shapley value solution for *n*-person games—within a coherent single model. Subsequent literature in the field then modified and extended my synthesis.

Now let me talk about another game theoretical problem that I tried to solve. Here the problem was to find a solution for games with incomplete information. Let me tell you what this involves. In classical game theory you always basically know what kind of opponent you have. You play, let's say, a tennis match against the other fellow, and you know what his abilities are. The outcome of the match will be partly a matter of chance, along with other conditions such as skill and training. But your strategy is based on complete information about the type of player you face. Of course, the theorist does not know beforehand the strategies each player will use against the other, but he does know that once player 1 uses the third strategy and player 2 uses the fifth strategy, the outcome is determined and known. This is what classical game theory always assumed.

My new problem was to find a mathematical model to represent games with incomplete information. The basic model is this: Let's assume there are, say, ten different types of possible Russian players and that the Americans can have eight different types. So, you have to develop such a mathematical model with ten different types for the Russians (types R1, R2, R3, up to R10) and eight different types for the Americans (types A1, A2, A3, up to A8). For example, type 1 of the Americans could meet type 5 of the Russians. We then form a model in which chance will decide which particular type of Russian will meet which particular type of American.

Once you define this clearly you can solve the problem. My work along these lines gave rise to a whole theory of games with incomplete information. I developed this theory in a long paper, which had to be published in three parts, in *Management Science*, because it was too long to publish in one issue ("Games with Incomplete Information Played by 'Bayesian' Players, I, II, III," 1967–1968). In these papers, I showed that any game with incomplete information can be transformed into a game with complete yet imperfect information. This was done as I have described, by this method of defining types for both players and asking what is the probability that a particular type of combination will come into being. I showed that once you use this model you can actually convert a game with incomplete information to a game with more complete information. Therefore the two are really equivalent, and it became possible to solve this problem with game-theoretic analysis.

After I published these papers it took some time, of course, for other game theorists to read the work and understand it. There was a lot of discussion, but by around 1975 the theory of games with incomplete information was increasingly used and after a while completely transformed game theory. It was this particular work of mine, whose last piece was published in 1968, which twenty-six years later the Nobel Committee cited when they decided to award me the 1994 Nobel Prize in Economics. As you know, I shared the 1994 Nobel Prize with John Nash and Reinhard Selten. Earlier in my essay, I spoke about the large impact that Nash's brilliant articles had in stimulating my early interests in game theory. Just as Nash greatly influenced my early work in game theory, I have had the privilege of working off and on with Reinhard Selten during much of my career. For example, early on we worked together for the

Arms Control and Disarmament Agency, described previously, and subsequently worked closely together during Selten's visits to Berkeley and my visits to the University of Bielefeld. Following my retirement, Selten, with the assistance of H. W. Brock, edited the volume *Rational Interaction* (1992) in my honor. The last book I published, *A General Theory of Equilibrium Selection in Games*, published in 1988, was co-authored with Selten following many years of joint work. Receiving the Nobel Prize has not only been a great honor, but sharing it with John Nash and Reinhard Selten provides a particularly fitting set of bounds that spans my life as an economist.

Note

1. The Harsanyi lecture is based on transcripts of his talk given at Trinity University. The opening section of his talk extends the brief autobiography that was provided to the Nobel Foundation.

John C. Harsanyi

Awarded Nobel Prize in 1994. Lecture presented March 5, 1997.

Dates of Birth and Death

May 29, 1920; August 9, 2000

Academic Degrees

Pharmacology, University of Budapest, 1944
Ph.D. Philosophy and Sociology, University of Budapest, 1947
M.A. Economics, University of Sydney, 1953
Ph.D. Economics, Stanford University, 1959

Academic Affiliations

University Assistant in Philosophy, University of Budapest, 1947–48
Lecturer in Economics, University of Queensland, Brisbane, Australia, 1954–56
Senior Fellow, Australian National University, 1959–61
Professor of Economics, Wayne State University, 1961–63
Visiting Professor of Economics and Business Administration, University of California, Berkeley, 1964
Professor of Economics and Business Administration, University of California, Berkeley, 1965–90
Visiting Professor, University of Bielefeld, 1973–74, 1978–79
Professor of Economics and Business Administration, Emeritus, University of California, Berkeley, 1990–2000

Selected Books

Essays on Ethics, Social Behavior, and Scientific Explanation, 1976
Rational Behavior and Bargaining Equilibrium in Games and Social Situations, 1977
Papers in Game Theory, 1982
A General Theory of Equilibrium Selection in Games, 1988 (with R. Selten)

Myron S. Scholes

I was born in Timmins, Ontario, Canada on July 1, 1941. My only brother, David, was born five years later. My father was born in New York City but moved to Toronto as a young man to live with his older brother. After graduation as a dentist and after a start as a teacher at the Eastman Clinic in Rochester, New York, that was cut short by the Great Depression, my father ventured to Timmins, a relatively prosperous gold mining region in northern Ontario, to practice dentistry in 1930. This was targeted as a temporary move until the Depression ended. His temporary move, however, lasted for twenty-five years. My mother had a longer journey to arrive in Canada. As a result of the many purges in Russia, as a two-year-old she had fled with her parents to Canada around 1908 and settled in South Porcupine, a very small town six miles south of Timmins.

As a young woman, my mother and her uncle established a successful chain of small department stores in and around Timmins. At its height, they employed over 1,000 employees in approximately ten stores.

In 1941, the year I was born, her uncle left by train for Toronto, 500 miles to the south, to formalize the legal relations among my mother and her family and her uncle and his family. Unfortunately, her uncle died on the train trip before any of the agreements could be formalized.

The death of her uncle resulted in a family dispute, my first exposure to agency and contracting problems. Although it was not an equitable distribution, her uncle's sons-in-law claimed all of the stores registered in his name as their own, forcing my mother out of a large fraction of the business. This episode always fascinated me. After turning over the stores that happened to be in her name to others on her side of the family who worked in the business, she devoted her efforts to raising me and subsequently my brother while running the rest of the family business on the side.

I was always very proud of my mother's business accomplishments. It was quite an achievement in those days for a woman to run an organization, let alone one in northern Canada. As you might imagine she was a powerful woman, a family leader, and insightful in subjects pertaining to business and in dealing with others.

My father was a scholar, an extremely intelligent man, who was well read in many diverse subjects. When I was young, he seemed to know everything. He was respected for his work; his personality was the exact opposite of that of my mother's. He was a quiet, gentle, but firm man. To my parents, education, learning, thinking, and discussing issues were of prime importance. And, given my love of participating and learning, I thrived in this environment.

Through my parents, especially my mother, I became interested in economics and, in particular, finance. As I mentioned, my mother loved business and discussed stocks, world events, and finance in general whenever there was an opportunity to do so. Before she died, she suggested that I consider joining her brother in his book-publishing and promotion business. During my teenage years, I was always treasurer of my various clubs; I traded extensively among my friends; I gambled to understand probabilities and risks. I invested in the stock market while in high school and university through accounts set up first by my mother and then by my father. I was fascinated with the determinants of the level of stock prices. I spent long hours reading reports and books to glean the secrets of successful investing, but, alas, to no avail. The Holy Grail still awaits me.

I decided to attend McMaster University, a school close to my home, for my undergraduate studies. McMaster turned out to be a fortuitous choice. Because it was such a small school, Professor McIver, a University of Chicago graduate in economics, worked closely with me in my studies. He directed me to read and understand the work of many classical economists, including the more contemporary teachings of Milton Friedman and George Stigler, two subsequent awardees of the Nobel Prize in Economics. I was impressed with their writings.

Upon graduation in 1962, I was deciding between entering law school or graduate school in economics. After considerable thought, I decided to follow my mother's wishes and join my uncle in his publishing business on the condition that I complete my studies in a graduate program. Because of my enjoyment of economics and my planned return to business, I decided on business school, not law school. Although my family wanted me to apply to other schools, such as Harvard, I wanted to go only to the University of Chicago, where Stigler and Friedman were teaching and conducting research.

I had learned an important lesson, maybe at McMaster University. Intuitively, I knew that if I wanted to grow and achieve my potential, I should learn and work with those who were the best and who could bring out the best in me. That strategy has become a cornerstone of my career. I have always tried to go where the best were located. My thought at the time was that this would enable me to "steal" knowledge from them, but I subsequently realized that I had to contribute to the interchange of ideas to enable me to learn from others.

Chicago was a marvelous school for me. I did not know what awaited me on my arrival. During my first year at Chicago, I met a few classmates, who would become life-long friends, and from whom I have learned and continue to learn a tremendous amount over the years. In particular, Michael Jensen and Richard Roll, both in the Ph.D. program in finance, who have become world-renowned scholars in their own right and should also be awarded the Nobel Prize, added immeasurably to my understanding of economics and finance. Marshall Blum and Joel Stern were significant contributors to my learning and growth. I credit Jack Gould, who later became dean of the Graduate School of Business, for helping me clarify many of the finer points of economic reasoning.

The summer of 1963, my first summer at Chicago, changed the direction of my life forever. During the first year at Chicago I had worked on a project for my uncle. I evaluated the possibility of buying a children's book company called Golden Books. My recommendation to buy what was then a wonderful franchise but a mismanaged company, was turned down for other than economic reasons. Once again I understood agency problems. As a result, I decided not to return to my uncle's company.

For that first summer, although I had never programmed before nor knew what a computer was, I secured a junior computer programming position at Chicago through the kindness of Dean Robert Graves. By the end of that summer, I was becoming a computer wizard, a skill that I would continue to develop over many years. If Chicago had had a computer science school, or if computer science had been a more developed field, I might have been tempted to become a computer scientist instead of an economist. Programming allowed me to conceptualize solutions to problems and then apply the solutions to demonstrate the actual results.

Another powerful force, however, had taken hold of me that summer: the love of economics and economic research. I was mesmerized by how the professors who were my computer clients created and addressed their own research projects. This was empowering. They enjoyed the process; they were absorbed by discovery. From time to time I ventured to ask them to explain their research, and occasionally I made suggestions on how to improve the research design. Lester Telser and Peter Pashigian were two of my clients. Merton Miller and Eugene Fama, two energetic and creative financial economics professors were clients as well. Merton Miller was awarded the Nobel Prize in Economics in 1990, and Eugene Fama certainly deserves the award as well. At times, they were quite frustrated when I provided them with research output that they did not seek, but I thought that they would find interesting. They became my mentors, shaping my understanding of finance. And, fortunately, both became life-long friends.

Either because of my scholastic qualities or because he did not want to lose me as a programmer, Merton Miller suggested that I enter the Ph.D. program. I did, and I came to love economics and its young new branch, which has come to be called financial economics. Chicago provided me with a wonderful learning environment. Miller and Fama were blazing ahead in financial economics. Stigler was leading the way in a new field of economics called "information economics." Friedman was fighting on in the macroeconomic front, persuading us that Keynesian economics was based on false economic rigidities.

I became interested in relative asset prices and the degree to which arbitrage prevented economic agents from earning abnormal profits in security markets. My province became risk and return. I concentrated my economics research during 1965–78 on attempts to understand the trade-offs between risk and return in both frictionless and friction-filled economies. I made tremendous progress in this area.

My Ph.D. dissertation, for example, attempted to determine the shape of the demand curve for traded securities. Since, as I reasoned, risk and return characteristics were the features that distinguish one security from another, the extent of the market was far greater than that of the individual stock. It was new information that would cause a change in the price of the security, information that was signaled by the large sale by an informed investor. This was the first statement in finance of a rational expectations approach to understanding economic activity. That is, only new information could change the demand for securities, not whether an individual wanted to sell more or less of a particular security.

After formulating the theory, careful empirical tests provided evidence that the prices of securities change not because of a movement along a demand curve with increases in supply, but because of changes in the information set that affect valuations. Temporary supply/demand imbalances exist because of the time necessary for speculators to assess the importance of the new information, not the size of the sale itself. Even to this day, there is considerable confusion between attributing movement along a demand curve and changes in the positioning of the entire curve. For example, the effectiveness of "operation twist" during the 1960s, wherein the U.S. Treasury attempted to encourage long rates to fall in order to foster investment while retaining higher short-term rates, is only one of many examples along these lines.

After essentially finishing my Ph.D. dissertation in the fall of 1968, I became an assistant professor of finance at the Sloan School of Management at MIT. I had two job offers in 1968, one at MIT for $10,000 and one at the University of Texas at Austin for $17,500. I told MIT that $10,000 was too low a salary, and they increased it to $10,500. I went to MIT, but not for the pay. My professors wanted me to go to MIT for seasoning and to grow on my own. The next year, when MIT gave me a raise of only $250, I thought that I had failed as an MIT professor. But, the dean informed me that, on the contrary, the faculty was proud of my successes and that I had achieved one of the highest increases in salary that year. Given my scholarships at Chicago, I had made more per year after taxes as a graduate student at Chicago. I knew that MIT was going to be expensive. And again, relative, not absolute, pricing came to the fore.

Paul Cootner, Franco Modigliani, and Stewart Myers became my colleagues at the Sloan School. During my first year at Sloan I met Fischer Black, then a consultant working for Arthur D. Little in Cambridge. We hit it off immediately. We had many lengthy discussions about financial economics and research needs in the area. As a result of these discussions, we started to collaborate on many research projects. It was an extremely productive relationship for both of us. We would spend endless hours discussing financial economics, its models, how to test economic relations and the failings of economics to incorporate risk into economic models with sufficient prominence. In our minds, risk was a first-order consideration.

Although Paul Cootner unfortunately left the Sloan School in 1969, Robert Merton joined our group at that time. As you are aware, Robert Merton was my co-recipient of the Nobel Prize in 1997. Essentially, the senior faculty members in finance were not available to work with us; that is, Franco Modigliani was involved in large macro projects and Dan Holland was involved in macro tax policy, so the young assistant professors controlled the development of the financial economics teaching and research program at the Sloan school. We were on our own in both the research and teaching domains.

Stewart Myers greatly influenced my thinking in the area of corporate finance, and Franco Modigliani on macro and asset-pricing models. Robert Merton, Fischer Black, and I were interested in asset pricing and derivative pricing models. It was through many interactions that the three of us developed and extended the field of contingent-claims pricing. In my Nobel address I explained how we developed the Black–Scholes model and how Fischer Black and I used our understanding of risk, return, and arbitrage to define a new method to value risk and to price options. Although some have surmised a different approach, we developed the model from our economic intuition. We were confronted with an interesting economic problem, how to value options. We found the tools to solve it. We did not have a set of tools looking for a problem to address.

In 1973, soon after the Black–Scholes model was published, Texas Instruments (TI) marketed a calculator containing our formula. Traders on the options exchange such as the CBOE could use the calculator to calculate Black–Scholes model values given their inputs. I called TI and asked them whether they would provide us with royalties for using the model. They said no, the model was in the public domain. I asked if they would be willing to send me one of the calculators. They suggested that I buy one using my own nickel.

During my years at the Sloan school, I worked on testing the capital-asset pricing model with Fischer Black and Michael Jensen, and on developing the option-pricing technology with Fischer Black, while continuing to work with Merton Miller on several research projects. Fischer Black and I were interested in all aspects of finance but loved the capital-asset pricing model as a way to describe the trade-off between risk and return. It gave us the insights to figure out how to value options. An option is the right but not the obligation to acquire or sell an asset. It is the value of flexibility. The more uncertain the view on future outcomes, the more valuable the option.

I learned a tremendous amount through many hours of discussion with Paul Samuelson, Robert Solow, and many others at the economics table in the faculty club at MIT. Although I knew that I would miss working on a day-to-day basis with Robert Merton, I returned permanently in 1973 to the Graduate School of Business at the University of Chicago after a visiting year. Although Robert and I are no longer at the same institution, we have remained life-long friends and continue to discuss economic problems.

Fischer Black took his first position in academics as a professor at the University of Chicago in 1972. I wanted to return to Chicago and, in particular, work with Fischer Black, Gene Fama, and Merton Miller. It was an important period in the life of the school, and I had the opportunity to interact with many interesting colleagues. Although Robert Merton was successful in luring Fischer back to Boston in 1974, I resisted taking the offer to return as well and remained at Chicago.

During my Chicago years, I started to work on the effects of taxation on asset prices and incentives. For example, I studied the effects of the taxation of dividends on the prices of securities in three papers, one with Fischer Black and two others with Merton Miller. Merton and I studied the interaction of incentives and taxes in executive compensation. Robert Hamada and I addressed capital structure issues with taxation, and George Constantinides and I studied the effects of taxes on the optimal liquidation of assets.

I became heavily involved with the Center for Research in Security Prices at the University of Chicago during the 1973–80 time frame. As director of the center, I led the development of large research data files containing daily security prices and related information on all New York and American Stock Exchange securities from 1962 to 1985 (now updated by others through the present), and merged these data with monthly data files back to 1926. This effort added immeasurably to the research output of colleagues around the world conducting research in financial economics. I believe that great empirical work leads to additional theory and new theory leads, in turn, to new empirical testing. With this in mind, Joe Williams and I wrote a paper on the estimation of risk parameters employing nonsynchronous data, the so-called "Scholes–Williams betas."

In 1981, I visited Stanford University and became a permanent faculty member of the Stanford Business School and the Stanford Law School in

1983. I believe to this day that re-potting oneself keeps the intellectual juices flowing. Staying put just became too comfortable for me. Even to this day, I love traveling and discussing new ideas with associates around the world.

The period at Stanford was a time of significant learning for me. My close colleagues in the business school included William Sharpe, James Van Horne, and a host of up-and-coming younger professors, most notably Jeremy Bulow, Anat Admati, Paul Pfleiderer, and Michael Gibbons. My close colleagues in the law school included Ronald Gilson and Kenneth Scott. With Jeremy Bulow, I wrote several papers on pension planning.

Most important, I was fortunate to work with and become a close friend of Mark Wolfson. We wrote several articles together on investment banking and incentives. We developed a new theory of tax planning under uncertainty and information asymmetry. Many of our published articles on these topics were rewritten and incorporated into our book, *Taxes and Business Strategy: A Planning Approach*, which was published in 1992.

In 1990 my interests shifted back to the role of derivatives in facilitating the financial intermediation process. I became a special consultant to Salomon Brothers, Inc., and continued on as a managing director and co-head of its fixed-income-derivative sales and trading group, while still conducting research and teaching at Stanford University.

My life as an economist was shaped by attempting to conceptualize and test real-world problems. My first consulting relation occurred in 1968 when I consulted with the management science department of Wells Fargo Bank on the efficacy of their security analyst system. I wrote a report suggesting that they abandon active management entirely and concentrate their efforts on evaluating risk and return, and how to create portfolios that would provide alternative risk and return trade-offs.

John McQuown, head of the management science group at the bank, asked me to consult with them on such a project. Since Fischer Black wanted to leave Arthur D. Little at the time, he joined me on the project. We invented the concept of the *index fund*. Many of our research projects were funded under this research agenda. Although it took many years before index funds became mainstream, an entire industry was built on our efforts. John McQuown was correct in pushing this vision forward.

I enjoyed working with the Chicago Board Options market and with the clearing members to use the options-pricing technology to establish risk-management systems for the clearing-member firms. The clearing-member firms and the traders adopted the option-pricing technology to build the first quantitative-risk-management systems. They did so not because some regulator told them to do so for accounting or for some other purpose, but because they could offer more competitive prices on their products. Lowering their capital costs improved their competitive advantage; using models gave them an edge to set tighter spreads. The technology reduced transaction costs.

Absent a model, traders could neither price securities with embedded options with sufficient accuracy to compete against other traders with models, nor could they reduce the risks of their positions to employ their capital more efficiently at a low enough cost to compete with other traders. Although it is hard to prove, I do think that the success of the CBOE, the other exchanges, and the trillion dollar over-the-counter market in derivative products can be attributed to option-pricing models. Financial theory has spawned the development of an entirely new industry and changed how finance is practiced around the world. And, the risk-management technologies have become the backbone to risk-management systems now used in the banking community around the world.

In late 1993, I joined with several colleagues, many from the Salomon Brothers Group, to become a principal and co-founder of a firm called Long-Term Capital Management (LTCM). This experience has shaped my research interests in the last few years. In joining LTCM, I had hoped to further the application of financial technology to practice. My reason for joining Salomon Brothers and then LTCM was to achieve a deeper understanding of the evolution of financial institutions and markets and the forces shaping this evolution on a global basis. I felt that to achieve that deeper understanding, I needed to immerse myself in the markets. My research papers in the last few years have focused on the interaction and evolution of markets and financial institutions. I will return to that research program in a moment.

During 1997–99 we have seen the movement of a financial crisis in the debt markets around the world. The Russian government default on their debt products in August of 1998 caused an increase in volatility and a flight to liquidity and to quality in markets around the world. The increase in volatility and the flight to liquidity around the world caused LTCM to experience an extraordinary reduction in its capital base in August and then again in September of 1998. The August loss was attributable to the Russian crisis; the September loss was attributable to LTCM's own difficulties. The position sizes were too large and too concentrated to liquidate into a chaotic market. Correlations that had been low in the past became extremely high in all asset classes around the world as investors tried to reduce risks.

Some attribute this collapse to a failure of models, and, in particular, option-pricing models. In my opinion, this is false. First, option-pricing models were not used to determine the lion's share of LTCM's positions, and second, did not come into play in the risk-management system. The Salomon traders assumed that correlations would remain low enough to share capital among the positions. Instead, the correlations approached one as all positions lost money at the same time. The firm could not liquidate its illiquid positions into a chaotic market and its capital disappeared.

This reduction in capital culminated in a form of non-fault bankruptcy. A consortium of fourteen leading financial institutions, with outstanding claims against LTCM, infused new equity capital into the firm and took over its assets. The consortium hired the LTCM team to manage the portfolio under their direct supervision. The Federal Reserve coordinated this takeover. Although some called this a bailout, I have called it a coordinated liquidation to avoid the snails-pace processes of the bankruptcy courts, institutions that are not geared to handle a capital market crisis in an efficient manner.

The last few years have been terrific for me. I have been working on a book that models and explains why the prices of risk transfer and liquidity change in the market. I believe that understanding risk transfer and liquidity in modern financial markets in light of unanticipated changes in the opportunity set is an important and exciting research area. The book will be published by Princeton University Press.

Although I have not been teaching full time at Stanford, I have been giving lectures around the world to students, academics, and practitioners. This is enjoyable and lets me address much larger audiences efficiently. I will continue in this vein, for I enjoy it.

Myron S. Scholes

Awarded Nobel Prize in 1997. Lecture presented April 7, 1999.

Date of Birth

July 1, 1941

Academic Degrees

B.A., McMaster University, 1962
M.B.A., University of Chicago, 1964
Ph.D., University of Chicago, 1969

Academic Affiliations

Assistant and Associate Professor of Finance, Sloan School of Management, MIT, 1968–73
Associate Professor, Graduate School of Business, University of Chicago, 1973–76
Director, Center for Research in Security Prices, University of Chicago, 1976–80
Professor, Graduate School of Business, University of Chicago, 1976–83
Frank E. Buck Professor of Finance, Graduate School of Business, Stanford University, 1983–96
Senior Research Fellow, Hoover Institution, Stanford University, 1985–96
Frank E. Buck Professor of Finance, Emeritus, Graduate School of Business, Stanford University, 1996–present

Selected Books

Taxes and Business Strategy: A Planning Approach, 1992, 2001 (with M. Wolfson)

Gary S. Becker

It is my pleasure to be here and to participate in the Nobel economists lecture series, a series that has had the great modern figures in economics speak, people such as Friedman, Samuelson, and Buchanan, among others. I'm supposed to talk about my evolution as an economist and the forces that influenced me. I will take that as my charge. Yet it is a difficult assignment. It is hard to assess the forces that have had a major influence on one's research. What I can do is to talk a bit about my development as an economist. I will emphasize the many instances where I was extremely lucky to come into contact with people—giants in the field—who had a great influence on me. I will also discuss instances where I started down research paths that at the time seemed to be rather natural and appropriate extensions of microeconomics; I was not fully aware that these would develop into more comprehensive, path-breaking, and often controversial contributions to economics and social science. Following very brief remarks about my days growing up, I will turn my attention to my student days at Princeton, where I first became serious about economics.

I was born in Pottsville, Pennsylvania, in 1930 but grew up in Brooklyn, New York, where our family moved when I was a young child. My father was a businessman and my mother was a housewife. My parents were very intelligent, I see in retrospect. I didn't always see that when I was growing up—they were not highly educated; neither one of them went beyond the eighth grade. My father, growing up in Montreal, Canada, left school because he was eager to make money, despite his mother's insistence that he remain in school. My mother's lack of schooling is not surprising since at that time most young girls were not expected to continue with their education. My parents did realize the value of a good education. They did not insist that we pursue higher education, although both my two sisters and my brother and I did so. We could tell growing up that there was an appreciation for education, in spite of the fact that there were not many books in our house and neither one of my parents read a great deal.

I was an excellent student, in general, at least to judge by grades, but up to the age of sixteen I was not what I would call a serious student. I was more interested in sports than in academic subjects. I did the amount of work necessary to get good grades. I was not intellectually inclined in high school, at least initially. For some reason, I cannot precisely state what the forces were, but at about the age of sixteen my interests began to shift. I date them dramatically to when I voluntarily gave up on the high school handball team of which I was a member (I probably could have been the number one player), but instead chose to become a member of the math team. They met during the same period, and I had to choose one rather than the other. I went through a little bit of uncertainty, but finally chose the math team. I am glad I did so, because my subsequent academic interests were centered on mathematics and science.

What I liked about the math team was that we actually had competitions. This was in New York City, and there were competitions among schools in which we had to solve problems, two tough problems at a time, and solve them within an intense time frame, usually ten minutes to do both problems. And while there was a lot of pressure and tension, particularly when you did not know the answers, it was a fun and collegial process, with five members on each team. The math competitions had an important influence on me, first in seeing other students who were quite good, and second in proving to myself that our team could do well against Bronx Science and Stuyvesant and the other specialized high schools in science and mathematics.

My senior year in high school I became concerned about doing something for society. Here I was interested in math and science and then, all of a sudden, my interests began to shift as I became more socially conscious. Like most young people at the time, I considered myself a kind of a socialist and felt that I should move toward politics or history or some field where I could make more of a contribution to society. I had a really mixed view, continuing to be strongly interested in math, but no longer really wanting to become a mathematician.

A Princeton Undergraduate

I went to Princeton when I was seventeen and had this conflict going on—a strong interest in math but the desire to make a contribution to society. As freshmen we had to choose some electives and were required to take a course in the social sciences. And for some reason (I have no idea why) I chose to take the principles of economics. And for me this turned out to be a very good, or basically lucky, decision. As you will see, this was just one of several lucky decisions that came at various times. We used as our textbook an early edition of Paul Samuelson's *Economics: An Introductory Analysis*. It certainly has been one of the best-selling textbooks in economics, or in any other field. It is still in use. What I liked about this book was the rather brief section on microeconomics— how prices operate in a market system. It appealed to me because of its more mathematical discussion; basically microeconomics seemed to have a very compact mathematical foundation. Given my previous interest in math, microeconomics had a natural attractiveness for me, while at the same time it was dealing with social problems. I was less taken by Samuelson's extensive discussion of macroeconomics, which seemed to me to be rather vague and not fully satisfactory. I still feel that way about it, although there has been some real progress in that area.

I graduated from Princeton in three years, but during that period I read as many articles and books on economics as I could manage—probably the most influential being Stigler's *The Theory of Competitive Price*, as it was then called, and Hicks's *Value and Capital*. I remember reading Hicks one summer. When I saw one of my teachers in the fall and he asked what I was doing, I told him, "I read *Value and Capital* this summer, but I found it very hard." He said, "Don't worry about that, none of the faculty understand it either." So I felt they didn't understand it and I felt I didn't understand it either, but at least I was close to understanding it (or so I thought at the time). So that gave me a little confidence—maybe I could get someplace in economics.

The paper I wrote for my junior year thesis (required at Princeton) was on classical monetary theory. I criticized some analysis of Leontief and others that had been in the literature and debated at the time. Several faculty members said that I was correct in my criticism, and I think, in retrospect, that I was correct. Eventually I collaborated with a teacher, William Baumol; we published the analysis from my junior thesis, plus other material, in the *American Economic Review* in 1952. The paper was titled "The Classical Monetary Theory: The Outcome of the Discussion." My senior thesis was also published in the *American Economic Review* during 1952, in a paper titled "A Note on Multi-Country Trade."

So I was doing well in economics. During my senior year at Princeton, however, I was losing interest in economics and began to think that I should go into something else. Economics seemed excessively formal to me. I'm sure that cannot be true of anything you have been reading as students nowadays, but then that is how it seemed to me. Economics appeared incapable of helping me understand the issues in which I had an interest: inequality, class, race, prestige, and similar issues that were important for society. A sociology professor at Princeton suggested I look at Talcott Parsons's *Structure of Social Action*. Parsons, then the dominant figure in American sociology, started his career as an economist and believed that social theory included economics as a special case. I tried to read this book, but it contained an enormous quantity of jargon that did not lead anywhere, or at least anywhere that I could follow. I concluded that sociology was too hard, and returned, somewhat reluctantly, to economics. I remained unhappy—unhappy by what seemed to me a disconnect between what economists would talk about in textbooks and elsewhere and what I wanted to talk about.

I decided nevertheless to go on for a doctorate in economics. Adlai Stevenson once defined a graduate student as someone who didn't know when the party was over. Well, I wanted to continue in this party atmosphere, so I went for a doctorate. Most of the faculty wanted me to stay at Princeton, though I had already taken many graduate courses at Princeton; I felt, and some of my teachers agreed, that it would be better if I went someplace else. I was choosing between Harvard and Chicago and, for a variety of reasons, I decided to go to Chicago.

Chicago: The Early Years

From a professional point of view, the decision to go to Chicago was probably the most important decision I ever made. The atmosphere at Chicago was enormously stimulating. Original work was going on in many different areas and by many economists there, most notably Milton Friedman. The Cowles Commission (which subsequently left) was very active in mathematical economics and econometrics.

Milton Friedman became the greatest influence on my development as an economist. Attending his graduate course in price theory was just exciting, and I would eagerly wait for that course to come twice a week. Some people would even ask my friends, "How can he be so excited about attending class?" A lot of the classes were boring, but that is nothing new for students. Friedman's class was different. Here I saw economics as a tool and not simply as a game played by clever academics, which is what had worried me most about economics. In Friedman's hands, economics was a powerful tool to understand a whole host of problems—in the class Friedman dealt with things such as birthrates, insurance and lotteries, personal and business responses to taxes, how labor markets functioned, and the effect of having unionized versus non-unionized markets. And, on and on, economics was used to understand business practices of all types. "Let's see," Friedman would have asked, "how can we understand what Microsoft is doing?" (had Microsoft existed at that time).

It was a great course that showed me what I thought was not possible. You can do economics and do it in a rigorous way and nevertheless talk about important problems. So my indebtedness to Milton Friedman, one of the greatest economists of the twentieth century, is unlimited.

There were other people in Chicago who were doing important, original work: Ted Schultz in human capital, Gregg Lewis in labor economics, Aaron Director in law and economics, L. J. Savage in statistics and probability. It was a wonderful intellectual environment, and as I developed within that environment, I no longer had this feeling that economics couldn't do it. Indeed I developed the Chicago chip-on-the-shoulder attitude that economics could unlock the mysteries of the real world. Right or wrong, it was a great feeling to have. Here I was being given this powerful tool and a belief that the mysteries of the social world could be unlocked if we applied this tool in some creative fashion. I began to believe this as a graduate student. I still believe that it is true.

I stayed at Chicago for six years, the first three as a graduate student. During the second year I was looking for a thesis topic and had already done some research on an economic approach to political democracy. My paper on this topic was almost published in the *Journal of Political Economy,* but one of my teachers, Frank Knight, was the referee, and he did not like it. I have kept his comments to this day. Knight was a great economist, but he looked at democracy with what I would characterize as a normative point of view. He defined democracy as government by discussion. I wanted to employ an approach to democracy that looked upon it as an institutional system operating in a particular way, for good or bad, which you could analyze using economic analysis. The approach I took in this paper was a very early work in what we now call public choice theory. The editor wanted to publish it in the *JPE,* but was persuaded not to by the referee. It eventually got published in 1956, in a shorter, toned-down version in the first issue of the *Journal of Law and Economics.*

I thought of developing this topic more broadly as one of my possible thesis subjects. But, finally, I hit on something in which I became more interested—an economic approach to the issue of discrimination against minorities, whether religious minorities, racial minorities, gender, or anything else. It was a topic that I had been interested in, of course, but never thought about systematically until I began to think in response to a question put to me by Friedman and Ted Schultz—how might we analyze the fact that there is discrimination in the economy? It occurred to me at the time, but again I am not sure exactly how, that we can associate with each person a taste for discrimination. This taste or prejudice would be measured based on how much income an employer is willing to forfeit in order to avoid hiring somebody who he didn't like from a group that he didn't like; or how much an employee is willing to forfeit to avoid working with a member of a group that he didn't like; or how much a consumer will pay to avoid a product that is served by or produced by a group that he didn't like. So my approach to discrimination was to look at the willingness to pay, or forfeit income, in order to exercise a prejudice. This is still the only right way that I can tell to look at discrimination in mortgage lending, searches for drugs in cars, and other issues that are of great contemporary interest right now. Once you took this approach, then you had to think about how to link the observed discrimination that we see in the marketplace to these personal preferences or prejudices.

To make the link between market discrimination (that is, market outcomes) and personal preferences for discrimination required that I provide a model and analysis. My Ph.D. thesis showed how the degree of market discrimination depended not only on the discriminatory preferences of employers, employees, and consumers but also on the degree of competition in product markets, production technologies, and many other economic variables.

As I was working on my dissertation, I was fortunate to get encouragement from my faculty advisers, but some members of the faculty were highly dubious whether this was an appropriate subject. Their attitude was: "What's a good economist doing working on discrimination?" They could not talk me out of this topic, however, so they insisted instead that a distinguished sociologist at Chicago, Everett Hughes, become a member of my thesis committee, just to make sure that I did not go off the deep end. I do not think Hughes was much interested in what I was doing. The nice part was that he did not object to anything I was doing either. I would go to see him once every nine months and he would say "okay" and that was it. That satisfied the faculty who were dubious whether this was a worthwhile project.

Prior to entering the academic job market, I went to Harvard to present some of my work and also to MIT to discuss this work with some people. I remember talking to a younger faculty member at MIT (a subsequent Nobel Prize winner who gave one of your lectures); he asked me what I was working on and I said "racial discrimination." He said, "I thought you were a neoclassical economist?" I said, "I *am* a neoclassical economist, but isn't this part of neoclassical economics?" But I could not convince him that discrimination was a legitimate subject for economists to work on.

And this was the general experience I had with my dissertation research on discrimination. Eventually a revised version was submitted to the University of Chicago Press. The press received very negative reviews on my manuscript when it was sent out to readers. The editor did not want to publish it. The economics department finally "bribed" the press. You see, Chicago believes in the market system. So the department said we would put up part of the cost and would share any profits on the book. The press agreed to publish my book, but only because of that bribe.

It gave me great pleasure that about ten years after the press published *The Economics of Discrimination,* the then editor of the press (who was also editor when my book came out) wrote an article, published in the *American Economic Review,* in which he admitted that my book was attracting sizable interest. It was not selling a lot—but it was creating a great deal of interest.

The negative reaction to my work on discrimination, coupled with Frank Knight's hostility toward my article on democracy, made it clear to me that using economic analysis to discuss social and political issues was not going to be welcomed with open arms by most economists. I initially had expected economists to applaud attempts to widen the scope of their field. I was surprised that the main hostility toward my work, at least as it was explicitly stated, came from economists, not noneconomists. I began to realize that my original view was naive. All disciplines have a strong and probably justified degree of intellectual conservatism. You do not give up ideas and concepts you have held for a long time without a fight. It is necessary to fight to get new ideas accepted.

Even after I became aware of the extent of the hostility, I remained confident that the contribution of the economic approach to broader problems would eventually be recognized. This confidence in what I was doing helped me persist against sometimes considerable and vicious opposition. There were two reasons why I remained confident. First, it just seemed to me obvious that economics could contribute to these areas. Economics was not the whole story, it was not the final word on discrimination, but how could economists justify that prior to my book on discrimination, with two or three exceptions, there was virtually no work by economists on a topic as enormously important as discrimination in the marketplace? I mean, it's incredible! So it seemed obvious to me that there was a role here.

That was one factor. As important as this was, I do not think that this would have been sufficient to enable me to persist against continuing hostility. The other factor was that I was fortunate to have intellectually powerful people on my side. I gained strength from the support of senior economists I greatly respected. Support came from my teachers, like Milton Friedman and Gregg Lewis, George Stigler—who soon effectively became my teacher—and other friends I had met along the way such as Armen Alchian and Jack Hirshleifer.

In short, this was a period in which my research and intellectual discourse encountered an enormous amount of opposition. There was little demand to hire me from the major institutions. After three years as a graduate student, I accepted an assistant professorship at Chicago. And these six years, looking back on it now, were perhaps the most important and most exciting of my career. I formed the foundation of what I was going to do later on. And I was learning at a rapid rate as I absorbed so many new things that were coming from people at Chicago and from others who came through Chicago. Four of my teachers went on to win the Nobel Prize: Milton Friedman, Friedrich Hayek, who was then on the Committee for Social Thought (I attended his seminars), Tjalling Koopmans, and Ted Schultz. And in addition to that, the Chicago intellectual vitality had many others, some mentioned here, who did not win the Nobel Prize but have done very important work that has been continually recognized.

Chicago wanted me to continue there after my three-year term was up, but I wanted to leave, even though Chicago offered me more money and a good chance of getting tenure. I felt it was more important for me to leave the nest and go out on my own. I had protection at Chicago with the likes of Friedman, Schultz, and Lewis, among others, and that was great, but I wanted to see if I could make it on my own. I said, in effect, "I appreciate the offer, but I really don't want to stay at Chicago." So I looked around, went on the job market, and as a lot of other students have experienced, I did not find an overwhelming demand for my services. Major universities such as Harvard, MIT, Berkeley, and Yale showed no interest in me and did not interview me at any of the meetings. This was probably because I was a Chicago graduate and Chicago at that time was an "outlaw" department in the profession. Its students were treated as suspect by representatives of most of the major institutions. It is not that extreme now.

I had only two interviews, with Johns Hopkins and Columbia. Hopkins decided not to make me an offer. So I considered all my choices and decided to choose among them and went to Columbia, which I was happy to do. I also was offered a position at the National Bureau of Economic Research, which was then in New York City, so I could combine the two. I spent a dozen highly productive years at both institutions.

Columbia and the National Bureau of Economic Research

I started my work on human capital at Columbia and the National Bureau of Economic Research. When I came to the bureau, the then director, Solomon Fabricant, asked me what I would like to work on. From my work on discrimination, I had seen that there were enormous gaps in earnings between workers with different levels of education, among both blacks and whites. I knew the work Ted Schultz had been doing on human capital, which I found to be of considerable interest. So I told Fabricant that I would like to do a study on the rates of return to education and training. This would be a new departure for the bureau, but he said, "I will see what I can do." He got a small grant for me to work on education and earnings, which I began in 1957.

I soon realized that much more was needed in the human capital field than to calculate rates of return. There were no foundations for the theory of investment in human capital. My study was intended to be empirical, but I set about trying to sketch out a small set of foundations to give the work theoretical content. As I was sketching out some basic theory, I had no vision at all of what this would lead to. Once again, here is an example of the role of luck. As I delved into the theory and tried to develop a basic foundation for human capital investment, it looked to me that the theory could explain the way earnings rise with age (a concave age-earnings profile), the effect of education on the distribution of earnings, externalities of human capital, and many other issues that continue to this day to be discussed and debated. I was amazed and then greatly excited when I began to realize that this framework could integrate scores of observations and regularities in individual earnings, occupational differences in earnings, and employment.

In 1959, I made the first public presentation of some of my results at a session of the annual meetings of the American Economic Association. I presented a short paper that compared rates of return to schooling and returns on physical capital in the United States. And the discussants, to my amazement, were absolutely outraged. Once again, I continued to be surprised by what I should have anticipated. What was it that so outraged my discussants? In retrospect it seems silly. They were outraged that I was treating education as an economic activity, believing that this assumption somehow denigrated the cultural or non-economic aspects of education. I replied with some fervor and bluntness to my critics. It was one of the more heated sessions of the meeting. I was taken aback, but, truth be told, I did not lose any confidence about what I was doing because their comments seemed so silly to me. I could not really believe that senior economists—I was twenty-nine years old at the time—were making such dumb comments on my paper.

I continued working on the economics of human capital and in 1962 published an article on it. It was in fact well received. Then, in 1964, I published a book called *Human Capital: A Theoretical and Empirical Analysis, with Special Reference to Education.* The long subtitle is now forgotten—it is now called *Human Capital.* Actually, I debated a long time before I used the title *Human Capital* because I had been aware that people said that if you call it "capital" you are treating human beings as if they had no soul. Some people would make fun of it and call it "human cattle," suggesting that one is not treating humans as individuals. I knew that, and could have weaseled a little and called it "human resources," a phrase that was becoming common at the time. I decided to take the bull by the horns and title the book *Human Capital,* although it had this long subtitle to protect myself a little.

By the time I finished this research, I was indeed convinced that human capital was a crucial concept to understanding economic and social issues in many areas of life. Still, and this I will also confess, I was not prepared for the magnitude of its impact. Eventually, it would be referred to endlessly, and by that language—human capital—not only in academic writing but by politicians of both parties, journalists, even in ecclesiastical encyclicals. After a while some of the people who had resisted using this term began to think, "Well, look, if we call everything human capital and say we are investing in people, this can provide a good rationale for obtaining public monies." I remember the superintendent of the Chicago school system at that time, Benjamin Willis, inviting me to deliver an address to a meeting of superintendents. He told me, "I don't know why people dislike that word; it can be a great tool for us superintendents to get more money." So I think that this partly explains its success. Everything is now called human capital, including some things that should not be so called.

At the same time that I was doing research on human capital, I was also working on the economics of the family and the demand for children. I began this work by asking what determines how many children that families have. I gave my first paper on this topic in the late 1950s, around the same time that I presented my early work on education. At a conference on the economic analysis on fertility, I drew an analogy between the demand for children by parents and their demand for durable consumer goods. I used that language in my paper. Well, you can imagine the reaction from my audience—as soon as I used this language everyone started laughing. Well, not everyone. This was a mixed audience of economists and non-economists. One economist who was the discussant on my paper, a youngish economist at Harvard, was very negative about it, stating that this approach could not explain much about the demand for children. I had learned over time to expect a negative reaction from the audience. But, once again, I was a little surprised by just how much hostility (and this was verbally expressed in public comments) my work aroused among some eminent economists. And yet again, this was an instance in which I feel indebted to Milton Friedman. Friedman had been a participant at the conference and was attending my session. He got up and vigorously defended my paper during the discussion period. I felt, well, there are these fools on the one side criticizing me, but I have people like Friedman defending me. And that is all I needed. I had enormous respect for Friedman—I still do—so I thought, "Now look, if Friedman is defending my work, there must be something to what I am doing."

At Columbia, Jacob Mincer and I jointly conducted a labor economics workshop that gained a large following among a new generation of labor economists. I greatly benefited from my colleagues at Columbia and the bureau; in addition to Mincer these included Victor Fuchs, Robert Willis, Finis Welch, and Sherwin Rosen. I had a remarkable group of students at Columbia, too numerous to mention here, that have gone on to make major contributions in the fields of human capital and labor economics, health, crime, and law and economics. So I was quite happy professionally at Columbia.

Return to Chicago

Yet, I decided I was a better fit at Chicago. Upon my return to Chicago, I found it to be at least as stimulating as when I was a graduate student. Friedman was still there in his prime, Stigler was doing very important work in industrial organization and political economy. They had Black, Fama, Miller, and Scholes working out rigorous approaches to finance and the evaluation of options. Coase, Posner, Landes, Demsetz, and others were doing law and economics, building on the pioneering work of Aaron Director. My work on the economics of crime fit in well with their interests. We had Bob Fogel doing path-breaking work in economic history—slavery at first and then other topics. It was a magical place!

While I was at Chicago, I decided to continue my work on the family. I remember sitting in a hotel room in New York and thinking about the question of marriage—who marries whom? Now why I started thinking about this at that time, I do not know. True, my first wife had died and I was unmarried at the time, so perhaps that had something to do with it. As I thought about the question of who marries whom, it seemed to me that there is something we might think of as a marriage market. Not a market à la Li'l Abner on Sadie Hawkins Day, if any of you remember Al Capp's comic strip *Li'l Abner*. It's not literally a market with explicit buying and selling, but you can think of the matching of partners as operating like a market—people make their choices, they date, and so on. I worked out some rules that would determine who would marry whom, threw in a couple of "theorems," and submitted a paper to the *Journal of Political Economy*. The same distinguished economist that could not accept my discrimination work ended up as a referee (George Stigler was the editor and told me this). This referee hated the paper, saying, "What is Becker doing wasting his time working on these questions?" Stigler disagreed. He told me that he liked the paper, to take account of the referee comments as best I could, and that they would publish the article, which they did. I then submitted a paper a couple of years later on the economics of divorce. Another very good economist wrote back and said they should not accept this paper. And Stigler again overrode the referee recommendation and, following revision, published my paper. Each of the papers turned out to have a good market, leading to a considerable body of subsequent research.

At about that time I decided that I should try to weave all this together into a book on the economics of the family. The book was to combine and integrate the topics of fertility, divorce, marriage, investment in children, and the evolution of the family over time. I even dealt with some nonhuman species. I worked very hard on this book for four or five years. I would wake up in the middle of the night, many nights, and work on it. It was very intense and, finally, in 1981, I published *A Treatise on the Family*. I was exhausted by that time, and it took me roughly two years to regain my mental energy. A comprehensive treatment of the family is inherently such a difficult problem, with so much history, so many cultures, and the like. I found it very difficult. And to this day the book remains controversial. When the Nobel Committee awarded me the prize in 1992, their news release stated, "Gary Becker's analysis has often been controversial and hence, at the outset, met with scepticism and even distrust." Nowhere has this characterization been truer than with my work on the family.

Writing for a Popular Audience

Throughout my career, I had worked on topics closely related to public policy—education, crime, the family, discrimination, addiction, and politics, for example—yet I remained aloof from debates over public policy. I had never given advice to any political figures. Prior to 1985, I had never written one single word in the popular media, not a word, be it a newspaper, magazine, or the like. By 1985 I was fifty-five, so I had gone through roughly thirty-five years of doing economic research, and not one single popular work. Nowadays, some economists hit thirty and begin writing op-ed pieces. I always felt it was a good division of labor on my part to concentrate on my research.

You can imagine then that it was a great surprise to me when in 1985 I received a telephone call from someone at *Business Week,* a magazine I had criticized a couple of years earlier because they misquoted me on something. Their representative said, "Would you be willing to write a regular column for the magazine—a one-page column every four weeks?" My initial reaction was to reject their proposal. But what I said was, "It is not something I have done, it would take me away from my research, but I will think it over and give you an answer." The response back was, "Oh good, I thought maybe you would turn us down on the spot."

So I went back and told my wife, Guity, and she said, "You should do it." She prevailed on me to try it for a while. She argued that the columns would help spread my ideas and might even have a small influence on public policy. And if I did not like doing it, I could always stop. Guity also promised that she would read my early drafts and provide comments. I am happy to say that she gave me good advice. And I might add at this point that I have been very fortunate for almost thirty years to be getting excellent advice and encouragement from her, both professional and personal. She has had an enormous influence on me.

So I got back to *Business Week* and said, "Okay, I am willing to write a column on a trial basis." They said, "Don't worry, we are looking upon it as a trial as well." And the contract sent to me stated that "either party can terminate the agreement with one month's notice." In academia we are used to tenure; there was no tenure here.

Writing for a popular audience, I have addressed a wide range of topics. My interests in economics are broad and my column has resulted in my interests becoming even broader. I have written about baseball, the unfairness of the NCAA in not allowing student athletes to be paid, marriage contracts and religion, immigration, education, and the policies of different presidents or political candidates. Once again, this was one of several lucky events that ended up having a positive and important effect on me.

The Prize

The final thing I will discuss is the Nobel Prize. When I entered economics there was no Nobel Prize in Economics; it is a recent award, having begun in 1969. There were two prizes awarded by the American Economic Association, the John Bates Clark Medal for economists under the age of forty (I was honored to receive this award in 1967) and the Francis Walker Prize for senior economists. The AEA abolished the latter once the Nobel Prize began.

By 1980 I began to be mentioned as a serious candidate for the Nobel Prize. I realized then that there were many older, highly deserving economists in the Nobel queue, mainly because the prize had not existed for very long. I realized that if I were ever to get the prize, and this was not assured, it would have to come later.

I admit that I wanted to be awarded the prize, and for several reasons. Clearly, the prestige and financial rewards were important. But there was another reason as well. I had a lot of students and others who had been pursuing research along the lines indicated by my work, often working outside the more narrow range of traditional economics topics. These economists were often given a tough time in the profession, and several had difficulty getting good jobs. One of my top students years ago, who worked on religion, generated almost no job market interest. Now he is considered a preeminent economist working in religion, perhaps the preeminent person in any field doing research on religion. But he had a difficult time getting a job. People would ask, "Religion, what kind of topic is that for an economist?" I wanted myself and others to get the validation that the Nobel Prize would provide—that the economic approach to human behavior is acceptable work and that we are doing real economics. Yet in 1992, my work continued to be controversial, especially in Western Europe, and I began to wonder whether I would ever receive the prize.

I thought there was no chance I would receive the prize in 1992. Economists from Chicago were among the three winners in 1990, and another Chicagoan, Ronald Coase, won in 1991. I concluded that the committee would never choose three Chicagoans in a row. In the fall of 1992, I had a terrible flu with a very high fever. Doctors wanted to put me in the hospital, but my wife resisted that move. For both these reasons, the last thing on my mind was the Nobel Prize. I had no idea when the announcement was coming. I had not been into school for a week and I was in bed at 5:30 on the morning of October 13, sleeping soundly for the first night in about a week. My wife, who had been up grading papers, answered the phone when it rang that morning, worried that it might interfere with my sleep. She was a bit nasty, she said to me later, but the caller said this was an important phone call for Professor Becker. My wife did not think it was the Nobel Prize, at least not for me. She went and woke me up and I kept saying, "I want to sleep, I haven't slept so well for a long time." "No, it's a call from Sweden," she said, and that was the magic word. A call from Sweden! I did not know that the prize was announced. But when I heard "a call from Sweden," I figured, "well, maybe" and picked up the phone. My wife subsequently said that she was sitting there as I was saying, "yes, yes" with no expression on my face, and she figured that they had called for my input on somebody else who was being considered. Finally, she hears me say "Thank you very much; tell the committee what a great honor it is that you have conferred on me." This of course was the call telling me I had been awarded the prize. The first thing Guity did was to let out a yell and the first thing I said was "I'm glad that monkey is off my back." We called our four children and then we took the phone off the receiver to have breakfast in some peace. Before 6:30 or so, the reporters, the *New York Times,* the university people, and so on, had found us.

The prize recognized my research in four broad areas: investments in human capital; behavior of the family (or household), including distribution of work and allocation of time in the family; crime and punishment; and discrimination in the markets for labor and goods. In private I was told that some members of the committee did not want to award me the prize. But because in the last couple of years I had been nominated the most often by the economists asked to identify potential recipients, the committee felt they had to give me the prize. Well, better than not. And so, it was a great week and a great period of recognition.

Gary S. Becker

Awarded Nobel Prize in 1992. Lecture presented April 13, 2000.

Dates of Birth and Death

December 2, 1930; May 3, 2014

Academic Degrees

B.A., Princeton University, 1951
M.A., University of Chicago, 1953
Ph.D., University of Chicago, 1955

Academic Affiliations

Assistant Professor of Economics, University of Chicago, 1954–57
Assistant Professor of Economics, Columbia University, 1957–58
Associate Professor of Economics, Columbia University, 1958–60
Professor of Economics, Columbia University, 1960–68
Arthur Lehman Professor of Economics, Columbia University, 1968–69
Ford Foundation Visiting Professor of Economics, University of Chicago, 1969–70
University Professor of Economics, University of Chicago, 1970–83
University Professor of Economics and Sociology, University of Chicago, 1983–2014
Senior Research Fellow, Hoover Institute (Stanford), 1990–2014

Selected Books

The Economics of Discrimination, 1957, 1971
Human Capital: A Theoretical and Empirical Analysis, with Special Reference to Education, 1964, 1993
The Economic Approach to Human Behavior, 1976
A Treatise on the Family, 1981, 1991
Accounting for Tastes, 1996
The Economics of Life, 1997 (with Guity Nashat Becker)
Social Economics: Market Behavior in a Social Environment, 2000 (with K. Murphy)

Robert E. Lucas, Jr.

1

I took a train trip east from my Seattle home in September 1955, when I entered the University of Chicago as a scholarship student. Like my parents, I had graduated from Roosevelt High School, but I did not want to follow most of my classmates to the University of Washington. My mother chose to view my first year at Chicago as a temporary stay, as her year in New York had been. I may have seen it this way myself at first: my letters home made references to a possible transfer to the University of Washington, to study engineering. If so, it was not for long. I was homesick, for sure, and had doubts about my ability to succeed, but when my first quarter transcript showed a couple of A's—not just in calculus, where I could coast on my high school training, but in Humanities I, where everything was new—I knew I was at Chicago to stay.

The only science course I took in college was Natural Sciences II—a biology course. We read a modern anatomy text and also selections from Darwin, Mendel, and others. I remember struggling over an incomprehensible paper on embryology by Spemann and Mangold and one by another German author called "The Continuity of the Germ Plasm" that had mysterious overtones.

2

The reality addressed by natural science always seemed to me someone else's province. In public school science was an unending and not very well organized list of things other people had discovered long ago. In college, I learned something about the process of scientific discovery, but what little I learned did not attract me as a career possibility. Introductory physics and chemistry were huge courses, designed to weed out pretenders, which I feared I would soon be discovered to be. More important, I think, was a sense that these areas were in good hands, that they would progress in pretty much the same way with my participation or without it.

What I liked thinking about were politics and social issues. My parents had become politically aware in the 1930s, and politics were always the leading topic of discussion in our house. My letters home, from undergraduate days through middle age, were full of politics and social commentary. I had read widely on these matters, and with this background, I got advanced placement in social science. It was not until my second year at Chicago that I could take Social Sciences III and the History of Western Civilization. I had never worked so hard or with as much enthusiasm as I did in these two courses.

I won a Woodrow Wilson Fellowship for graduate study in history, and was admitted at the University of California at Berkeley. The trip west was my honeymoon: Rita Cohen and I were married in New York in the summer of 1959. My weakness in languages—a classical historian needs five—discouraged me from pursuing my interests in ancient and medieval history. I took an English history seminar course—tweedy students imitating every mannerism of their tweedy professor—and courses in economic history from Carlo Cipolla and David Landes. For Landes, I wrote a bibliographical paper on nineteenth-century British business cycles—a topic I chose from Landes's list because it looked like the most theoretical, and so it was. I could see that without a better economics background I would always be on the fringe of a topic like this. I wanted to transfer into economics, but even with Landes's support the Berkeley economics department was not encouraging.

Rita and I were also homesick for Chicago. I talked the Social Sciences Division at Chicago into accepting me back as a graduate student. I talked the Woodrow Wilson Foundation into transferring my fellowship to Chicago. With the help of my brother Pete, who passed through Berkeley on his way to the Rose Bowl in Pasadena, we loaded a rented trailer and headed back to Chicago.

3

By the summer of 1960 my young wife was pregnant, I had lost my Woodrow Wilson Fellowship, and I had spent the better part of the year making up for the fact that I had had no economics as an undergraduate. But I had found a field that I loved and was good at, and I could hardly wait to start the regular first-year graduate program with Milton Friedman and the rest of Chicago's faculty.

4

Before the various University of Chicago libraries were consolidated in Regenstein Library, economics Ph.D. students studied in the business and economics library, on the top floor of what is now Stuart Hall. The room had been designed as the law library, and its Gothic arches and leaded glass windows lent a welcome seriousness to our efforts to gain some intellectual control over the vastness of economic knowledge. In this room, Neil Wallace set an issue of the *Review of Economics and Statistics* on the table in front of me: "Look at this." The issue contained a symposium on monetary policy, including the papers that had been presented along with commentary by assigned discussants. Neil had opened it to the opening paragraphs of Milton Friedman's comments on a paper by the Harvard economist Seymour Harris. I read the introduction, in which Friedman criticized Harris for mixing "prediction and prescription so thoroughly that it is difficult to tell when he is recording what is going to be done and when recommending what should be done." Section II then began,

> The role of the economist in discussions of public policy seems to me to prescribe what should be done in the light of what can be done, politics aside, and not to predict what is "politically feasible" and then to recommend it. Accordingly, I shall not attempt a detailed criticism of Harris' comment.[1]

What excited me about this passage—and what I knew had excited Neil—was the confidence of Friedman's dismissal of Harris in this public, face-to-face interchange, and his own focus on what he saw as the economics of monetary policy without regard for how popular he or his analysis would be with his listeners. This focus and fearlessness was what we admired in Friedman's class: he was a moral example to us, just as Frank Knight had been for him and George Stigler.

Friedman rarely lectured. His class discussions were often structured as debates, with student opinions or newspaper quotes serving to introduce a problem and some loosely stated opinions about it. Then Friedman would lead us into a clear statement of the problem, considering alternative formulations as thoroughly as anyone in the class wanted to. Once formulated, the problem was quickly analyzed—usually diagrammatically—on the board. So we learned how to formulate a model, to think about and decide which features of a problem we could safely abstract from and which we needed to put at the center of the analysis. Here "model" is my term: it was not a term that Friedman liked or used. I think that for him talking about modeling would have detracted from the substantive seriousness of the inquiry we were engaged in, would divert us away from the attempt to discover "what can be done" into merely a mathematical exercise.

5

I couldn't wait to finish my thesis on capital-labor substitution and get on to something more interesting and ambitious.

The example I wanted to follow was the work of Dale Jorgenson, who was visiting at Chicago during my last year there. His study of the investment decision of the firm mixed theory, econometrics, and careful measurement in a way that I much admired (and still do). The modeling of firm and industry dynamics was at the top my agenda in 1963, when I became an assistant professor at the Graduate School of Industrial Administration (GSIA), the business school at Carnegie Tech.

Jorgenson had derived a formula for a firm's long-run capital-output ratio, but the theory did not explain why the adjustment to such a long-run target should be slow, as it appeared to be in the data. I modified the model by adding a penalty for rapid change—an adjustment cost—and used the calculus of variations to derive both the long-run target and the gradual approach to it from a single set of assumptions. I sent the paper to Dale, who directed me to an earlier paper by Eisner and Strotz that contained everything I had done. This was a setback, but somehow a stimulating one. I worked out a theory of firm-determined technological change, using the same variational methods. I generalized the Eisner–Strotz theory to many capital goods. It seemed there were enough unsolved problems in firm dynamics to support a lot of theorists.

Dick Schramm's GSIA thesis showed how to make a multiple capital good model operational econometrically. His model involved a lagged adjustment of price expectations to movements in actual prices. I remember a seminar presentation of Schramm's at which Jack Muth asked Dick why he had not assumed rational expectations. Of course, we all knew and admired Jack's paper "Rational Expectations and the Theory of Price Movements," but none of us knew how to exploit this idea econometrically. At that time, I thought of rational expectations as an elegant rationalization of the kind of lagged adjustment of expectations that Schramm assumed in his thesis, not as an alternate model. This was a half-truth that kept me from seeing the force of Jack's objections.

Schramm's thesis dealt with decisions of competitive firms, taking prices and expected future prices as given. So did the Eisner and Strotz paper, and my extensions of their work. Since these theories did not treat the determinants of prices, there was no internal inconsistency in the nonrational expectations they assumed. Serious inconsistency did emerge, though, when I made an entire Marshallian industry the unit of analysis, instead of the individual firm. In my "Adjustment Costs and the Theory of Supply," I took the industry demand function as a given, and solved for the time path of prices along with the paths of production and capital stock. I postulated "myopic" expectations—price expectations formed by simply extrapolating the current price into the future—and then deduced from this and other assumptions an equilibrium price path that was not constant but rather grew or declined in a predictable way. In such a model, you could *see* the profit opportunities that firms were passing up. Why couldn't they see these opportunities too? But if they did, the model couldn't be the right way to describe their behavior. Now I could go back to Muth's 1961 paper and see that this inconsistency was exactly his argument: In his words, "the marginal revenue product of economics" should be zero, or close to it. If your theory reveals profit opportunities, you have the wrong theory.

The context in which I came to this understanding was deterministic, so the assumption of rational expectations reduces to perfect foresight, using a terminology that I take from Buz Brock. Calculating a perfect foresight equilibrium for an industry, say, sounds as though it should involve solving a fixed point problem in a space of price paths: the actual path implies a forecast path, which in turn implies an actual path. This sounds hard, and it can be. But under competitive conditions, one can show that an industry over time will operate so as to maximize a discounted, consumer surplus integral—a problem that is mathematically no harder than the present value maximizing problem faced by a single firm. Who, exactly, is solving this planning problem? Adam Smith's "invisible hand," of course, not any actual person: but the mathematics of planning problems turned out to be just the right equipment needed to understand the decentralized interactions of a large number of producers. One can calculate equilibrium quantities over time using this fact and then read the equilibrium prices off the demand curve. I saw this in a particular context just by comparing the Euler necessary conditions for the equilibrium problem to those from the consumer surplus maximization problem. In fact, it is a consequence of one of the classic theorems of welfare economics.

In my first years at GSIA I worked furiously to pick up the mathematics of optimization over time—calculus of variations, the maximum principle of Pontryagin, Bellman's dynamic programming—and of the differential equations systems these optimization problems produced. I worked on applications of these methods to problems in economics and operations research. Theoretically minded economists of my cohort were doing the same thing all over the world. I was studying the dynamics of investment at the firm and industry level, as were many others. Still others were studying optimal growth of an economy, optimal accumulation of human capital, optimal advertising and R&D investment, and so on.

In 1966 I was invited to a workshop on economic dynamics, conducted in Chicago by Hirofumi Uzawa, that involved some of the best people in this group of younger theorists. Uzawa was a charismatic figure, an enormous influence on theoretically minded students, who had moved to Chicago from Stanford just after I had left. The seminars ran all day, through dinner, and into the evening. Discussions were noisy and intense, but friendly and constructive: I remember people going to the blackboard in the middle of a talk, to show how a speaker's argument had gone wrong and to try to help fix it.

Dave Cass spoke about work that he and Menahem Yaari were doing, trying to understand the logic of a model of an economy with an infinity of overlapping generations that Samuelson had published in 1958. This paper had not been on reading lists of mine, but I was immediately attracted by its simplicity and the role it had for money. This was the first model I had seen in which paper money had a useful role to perform and had a command over goods in equilibrium. This was exciting, and the following fall I began to use this setup in my graduate courses in macroeconomics.

The paper I had written for the Uzawa conference was never finished: I couldn't establish the mathematical result that was to be the paper's centerpiece. I proposed to Ed Prescott, a friend of mine from his student days at GSIA who was then on the faculty at Penn, that we work together on it. Even with Ed's help, the original problem proved intractable, but we found ourselves thinking together about the behavior of firms in a competitive industry that is subject to unpredictable demand shocks. Ed had used dynamic programming methods in his thesis, and introduced me to a paper by David Blackwell that worked out the underlying mathematics in a useful and beautiful way. We applied these methods to the problem of maximizing expected, discounted consumers' surplus in the industry. The solution takes the form of a Markov process or stochastic difference equation describing the evolution of capacity and production in response to recurring shocks to demand. Buz Brock and Leonard Mirman were thinking about optimal growth in similar terms at about the same time.

But then how can the solution to this maximum problem be related to a competitive equilibrium in which firms have rational expectations? Part of the answer lay in reformulating the rational expectations hypothesis in a way that did not require the linearity Muth had assumed in his analysis. The other part of the answer came from applying the competitive general equilibrium theory of Arrow, Debreu, and McKenzie, theory developed in the 1950s and gradually being extended to ever more general mathematical contexts. The potential of this body of theory for more applied work was, at that time, unrecognized. Prescott and I saw that it would be helpful to us, and plunged into a self-taught crash course. Putting the pieces together, we wrote "Investment under Uncertainty."

In 1963, I had thought of a competitive industry in terms of firms solving short- and long-run, deterministic profit-maximization problems, under the (false) belief that current prices would maintain their current values forever, and with the passage from one to the other and all the effects of unpredictable shocks tacked on as afterthoughts. Five years later, I thought of the same economics in terms of firms maximizing expected discounted present value, with rational expectations about the probability distributions of future prices, and with stochastic shocks and adjustment costs both fully integrated into the theory. From an objective point of view, this transformation can be viewed as a product of decades of research by many economists. From my subjective viewpoint, it was the most rapid, radical change of view I have ever experienced as an economist.

6

In those early years at GSIA, my closest friend was Leonard Rapping, a Chicago Ph.D. about two years ahead of me. As Leonard said in a 1982 interview,

> I expect that we talked once or twice every day from '63 to '68. We talked about everything: about economics, about politics, about business school problems, just about everything. We would have coffee from about three until five. We were the two people who would always be at the afternoon coffee hours. Everyone else would be back at their offices.[2]

Maybe it was inevitable that we would do joint research, but it was surprising that this should turn out to be research in macroeconomics—a field in which neither of us had even taken a prelim. We got there by the back door, through labor economics: at Chicago; we had both studied with Gregg Lewis.

At that time, many people were regressing changes in nominal wages on the unemployment rate, a statistical relation known as a Phillips curve, interpreting the negative coefficient of unemployment as describing a trade-off: lower unemployment means higher wage inflation. People had just begun to consider what kind of economics might underlie this statistical connection. Leonard and I started discussing supply and demand models of joint wage and employment determination, and tried these out in the classroom. We decided to formulate and test such a model more carefully. To get an aggregate time series of decent length, back then, one needed to go back to 1929, so our project turned into an attempt to understand wage and employment behavior through the Depression and war years.

Like everyone else, we thought that the ultimate source of employment fluctuations in both these periods came mainly from the demand side: fluctuations in spending on goods and services. But all the evidence we knew about indicated that labor supply was very inelastic. How could we get large employment swings out of demand shifts in such a setting? We used a device based on the old Keynesian idea of "money illusion": people in booms (as after World War II) are willing to supply a lot of labor temporarily at the high money wage rates available then, without realizing that when they spend these dollars it will be at higher prices. Symmetrically, people in depressions temporarily pass up jobs at low money wages, not realizing that these low wages will buy a lot more goods than they would have two years earlier. This was the idea we used to reconcile an elastic short-run supply of labor with an inelastic long-run supply. I thought of my parents, both working throughout the war and saving most of what they made to build up a down payment for the house they bought when the war was over.

In our model, wages and employment levels were always in a kind of temporary equilibrium, and this equilibrium had the property that inflation would stimulate employment. What about *un*employment? We added a labor force participation equation that, combined with the rest of the model, gave us a Phillips curve.

Leonard and I did a careful job of working through the decision problems of households and firms in a world subject to these "illusions," and another careful job putting together a set of compatible time series. The econometric work came out well, and the ambitions of the project began to dawn on us. "Bob, we're going to be famous!" Leonard would say. It frightened me, and I managed to be out of town on the day that Leonard presented the paper to our colleagues at a GSIA seminar. We were both right. Albert Rees refereed the paper at the *JPE*: his outraged reaction was later published as a comment. But why outrage? Another economist, we heard, called the paper "fascist economics." Fascist! For writing down a labor supply curve and taking it seriously!

Before our paper was finished, Milton Friedman had used his presidential address to the American Economic Association to argue that in the long run, the unemployment rate would be independent of the inflation rate: there would be no Phillips-like trade-off between inflation and unemployment. Friedman's argument was theoretical, but his premises all seemed to Leonard and me to hold for our model. Yet our model *did* imply a long-run trade-off. Later, we came to see that this difference was due to our use of adaptive, rather than rational, expectations, but at the time we simply accepted it as an unresolved puzzle.

Edmund Phelps had been trying to use an equilibrium framework to think about unemployment and wage determination at about the same time, and he had reached the same theoretical conclusion that Friedman had. While making the rounds of the seminar circuit he had run across others engaged in the same kind of investigation he and Rapping and I were engaged in. He assembled these papers in a 1970 book, *Microeconomic Foundations of Employment and Inflation Theory*, now universally known simply as the "Phelps volume." This was the kind of fame that Leonard and I had dreamed of, and the book and the conference Ned organized around it gave us the first experience either of us had had of being at the forefront of an important research area.

In an early draft of the introduction to the volume, Phelps had written that "perhaps Lucas and Rapping are 180 degrees to the truth," by which he meant that perhaps we should have emphasized income effects in our theory of employment fluctuations rather than the substitution effects we did emphasize. On a social occasion soon after the conference—when Leonard and I were still high—we joked about this remark. This shocked Elayne Rapping. She said, "All you two care about is being cited by a well-known economist, about being famous. It doesn't matter to you whether you are right or 180 degrees off." Elayne's remark stung, and she was certainly right that the source of our good mood that evening was the boost the conference had given to our ambitions. The desires for fame and truth are not inconsistent, though, and in fact we were laughing because we were so sure that Phelps's criticism could be dealt with. But this was not the occasion to try to explain income and substitution effects to Elayne, and anyway we knew that she was as pleased with our success as we were.

Not long after this occasion, Leonard and Elayne were swept up in the opposition to the war in Vietnam and moved far to the left politically. Leonard lost interest in the kind of economics we had done together. When the *JPE* published Rees's comment on our paper, both of us signed the reply, but I had written it alone. Our friendship had been based on conversations that ranged much more broadly than our joint work, and we tried to maintain them, but without success. Soon after, Leonard moved to the University of Massachusetts, which was then becoming a center for radical economics.

7

By the end of the '60s, I was leading two lives as an economist. With Rapping, I was an empirical macroeconomist, estimating Phillips curves and aggregate labor supply functions. Working with Prescott, I had immersed myself in the mathematics of dynamic programming and general equilibrium theory and was applying these methods to construct tractable, genuinely dynamic models. In my graduate teaching, I was putting these elements together, using the overlapping generations models that I had learned about from Cass, to build models of monetary economies that would, I hoped, be helpful in addressing questions of macroeconomic policy.

At the Phelps volume conference, Ned Phelps had pushed one such question to the front of my thinking: if Rapping and I were right that monetary shocks affected people's willingness to supply labor by "fooling" them about their future options, then we needed to explain why everyone gets fooled in the same direction. Why isn't the worker who is over-optimistic about his job prospects offset by another who is too pessimistic? Phelps outlined an answer to this question in his essay in the volume, based on the idea that workers at any one location are short on information about what is happening elsewhere. When a worker sees a wage change, he thinks it is specific to his own market, not realizing that the same thing might be happening everywhere. I thought I could capture this effect with the kind of overlapping generations models I was using in class. I tried out one version in 1968. Further work led to "Expectations and the Neutrality of Money," submitted to the *American Economic Review* in 1970 and finally published in the *Journal of Economic Theory* in 1972.

The paper contained a careful and explicit construction of a theoretical example of an economy in which the motives, opportunities, and information of every economic actor were unambiguously spelled out. Expectations were rational. In this setting, as in Friedman's AEA address, there was no long-run trade-off between employment and inflation. Yet the model also implied the kind of correlations between employment and inflation that were then widely interpreted as hard evidence that such trade-offs did exist. I felt I understood for the first time both why Friedman and Phelps were right in arguing there was no long-run trade-off between unemployment and inflation and why econometric tests continued to reject this "natural rate" view.

Working out this example took me to the limit of my technical skills and beyond: it was not easy reading, nor had it been easy writing. It built closely on Rapping's and my view of the labor supply decision, as well as on the formulation of rational expectations that Prescott and I had developed working on "Investment under Uncertainty." It is easy for me to see the influences of Phelps, Rapping, Prescott, and Cass in this paper, but the combination was new and striking: no one else was doing macroeconomics this way in 1970. The paper made my reputation.

8

My family and I spent the summer of 1970 in Seattle, driving our underpowered Plymouth Valiant into the headwind for days to get there. I had an office at the University of Washington. My ambition for the summer was to write a paper on Phillips curves for a conference to be held that fall at the Federal Reserve Board. I had been invited, I assumed, as a spokesman for the Friedman–Phelps position that there was no long run trade-off between unemployment and inflation. My plan was to translate what I had learned from writing "Expectations and the Neutrality of Money" into linear examples that would make it clear to a much wider readership why the standard tests for "long-run" effects—tests of the sort Rapping and I and dozens of others had used—were not informative about the Friedman–Phelps hypothesis. This paper became "Econometric Testing of the Natural Rate Hypothesis."

The stay in Seattle was a pleasure—I enjoyed being close to my Seattle family—but by the summer's end, I found I missed the more intense atmosphere of GSIA and was eager to get back to Pittsburgh. On my first day at the office Marty Geisel handed me a working paper by Tom Sargent, saying only, "I think you will be interested in this." Sargent's paper involved exactly the logic of the paper I had just completed (which of course Tom hadn't seen), applied to Irving Fisher's predicted relation between expected inflation and interest rates. Rational expectations connected expected inflation, which we cannot observe, to actual inflation rates, which we can, in just the right way to give Fisher's idea content. Sargent had based a test of Fisher's theory on this observation—the first econometric application of Muth's idea.

I gave my paper in Washington in the fall. It was the first time that many in attendance had heard of rational expectations. James Tobin gave it a generous review when he summed up the proceedings of the conference: it was clear that I had made my point. When my session ended, an economist of about my age whose work on Phillips curves I knew and respected came up to the podium and told me, "You just explained why everything I've done in the last few years is worthless." This shocked me: I was viewing myself as an underdog in the conference setting and was not prepared to assume this very different role. I protested, "Oh no, that wasn't what I said at all." He insisted: "Yes, it was. It was exactly what you said. And you were right." I had not experienced anything like this before.

As Sargent's test of the Fisher hypothesis showed, the idea that rational expectations implied restrictions across equations was not special to Phillips curves. When Allan Meltzer and Karl Brunner asked me to give a paper on empirical Phillips curves for the first meeting of the Carnegie–Rochester Conference Series, I decided to try to illustrate this fact with a variety of econometric applications. The resulting paper, "Econometric Policy Evaluation: A Critique," explained in detail how rational expectations undermines the then-conventional uses of econometric models in simulating the effects of policy changes. This "Lucas critique," as it came to be known, is probably the most influential paper I have written.

My critical writing on the Keynesian macroeconometric models of the day showed that simulations of these models could not be expected to give accurate answers about the effects of changes in economic policy. Parallel work by Sargent, and Sargent and Neil Wallace, showed the same thing. These demonstrations effectively ended the role of these models in policy debates and eliminated the main intellectual basis for monetary and fiscal fine-tuning of the economy. We were certainly not the first economists who were skeptical of Keynesian econometric models—the whole monetarist tradition of Milton Friedman, Allan Meltzer, and Karl Brunner anticipated our conclusions—but Sargent and Wallace and I were critics from *within*. We were committed to the use of explicit models to evaluate policy changes; we knew the work we were criticizing in detail, and we could articulate the reasons for our skepticism in a way that those we criticized could see the arguments and respond usefully to them. Macroeconomic debate had changed course.

9

Not long after "Investment under Uncertainty" was finished, Ed Prescott returned to GSIA as a faculty member. I was working on monetary theory, a topic that Ed had never been much interested in. I was also thinking about unemployment, using a theoretical setting in which workers are distributed over a large number of distinct markets, and these markets are subject to persistent shocks to demand. If your market is hit with a bad shock, wages are likely to be low for a while. You are tempted to leave, to set out for brighter prospects elsewhere, but this will entail a spell of unemployment. The risks must be balanced and how this balancing comes out depends on what everyone else is doing. After some weeks of work, I felt I was very close to having a successful mathematical model of this situation, a theory of what Milton Friedman had called the "natural rate of unemployment."

But the pieces would not fall into place. I believed that my formulation had the economics of these interactions just right and that the problem was that I didn't know and couldn't invent the mathematics to work out the implications of the theory. Once again, I asked Ed to collaborate, and after I had taken him through the model, he agreed. This was late on a

Friday afternoon, so we stopped working and went downstairs to the faculty–student TGIF.

After the party, walking home by myself through the Schenley Park golf course, thoughts of regret came over me. I had formulated, on my own, a great theoretical problem and had carried the analysis of that problem close to completion. Now I had shown the problem to Ed, who would surely see a quick resolution of the mathematical issues that I had been stuck on. He could write the paper by himself and since I had shown him no actual results, claim credit for himself. He might not even thank me for "helpful discussion" in his opening footnote! As soon as I got home I took out my typewriter and, in a kind of paranoid frenzy that lasted through the weekend, I wrote a draft of the entire paper: Introduction, Theorem 1, Theorem 2, and so on, right through to the end.

On Monday I felt foolish as soon as I saw Ed, but I handed him the draft anyway. Of course we soon discovered that most of the results stated in the draft were false and that we had no idea how to prove the theorems that were possibly true. How could it have been otherwise? If I had really known how to finish the paper I wouldn't have asked Ed to work with me! So we began work in earnest.

Some days, perhaps weeks, later I arrived at the office around 9 and found a note from Ed in my mailbox. The full text was as follows:

Bob,
This is the way labor markets work:

$$v(s, y, \lambda) = \max\{\lambda, R(s, y) + \min[\lambda, \beta + v(s', y, \lambda) f(s', s)ds']\}.$$

—Ed

Of course since our project was well under way, we had agreed on notation: s stood for the state of product demand at a particular location, y stood for the number of workers who were already at that location, $R(s, y)$ was the marginal product of labor implied by these two numbers, and $v(s, y)$ stood for the present value of earnings that one of these workers could obtain if he made his decision whether to stay at this location or leave optimally. Other features of the equation were as novel to me as they are (I imagine) to you.

The normal response to such a note, I suppose, would have been to go upstairs to Ed's office and ask for some kind of explanation. But theoretical economists are not normal, and we do not ask for words that "explain" what equations mean. We ask for equations that explain what words mean. Ed had provided an equation that claimed to explain how labor markets work. It was my job to understand it and to decide whether I agreed with this claim. This took me a while, but I saw that Ed had replaced an assumption of mine that workers who leave any one location hit on a new location at random—maybe a worse location than the one they had left—with the alternative assumption that searching workers were fully informed about options elsewhere and bee-lined for the best destination. Mathematically, this meant that a single parameter—Ed's λ—stood for two different things: the present value of earnings that all searching workers would have to expect in order to leave a location and the present value that a particular location would need to offer to receive new arrivals.

Mathematically, Ed's equation was a very familiar, comfortable object for me to analyze: once I convinced myself that it described some sensible economics, it took a few minutes to see that its properties could be established by standard methods and that these properties were interesting and reasonable. By lunchtime, I could see that I was to be a co-author of a very sharp paper, unlike anything anyone had seen before, a paper with a potential for helping us to think about important events.

If I had to pick a single day to represent what I like about a life of research, it would be this one. Ed's note captures exactly why I think we value mathematical modeling: it is a method to help us get to new levels of understanding the ways things work. No one could have written Ed's equation down at the beginning of an inquiry into the nature of unemployment: it is too far from earlier ways of thinking to be grasped in one step. The new understanding that this equation represents could be gained only through a trial-and-error process, involving formulating and analyzing explicit models. It is this struggle to capture behavior in tractable models that leads us deeper into the economics of market interactions and forms the progressive element in economic thought.

10

In October, 1978—leaf season—the Federal Reserve Bank of Boston sponsored a conference at the Bald Peak Colony Club in New Hampshire. Ed Prescott and I rented a car at Logan Airport and drove up together. Night fell before we reached the conference center, and we got lost on country roads. We stopped for directions at a crossroads store, but after a few minutes of laconic "Nope, yep" New England conversation we realized that the two old men in the store were amusing themselves at our expense, conveying no information. We left in disgust and anger. The incident heightened my sense of entering foreign territory.

On the drive, neither Ed nor I discussed the papers we were to give at the conference. Ed had been reading Simon Kuznets's work and treated me to a review of Kuznets's main findings. I was grateful for the chance to learn something from this central figure in research on economic growth without actually having to read him. We talked about the kinds of theoretical models that might fit the regularities that Kuznets had documented. What better and more productive way to deal with anxieties about how one's work will be received than looking beyond to the next project?

When the conference began, the next day, it became clear that this was not the occasion for such anxieties. The attenders included representatives of the Keynesian establishment—including Paul Samuelson himself—and some "new classical" rebels. In my memory, the conference was a kind of triumph of the new classical views. My own paper was a reprise of Milton Friedman's 1948 paper, "A Monetary and Fiscal Framework for Economic Stability," emphasizing the support that recent research provided for Friedman's positions, with no pretense of new findings. I viewed it as my day to stand up and be counted as a Chicago economist. I later wrote to my parents:

> The influence my work has had was astonishing to me. I was very nervous about my presentation, which was extremely negative on what most of this group is up to, yet people were lining up in the question period to take their turn to say how right I am.

The question period I referred to was chaotic, and I remember people calling for me to denounce work by John Taylor and Stan Fischer that, like some of my own work, attempted to account for real effects of monetary instability. I also preferred my approach, but I understood that this preference was not really defensible empirically. I said that on the basis of the evidence available now, I did not see how it was possible to distinguish between my views and Taylor's. Looking back on the occasion, an exciting one for me, I am pleased and a little surprised that I managed such a level-headed reply.

Though I did not see it at the time, the Bald Peak conference also marked the beginning of the end of my attempts to account for the business cycle in terms of monetary shocks. At that conference, Ed Prescott presented a model of his and Finn Kydland's that was a kind of mixture of Brock and Mirman's model of growth subject to stochastic technology shocks and my model of monetary shocks. When Ed presented his results, everyone could see they were important but the paper was so novel and complicated that no one could see exactly what they were. Later on, as they gained more experience through numerical simulations of their Bald Peak model, Kydland and Prescott found that the monetary shocks were just not pulling their weight: by removing all monetary aspects of the theory, they obtained a far simpler and more comprehensible structure that fit postwar U.S. time series data just as well as the original version. Besides introducing an important substantive refocusing of business cycle research, Kydland and Prescott introduced a new style of comparing theory to evidence that has had an enormous, beneficial effect on empirical work in the field.

11

By the time of the Bald Peak conference, I had moved from Carnegie Mellon to the University of Chicago. I was just over forty years old. The work that was later recognized by the Swedish Academy of Sciences was done. I had arrived at a research style that has continued over the years to lead me into new ways of seeing things.

In the more than twenty years since, I have continued to devote virtually all of my time to teaching and research. I have written on many subjects and participated in collaborations with Andy Atkeson, Esteban Rossi-Hansberg, and, especially, with Nancy Stokey, that have been as interesting and fruitful for me as those with Leonard Rapping and Ed Prescott. Perhaps at some later occasion I will review these years, too: I have enjoyed them, produced some work I am proud of, and accumulated enough memories for many more memoirs.

Notes

1. Reprinted in *Milton Friedman, Essays in Positive Economics* (Chicago: University of Chicago Press, 1953).
2. Arjo Klamer, *Conversations with Economists* (Savage, MD: Rowman and Littlefield, 1983), 223.

Robert E. Lucas, Jr.

Awarded Nobel Prize in 1995. Lecture presented April 5, 2001.

Date of Birth

September 15, 1937

Academic Degrees

B.A., University of Chicago, 1959
Ph.D., University of Chicago, 1964

Academic Affiliations

Lecturer, Department of Economics, University of Chicago, 1962–63
Assistant Professor of Economics, Carnegie Institute of Technology, 1963–67
Associate Professor of Economics, Carnegie Mellon University, 1967–70
Professor of Economics, Carnegie Mellon University, 1970–74
Ford Foundation Visiting Research Professor of Economics, University of Chicago, 1974–75
Professor of Economics, University of Chicago, 1975–80
Visiting Professor of Economics, Northwestern University, 1981–82
John Dewey Distinguished Service Professor of Economics, University of Chicago, 1980–present

Selected Books

Studies in Business-Cycle Theory, 1981
Models of Business Cycles, 1987
Recursive Methods in Economic Dynamics, 1989 (with N. Stokey and E. Prescott)
Lectures on Economic Growth, 2002

Vernon L. Smith

Limestone is something you get interested in and something you learn to like. And then you become part of it. You know every move to make: just how to mark it off, drill it, load it, shoot it and then you see a real straight break, and you feel good.
—McClure Stilley, Chase County Kansas quarry man, as quoted in W. Least Heat-Moon, *PrairyErth*, 1991

One cannot take advantage of his fellowman and come out ahead. It just cannot be done.
—Quintin Lomax, 1947

Prison guard: "Don't you know that you can't change the world by carrying that sign."
Lone picketer, protesting capital punishment: "I'm not trying to change the world. I am just trying to keep the world from changing me."
—Dialogue in movie, *The Hoodlum Priest*, 1961

You Can Go Home Again[1]

I want to begin by letting you walk through a part of my childhood home as it would have appeared that day in 1927 when I was born.

Walking west through the front door you enter the living room. You see my mother's old, but always-tuned, solid walnut upright piano on your left, facing north in the southeast corner. When you sit on the piano bench there is a window on your left, bathing the piano and sheet music with daylight, even on one of those rare cloudy days in Kansas—a condition that has already attracted the attention of the great entrepreneurs who would make Wichita the center of the light airplane industry.

Lifting the hinged lid on the piano bench you find it stuffed with Bach, Beethoven, Stephen Foster, and Hoagy Carmichael sheet music, along with the complete scores of *Cavaleria Rusticana* and *HMS Pinafore*, to name only a few of my favorites in that treasure chest. Decades later, when I write my memoir, I will still have a cardboard box full of those musical scores. If I pull out three of those yellowing old scores and read lines like, "I am the builder, come walk with me," "I am the very model of a modern major general," or "When the deep purple falls over sleepy garden walls," the memory of that piano bench will be fresh, sharp, and black.

To your right on the north wall of the living room you see an open ceramic grated gas fireplace, a mantel, and glass-enclosed bookcases containing my father's set of rust red Harvard Classics. My father had an eighth-grade education, and has always needed to work long hours for a living. He aspired to read more, but actually read little that was not related to earning his bread and butter. For me, however, these books will come to symbolize the immensity of that which is knowable, and I will keep them all my life. One of the classics, volume 17, will become severely worn and frayed, with a shredded, loose, dangling binding from being read over and over again by me—Grimm, Andersen, and Aesop tales.

In my early childhood years I will think of libraries as infinite extensions of my father's bookcase; libraries surely contain all that is known, and I will aspire to go to college because that is where one learns all that is known, which is everything. Nothing is unknowable; you had only to seek it in a book or some source somewhere. I will know so little and be hungry to know, but I will gradually learn that the action—all the learning and understanding—will be in the pursuit, not in the consummation of knowledge, and that the questions always grow faster than the answers. Every answer sprouts multiple questions so that knowledge becomes an unending quest, but therein lays its charming challenge. I will learn that any three-year-old can force you to the outermost limits of your knowledge on any topic by asking "Why?" three times in response to each of your answers. It is a sobering observation that every child passes through a short "repeat-why" stage, pressing to identify the limits of what is known, before learning to stop asking, and arbitrarily to accept living with less—a state that I will find troubling again and again throughout my life.

I will learn to read early and well, and Harvard Classics volume 17 will become one of my two childhood treasures. The other will be Tal: His Marvelous Adventures with Noom-Zor-Noom *(1929, 1937, 2001) by Paul Fenimore Cooper, whose great-grandfather was James Fenimore Cooper, novelist of the American wilderness. I will read* Tal *to all my children, and my copy will come to have no binding left to dangle, so thoroughly will it be consumed, loved, and enjoyed. My oldest daughter, Deborah, will name her son Tal (Taliesin). Sixty years after first reading* Tal *I will conceive of the idea of having the book reprinted at my own expense, believing that no one else would have such an interest. I will procrastinate and be pleasantly surprised to discover a third edition inspired by the author's nephew, Henry S. F. Cooper, Jr., appearing in 2001, with an introduction bearing testimony to its loyal and dedicated readership. I will have no idea that I was far from alone in loving that book. Fantasy is important to the child. Dreams are fashioned of fantasy, and out of dreams come the desire for adventure, for learning, and ultimately the realization that learning is about learning to learn, and is a self-teaching process. In dreams and fantasy nothing is unattainable, and this is a model for seeking, overcoming, and coming to know, but most important a model for life.*

To the left of the fireplace is an open light oak staircase, which you ascend facing west, that immediately circles left up to a landing with a balcony overlooking the living room. Two or three years later, if it is 7:00 p.m., you might see my father standing in the living room, facing the balcony, singing an Irish ballad for me just after I have retired to my bed upstairs. There are no upstairs bathrooms, and the closets are very small, closely matching our clothes, toy, and "things" budget. Toys, I will learn to design and make, much as my father learned to design and make machine tools.

If it is a hot summer day, the "evaporative cooler" may be set up and running in the middle of the kitchen floor, or behind you in the dining or living room. The evaporative cooler consists of an ancient oscillating fan with a line strung between two chairs in front of it for hanging wet tea towels. The fan air evaporates the water from the towels and cools the room. This is an effective air cooler in the 1930s' climate of Kansas with single-digit humidity, but the towels require resoaking often, so quickly do they dry out. You cannot help but notice from the faded colors and printing on all our tea towels that they have been made from old, worn, and empty twenty-five-pound cotton flour bags by removing the stitches. I will discover that we were poor and governed by the maxim "Waste not, want not."

Straight west of the back door behind the clothesline is a chicken yard. You may wonder why there is a large chopping block behind the garage with a big ax stuck into it. That is for dispatching one of the chickens for a regular Sunday or a special dinner.

Before Me

> We hadn't received any more orders. Down the track we went, approaching Vaughan, which is twelve miles from Canton. Vaughan was at the lower end of a double S curve. The north switch was just about the middle of the first S, and as we roared down on it we saw two big red lights ... it was a train not in the clear. I could see the lights, but Mr. Casey couldn't because there was a deep curve to the fireman's side. I yelled to Mr. Casey, "look out! We're gonna hit something!" "Jump Sim!" he shouted, and these were his last words. I heard him kick the seat out from under him and apply the brakes ... I swung down ... and hit the dirt. When I came to ... Mr. Casey was dead. Our engine had ploughed through the caboose of the freight, and ... a car of shelled corn and a car of hay. When Casey's body was found in the wreckage, an iron bolt was driven through his neck, and a bale of hay rested on his chest.[2]

Grover Bougher, my mother's first husband and father of her two oldest children, was a fireman on the Santa Fe Railroad. For those not brought up on railroad lore, a fireman puts on, not out, engine fires; he makes and stokes the locomotive's boiler fire by shoveling coal and maintaining the locomotive's steam pressure. A fireman was commonly a locomotive engineer apprentice; you served time in the cab mastering the engine's operations and learning from the engineer, who is essentially the captain of his train. This subordinate role is clearly indicated in the exchange recorded above with the famous Casey Jones, "Mr. Casey," as his fireman, Sim Web, called him. At some point, after getting added experience in the cab as an engineer by working the extra board, if you were proved fit for the task and were of a mind to continue, then you were promoted to engineer. An engineer lived by the maxim "Get her there and make time or come to the office and get your time."

I have a letter Grover wrote to his brother, George, a private in the American Expeditionary Force serving in France, dated October 3, 1918. Two days later Grover was killed instantly in a train wreck when his passenger train engine and its cars were diverted by a manual cutover switch that had been inadvertently left open on to the sidetrack, colliding with a waiting freight engine. A similar type of incident is what killed Casey Jones in the wreck of the Cannonball in 1906.

The letter was returned to Newton, postmarked the following April and forwarded to Wichita, where my mother had moved, with a notation by the command post office that George had been killed eight months earlier, before Grover had written to him, on September 17, 1918, fighting the war in France. Thus, neither brother knew of the other's death. When Grover was killed, my grandfather-to-be, Aseal Lomax (1874–1945), had been laid up for some period with a badly injured leg caused by a railroad accident. He was an engineer on the Missouri Pacific Railroad, and was injured on a straight track accident, not an S curve as in the spectacular Cannonball wreck, when one of the rods on the great drive wheels bolted loose from the drive wheel and flailed up through the cab's wood flooring. Grandpa Lomax and his fireman both "hit the dirt" from each side of the cab, enabling them to escape the likelihood of death. On a straight open track the train will come to a stop without assistance by the engineer, and you can be heroic not a bit from the inside of a demolished cab. He often said that years later his leg still contained splinters that had erupted from the floor of the engine cab.

Enter My Father

Unemployment occurs when large numbers of people can't find work.
—Calvin Coolidge

Fortune smiled for us all when my father, Vernon Chessman Smith (1890–1954), a machinist who had apprenticed in Cleveland, Ohio, met my mother, Lulu Belle Bougher (Lomax) (1896–1957) in Wichita, and was delighted to find a warm and caring woman already with a family. They were married on August 16, 1921. Her diary entry for August 16, 1944, states, in beautifully simple language, "Our 23rd wedding; thought of it Monday—forgot it today. Vern (my father's spoken name) remembered today. A wonderful 23 years. I love him." I will say more of my parents, and what kind of people they were, but this closet diary entry, a private and unadorned personal message, says almost everything there is to say.

In 1932, my father was laid off for lack of enough work and became one of many who fitted Cal Coolidge's definition of "unemployment." The three of us moved to the farm located near Milan (pronounced "mile-n," in them there parts, not "mil-awn"), Kansas. The farm had been purchased earlier with the insurance money my mother had received from the Santa Fe Railroad after Grover's death.

The farm brought new dimensions of hard work and hard times for my parents, but also survival for two years when there was no acceptable alternative. Farming was not yet hydrolyzed, electrolyzed, or mechanized. Neither was our house, which had no indoor drinking water, electricity, central heating, or toilet facilities.

For me, however, if not for my parents, the farm yielded trivial memories of personal inconvenience for the simple reason that there existed no alternative known to me. This was life, and you were here to make the most and best of it without bellyaching. I always seemed to minimize any discomfort from most things that were less than the best. That farm was a great place and time to be a kid looking for adventure. For me it was not "hardship"; it was more like high-class "camping out."

In autumn 1932, at age five, I took my place in the first grade alongside more seasoned farm children for primary education in the classic rural one-room schoolhouse. A neighbor, Mr. Hemberger, part of a German community, had the distinction of being able to speak, read, and write English, knew arithmetic, and therefore was deemed fully equipped to be our grade-school teacher. A wise decision, I think, although my mother was always a bit irritated when he used the word "ain't," a completely grammatical contraction of which English has many; mom was something of a language maven, as Steve Pinker would say. Each morning my teacher/neighbor faced rows of old-fashioned desks with lids that could be raised to take out your books, notes, and paper, always stored in your desk. "Homework" was farmwork, as you never were asked to take home any schoolwork described by that term; otherwise what the hell was the classroom for if education could not be fully and completely accomplished there? A quarter century later, when my own children were in public school, I found myself naturally resistant to the concept of homework in first grade.

The first row on Mr. Hemberger's right as he faced the class, where I sat, was grade one, the second row grade two, and so on for all the grades. I sat in the front of row one because I could not see the blackboard—no one knew yet, and it would be two years before anyone knew, that I was severely myopic, and nothing written on that blackboard had any meaning for me. At the end of grade one, Mr. Hemberger gave me a note to take home to my mother stating unceremoniously that "Vernon can read the second-grade reader and therefore next year he will be in the third grade." There were of course only three subjects—reading, writing, and arithmetic. Reading seemed to be the litmus test; if you were less strong in arithmetic or writing, the next year you could participate along with those in the row on your left before Mr. Hemberger got to your row. The whole purpose of this management style was to move each person along at her own pace of accomplishment, get her through school and into farmwork, where she could be useful. I understand that the earliest achievement tests showed high performance in Kansas and Nebraska because of these rural schools. It's no wonder to me that Kansas bred the Eisenhowers, William Allen Whites, Beeches, Garveys, and so on, by the hundreds, maybe thousands.

City Lights Again

In 1934, my father returned to the Bridgeport Machine Company for alternate-week half-time work and subsequently full-time work. This was fortuitous, as we lost "ownership" of the farm to the mortgage bank, with which we had always shared ownership, unable to meet payments on the loan. We would have had to move back to Wichita, whether Dad had employment or not. We would also have lost our home in Wichita, but my parents recognized this possibility and earlier had temporarily deeded the asset in the name of Grandpa Lomax to protect it from being added to the default obligation; so the issue never arose—probably some kind of horrible criminal offense.

We were returning from the farm world of personal exchange through the trading of favors to a world of impersonal exchange through markets. More, but far from all, of our needs would be met by store-bought goods, and that world would gradually be emerging, reinvigorated, from the Great Depression.

In 1920, my mother cast her first vote for Eugene Victor Debs, the socialist candidate for president who was campaigning from jail, where he had been sentenced as a result of his opposition to World War I. Bertrand Russell once said that there had been only two wars worth fighting: the American Revolution and World War II. He was surely right about World War I: we won the war, but then lost the peace in a fit of retribution that set the stage for the rise of Hitler and World War II, which we had to fight to stop the beast. Russell did not live to see the Vietnam War that Eisenhower avoided. Russell's favorite war (and mine) has always been the American Revolution. Our ancestors were doing God's work when they threw the redcoats out of this land. Going after the Tories in Canada was a little headstrong, but the War of 1812 might well have been another good one for the arrogant Americans to win.

When I entered the voting booth for the first time in 1948, at age twenty-one, I repeated my mother's history of 1920, and cheerfully voted socialist, for Norman Thomas. I doubt that I have voted for anyone since who approached Thomas's incredible integrity and compassion for humanity. Remarkably, I still have a warm memory of that experience, although intellectually, of course, command-and-control systems do not and cannot work, and demonstrably cannot manage the economy. They perpetuate poverty, destroy freedom, subordinate the individual to a mindless bureaucracy of doublespeak, and in their worst incarnations, brutalize their most imaginative and independent citizens, all the time claiming otherwise. An understanding of why I could feel warmly toward that first voting experience would go a long way to explaining why in the name of freedom, fairness, and justice we realize less and less of all three; why, even when liberalization efforts break through the political process—for example, the worldwide privatization and decentralization movement of the 1980s—the pendulum also swings back and gradually undermines wealth-creating as well as poverty-reducing reforms.

The answer, I think, based in ongoing behavioral research with my colleagues, is found in an inherent tension between the individual's experience in social exchange and the requirements of freedom in the external order of impersonal exchange through markets. As I have written in my research, you can make the case that the collectivist individual impulse is nourished by the human perceptions and understanding that comes experientially from what the economic historian and Nobel laureate Doug North calls "personal exchange." Personal exchange is what was prominent on the farm, and takes the form of trading favors and barter in close-knit communities based on trust, trustworthiness, and reputations for being a reliable social exchanger. In this more intimate environment, our individual experience is that good comes from reciprocity—doing good and receiving good in return—being cooperative, and a good neighbor. At the level of the family, extended family, and our social groupings, our direct experience is that you produce good by intentional acts of doing good.

In impersonal market exchange through prices, we do not see that it involves the same reciprocal benefits for buyer and seller that characterize personal exchange. Neither do we see that specialization—or task subdivision—derives from and is supported by markets. We do not experience the fact that

*millions of people, with differing cultures, languages, skills, and resources,
cooperate through long networks of interdependence connected by prices. If
the price of gasoline increases, we see that the oil companies get more money
and we get less, and that is not "fair." What we do not see is that some remote
disruption of a source of supply has caused the price increase, and that this
sets in motion an adjustment process providing incentives for supplies going
elsewhere to be rediverted to us—or one of dozens of other causes and effects.*

*Consequently, we readily come to believe that markets perform badly,
and by better planning and intervention we can make them work better—
for us—but such a myopic policy has unintended consequences, making us
worse off, and these consequences are invisible to our experience. Emotionally, we easily and warmly relate to programs of redistribution and control
in political economy that can unintentionally do far more harm than good.
Any human good that is claimed will flow from some interventionist scheme
seems to ring true, but the creeping and accumulating harm it causes in limiting the growth of wealth and welfare is not plainly visible to our experience.*

In 1940, my father lost his job permanently when the independent
entrepreneur owner of Bridgeport, A. A. Bushaw, closed his factory rather
than cede control of his oil field equipment factory to President Franklin
Roosevelt's defense industry production. (Bushaw's Bridgeport plant was
taken over by another company and of course used for defense, then
war production; markets are not sympathetic to waste, unless someone
is willing to pay for their preferences.) My father changed employment
to the Coleman Lantern Company for less than a year. Then on October
24, 1940, he hired on at Stearman Aircraft, on the east side of town; it
had been purchased by Boeing in 1938, the year that Hitler marched
into Poland. I remember the larger-than-normal headlines in the *Wichita
Beacon* proclaiming Hitler's unopposed invasion.

Sixty-six years later Boeing has come full circle. As of April 2004, the
company is looking for a buyer of its Kansas and Oklahoma production
facilities.

After my stellar first-grade academic achievements, I continued to
perform well in the city elementary schools. My school performance,
however, deteriorated beginning in the eighth grade and all through high
school. I found high school very uninspiring—"girls," as they were known
as in them there days, were far and away more interesting—but I always
expected to go to college. My inspiration was just temporarily diverted,
as is common with teenagers. I vividly recall that my mother helped me
with my English homework when we were learning to diagram sentences
in the tenth grade. I also recall her complaints about the deterioration

in the quality of the public schools, circa 1941–1942. She had learned to diagram sentences in the eighth grade. It was not evident to me why one should learn it in any grade, but what did I know? I never got the point of diagramming, nor did I ever understand what language was all about, until fifty-odd years later I had the great pleasure of reading Steve Pinker's *The Language Instinct* (1994).

College Years: From Friends U to Harvard U

Great teachers are valuable not only for what they teach but more so for the pattern they put on one's life.
—Personal letter from Dr. Arthur E. Hertzler, 1945

A small, very serious Quaker college, Friends University, was located near my home in West Wichita. I enrolled in physics, chemistry, calculus, astronomy, and literature courses for one year, earned top grades, and at eighteen sat for the entrance exams for Caltech in spring 1945.

My attitude at Friends University was 180 degrees opposite to what I had nurtured in high school. I was a very serious and highly motivated student. I knew what I wanted. I was there to make up for my high school shortcomings and to enter Caltech.

Returning to my preparations for entering Caltech, there was only one hurdle: the entrance exam embracing physics, chemistry, and mathematics. This exam was a unique creation of the Caltech faculty, and the entry decision was famously dependent on how well you performed on that examination and not on prior grades. The exam consisted of problems: How fast is a snowball thrown against a wall if the snowball melts on impact? Let's see now, if the mass of the snowball is m, and its velocity, v, then its kinetic energy is $(1/2)mv^2$. Since it takes C (was it 528?) calories of heat energy to convert each gram of snowball (ice) into water, you had only to equate the meltdown energy with the kinetic energy and solve for v with suitable account taken of the units of measurement. The exam went to the heart of basic principles, and although a working knowledge of mathematics was essential, it required no special mathematical virtuosity.

I passed, took the Santa Fe's California Limited (the Chief and Super Chief were out of our ticket class) passenger train west out of Newton through La Junta, Colorado; Tucumcari, Clovis, Gallop, and Albuquerque, New Mexico; Winslow, Flagstaff, and Kingman, Arizona; then Barstow, California, arriving in Los Angeles in September 1945. It was "all the way, on the Santa Fe" as the concessionaire would announce in each car as he went through with peanuts, gum, candy, pop, and cigarettes. This route would become familiar in the next four years, whether I was traveling by train or driving on the parallel famous Route 66. Forty-six years later, curious about the bar in Wellington, New Zealand, named Route 66, I walked in, and asked the small coterie of customers and service persons clustered in the rear, "Anyone here who knows where Route 66 is?" The friendly reply, "Where is it, Yank?"

Caltech was a meat grinder like I could never have imagined. The first thing to which one has to adapt is the fact that no matter how high people might sample in the right tail of the distribution of intelligence or whatever it is that measures college performance, that sample is still normally distributed in performing on the materials in the Caltech curriculum. The second thing you learn, if you were reared with my naive background, is the incredible arrogance that develops in conjunction with the acquisition of what you ultimately come to realize is a really very, very small bit of knowledge compared with our vast human ignorance. My new awareness was captured years later in the story I heard about the difference between Harvard and Caltech: "at Harvard they believe they are the best in the world; at Caltech they know they are the best in the world."

I studied night, day, and weekends, and survived hundreds of problems, but what a joy it was to take freshman chemistry from the inspiring Linus Pauling, who would be given standing ovations occasionally at the end of class (Bohnenblust, the differential geometer who we called "Bony," would also receive such ovations in freshman calculus); hear physics lectures by J. Robert Oppenheimer on his frequent visits to Caltech; attend a visiting lecture by Bertrand Russell; and regularly see von Karman, Anderson, Zwicky, Tolman, Millikan, and other legendary figures of that time on campus. I discovered that one kind of great teacher is the kind that simply thinks out loud, in commonsensical terms of basic principles, and you easily can read his thought processes.

I was majoring in physics, but switched to electrical engineering (EE), which was then in the same division (of mathematics, physics, and electrical engineering), as a senior. In this way, I did not have to take the dreaded "Smyth's course." It was rumored that Carl Anderson, awarded the Nobel Prize in Physics for discovering the positron, had flunked Smyth's course. The course was required for physics majors but not EE majors, so I received my B.S. (in EE) on schedule in 1949, unmoved by those for whom it was a big ego trip to take Smyth and pass it. But it was Anderson whose contribution people came to know, not the egocentric smart alecks. I'm sure glad I learned that lesson early enough to save my soul in the here and now, and therefore in the future.

I relished the unbending rigor of mathematics, physics, and engineering, but then, as a senior, I took an economics course and found it very intriguing—you could actually learn something about the economic principles underlying the claims of socialism, capitalism, and other such "isms." I knew little, but I was intrigued. Curious about professional economics, I went to the Caltech library, stumbled on Paul Samuelson's *Foundations of Economic Analysis* and, later that year, Ludwig von Mises's *Human Action*. From the former, it was clear that economics could be done like physics, but from the latter there seemed to be much in the way of reasoning that was not like physics. I also subscribed to the *Quarterly Journal of Economics*, and one of the first issues had a paper by Hollis Chenery on engineering production functions. So economics was also like engineering. I had not a hint then as to how much those first impressions would be changed in my thinking over the decades to follow. But in 1962, my book *Investment and Production* would have a chapter on engineering production functions. Later, since I taught it as part of the graduate theory course at Purdue, the graduate students would call it "enginomics."

From Caltech I returned to Kansas, took an M.A. in economics, then went to Harvard for a Ph.D., and on to Purdue and a career in the study of markets. I was not a likely person to develop a career in the study of markets. I had to overcome two severe handicaps: my mother was a socialist, and I had a Harvard education.

In closing I have learned a few maxims along the way that I like to share with students when possible. Here are three:

First, it's not what you know that counts; it's what you can do with what you know. Education, science, and the performance of the economy are all about the utilization of knowledge.

Second, by far the most important thing to learn is to learn how to learn.

Third, if you are not learning, then you are not teaching.

Notes

1. This essay is based on an edited excerpt from *Discovery: A Memoir* (Bloomington, IN: AuthorHouse, 2008).

2. Quoted in Alan Lomax, *The Folks Songs of North America* (New York: Doubleday, 1960), 554. Reported by Sim Webb, fireman for Casey Jones—crack passenger engineer at age twenty-six for the Cannonball Express—on the spectacular wreck of the Cannonball on April 30, 1906. The great Negro ("black" today) folk poet and roundhouse worker Wallace Saunders began composing the ballad of Casey Jones as he wiped Casey's blood off No. 382.

Vernon L. Smith

Awarded Nobel Prize in 2002. Lecture presented April 14, 2004.

Date of Birth

January 1, 1927

Academic Degrees

B.S., Caltech, 1949
M.A., University of Kansas, 1952
Ph.D., Harvard University, 1955

Academic Affiliations

Assistant Professor, Krannert School of Management, Purdue University, 1955–58
Associate Professor, Krannert School of Management, Purdue University, 1958–61
Professor, Krannert Outstanding Professorship, Purdue University, 1961–67
Professor, Brown University, 1967–68
Professor, University of Massachusetts, 1968–75
Professor, University of Arizona, 1975–98
Regents' Professor of Economics, University of Arizona, 1998–2001
Professor of Economics and Law, George Mason University, 2001–08
Visiting Rasmuson Chair in Economics, University of Alaska, 2003–present
Professor of Economics and Law and George L. Argyros Chair in Finance and Economics, Economic Science Institute, Chapman University, 2008–present.

Selected Books

Economics: An Analytical Approach, 1958, 1962 (with R. Davidson and J. Wiley)
Investment and Production: A Study in the Theory of a Capital-Using Enterprise, 1961
Economics of Natural and Environmental Resources, 1977 (ed.)
Research in Experimental Economics, Vols. 1–3, 1979, 1982, 1985 (ed.)
Experimental Economics, 1990 (ed.)
Papers in Experimental Economics (collected works), 1991
Experiments in Decision, Organization, and Exchange, 1993
(ed. with R. Day)

Bargaining and Market Behavior: Essays in Experimental Economics (collected works), 2000
Law and Economics of Irrational Behavior, 2005 (ed. with F. Parisi)
Discovery: A Memoir, 2008
Handbook of Experimental Economics Results, Vol. 1, 2008
(ed. with C. Plott)
Rationality in Economics: Constructivist and Ecological Forms, 2008
Rethinking Housing Bubbles: The Role of Household and Bank Balance Sheets in Modeling Economic Cycles, 2014 (with S. Gerstad)

Clive W. J. Granger

Overview

I am not sure that I ever did become an economist. I started as a statistician and have ended as a time series econometrician. I have picked up some economics on the way, and the field of econometrics has itself evolved to be closer to my interests as I have moved closer to the core of econometrics.

Thus there are two components to my intellectual journey, from being a statistician to being something of an economist, and within econometrics, from being purely a time series econometrician to having greater appreciation for other components of the field of econometrics.

I started as the first undergraduate student in a joint degree in mathematics and economics at the University of Nottingham in England. It was also the first degree of its kind in the country. The first year of study for the degree consisted of two-thirds mathematics and one-third economics—the economics being equal parts of macroeconomics, microeconomics, and statistics. The microeconomics course used the well-known textbook by James Henderson and Richard Quandt, which I found to be excellent. The macroeconomics course used a book by the teacher, Brian Tew, which was fine, but used no mathematics. The statistics course considered

some basic concepts, but concentrated on data availability and definitions, such as the national accounts, which has proved to be very useful
to me in later years.

At the end of the first year, I became a full-time student in the mathematics department. My two first-year undergraduate economics courses
were the only formal training that I have ever received in economics, and
all that I needed apparently. I have lived among economists all during my
career, and picked up some knowledge by osmosis, through reading, and
by attending seminars.

As an aside, after winning the Nobel Prize, I returned to the University
of Nottingham to give a lecture. I told the students that the only economics required to win the prize were the first-year courses at Nottingham,
which were really good; the students were delighted, but the faculty was
less than pleased.

Because of the rapid expansion of British universities, I quickly
obtained a teaching position at Nottingham. Very early in my career as a
faculty member I learned an important lesson about applied economics
and theory. I had done a small empirical study on a subject that I can
no longer remember. A critical coefficient had come out clearly negative,
and I showed the result to my professor, Brian Tew, and asked for his
reaction. He said that he was not surprised and produced a piece of economic theory to support his statement. That evening I discovered that I
had made a substantial mistake in the calculations, and when corrected,
the coefficient of interest now became positive. I showed it to Brian, and
again he said that he was not surprised and produced a new piece of
theory to support that viewpoint. What did I learn from the situation?
Economic theory can be very flexible and can be used to support almost
any empirical finding, and that empirical results can be changed by incor-
rect analysis.

For my Ph.D. subject, I chose to work in the area of time series analysis as I thought it would be relevant for economics as much important
economic data takes this form.

My next main dose of economics was obtained at Princeton, which I
attended on a Harkness Fellowship as a postdoctoral student. I was at
the Econometric Research Project headed by Oskar Morgenstern. The
majority of the group worked on game theory, and just a few of us on
time series. One exciting period occurred in 1960, when Morgenstern
was asked by President Eisenhower to very quickly produce a report on
"bargaining." The president had agreed to meet with the Russian premier
for a debate, but he decided that he did not know how to bargain. All

game theorists at Princeton and many others in the project dropped all work for a couple of weeks to consider the topic. We did find a few relevant ideas, but then the U-2 spy plane incident occurred, so the U.S.-Russian meeting was canceled. At least I discovered that economics could potentially be both very important and exciting when coupled with politics, but that eventually the political aspects of a situation would dominate.

An area of application of the new time series techniques that we developed at that time was to stock market prices; this was at the start of the period when the random walk model was being tested. This model states that a return cannot be forecast from previous returns. It soon became clear that the model held true for most time periods and markets. Later, the "Efficient Market Theory" gave a theoretical basis for these empirical results. This indicates that the process toward discovery need not start with a theory, although certainly could do so. This work eventually produced two of my applied books, one with Morgenstern on stock prices, and another with Walt Labys on commodity prices, plus my first theory book, with an excellent Japanese econometrician, Michio Hatanaka, on spectral analysis.[1]

Throughout my career I have usually worked with others. I find that the interaction and discussion is stimulating. I think that I have accumulated about eighty-five co-authors by now.

Forecasting

Of all the topics that I have been involved with throughout my career, I suppose the area that has changed the most is economic forecasting—and it is still evolving. Throughout econometrics, the methods developed and used are constrained by the properties of the available data: their form, quantity, and quality. For forecasting you need an information set available today that can be used to project into the future. As a starting point, this information will include the past and previous values of the series being forecast (say, the unemployment rate), together with past and present values of other relevant series (say, consumption and inflation). As time has passed, we have had available more series of a longer duration, although the quality of the data, at the macro level at least, may not be getting better. We have also learned to search for more plausible features of the data, not only trends and seasonal surveys, but also time-changing or nonlinear effects, plus features such as long memory and breaks. All lead to more sophisticated models and, sometimes, improved forecasts.

One area where we have clearly improved is in knowing how to evaluate our forecasts, how to decide if one method of forecasting is better than another, or whether some combination of the two may be better than both, as is usually the case.

Many of these developments are possible because of the enormous increase in computing power—both in speed and memory size—that has occurred during my career. I started with electric calculators and then moved to the IBM 650, which had a thousand slots to store the program statements and the data set—one number to a slot. As computing has gotten faster and cheaper, I think that we have gotten further from our data, and are less aware of its properties and subtleties.

We can also attempt to forecast more things, very high-frequency data, such as each trade on the stock market, or over longer horizons, perhaps up to a quarter century ahead, and breaks or sudden changes in the economy, such as a financial crisis. These are all very difficult, and we do not forecast them very well, but are improving, and by trying we are learning something about how we can approach such problems. We are also forecasting things that are difficult to quantify, such as risk, which has become a major subject area.

Over the years, techniques and appreciation of the problem has certainly improved, and some forecasts are clearly better, but many important economic series remain very difficult to forecast. As an example of a success, a group of us at San Diego, including two future Nobel Prize winners, were asked to model short-term electricity demand in a particular U.S. city. At 9:00 a.m. on one day—say, Tuesday—we had to forecast electricity demand for each hour, from 1:00 a.m. until midnight for the next day, Wednesday. We used twenty-four simple models involving the previous day's electricity consumption, the weather forecast, and known daily patterns of consumption from earlier years, plus previous temperatures. The forecasts won a competition against methods based on more complicated techniques, including neural networks and state-space models. The lessons were several: a simple methodology should always be tried (and may well be difficult to beat); and economists *can* forecast, and in ways that are certainly useful to an important industry. It is worth noting that over the four months of the project, electricity prices and the efficiency of electric appliances do not change appreciably, so they did not need to be considered in the model. A forecast based on a simple economic theory would concentrate on price and appliance efficiency changes.

Time Series Theory

Interspersed with the applied projects, I have also been involved in a long-term program that attempts to develop parts of time series analysis and econometrics. In my early years as a researcher I observed that econometrics did not emphasize the temporal aspects of economics, possibly because the time series data available were rather short and thus difficult to analyze. Slowly it was realized that time series methods were important, particularly in macroeconomics and finance, and coverage of them started to appear in the major textbooks. From data analysis it also became clear that economic time series did not obey the standard assumption that they were stationary. Many series needed to be differenced to make them stationary. This made them "unit root processes." This observation implied that many standard statistical procedures, such as regressions, could not be used without interpretational problems. New procedures and models had to be devised, and widely applied, and economic interpretations had to be found.

The Growth of Time Series Econometrics

While I was involved in the theoretical econometric developments and a variety of applications, my knowledge of economics certainly widened and possibly deepened. Simultaneously, I moved from being interested only in time series econometrics to gaining an appreciation for other parts of econometrics, including cross-sectional models, the classical large-scale macro models that emphasized simultaneous relationships between many variables and the later developing panel models. Each area deals differently with the dynamics of the economy, but cross-sectional analysis largely ignores it. The very early econometric models had little dynamics, and mostly in their error terms to ensure that coefficient estimates have satisfactory properties. Panel models would prefer to have sophisticated dynamics, but traditionally had available only short time series and so could not explore this possibility very extensively.

Attitudes toward dynamics thus depended on the original training of the group of researchers, the type of question asked, and data availability. Macroeconomists were often interested in questions about equilibria; such questions were of little interest to time series economists under the original standard assumption of stationarity, but gained much more interest when it was found that variables were I(1) and co-integrated.

When I first came to teach in the United States in 1974, there were few time series econometricians in major economics departments. In the intervening years, the subject matter of econometrics has drifted closer to my interests, so it has not been necessary for me to learn a lot about other areas to stay fairly central. As I have become more interested in methodology, however, particularly the areas of model building and evaluation, one needs to be aware of the major strengths and weaknesses of the various available approaches. I have found that thinking about evaluation to be very helpful in my growth as an econometrician and, hopefully, an economist.[2]

Causality

Throughout my career I have been involved with the important concept of causality in economics, although to varying degrees at different times. I entered the arena naively needing a definition in connection with an interpretation of a technical concept known as the cross-spectrum. I was directed to a paper written by a very eminent mathematician, Norbert Weiner. There I found the definition that I later expanded and proposed in chapter 7 of *Spectral Analysis of Economic Time Series*.[3] The definition is rather simple in terms of three variables: X_t, Y_t, and Z_t (the last may be a vector). If one is interested in the question "Does Y cause X?" then consider only Y_t and X_{t+1}, so that the "cause" Y_t occurs before the "effect" X_{t+1} (the length of the lead is not important for the definition as long as it is positive) and provided if we try to explain X_{t+1} from Z_t then we do better explaining X_{t+1} with Z_t *and* Y_t. Thus, Y_t contains relevant information about X_{t+1} not contained in Z_t.

Initially the definition was slow to be accepted, but later the application by Christopher Sims produced a great deal of discussion.[4] Soon, many alternative tests became available and applications appeared, although most writers did not quite accept the definition of causality, saying that the definition used was not "real causality but only Granger causality," even though no one would define "real causality" for me. The definition I provided was pragmatic and easy to implement, but the insistence that it be associated with my name made me famous and many editors annoyed. Occasionally alternative phrases were considered, such as "exogeneity" or "feedback free," but they never caught on. I have since become involved in fairly heated debates about what is causality, and there are now various alternative definitions available to applied economists. But I let demand for the product determine its current worth and continue to maintain a belief that whatever the final definition that we all agree on might be, it will contain my own as a component.

Space and Time

One's knowledge develops over time but also over space. I always found one of the big advantages of being an academic—with long summer breaks, the occasional sabbatical leave, and the opportunity to attend conferences in attractive places—was that I could visit many countries, sometimes with the family. In total I have visited over thirty countries, some just for a day or two, but many for at least a month, so that one can get a feel for the pace of life, the standard of living, and what are the economic topics of critical importance to that economy. Although standard economic theory should hold the same everywhere, some basic attitudes do vary across societies, such as toward being unemployed, and of course the major institutions in the economies can differ in significant ways. Not all economies are the same, and we learn a lot by discussing the differences.

To an applied econometrician, a major difference has been in the data: its availability and quality. When doing cross-country studies, it is often surprising to find that even simple values like an interest rate or a stock price index were not available until the mid-twentieth century (or later) as the country's banking system and stock market had to be set up.

What I have appreciated from my travels is that the standard measure of the economic quality of life, GDP or GDP per capita, is not really an appropriate measure of economic "well-being" that is applicable every-where. Some societies do not emphasize wealth or consumption as the ultimate objective. Having stated that, it is unclear how to find a suitable, easily collectible measure that is widely accepted. I realize that there is a lot of research ongoing in this important area, and hopefully a useful conclusion can be achieved. Finding a new measure of well-being may require a complete re-structuring of the national accounts to emphasize the increasing importance of service industries.

Conclusion

I find economics to be a deep and challenging area, continually chang-ing and developing new important problems. I think that econometrics, including time series econometrics, will play a central role in future devel-opments, both in practical relevance and methodology. In recent years I have been the president of the Western Economic Association, elected distinguished fellow of the American Economic Association, and now been awarded the Nobel Prize in Economics. I should now feel accepted as an economist, but I do not believe that I think like an economist. I suspect that it may be good for the discipline of economics to contain some workers with different backgrounds; diversification is probably always a good idea. In fact, Paul Samuelson proved just that.[5]

Apparently, there is a belief about the winners of the Nobel Prize in Literature that after they win the prize, they never write anything worthwhile. I am sure that this is not true for literature and am convinced that it is certainly not true for economists. Having now won the prize, I get the opportunity of meeting other winners, and they are usually very occupied with important studies and projects. One does get many opportunities to lecture and write on a variety of topics; my present list includes "The Economics of Peace," "The Philosophy of Forecasting," "Global Econometric Models as a Research Tool," "The Future of Forecasting," and "The Evaluation of Economic Models."

Notes

1. Clive W. J. Granger and Oskar Morgenstern, *Predictability of Stock Market Prices* (Lexington, MA: Heath Lexington Books, 1970); Walter C. Labys and Clive W. J. Granger, *Speculation, Hedging, and Commodity Price Forecasts* (Lexington, MA: Heath Lexington Books, 1970); Clive W. J. Granger and Michio Hatanaka, *Spectral Analysis of Economic Time Series* (Princeton, NJ: Princeton University Press, 1964).

2. Some remarks of mine in this area can be found in Clive W. J. Granger, "Evaluation of Theories and Models," in *Econometrics and the Philosophy of Economics*, ed. Bernt P. Stigum (Princeton, NJ: Princeton University Press, 2003), 480–498; Clive W. J. Granger, *Empirical Modeling in Economics* (Cambridge: Cambridge University Press, 1999).

3. Granger and Hatanaka, *Spectral Analysis of Economic Time Series*.

4. Christopher A. Sims, "Money, Income, and Causality," *American Economic Review* 62 (September 1972): 540–552.

5. Paul A. Samuelson, "General Proof That Diversification Pays," *Journal of Financial and Quantitative Analysis* 2 (March 1967): 1–13.

Clive W. J. Granger

Awarded Nobel Prize in 2003. Lecture presented February 16, 2005.

Dates of Birth and Death

September 4, 1934; May 27, 2009

Academic Degrees

B.A., University of Nottingham, 1955
Ph.D., Statistics, University of Nottingham, 1959

Academic Affiliations

Assistant Lecturer, Mathematics, University of Nottingham, 1955–1957
Lecturer, Economics, University of Nottingham, 1958–1963
Visiting Professor, Economics, Princeton University, 1959–1960 Visiting Professor, Economics, Stanford University, 1963
Reader, Mathematics, University of Nottingham, 1964–1965
Professor, Applied Statistics and Econometrics, University of Nottingham, 1965–1974
Professor, Economics, University of California at San Diego, 1974–2003
Visiting Professor, Economics, Australian National University, 1977
Visiting Fellow, Economics, All Souls College, University of Oxford, 1994
Visiting Fellow, Economics, Trinity College, University of Cambridge, 1996
Professor Emeritus and Research Professor, University of California at San Diego, 2003–2009

Selected Books

Spectral Analysis of Economic Time Series, 1964 (with M. Hatanaka) *Predictability of Stock Market Prices*, 1970 (with O. Morgenstern) *Forecasting Economic Time Series*, 1977, 1986 (with P. Newbold) *Forecasting in Business and Economics*, 1980, 1989
Modelling Economic Series: Readings in Econometric Methodology, 1990
Long-Run Economic Relationships: Readings in Cointegration, 1991 (ed. with R. Engle)
Modelling Nonlinear Dynamic Relationships, 1993 (with T. Teräsvirta)
Essays in Econometrics: Collected Papers of Clive W. J. Granger, 2001 (ed. E. Ghysels, N. Swanson, and M. Watson)

Edward C. Prescott

But do let me say something: Thanks so much for being a great adviser. You have always made economics exciting, exciting, exciting. And whatever strange little ideas I've had, whatever direction my research has gone, you have always been incredibly supportive (while at the same time challenging my ideas to improve them).
—James Schmitz, congratulatory message, October 11, 2004

The Joy of Being a Teacher-Researcher

I was asked to lecture on my development as an economist, and this is what I will do. Before doing this, however, I will introspect a little on the related question of why I turned out to be successful as a teacher-researcher. I hyphenate teacher and researcher because in my case these two activities are joint activities, and cannot be separated. I love the enthusiasm of former students for economic research and teaching, as shown in the above quotation. In this essay, I will be discussing several collaborations with past teachers and students. I have a great debt to my students, from whom I have learned so much, and I think they have learned from me. There are many students whose dissertation I signed or played a major role in thesis supervision. I dedicate this essay to these special people.

Virtually all my research is joint research, and when I say "joint," I mean with one other equal collaborator. Both collaborators contribute to all phases of the research, and both are senior authors on the resulting paper or papers. These collaborations typically originate in discussions that give rise to an economic problem that warrants analysis. My style is to get things done in the morning and wander the halls talking to people in the afternoon. In these talks a good research problem sometimes arises. Even when it doesn't, I often learn something that enhances my stock of useful economic knowledge. I emphasize that discovery of a problem is a joint activity, and assigning credit for discovering a good research problem is impossible.

A little about my personality, which is related to why I gravitated to economics, is as follows. Throughout my life I liked figuring out puzzles, and making complex things simple and orderly. I get joy out of understanding why something is true, and I am not content to just know that it is true. As an example, I played a fair amount of bridge in high school. I remember when my partner, Joseph Dodge, stated the principle of restricted choice for finessing. I just had to either disprove the principle or understand why it was true. In the process of figuring out why the principle is true, I rediscovered Bayes's theorem for the case where the probabilities are rational numbers, as they are in bridge. Understanding the theory underlying the principle of restricted choice put my mind at ease.

Another feature of my personality is that I am a skeptic; I have to be convinced. I remember many arguments with my father, who was also a skeptic. This personality trait has served me well, because often what is generally accepted economic knowledge should not be. When working on a problem with someone, I have intense concentration, and solving the problem becomes important to me. In these joint efforts, it does not matter who has the insight that leads to the solution to each of the many subproblems that come up along the way to solving the problem. What matters is that the problem gets solved.

I am a bit of a dreamer, and in high school I wanted to be a rocket scientist. It was the Sputnik era, so the fact that I dreamed of being a rocket scientist is not surprising. This dream led me to major in physics my first three years at Swarthmore College, a small liberal arts college eleven miles southwest of Philadelphia. A number of lucky events led me to becoming an economist. One stroke of luck occurred in my junior year at Swarthmore. That year I had two all-day honors laboratories—one in physical chemistry, and one, I believe, in electricity and magnetism. I did not like the all-day laboratories, and this led me to drop out of the physics honors program and major in mathematics. Another lucky event was that I took a course in the engineering department in my senior year. The course was taught by an enthusiastic, supportive professor named Sam Carpenter. This course influenced me to go to graduate school in operations research—a discipline that brought mathematical modeling into management. This was then a new and exciting field. I attended Case Institute of Technology for graduate studies.

At Case I learned recursive methods, which proved so useful when made applicable to economics. On a methodology note, a statement made by Russell L. Ackoff, then the head of the operations program at Case and one of the fathers of operations research, sticks in my head to this day and continues to influence my approach to research. He said that there is no theory without measurement, and no measurement without theory. He went on to say that a science progresses through the back-and-forth between theory and measurement.

I was lucky that experimental physics was not to my liking and that I took the engineering course that led me to Case, where I learned a set of tools that proved to be invaluable in helping to make macroeconomics part of economics. At Case I decided to go on for a Ph.D., and my choice set was Case and the Graduate School of Industrial Administration (GSIA) at the Carnegie Institute of Technology. The program at GSIA was multidisciplinary, not interdisciplinary. My program was economics, statistics, and industrial administration. The latter field included accounting, finance, and marketing, which in large part are subfields of economics. I am not sure why I chose GSIA, but I was lucky I did. Otherwise, I would not have become an economist.

My Development as an Economist as a Student at GSIA

Michael Christopher Lovell, Teacher and Collaborator
When I arrived at GSIA, the dean was Dick Cyert. He had the policy of matching, in an informal way, an incoming Ph.D. student with a faculty member. I was matched with Mike Lovell, another stroke of luck. Mike helped me so much to gain confidence in my ability to do research. We wrote two joint papers, one in the old business cycles tradition of Samuelson's multiplier-accelerator model, but with money. The primary contribution of the paper was to make a point in a debate that was then ongoing in macroeconomics. But we innovated methodologically in that paper in assuming rational expectations for the targeted capital stock,

which was an argument of the investment equation in the model we developed and used. We determined the operating characteristics of the model for various monetary and fiscal policy rules. This model was not a dynamic general equilibrium model and therefore not in the tradition of what has become macroeconomics (or for that matter, what virtually all of aggregate economics has become).

The other paper was a statistics paper in which we analyzed least squares estimators with linear inequality constraints. It turns out that proving the obvious—the constrained estimator is better than the unconstrained estimator—was very difficult. Indeed, in the process of trying, we proved that the obvious was not true in general by coming up with a counterexample. We did prove that under weak conditions, the restricted least squares estimator was better than the unconstrained estimator. We conjectured but did not prove that the result holds under more general conditions. I must admit that not being able to prove the conjecture has bothered me for over forty years. Sometimes when I'm on an airplane and I have some time to waste, I come back to this problem. This says something about my personality, I guess.

The skills I learned from Mike Lovell have contributed to my success as a teacher, and I owe a big debt to him for what I learned. Unlike factors determined by the genes, the skill in helping students develop into teacher-researchers has been transmitted to my students and to students of their students. Key is helping students to believe in themselves and be honest with themselves.

An important event in my development as an economist was meeting Janet (Jan) Simpson in Pittsburgh in 1964. She became my wife a year later. She has always had a nonconformist streak and did not expect me to make much money. She was more interested in having a family and a career than in having high consumption levels. She raised three children, got a Ph.D. in industrial psychology after the children were all in school, and then had a successful career working for an industrial psychology consulting firm.

I was lucky that she is adventuresome. In 1974, I obtained support from the Guggenheim Foundation and the National Science Foundation for a year's leave. I was advised to take this opportunity to visit MIT, which was a very attractive possibility, but at Jan's urging decided to visit the Norwegian School of Business and Economics (NHH), where Finn Kydland was then a faculty member. Going with three young children aged seven, five, and one to a city with no English-speaking school was quite an adventure. Nobody in the family spoke Norwegian when we arrived, although by the time we left my oldest son was fluent, my daughter understood it but wouldn't speak it, and my wife could communicate a little.

It was a crazy career decision, but that year at the NHH working with Finn proved to be a productive one. Finn and I wrote our paper "Rules Rather Than Discretion and the Time Inconsistency of Optimal Plans," one of the two papers for which we were awarded our Nobel Prize. I guess being away from the mainstream has some advantages. We were relatively free to think differently and go our own way. It turned out that visiting Norway was not a career sacrifice as I, and my colleagues, thought would be the case.

Robert E. Lucas, Jr., Teacher and Collaborator

Robert (Bob) E. Lucas, Jr., and I arrived at GSIA in fall 1963, he as a new assistant professor and I as a Ph.D. student. I was fortunate to take two of Bob's courses at GSIA. The first was econometrics, where I learned some of the principles of using the statistics discipline to draw scientific inference in economics. The second was a capital theory course, where I learned some invaluable economic theory. Many of the things he said with respect to methodology I learned to appreciate only later.

There were many methodological discussions at GSIA. Herbert Simon, who was awarded a Nobel Prize in 1977, would argue that firms face mathematical problems that are unsolvable and therefore the assumption of profit maximization in economics should be abandoned. Herb was right about firms facing combinatorial problems that are unsolvable. Bob accepted this fact, and went on to argue that the way to proceed is to treat firms *as if* they maximized and, for that matter, to treat all decision-makers in economic models *as if* they consistently maximized. This led to the then-radical view that assuming maximizing behavior is the way to proceed even when agents are faced with dynamic problems and there is uncertainty. I learned from Bob that we have to build our economic intuition from the study of model economies that we can analyze.

The history of our collaboration is as follows. Edmund (Ned) Phelps, who was at the University of Pennsylvania when I was, identified a number of papers concerned with laying the micro (which now means neoclassical) foundations for macroeconomics and put together the book *Microeconomic Foundations of Employment and Inflation Theory*. Ned brought the authors of these papers to a meeting at Penn, where the authors presented their papers and were subject to the constructive criticism of the other contributors.

I was not an author and so did not participate, but I did go to the reception after their long day. At that reception, I talked with Bob Lucas about an interesting problem. We thought that we could solve it, and we decided to submit our idea to the North American Summer Meeting of the Econometric Society. Submission meant writing up and sending in an abstract for a paper. The paper was accepted for presentation. The problem turned out not to be straightforward, and as a fallback Bob proposed extending his 1967 "Theory of Supply" paper to uncertain environments in order to develop an investment equation. The paper did much more than extend his paper to uncertain environments. The concept of recursive competitive equilibrium, a tool needed to apply the dynamic economic theory to modeling aggregate phenomena, is developed there. Equilibria are Markov processes with stationary transition probabilities, and the behavior of model time series can be compared with the behavior of the time series of the economy being studied.

With this collaboration, I understood the comment he made after I defended my dissertation. He was telling me to use dynamic economic theory to model aggregate phenomena. I became a Bob Lucas student and an economist. To return to the theme of this lecture, Bob Lucas is the most important person in my development as an economist. Having been at the right place at the right time was another stroke of luck.

The principle guiding my research is the importance of theory interacting with measurement. I came to the conclusion that there was no hope for the approach being used in macroeconomics of empirically searching for the policy-invariant laws of motion of the economy. I had read the Lucas critique. Something else was needed. Given this, I stopped teaching what was then called macroeconomics and began using dynamic equilibrium models to study aggregate economics as practiced by Bob Lucas.

I disagreed with Bob on one point: the importance of the national accounts, behind which there is a lot of theory. These accounts are based on a recursive capital theoretic framework for technology, which is the framework used in capital theory, which in turn is the theoretical framework used in aggregate economics. I made the big switch from organizing empirical knowledge around equations to organizing empirical knowledge around preferences and technology, or in layman's terms, around the ability and willingness of people to substitute. Supply and demand in general equilibrium theory have no empirical counterparts, and are used only to establish the existence of equilibrium. I love the title of Tom Sargent's paper "Beyond Supply and Demand." Tom was my valued colleague for one year at Penn and five years at the University of Minnesota.

My Development as an Economist at the University of Pennsylvania

My first academic position was at Penn, where I began my shift from statistician to economist. A group of exceptional young economists there contributed to my transformation. I also interacted with a number of talented students there. One of those students, in particular, influenced my development as an economist.

Thomas F. Cooley

The one student at Penn with whom I subsequently collaborated is Tom Cooley. We became friends, and over a beer would talk about some of the practices and problems of economic forecasting. We subsequently wrote a series of papers in which we built on the ideas that arose in our discussions.

My Years at GSIA as a Carnegie Mellon Faculty

Finn Kydland

After returning to GSIA in fall 1971 as a faculty member, I met Finn Kydland, a truly great stroke of luck. He had completed his qualifying examinations and was writing a dissertation. He was not in the best of positions because his mentor, Sten Thore, with whom he had come to GSIA, had gone back to Norway. Both Finn and I were out of the operations research tradition. We knew recursive methods and could use the computer to solve maximization problems. I gave Finn feedback on the third essay of his dissertation dealing with a dominant firm problem. I remember so distinctly when he made a claim to which I said, "That can't be right." In the most confident way, Finn said, "I don't make mistakes," and he doesn't. He has to be certain of something before he will make a statement.

The year before he returned in fall 1973 to NHH, we began working on the use of recursive methods to evaluate policy rules. I joined him in Norway a year later. The lifestyle at NHH was then very different from what it is at other academic places I have been. Lunches were tea and a piece of goat cheese on a piece of bread. In the late afternoon, there were only three people in the building: Finn, me, and the woman who waxed the floors. That woman was annoyed by us getting in the way of her doing her job. Everyone else was home working on their house. A common sight in the Bergen area was a cement mixer in the front yard, along with a pile of stones and a half-built stone wall. They called the area along the fjord, just a little way from NHH, Porridge Hill, because most of the disposable income of the people living there was going to making mortgage payments. There was very little left to spend on food, which was very expensive.

The first half of that year at NHH, I did a lot of thinking about economics, but did not get much done. Then it dawned on Finn and me that the fact that the time consistent policy rules we had been computing are not optimal was an important finding. In the spring, we sat down and showed how bad outcomes could be if there is discretion, and best action is chosen in the current situation given the state of the economy. We wrote the first draft of the paper "Rules versus Discretion: The Time Inconsistency of Optimal Plans," an extended version of which appeared in 1977.

This was not the last of our major collaborations. Finn visited GSIA in 1977–78 after visiting Minnesota the previous year. We became more interested in a positive theory of business cycle fluctuations than in a theory of policy. We started interacting theory with observation, but were not that successful in that endeavor because we were beginning modeling at the linear-quadratic economy level.

Academic year 1978–79 was my turn to be on leave. I had presented our not-very-successful paper at Northwestern that year and received some criticism. Back at GSIA for the summer, Finn and I had extended discussions about what to do differently. We decided to investigate if beginning with the neoclassical growth model as the starting point would be more fruitful. We had to extend that model to include the labor-leisure decision, because business cycles were fluctuations largely accounted for by fluctuations in the labor input. Starting out with the extended neoclassical growth model turned out to be incredibly fruitful.

This exploration was carried out in summer 1979 at GSIA. Finn and I worked away with the programming in the basement of GSIA, and developed a new methodology that has proven so useful. We found that if people are highly willing to intertemporally substitute market time or, in more popular jargon, "make hay while the sun shines," and if productivity shocks are persistent and of a certain magnitude, business cycles of the nature observed are a prediction of the extended neoclassical growth model. I used the tools of statistics to estimate the parameters of the process governing the productivity shock. I found that the process was highly persistent and that the shocks were of the magnitude that gave rise to fluctuations of the magnitude observed.

Whether people were as willing in the aggregate to reallocate their work effort over time as needed for the neoclassical growth model to predict business cycles was the open question. Finn and I knew we could get a good fit to the aggregate observation by choosing a high value for the parameter governing this willingness. The needed number was far larger than the one that economists had estimated using panel observations for continuously employed, full-time, prime-age males. A fact for this population was that when compensation per hour worked went up, market hours increased little. This conflict between individual and aggregate behavior was subsequently resolved, and I will come back to this point when I discuss another student with whom I only recently collaborated.

Rajnish Mehra, Student and Subsequent Collaborator

Another student at GSIA with whom I have had subsequent fruitful collaborations is Rajnish Mehra. He is the antithesis of Finn. In each of our three collaborations, he initiated the project and stuck my name on the paper at an early stage. Each of these papers addressed a good problem, but the early papers had flaws and required a sizable effort before we had something worth reporting to the profession.

Our "Equity Premium Puzzle" paper, written in 1979 and appearing in 1985, was important in my development as an economist. There we used theory to determine how much of the historical difference in the average return on the stock market and virtually risk-free short-term debt is a premium for bearing nondiversifiable aggregate risk. Our finding was that nondiversifiable risk accounted for only a small part of the difference in historical average returns.

The reason this paper was important in my development as an economist was that it led me to stop thinking in terms of finding the model to *fit* some data set to simply using theory and measurement to make quantitative statements. Given that the big difference in these average returns was not a premium for bearing aggregate risk, Raj and I concluded that it had to be for something else. Recently, important progress has been made on finding what other features of reality account for most of the difference in average returns.

We had problems getting the paper published and had given up trying. Robert King and Charlie Plosser came into my office at the Minneapolis Federal Reserve Bank and encouraged the submission of the paper to the

Journal of Monetary Economics, which we did. This was another stroke of luck. The paper turned out to foster a considerable body of very interesting research.

My Years at Minnesota

In late fall 1979, to my joy, I received an offer from the University of Minnesota, which was then the best place in macroeconomics and a great match for me, given its abundance of smart, adventuresome students who were well trained in economic theory. I have Tom Sargent to thank for engineering this appointment, along with Walter Heller, who provided some crucial support. This was another stroke of luck.

Stephen Parente

At Minnesota I did not teach macroeconomics. I taught a valuation equilibrium and recursive methods course in the macro theory sequence. I taught the students the language of economic theory, not how to use it. You have to know the vocabulary and grammar of a language before you can use it productively. I also taught an industrial organization course where a variety of economic questions were addressed.

In the 1980s, growth and development returned to center stage in economics. I had read Paul Romer's economic development paper and Bob Lucas's mechanics of economic development paper on endogenizing growth, and wanted to develop some aggregate models with explicit micro foundations. Some students became very interested in this topic and requested that Minnesota again have a field exam in this area. I shifted my teaching to that area to fill a need, as Minnesota had enough good people willing and able to teach industrial organization.

At that time, everyone was emphasizing the importance of the savings rate and the accumulation of factors of production, including not only physical productive assets but also human capital. Stephen Parente, in a highly original dissertation, took another approach that focused on the role of barriers to efficient production. Countries were poor because they were good at setting up barriers to efficient production. He developed a dynamic micro-based general equilibrium model where barriers were key in determining living standards. After he wrote his dissertation, we began to talk about how to modify his model so that it could be quantified in the hopes of replicating the success of the extended neoclassical growth models in the study of business cycles. This turned out to be a ten-year collaboration that resulted in our book *Barriers to Riches*.

More Ambitious Exercise

In our business cycle research, Finn and I focused on the business cycle facts, which were a set of statistical properties of the economic time series. Along with Gary Hansen and Tom Cooley, I addressed the question, Did technology shocks cause the 1990–1991 recession? The answer is yes, but the behavior of these shocks in that period implied a recovery much sooner than occurred. The fact that there is a deviation from theory is evidence that macroeconomics has become a hard science like the natural sciences had become many years before. No longer was macroeconomics an exercise in storytelling with many explanations of every observation. Incidentally, this deviation from theory has been resolved with the inclusion of tax rates, which were increased in the early 1990s, but the importance of taxes for business cycles was only later evaluated and measured.

The Federal Reserve Bank of Minneapolis

Ellen R. McGrattan

Ellen McGrattan and I presented a paper in a bag lunch seminar at the Minneapolis Fed. These seminars get a bit wild. Tim Kehoe attacked the findings by pointing out that our theory predicts that the value of the stock market should have been twice as high as it actually was in the 1960s. Tim's point was well taken. Ellen and I asked each other, What could account for this huge deviation from theory in the 1960s? We spent a week working on the problem. Then Ellen came running into my office with a big grin on her face. She said it was taxes. We, of course, had corporate income taxes and taxes on corporate property in the first version of the neoclassical growth model that we were using. But we had omitted taxes on distributions to owners. Consequently, our estimate of the fundamental value of corporations is a good one only when the tax rate on distributions to households is near zero. At the end of 1999, tax-deferred accounts included pension fund reserves, IRAs, 401(k)s, and the like; taken together they held the majority of corporate equity. Because of these accounts, the tax rate in 1999 was low, and introducing taxes on distributions (dividends plus part of buybacks) would have decreased the predicted value of the stock market by only about 5 percent. This was not the case in the 1960s, however, when the tax rate on distributions was closer to 50 percent than to 5 percent. With this correction to our model, the value of the stock market in the 1960s is very close to, rather than far lower than, that predicted by the model.

Our paper was rejected by an American journal so we sent it to a British journal, the *Review of Economic Studies*. The editor wanted to see the analysis done for the British economy, which we did. This was a stroke of luck. The United Kingdom had even bigger movements in the value of its stock market relative to GDP than did the United States—a factor of 3 for the United Kingdom versus a factor of 2.5 for the United States. The theory predicted the behavior of the British stock market even better than it predicted the behavior of the U.S. stock market. On this one we owe a debt to the editor for requiring us to use our analysis for the United Kingdom.

Another question that arose at some Minneapolis Fed policy briefings in the late 1990s was why people were working so much. My finding was that cross-country differences in tax rates account for much of the huge differences in market hours per working-age person. These inter-national observations are well designed to estimate the key parameter because predictions depend on tax rate differences, and these tax rate differences are larger. The marginal effective tax rate includes all factors in the budget constraint that affect the relative price of consumption and leisure. We now know why Europeans work so little in the market sector relative to residents of other advanced industrial countries. Their tax rates are much higher.

Conclusion

In this essay, I reviewed my development as an economist. I see my and Finn's key contribution as developing a methodology for the study of dynamic economic phenomena. Using this methodology, so many people have contributed so much to advancing our economic understanding. This is the golden age of economics with numerous advancements being made using these tools and extensions of these tools. A rich class of important problems remain that can be addressed using our existing tools of anal-ysis. Another important development is that the data sets available have become richer and have made it possible to address questions quantita-tively. I cannot underestimate the importance of measurement in drawing scientific inference.

A number of other valued collaborators were instrumental in my con-tinual development as an economist. They include John H. Boyd and Harold Cole at the Federal Reserve Bank of Minneapolis, and Ayse Imro-horoglu, Javier Díaz-Giménez, Hugo Hopenhayn, and Victor Rios-Rull, who were my advisees at Minnesota.

Edward C. Prescott

Awarded Nobel Prize in 2004. Lecture presented April 10, 2006.

Date of Birth

December 26, 1940

Academic Degrees

B.A., Swarthmore College, 1962
M.S., Case Western Reserve University, 1963
Ph.D., Carnegie Mellon University, 1967

Academic Affiliations

Assistant Professor of Economics, University of Pennsylvania, 1967–71
Assistant Professor of Economics, Graduate School of Industrial Administration, Carnegie Mellon University, 1971–72
Associate Professor of Economics, Graduate School of Industrial Administration, Carnegie Mellon University, 1972–75
Visiting Professor of Economics, Norwegian School of Business and Economics, 1974–75
Professor of Economics, Graduate School of Industrial Administration, Carnegie Mellon University, 1975–80
Professor of Economics, University of Minnesota, 1980–98
Senior Adviser, Research Department, Federal Reserve Bank of Minneapolis, 1980–2003
Professor of Economics, University of Chicago, 1998–99
Professor of Economics, University of Minnesota, 1999–2003
Senior Monetary Adviser, Research Department, Federal Reserve Bank of Minneapolis, 2003–present
W. P. Carey Chair and Professor of Economics, Arizona State University, 2003–present

Selected Books

Contractual Arrangements for Intertemporal Trade, 1985 (ed. with N. Wallace)
Recursive Methods in Economic Dynamics, 1989 (with N. L. Stokey and R. E. Lucas, Jr.)
Barriers to Riches, 2000 (with S. L. Parente)
Great Depressions of the Twentieth Century, 2007 (ed. with T. J. Kehoe)

Thomas C. Schelling

In reflecting on this autobiography I have two impressions. They will appear, but I want to acknowledge these in advance and alert the reader.

One is that I have been blessed with all kinds of advantages and opportunities. I grew up immune to the depression of the 1930s. (My father was a naval officer.) I had great school teachers at San Diego High School, especially Miss Olson, who spent two years teaching me to write a five-paragraph essay and so on, in college and graduate school, and in my first professional job, and my second and third. Everything good that might have happened to me did. I had splendid colleagues everywhere I went. Most of what I accomplished intellectually depended on opportunities. And the opportunities came.

The second, related impression is that nearly everything I've done was stimulated by opportunities I didn't seek but came to me, and many things I've done, including some of the things I'm most satisfied with, I did at the suggestion of somebody else or as a result of some unsolicited invitation.

For example, I was invited—I've never known why, or who suggested me—to join a committee of the National Academy of Sciences on "Substance Abuse and Habitual Behavior," on which I was surrounded by experts in heroin, alcohol, marijuana, nicotine, eating disorders, and various self-destructive habits. It was believed that every committee needed an economist, in case economics became pertinent. Economics never became salient, but I became, over a period of five years and fifty days of meetings, a wonderfully educated amateur. It was doctrine among the experts that nobody could cope with addictions without professional help. I thought there were things people might do to help themselves, and said so, and was challenged to put something on paper. My earlier work on "commitment"—about which more later—led me to some tactics that seemed likely to be at least occasionally helpful. What I wrote got published, as "The Intimate Contest for Self-Command," and led to six or seven more publications over a decade or so. I called it "self-command" (and even coined the phrase "egonomics") to separate it from "self-control," which usually meant something else. Somebody somewhere is responsible for my ever having got into the subject.

Again, I happened to run into Kenneth Boulding outside the Yale Cooperative Store in New Haven one afternoon. Ken had been the referee for an article I'd submitted to the *American Economic Review*—actually, the best article I ever wrote—and he'd been so enthusiastic that the editor printed it verbatim (except for asking me to eliminate the term "threatee," for one who is threatened). I told Ken that there was one topic I'd wanted to include in the article that I couldn't get a grip on, and I tried to express what it was. I couldn't be explicit or else I'd have been able to deal with it in the article. Boulding said something to me—I've never been able to reconstruct what it was—that clicked in my brain and revealed what it was I was trying to formulate. Just one sentence on a sidewalk in New Haven and I had the grasp I needed. His suggestion—actually, it wasn't a suggestion, just a hint of some kind—led me to the idea of a "focal point," and the concept of tacit bargaining and its influence on explicit bargaining.

I left the University of California at Berkeley in the middle of my junior year to go to Chile. I wanted a year abroad but there was a war in Europe, and a Chilean housemate sold me on Chile. After Pearl Harbor, I was "frozen" in my job at the U.S. embassy for two years—actually exciting years, mostly as a personal assistant to the FBI agent who arrived to set up a counterespionage office. I developed stomach pains; the ambassador returned my passport; the Navy got me onto a ship to the States; my former roommate, now a medical student, put me in touch with an internist, who diagnosed a duodenal ulcer; and I learned that neither the

Army nor the Navy would touch me. I was Section Eight of the draft code: psychoneurotic and likely to hemorrhage under stress.

I re-enrolled at Berkeley and majored in economics. There were few men on campus; it was 1943, the draft age had been lowered to eighteen, and except for a naval officers' program, few healthy men were enrolled. Few women did economics, so economics classes, in the largest university in the world, were small, sometimes intimate. It was an excellent faculty, mostly no longer remembered, but William Fellner held a graduate theory seminar that was conducted so modestly, so inquiringly, so invitingly, that I was charmed, intrigued, and persuaded I wanted to be an academic economist.

I chose Harvard for graduate study and had so many influential contacts in Washington that I was able to become a full-time teaching assistant and resident tutor at Kirkland House—free room and board, and a decent salary. I already knew a lot of economics, but teaching the elementary economics course taught me a lot more. I attracted the attention of the faculty, and in my second year was asked by Alvin Hansen, Gottfried Haberler, and Edward Chamberlin to be their teaching assistants. In 1948, I passed my oral exams and the economics department nominated me for a junior fellowship with the Harvard Society of Fellows—a three-year fellowship with a good stipend. The prestige was considerable. I was all set when I got a phone call from Sidney Alexander, an instructor at MIT with whom I was acquainted, who said he was in Washington with the new Marshall Plan. He had an opportunity to go to Paris but needed a replacement. Would I come spend the summer in Washington with the Marshall Plan, which had commenced in April of that year, 1948. (You will notice how a phone call from an acquaintance changed my life forever.)

I said yes; my wife and I spent the summer in Washington; my boss was named program officer for the Marshall Plan in Copenhagen and asked me to join him; I said yes. After a year I was ready to resume my junior fellowship at Harvard, but was invited to join the central European office of the Marshall Plan in Paris. Paris sounded good, the work sounded interesting, and I resigned my junior fellowship. (Another opportunity out of the blue!)

Ambassador W. Averell Harriman, who headed the Paris office, left in the summer of 1950 to become White House foreign policy adviser to President Truman and took my boss, Lincoln Gordon, with him. By November the EPU was locked up, and Gordon arranged for me to join the Harriman office in the White House. We sailed first class on the

Île-de-France, and I was back in the building I'd always known as "Old State"—it is now the Old Executive Office Building at 17th and Pennsylvania, the loveliest building in Washington. In 1945–46 I'd been on the fourth floor, looking over the White House; now I was on the second floor, looking over the White House again. (My career had reached its pinnacle at the end of 1950, when I had a personally assigned parking space on West Executive Avenue, the short guarded street between Old State and the White House.)

The European Recovery Program, as the Marshall Plan was called, became the Mutual Security Program in spring 1951; Harriman became the director of mutual security, I became the officer in charge of European program affairs, and essentially we were the budget bureau for foreign aid.

With the election of Dwight Eisenhower, Harriman was replaced by Harold Stassen in January 1953. (Stassen had been a youthful governor of Minnesota, nominator of Wendell Wilkie at the Republican National Convention in 1940, and the naval officer who led the navy contingent that rescued the POWs interned by the Japanese in the Philippines.) By that summer I was ready to leave, had an invitation from the Yale economics department, and told Stassen of my decision. He approved, saying that if I wanted a career in government, I should establish a firm base outside so that whenever, or if ever, I wanted to resign in protest, I'd have a secure profession to repair to.

At Yale I was surrounded by a distinguished faculty. William Fellner, whom I've mentioned, was there; James Tobin, whom I'd known in graduate school at Harvard; Robert Triffin, with whom I'd worked in Paris on the EPU; Tjalling Koopmans and Jacob Marschak, who moved to Yale from Chicago with the Cowles Foundation; and of course distinguished scholars in political science, psychology, and other social sciences. One of my first graduate students was Ned Phelps, who received the Nobel Prize the year after I did.

At Yale I taught international economics and embarked on a textbook. It was finished in 1958, just as I left Yale. I tried to make it a "modern" textbook, treating foreign aid, strategic trade controls, international cost sharing, national security trade controls, economic integration (as appeared to be imminent in Europe), international investment, and even protectionism (of which the international was only one dimension) as needing theoretical analysis on a par with traditional trade theory. I hoped to broaden the subject from traditional trade theory. I also hoped to make some money. I accomplished neither.

The Yale years produced what I believe were the main contributions that appealed to the Nobel selection committee. I had decided, on leaving government, to make "bargaining theory"—as I called it, for want of a better term—my primary theoretical interest, thinking my years in international negotiation had given me insight. I spent two years producing a manuscript of some 250 pages, mainly developing the idea of commitment as applied to threats, promises, and negotiation. It occurred to me that an article in a major journal would reach more readers than a book; I decided to see whether I could compress the 250 pages into something article length.

I spent the better part of three months trying to convert pages into paragraphs, paragraphs into sentences, and finding simple examples that illustrated complex ideas, and in the end had a manuscript that as far as I could tell, had sacrificed nothing in the compression to what was eventually about thirty printed pages. I called it "An Essay on Bargaining," and it appeared in the June 1956 *American Economic Review*.

I later enlarged on that essay in London in 1958; I'll come to that later. What I did next was the article on focal points that was triggered by that conversation with Boulding. It was my only foray into "experimental" research. I decided to test whether people can actually concert their intentions by some process of logic or imagination, by recognizing a need for clues or hints or some process of convergent expectations. I referred to this as "coordination," and I tested, by a questionnaire mailed to some sixty friends and colleagues, whether people could coordinate when their interests were identical—"pure coordination," I called it—and then whether they could coordinate when their interests diverged, as between alternative choices but they had to choose identically to succeed at all.

Actually, I was led to this inquiry not through an interest in tacit bargaining but in the belief that the phenomenon I was looking at was crucial in arriving at agreement in explicit bargaining. I had observed that the results of bargaining were often a convergence on some solution that had become "mutually expected," often on some salient outcome qualitatively distinct from most alternatives, or reflecting some precedent or tradition. (Splitting fifty-fifty is an example.) I thought a demonstration that people actually could intuit their way to a common expectation in the tacit case would establish the psychological phenomenon that I was trying to describe. I evidently succeeded in persuading my audience that the tacit case was real; I'm not sure that my original major point was similarly appreciated.

Evidently both the "Essay on Bargaining" and the tacit bargaining article (which appeared as "Bargaining, Communication, and Limited War" in the inaugural issue of the *Journal of Conflict Resolution* [March 1957], which Kenneth Boulding edited) can be construed as game theory. At the time I composed them I didn't know enough game theory to appreciate that. The idea of commitment, whether to an unconditional or a conditional choice, can be construed as reducing selectively some of one's own payoffs in a matrix; a coordination problem can be portrayed as a matrix in which all the payoffs are zero except in a diagonal where they are all equal. According to the Nobel Committee, I must have been doing game theory without knowing it.

One result of my "Essay on Bargaining" was that people at the RAND Corporation saw it, and I was invited to spend the summer of 1957 at RAND. Several people at RAND were working on the theory and practice of "limited war"—that is, a non-all-out war—of which Korea was the outstanding example. I had already become interested, as my focal point article indicated even in its title. I left RAND thinking I'd do some work on the subject.

Then, in the fall of 1957, R. Duncan Luce of Harvard's psychology department and Howard Raiffa of the Harvard Business School published *Games and Decisions*, and my education began. It was not only a superb introduction to game theory, it was a comprehensive survey of the subject. I spent at least a hundred hours over it—probably two hundred. I learned how to formulate most of what I was doing or wanted to do with the help of matrices. I had never published a matrix, never used a matrix to order my own thoughts. At last I had a versatile tool that could expand my capabilities.

Armed with what I'd learned from Luce and Raiffa, I took my family to London from February to September 1958. There I enlarged on what I'd done in those two "game theory" articles, this time taking advantage of matrix notation. I was under the impression that the kind of game theory that I was doing was relevant to all kinds of situations that formal game theory was somewhat aloof from. I quote the introduction to what I produced during our stay in London.

On the strategy of pure conflict—the zero-sum games—*game theory* has yielded important insight and advice. But on the strategy of action where conflict is mixed with mutual dependence—the non-zero-sum games involved in wars and threats of war, strikes, negotiations, criminal deterrence, class war, race war, price war, and blackmail; maneuvering in a bureaucracy or in a traffic jam; and the coercion of one's own children—traditional game theory has not yielded comparable insight or advice. These are the "games" in which, though the element of conflict provides the dramatic interest, mutual dependence is part of the logical structure and demands some kind of collaboration or mutual accommodation—tacit, if not explicit—even if only in the avoidance of mutual disaster. These are also games in which, though secrecy may play a strategic role, there is some essential need for the signaling of intentions and the meeting of minds. Finally, they are games in which what one player *can* do to avert mutual damage affects what another player *will* do to avert it, so that it is not always an advantage to possess initiative, knowledge, or freedom of choice.

I went on to propose that we disaggregate non-zero-sum, recognizing that the coordination game was the limiting case opposite to the zero-sum, and that it might be called the zero-difference game, and we needed another name for those in which the conflict and common interest were embedded.

I actually had the temerity to subtitle my article, which appeared as a whole issue of the *Journal of Conflict Resolution,* "Prospectus for a Reorientation of Game Theory." With the exception of a few friends like Howard Raiffa, I don't think I converted any game theorist to my "reorientation," but in psychology, sociology, even anthropology and political science, scholars tended to be comfortable with my kind of game theory.

I then spent a year at RAND, September 1958 to September 1959. I learned and produced a lot. It was my first introduction to classified information about nuclear weapons and my acquaintance with the foremost theorists on nuclear issues: Bernard Brodie, William Kaufmann, Albert Wohlstetter, and Herman Kahn. Wohlstetter had just finished his article, published the following January in *Foreign Affairs,* "The Delicate Balance of Terror," establishing the crucial criterion for a deterrent force—namely, that it be invulnerable to attack—and arguing that U.S. strategic forces were not. By fall 1958, Eisenhower and Khrushchev had agreed to an international conference on "Measures to Safeguard against Surprise Attack"; five Eastern and five Western nations were engaged, and the five Western—Canada, France, Germany, the United Kingdom, and the United States—met in Washington to prepare.

Also at RAND I got an idea—it just sprang into my head while I was musing about something else—that I named "The Threat That Leaves Something to Chance." In my work on threats, I'd always argued that a threat required a commitment—a threat, I argued, was always painful or expensive to carry out, something the threatener would not be motivated to do, otherwise it was just a "warning"—and to allege that one would "probably" indulge in painful or expensive retaliation, as in "come one step closer and maybe I'll shoot you," left open the clear choice not to. But I saw, in this epiphany, that one could maneuver into a position in which there was a risk of mutual harm that was not altogether under one's control.

I use tailgating as an example. If somebody gets his front bumper eighteen inches from my rear bumper, he threatens to kill us both unless all goes well. He will surely use all his skill to make sure nothing goes awry, but at that short interval something can go wrong and we both suffer. The threat is "probabilistic." The same thing occurs when one "buzzes" an airplane to make it change course or land; one gets close enough that all one's skill cannot absolutely guarantee that nothing will go wrong. Later I used the example of President Kennedy's putting a navy quarantine around Cuba during the crisis of 1962: the Soviets knew that any military response carried some risk that though the last thing either party wanted was war, things might erupt into war that neither intended. I even argued that sometimes the purpose of initiating a crisis might be to create a situation that carried the risk of unintended expansion.

As my year at RAND closed, I put some of my work into a book. Submitted to the Harvard University Press, it was accepted (maybe because I was already on the Harvard faculty) and published in 1960. I called it *The Strategy of Conflict*, the same title I'd used for my journal-size article in the *Journal of Conflict Resolution*. It has had a good career, recently boosted by my Nobel Prize.

In September 1959, I joined Harvard, half in the Department of Economics and half in the Center for International Affairs. At the center I taught, with Henry Kissinger, a seminar on foreign policy; in the department, I shared a seminar on international economics and taught a seminar on defense economics.

For the summer of 1960, the Twentieth Century Fund financed a "summer study" of arms control. Some twenty of us spent two months at a resort owned by MIT; another twenty showed up for a day or a week. I had earlier visited Yale and met a graduate student, Morton Halperin, who so impressed me that I offered to finance his dissertation for a couple of years at the Harvard Center; I then suggested he join the summer study as rapporteur, and he did. At the end of the summer he and I decided to write a book together, reflecting the consensus that the group had reached.

Meanwhile, the MIT Center for International Studies and the Harvard Center for International Affairs had organized a joint center on arms control that met every three weeks for dinner and discussion. Halperin and I managed to write enough to provide a chapter at just about every meeting, for discussion and criticism. By December, we had a book that had been thoroughly discussed by a select group of academics (and a few non-academics), and the Twentieth Century Fund arranged for a printer to do a six-week printing job, and we had copies just about the time that John F. Kennedy was inaugurated. The fund gave us something like a hundred copies, which we circulated within the federal government.

Meanwhile, McGeorge Bundy of Harvard, who had been in our arms control group, had become national security adviser to the president; Jerome Wiesner, a member of the group, had become the White House science adviser; Walt Rostow, a member, had become assistant secretary of state for policy planning; Henry Rowen became deputy assistant secretary of defense for international security—he was a RAND colleague whom I had attracted to Harvard; Abram Chayes of Harvard Law School, another member of our group, became general counsel to the Department of State; John McNaughton of Harvard Law School became, at my suggestion, deputy assistant secretary of defense for arms control, and though he'd not been a member of the group, he knew us all and had the little Schelling–Halperin book to bring him up to date. As you can see, this was quite a potentially influential group, all of whom had been part of a study group on arms control.

In spring 1961 Lincoln Bloomfield, with whom I had established the Harvard-MIT arms control seminar, and I invented a new kind of game. There had been a few foreign-policy games, at RAND and elsewhere, usually with individuals playing "roles"—that is, secretary of state (foreign minister) or defense, senator, etc. We composed two teams, a blue (U.S.) team and a red (USSR) team, with no role-playing. The whole team was responsible for reaching decisions, and both were instructed not to second-guess what a U.S. or USSR leader or government would do, but to attempt to reach the best possible outcome for the United States or the Soviet Union.

Each team was given a "scenario" that presented a crisis at a date in the near future—near future so that teams didn't need to be given hypothetical future events—and was to produce a decision document indicating what actions it would take immediately or in response to what the other side did. A "control" team then matched the decisions of the two teams, and extrapolated the scenario to take account of what they had indicated they would do unconditionally or conditional on the other team's actions. They were given this extrapolation, and repeated the process. And again. It went on for two days, fifteen hours a day, and usually there were four or five iterations. The control team made a final extrapolation, and all three teams conducted a postmortem examination.

During the 1960s, nearly all my work was on nuclear weapons policy. I was invited to offer a seminar series at the Institute for Defense Analyses in Washington, DC, and gave eleven weekly lectures that after an eight-month sojourn at the Institute for Strategic Studies in London, became a book, *Arms and Influence*, published by Yale University Press in 1966. I began the preface as follows:

> One of the lamentable principles of human productivity is that it is easier to destroy than to create. A house that takes several man-years to build can be burned in an hour by any young delinquent who has the price of a box of matches. Poisoning dogs is cheaper than raising them. And a country can destroy more with twenty billion dollars of nuclear armament than it can create with twenty billion dollars of foreign investment. The harm that people can do, or that nations can do, is impressive. And it is often used to impress.

The book has had a good career, still selling after forty years, and a handsome Chinese edition appeared in 2007 from the Military History and Translation Division of the Ministry of National Defense, Taipei. Some of the chapters are "The Art of Commitment," "The Manipulation of Risk," "The Idiom of Military Action," and "The Dynamics of Mutual Alarm."

I published "Dynamic Models of Segregation" in the first issue of the *Journal of Mathematical Sociology* in 1971, and an abbreviated version (using an eight by eight board for typographic convenience) in my 1978 book *Micromotives and Macrobehavior*. An unexpected consequence was that as I learned about twenty-five years later, I was a pioneer in what became known as agent-based computational modeling.

I also, in that 1978 book, developed a diagrammatic analysis of binary choices among large groups of individuals, beginning with the "multiperson prisoners' dilemma" and embedding that in a large set of situations, some of which shared with the multi-person prisoners' dilemma a unique inferior equilibrium, some with happy equilibriums, some with two equilibriums, and eventually a total of some eleven different multi-person binary choice situations. I worked hard at it and was pleased with the results.

The question arises, was that book, *Micromotives and Macrobehavior*, game theory? If so, what makes it game theory?

I didn't think so at the time—it just didn't occur to me—but there were hints in the Nobel Committee's remarks that the committee thought it was. And I see now that everything in that book had to do with individuals' adjustment to or anticipation of the choices of others, and with needs and opportunities for coordination, formal cooperation, or submission to direction or regulation.

I've now concluded that this is game theory. Game theory, I find (or choose to define), is very much about *situations*. What is prisoner's dilemma but a situation? The logic of choice is central to game theory, but what game theory—again, I'm thinking about the invention of matrices—is often critical for is identifying situations in which choice is somehow puzzling, problematic, or challenging, and in identifying how many distinct situations of a certain kind there may be.

I've gone into some detail in order to demonstrate what I mean by game theory having to do with the analysis of situations, and how matrices can be essential to any exhaustive exploration of those situations. An ironic footnote here is that the essay I produced was being published by a journal, which shall be nameless, the editor of which insisted I delete all the matrices. I said nobody could follow the argument without the matrices; he said he'd rather have his subscribers perplexed than intimidated. Out they went, but I shortly published the comprehensible version elsewhere. (It is in my 1984 book, if your interest is arms control as well as game theory.)

Pursuing the idea that my interests were often exogenous, I could mention that I was invited by someone I hadn't known to participate in the 1967 President's Commission on Law Enforcement and the Administration of Justice. The thought was that my experience with "deterrence theory" would make me valuable to the Internal Revenue Service. I got sidetracked into "organized crime," became fascinated—a couple of congressional committees had recently held intensive hearings on the subject—and wrote a report that led to two publications (both in my 1984 book). For several years, I was regularly invited to the annual convention of chiefs of police.

In 1966, I was invited to contribute a chapter to a Brookings Institution book on public expenditure; my topic was how to value lives. I had earlier had an air force Ph.D. student who did his dissertation on government evaluation of lifesaving—for example, when the pilot should bail out to save himself, and when to try to land to save the expensive aircraft. The topic had been my idea, and maybe somebody knew of my interest.

Anyway, I wrote what I think was the first notion that lifesaving, in the form of modest reductions in risk to people's lives, might well be valued by how they would respond to opportunities to pay for reductions in risk to their own lives. This has always been controversial: Is a poor person's life worth less than a rich person's? My answer was "yes," if the issue were to require the poor person to pay for the same lifesaving as a rich person would willingly pay for, or to offer the poor person an increment of life safety at public expense when he'd rather have something else. It's still controversial.

Finally, climate change has occupied me for almost thirty years. I answered the phone in 1980, and was asked whether I would receive a delegate from the National Academy of Sciences who wished to recruit me to chair a committee on global warming and climate change. I said I'd heard of the subject but knew nothing; he said he'd like to come talk to me anyhow and buy me a drink. I said OK; he flew up from Washington with a senior staff person; I had my drink and said, again, that I knew little. He said all that was known I could learn in the six weeks before the committee could meet and he'd provide knowledgeable people to teach me. I said OK, spent some weeks learning what there was, had a great committee, and produced a report.

This issue was that President Carter was scheduled to attend a "summit" in Venice, and the German chancellor had put "the carbon dioxide problem" on the agenda. The White House asked the National Academy of Sciences to give a quick answer as to what to do about that item on the agenda. My committee recommended, sensibly, that the thing to do was to get it off the agenda, that the U.S. government was not ready to face the issue.

Congress then passed a resolution asking the National Academy of Sciences for a major assessment of the carbon issue, mainly because the president's program for coal-based liquid fuel would produce a highly carbon-intensive product. Because I'd done something already on the subject, I was naturally on the new committee, which—rather like my experience with drugs on that earlier committee—contained experts in fifteen pertinent scientific fields and one amateur, me. Two years later, I was about the best-educated amateur in the country; I wrote the chapter on the policy and welfare implications of climate change, and from then on never managed to drop the subject. My latest book reproduces three of my many publications on the issue of climate change.

I trust I've demonstrated what I said on my first page: how much of my career, indeed my intellectual life, has been determined by opportunities unexpected and suggestions unsolicited.

I'll close with two observations—one about game theory, and one about policy.

Game theory is usually defined as concerned with how individuals should choose rationally in situations in which the optimal choice for each depends on the choice of another or the choices of others. I have been, I believe, more concerned with how to select a behavior that will *influence* another or others—how to influence others by constraining their expectation of how oneself will act. This has led me to consider the institutional, legal, cultural, sometimes physical circumstances that make it possible to commit and reliably signal promises, threats, negotiating positions, and other kinds of commitments, and to appreciate when inability or disability, even deliberately incurred, may induce the favorable behavior of others. This is still game theory, but with a different slant.

My final observation is that one of my favorite applications of a focal point was in an appendix to my 1960 book. That appendix considered what constraints or restrictions on the use of nuclear weapons might ever become appealing, or compelling, and it concluded, via focal point analysis, with an analogy to the non-use of gas in the Second World War, that the only constraint likely to be stable would be absolute non-use. During the Eisenhower administration, both the president and his secretary of state repeatedly spoke of the "taboo" against the use of nuclear weapons, and the need to "break down this false distinction" (between nuclear and other weapons.) The official U.S. position was that nuclear weapons "must now be treated as in fact having become conventional."

In contrast, President Johnson in 1964, when asked about nuclear weapons in relation to Vietnam, said, "Make no mistake. There is no such thing as a conventional nuclear weapon. For nineteen peril-filled years no nation has loosed the atom against another. To do so now is a political decision of the highest order." The taboo survived the Korean War, the war in Vietnam, the war in the Falklands, the Yom Kippur War of 1973, and the hugely demoralizing war of the Soviet Union in Afghanistan. In each case, one party in the war had nuclear weapons.

For more than sixty years, since August 1945, no nuclear weapon has been used in conflict. My current interest, in the second half of my eighties, is to encourage appreciation of the value of that taboo for the next sixty years. That was the subject of my Stockholm lecture in honor of Alfred Nobel.

Thomas C. Schelling

Awarded Nobel Prize in 2005. Lecture presented April 18, 2007.

Dates of Birth and Death

April 14, 1921; December 13, 2016

Academic Degrees

A.B., Economics, University of California at Berkeley, 1944
Ph.D., Economics, Harvard University, 1951

Academic Affiliations

Associate Professor of Economics, Yale University, 1953–57
Professor of Economics, Yale University, 1957–58
Professor of Economics, Harvard University, 1958–90
Professor of Economics, John F. Kennedy School of Government, Harvard University, 1969–90
Distinguished University Professor, Department of Economics and School of Public Affairs, University of Maryland, 1990–2005
Lucius N. Littauer Professor of Political Economy, Emeritus, Harvard University, 1990–2016
Distinguished University Professor, Emeritus, Department of Economics and School of Public Affairs, University of Maryland, 2005–2016

Selected Books

National Income Behavior, 1951
International Economics, 1958
The Strategy of Conflict, 1960
Strategy and Arms Control, 1961 (with M. Halperin)
Arms and Influence, 1966
Micromotives and Macrobehavior, 1978
Thinking through the Energy Problem, 1979
Choice and Consequence, 1984
Strategies of Commitment and Other Essays, 2006

Edmund S. Phelps

Amid the "Theory Wars" in Twentieth-Century Economics

Any account of my evolution as an economist must narrate my early struggle to depart from the scientism and determinism of the neo-Keynesian school—repairing as best I could their omission of expectations, learning, and knowledge creation—only to find myself bypassed by a new classical school founded on a belief in "rational expectations." In the next decades, I struggled against the scientism and determinism of the new classical school—emphasizing their omission of Knightian uncertainty, Keynesian indeterminacy, and Hayekian discovery. Then I was rescued by fervent supporters and an august body from domination by the neo-neoclassicals, and am called "revolutionary." This biography will be tightly focused on that story line.[1] It is, I would say, a part of the story of twentieth-century economics.

Background

When I was a student of economics—from my first course in economics at Amherst College in fall 1952 to my doctorate at Yale in spring 1959—I could see that some fundamental departures in economic theory had taken place in the interwar years of the twentieth century. I sometimes went into the stacks of the library at Amherst to watch the sparks fly in the debates between Friedrich Hayek and John Maynard Keynes in the early 1930s. They were the pioneering architects of a modernist economic theory. Frank Knight, in his 1921 book *Risk, Uncertainty, and Profit*, had argued that what we now call *Knightian uncertainty* was endemic in market economies—a kind of uncertainty in which we *do not know* the quantitative probabilities to attach to each of the known contingencies or even what all the possible contingencies are. The same year, Keynes in his *A Treatise on Probability* sought to model aspects of how a rational person responds to such uncertainties. But it was Hayek, from his *Monetary Theory and the Trade Cycle* (1928; Eng. ed., 1933) to *The Pure Theory of Capital* (1941), and Keynes, with his *The General Theory of Employment, Interest, and Money* (1936), who began a movement to take account of Knightian uncertainties in macroeconomic models of investment and employment.

I noticed that both Hayek and Keynes showed awareness of *incomplete information* in real-life market economies. Keynes pointed out the "uncoordinated" character of decisions in real-life market economies. Hayek had the vision that in advanced economies and especially creative ones, where novelty and evolution are occurring, each manager and employee possesses little "information" about how the myriad goods are produced (i.e., the formulas), and what the cost of producing each would be. Their information is mostly specialized to one or a very few products. Hayek makes the process of "coordination" of these participants' individual activities in the face of such *private information* a cornerstone of his theory.

I also noticed that both Hayek and Keynes brought *imperfect knowledge* into their models—an even more radical step. Hayek built on the idea that faced with uncertainty, producers and investors may make mistakes in the directions of their investments, with consequences for both employment and growth. (Later, in the 1960s, he built on the uncertainty faced by innovators about the reception of prospective users to a new product or new method.) Keynes in the same decade built on the idea that the visions of entrepreneurs are unobservable, and even if they were observed, entrepreneurs' responses would not be subject to a known probability distribution. Keynes's reference to the "animal spirits" of entrepreneurs conveys the thought that entrepreneurs may exhibit spontaneity and perhaps innovativeness in their investment decisions. Entrepreneurs might take their cue from share prices, but the stock market was flakier than entrepreneurs, basing its current valuations on some fashionable but "flimsy" notion of what was driving the economy, and what would be the next thing.

But by the end of the 1950s, I saw signs of a retreat from this modernism. One sign was that the animal spirits driving investment demand were banished as a source of instability in the Keynesian system. James Tobin in 1955 built a neo-Keynesian model in which investment demand is a sort of residual, not a causal force: if consumption demand should drop, some of the employed move over to producing more of the capital goods; the market for houses and other capital goods willingly buys the additional output. If they were not to do so, interest rates would sag and the prices bid for capital goods would lift up above the opportunity cost of their production, leaving opportunities for a pure profit—a free lunch—by producing capital goods at an infinite rate. (This was the "Q-theory of investment.") Succeeding models provided for rising marginal costs in the capital goods industries. If prospects dimmed for future profits from new investments, the valuations put on having additional units of the capital good would drop, which would reduce production activity and employment in the capital goods sector. Thus, the animal spirits were caged and tamed. Autonomous individuals acting on their individual insights, hunches, and originality could not be a prime mover, sparking fluctuations. It was only changes in *fundamentals*, such as changes in prospects for future profit, which could drive movements in investment activity.

Neo-Keynesians next dissented on the matter of the average money wage. In Keynes's thinking, the wage possessed an element of indeterminacy—it could, for example, hang too high for a time or go into a shuddering descent. Yet the short-run models by John Hicks and Paul Samuelson in 1939 (and the latter's influential 1948 text *Economics*) went so far as to treat the money wage as a constant. A modification by A. W. Phillips in 1957 hypothesized a stable relationship between the rate of wage inflation and the level of unemployment, to be dubbed the Phillips curve by Samuelson and Robert Solow. This had the implication in the Keynesian model that the wage level would gradually adjust to a shift of "aggregate demand" until it had forced the resulting unemployment rate back to its long-run resting place. (So if investment demand is weakened, interest rates must drop as required to prop it back in order to restore [un]employment.) Thus, there exists in this model an equilibrium level—in the expectational sense—that is determinate, being determined by the height of the Phillips curve.

Almost the last remaining entry point for uncertainty was closed in the 1955 growth model by Solow. The basic model offered insights into the effects of slower population growth, but economists took greater interest in extended versions of the model showing effects of slower technical progress. Although it is doubtful it was Solow's purpose, the growth model described the complete determination of the economy's path over the indefinite future: the course of the capital stock, output, consumption, and the corresponding wage and interest rates. This is all driven by a "forcing function" that takes the course of technical progress to be exogenous to the economy, to be free of Knightian uncertainty, and to be known by all participants when they make their decisions. (It is true that one could ask the model what the implications are of a change from one path of technical progress to another. But do the prevailing expectations for technical progress change the same way? Where are the uncertainties in any real-life generation and implementation of technical progress?)

Putting People In

It was with this background that I began my career in economic research. Of course, I did not see immediately or simultaneously all or even most of the things that were unsatisfactory about this new development in economic theory. But having read Hayek's *Prices and Production* (2nd ed., 1935) and Keynes's *General Theory*, I could sense that the neo-Keynesian research, though intriguing and possibly useful in some ways, had utterly abandoned the modernist emphasis on incomplete information and imperfect knowledge in favor of some new method or methodology with which I was not at all comfortable. Instinctively, as Keynes would have said, I understood that the neo-Keynesian models, in abstracting from these things, inadvertently left no role for humans to play. There could be no beliefs as distinct from what is true, no expectations as distinct from what is or will be, no mental stimulation and challenge, no problem solving, no creativity, and no discovery. I remember having a good laugh when Robert Summers, my first statistics teacher at Yale, told the anecdote, which may be apocryphal, of the earnest young student reaction to the formal model the lecturer had just laid out: "But sir, where are the *people* in that model?"

My first efforts to put "people" into the models lay in the area of productivity growth. At Amherst, I had heard more than once the motto that education teaches us to learn. (The thesis, which referred to college education, is associated with Alexander Micklejohn, who was in fact president of Amherst College for a time in the 1920s.) So, on hearing my friend and Yale colleague Richard Nelson arguing one day that a farmer would be better able to learn which fertilizer is best for him if he had a college education, I thought of Micklejohn, and of my mother's brothers and sisters who ran the family farm in downstate Illinois, all of whom had gone to college. When I proposed an algebraic model different from Nelson's, he kindly invited me on board to do another version with him. (But he refused to scrap his own model.) My idea was that the best-practice technology in a country would approximate to the best-feasible technology at a *faster rate* the higher the proportion of the economy's participants having a college degree. This proposition has stimulated volumes of research, with a certain amount of confusion (possibly extending to me).

Next, I aimed to develop a model in which technical progress does not occur exogenously at the hands of explorers and scientists who do it without regard for costs and possible revenues. Technical advances require people. In the view I took for the sake of simplicity, it requires technical researchers (and only them). This model too yielded some refreshing results. It turned out that according to the model, the explosion of the population in the nineteenth century must have had something to do with the burst of technical progress from 1870 to 1940. I want to add that this framework is still too narrow, since it overlooks the creation of commercial ideas by businesspeople. (It is commonly said that the big new ideas come from technical people, while the little, "incremental" ideas come from businesspeople, of whom there are a huge number. But I am not persuaded that science generates the preponderance of big ideas and business the little ones.)

I thought these two papers were big steps away from the mechanical approach of the Solow model. That does not mean, though, that we cannot find promising ideas in the Solow model; it does mean that we can develop and work with richer models in which some real-world aspects of the innovation process are present.

My next efforts to put people into models lay in the area of employment and inflation dynamics. For me, the Phillips curve could be neither theoretically acceptable nor empirically reliable, since it took no account whatsoever of what may happen to various *expectations* when monetary policy or a banking development pushes up or pulls down the inflation rate. My 1967 paper arguing that "disinflation" requires the monetary authority to drive down "expectations" of inflation, and my 1968 paper on "money-wage dynamics" and "labor-market equilibrium," were the seminal papers out of which the others sprung. My 1969 paper outlining

my "islands parable" had an important influence—too much in some
respect, as it took attention away from the incentive-wage theory developed in the 1968 paper. The *Microeconomic Foundations* volume of
1970 signaled the arrival of a micro-macro movement in economics.

Return of the Determinists and Rationalists

The heading for this section recalls the panicky titles of the old horror
movies. In fact, it has been a little frightening and not a little dishearten-
ing to see virtually the entire economics profession rushing to embrace
the rational expectation axiom of neo-neoclassical economics like lem-
mings in a suicidal jump into the sea.

At Carnegie Mellon, just after giving a paper, I met for the first time
Jack Muth, who told me of his paper on what he called "rational expectations." Of course I was intrigued by it. In my 1966 book *Fiscal Neutrality* I had explored the case of "perfect foresight" (rational expectations
without any probabilistic element), though with skepticism and not
exclusively. I collaborated with John Taylor on a 1977 paper in which
rational expectations were used, and I adopted the premise again in my
1978 paper on "disinflation without recession." It was intellectually
interesting—even fun. I still think back once in a while to some theoretical results I obtained with rational expectations.

I want to add that the probabilistic aspect that the neo-neoclassicals
introduced added to understanding, with or without the rational expectations. My theory implied that, say, employment bulges during a war
because wages do not go up enough to prevent it, since wage setters are
slow to realize that wages at their competitors have increased as fast as
their own. The probabilistic models implied that wages do not go up
enough because wage setters take the probability that the war will go
on at least another period to be less than one. (This is related to Milton
Friedman's distinction between temporary and permanent disturbances.)
The rational expectations premise carried the idea to an extreme, imply-
ing that the *expected value* of employment in the upcoming period, after
wages are set, is equal to the *natural* level (or if there are hiring costs,
some natural path back to the medium-term natural level).

But the theory of rational expectations—the idea that the knowledge
of every participant about how the economy works could with some
generality have converged to something that is complete and right, at
least roughly so—seemed surrealistic to me and likely to be dangerously
wrong in some contexts. I kept in mind my 1959 doctoral dissertation

in which I pointed out that to test a hypothesis statistically, we have to specify one or more auxiliary hypotheses; you can't test in a vacuum, with no model whatsoever. If one or more of the latter are bad hypotheses, we may obtain statistical results that cause us to accept the hypothesis when in truth it is false; it would have been rejected had we embedded it in entirely correct auxiliary hypotheses. Some of the "knowledge" we think we have is a "house of cards" that will collapse if and when the right statistical test is performed. (I would add that Roman Frydman published in 1981 a paper with a formal argument that the individuals in a market economy will not tend to converge to one model: if perchance they had all been following one model, individuals, one after another, would sooner or later try out departures from that prevailing model— even if it were the right model by some miracle. Another discussion of the fallibility of human knowledge appears in a 1986 paper by James Heckman and Richard Robb.)[2]

In the 1981 conference that Roman Frydman and I organized, and the ensuing 1983 conference volume *Rational Expectations Re-examined: Individual Forecasting and Aggregate Outcomes*, my paper started from the point that a participant in the economy will not adopt the "rational expectation" derivable from the model to which he or she subscribes if it is believed that most or all of the others in the economy are basing their expectations on a different model. It is only in very special cases, I have found, that the models converge to one model after some amount of evidence has been observed.

So I conclude that rational expectations are not rational at all.

The Costs of Neo-neoclassicism

You may question whether, in fact, the long dominance of neo-neoclassical thinking has had any serious practical cost. I believe it has.

There is no question that "financial engineering" has brought benefits. It has improved the matching of investments to the needs of savers and extended financing to the smallest grains of sand in the economy. (The word *granular* is apt to turn up here.) Yet since August 2007 up to this writing in April 2008, the financial sector has been in near paralysis. In my judgment, this failure is the result of a sort of misfeasance on the part of the leaders at many of the investment banks. Much of this management failure, I believe, can be laid to a dearth of understanding of applicable economics. And some of that ignorance or obliviousness is the result, in turn, of the shortcomings of the neo-neoclassical models used on Wall Street for purposes of "risk management." A paragraph from a piece of mine in the *Wall Street Journal* of March 14, 2008 (with minor edits and an additional point in brackets) suggests some of the failures:

> Subprime lending and the securitization of debt were innovations that, it was believed, offered the prospect of increased homeownership. But "risk management" was out of its depth here: It had no past data from which to estimate needed valuations of the novel assets; [it appeared to suppose that diversification would eliminate systemic risks, including the Knightian kind;] it did not allow for possible macroeconomic swings; and it took inadequate account of the system effects when unknown numbers of financial companies enter the new business all at nearly the same time.

I have come across a catchword that nicely captures most, if not all, of what I was saying: *strategic vision*. The term has been used recently in discussions of what has gone wrong at some investment banks by both Luqman Arnold, chief of UBS in 2001, and Leo M. Tilman, senior strategist at Bear Stearns.

Dynamism

The most awful thing about determinism and the idea it inspires, rational expectations, is that they preempt all originality and thus leave no role for creativity in the business world—basically, this world. If everything were determinate or knowable, and it were in fact known by now, then there would be nothing yet to discover or invent. There would be nothing about which to be creative; nothing to create.

This doctrine is not only an affront to humanism, from the ancient Greeks to the present time. It is pretty obvious that it is very bad economics.

In reply, the neo-neoclassicals might suggest that innovators only seem to be prime causes of innovative forces; that, in reality, the conceptions of individual innovations are governed by a selection mechanism based on probability distributions, which are so detailed and granular that we cannot in practice estimate them. Schumpeter's great 1911–1912 book *Theorie der wirtscharftlichen Entwicklung* (*Theory of Economic Development*, trans., 1932) has that flavor, as do the avowedly "Schumpeterian" models by Philippe Aghion and Peter Howitt. That theory looks to be untestable, even metaphysical. Even if it were true or could be true in some cases, most of us appear to share the sense of having *free will*—to be able to choose a life of challenge and creativity in preference to a more passive, safe sort of life—and having *powers of imagination*—to have ideas that no one else has thought up, ideas that are contingent on our imagining. And many societies structure the economy for innovativeness because they desire it. It would be a pity, perhaps disastrous, if we lost that sense of autonomy.

In the view I have taken in several papers and lectures in the present decade, such as my 2002 Munich lecture and my 2005 lecture at the International Economic Association World Congress in Marrakech, the American economy and a few other national economies, defined as a structure of institutions and attitudes, are *mechanisms* for the generation—always with lots of unknown probabilities—of novel commercial ideas. As a result, the American economy can be seen as driven by the occurrence of such ideas, and much of its activity revolves around their financing, development into workable products, marketing, evaluation by prospective end users, and if they get that far, commercial adoption and final acceptance. (This is a straightforward elaboration and articulation of what Hayek called the "discovery procedure.") I have been using the word *dynamism* to refer to the *power* or *propensity* of the economy to generate novel products that are commercially successful—thus, the fertility and aim of the economy in producing new ideas. (Think of some value-weighted index of the discoveries per year over some long span as measuring this dynamism. Of course, there are many pieces of circumstantial evidence of an economy's dynamism.) As I see it, this mechanism is the essence of *capitalism*.

Inclusion and the Good Economy

Starting with a Paris lecture in the summer of 2006 and my Aristotle lecture in 2007, my thesis has been that problem solving, exploration, and intellectual growth—the attributes to which I referred above—are, for most if not all people in any country, *essential* for self-realization, self-actualization, or self-discovery; and that this experience or development is the essence of the *good life*, as humanist philosophers have proposed, from Aristotle to Dewey and Rawls, and from Cervantes to Nietzsche and Henri Bergson. Further, since a good economy must serve the good life, these attributes must be essential to the *good economy*.

I have argued in my Nobel Prize lecture, published in 2007, that we do not need to *choose* between inclusion and dynamism. It may very well be that continental Europe kept taking state and community measures to push up inclusion—and solidarity—until it damaged its already questionable dynamism. I argue that, in general, introducing institutional structures for greater dynamism, however, does not only serve the self-realization of the more advantaged. Such structures are job creating, and in pulling up employment as well as self-support and respect among the disadvantaged, serve to increase self-realization among the disadvantaged as well. Economies without dynamism cannot be just.

Reversal of Fortune

While happily embarked in new directions with the work on structuralism between 1985 to the mid-1990s, the work later in the 1990s on inclusion and the work in the 2000s on dynamism, I was aware that I had again left the mainstream—and the mainstream showed no sign of following me.

In the 2000s, however, my standing and visibility shot up, first when named a distinguished fellow of the American Economic Association in 2000, then with the massive *Festschrift* conference in my honor that was organized by Philippe Aghion, Roman Frydman, Joseph Stiglitz, and Michael Woodford. The award of the Nobel Prize in the fall of 2006 brought a renewed recognition of my research stretching from the 1960s to my differences with the new classical school in the 1980s.

With the Nobel Prize, I find myself with a platform that is more amazing than I could have imagined. I have had the opportunity to speak about my distinctive views all over the world. This has kindled the hope that the new theories I constructed in the past two decades and the new dimensions I have tried to introduce into economics will yet win a hearing among economists. Fortunately, I am joined by a band of like-minded economists, and we will make every effort to persuade the profession of the merits of our views.

Notes

Photograph of Edmund S. Phelps by Ramin Talaie.

1. Four earlier memoirs are "A Life in Economics," in *The Makers of Modern Economics*, ed. Arnold Heertje (Aldershot, UK: Edward Elgar, 1995); "The Origins and Further Development of the Natural Rate of Unemployment," in *The Natural Rate of Unemployment: Reflections on 25 Years of the Hypothesis*, ed. Rod Cross (Cambridge: Cambridge University Press, 1995); "Recollections of My Past Research in Economics," Beijing Technology and Business University, June 2005; "Becoming an Economist," in *Les Prix Nobel 2006* (Stockholm: Nobel Foundation, 2007). These documents and some other data, including my curriculum vitae, are on my personal website, available at http://www.columbia.edu/~esp2.

2. The reference is James Heckman and Richard Robb, "Alternative Methods for Solving the Problem of Selection Bias in Evaluating the Impact of Treatments on Outcomes," in *Drawing Inferences from Self-Selected Samples*, ed. Howard Wainer (New York: Springer, 1986).

Edmund S. Phelps

Awarded Nobel Prize in 2006. Lecture presented April 9, 2008.

Date of Birth

July 26, 1933

Academic Degrees

B.A., Amherst College, 1955
Ph.D., Yale University, 1959

Academic Affiliations

Assistant Professor of Economics, Yale University and Member, Cowles Foundation, 1960–62
Visiting Associate Professor of Economics, Massachusetts Institute of Technology, 1962–63
Associate Professor of Economics, Yale University and Member, Cowles Foundation, 1963–66
Professor of Economics, University of Pennsylvania, 1966–71
Professor of Economics, Columbia University, 1971–82
Professor of Economics, New York University, 1978–79
McVickar Professor of Political Economy, Columbia University, 1982–present
Director, Center on Capitalism and Society, Earth Institute, Columbia University, 2001–present

Selected Books

Fiscal Neutrality toward Economic Growth, 1965
Golden Rules of Economic Growth, 1966
Microeconomic Foundations of Employment and Inflation Theory, 1970 (with A. Alchian, C. Holt, et al.)
Inflation Policy and Unemployment Theory, 1972
Studies in Macroeconomic Theory, Volume 1, *Employment and Inflation*, 1979
Studies in Macroeconomic Theory, Volume 2, *Redistribution and Growth*, 1980
Individual Forecasting and Aggregate Outcomes: "Rational Expectations" Examined, 1983 (ed., with R. Frydman)
Political Economy: An Introductory Text, 1985

The Slump in Europe: Open Economy Theory Reconstructed, 1988 (with J.-P. Fitoussi)
Seven Schools of Macroeconomic Thought: The Arne Ryde Lectures, 1990
Structural Slumps: The Modern Equilibrium Theory of Employment, Interest, and Assets, 1994
Rewarding Work: How to Restore Participation and Self-Support to Free Enterprise, 1997
Enterprise and Inclusion in the Italian Economy, 2002

Eric S. Maskin

When I went to college, I had no intention of becoming an economist. In fact, I scarcely had any idea at that point what economics was all about. I was a mathematics major in college, and I studied such things as group theory and analysis with some superb but occasionally rather eccentric math professors. To give an example, I once bumped into my real variables professor, George Mackey, in the hallway. We talked for a while, and at the conclusion of our chat he asked me what direction he had been going in when we met. I was a bit startled by the question, but I indicated the direction, and he said, "Good. That means I must have had lunch already."

Notwithstanding such odd episodes, I found mathematics a very attractive subject, and I might well have stayed a mathematician had I not wandered almost by accident into a course in economics that the great economist Kenneth Arrow was offering on the economics of information. I didn't know who Arrow was at the time, and I certainly didn't know what the economics of information was, but I thought the class should at least be informative. Arrow's lectures were improvisational. He appeared to have thought up what he was going to talk about on the way over to the lecture room from his office, and sometimes not even then. But in addition to being improvisational, they were inspirational. The list of

topics was a bit of a hodgepodge. There was some information economics, as the name of the course suggested. There was some team theory,
there was a unit on planning procedures, there was a discussion of moral
hazard and adverse selection. But the highlight of the course, and the part
that changed my life, was Leonid Hurwicz's work on mechanism design
theory. Leo shared the 2007 Nobel Prize with Roger Myerson and me for
mechanism design, but he was the founder of this field, and Roger and I
simply followed in his footsteps.

I found the course so riveting that I decided to switch out of math
and into economics. I did a Ph.D. with Ken Arrow as my supervisor,
and a lot of my early work was on mechanism design. And before too
long, Ken had introduced me to Leo Hurwicz in person. One of my first
research projects was a collaboration with Leo and the economist Andy
Postlewaite.

I'll try to provide a one-paragraph definition of mechanism design,
but the best way to understand what the theory is aiming at is through
examples, so I will spend more time on those. Here is the short definition:
mechanism design is the engineering part of economic theory. Most of the
time in economics we take existing economic institutions and either try
to predict what outcomes they will give rise to (although that's especially
hard) or look back on past outcomes and try to understand why they
occurred. This is the so-called *positive* or *predictive* part of economic
theory. But what I am personally most interested in—and what mechanism design concentrates on—is just the opposite. We first identify what
outcomes or goals we want to achieve, and then we work backward and
ask whether institutions or mechanisms or procedures could be designed
to achieve those goals. If possible, we also try to describe what form
these institutions will take. This is the *normative* or *prescriptive* part of
economics. It's a much smaller part of economics than the positive part,
but it's the part I like best.

Here's an example that's likely familiar from your own domestic
experience. Let's imagine there's a parent—a mother, say—who wants
to divide a cake between her two children, Alice and Bob. If you've ever
done this in your own family, you know that it's absolutely critical to
divide the cake so that each child is happy with the piece he or she gets.
That means Bob should think he's got at least half, and Alice should
think *she's* got at least half. If we achieve this goal, then we say we have
a *fair division.* You'll know, if you've tried this at home, that not getting
a fair division is a catastrophe. So the mother certainly wants to get
it right.

How does the mother do this? If she knows the kids see the cake the way she does, then there's a very simple solution. She just takes a knife and cuts the cake exactly equally in her view, and gives each child a piece. Because the kids see the cake the same way, they both realize they each have half, and that's the end of the story.

But what if Bob or Alice sees the cake differently from their mother? In fact, this is what inevitably happens in any real home. The mother might think she has divided it exactly equally, but Bob will think that his piece is smaller than Alice's, or Alice will think her piece is smaller than Bob's. The problem is that the mother doesn't have enough information to achieve a fair division by herself. She, in effect, doesn't know what division is fair. Hence the mechanism design question: *Is there an indirect way of proceeding that will generate a fair division, even though the mother herself doesn't know what is fair?* It turns out that this is a very old question.

If you've read or heard Bible stories, you'll recognize that the question I've posed is exactly the same as the one Lot and Abraham faced when they were trying to figure out how to divide up grazing land between the two of them; it's the same question of fair division. This question, then, goes back at least a couple of thousand years, and as usual, the Bible doesn't just pose the question, it provides an answer. Here is the translation of the answer into "cake."

The mother should have one of the children (say, Bob) divide the cake in two, and have the other child (Alice) choose which piece she wants for herself. Very simple. Why does it work? It works because it exploits Bob's incentives to divide the cake equally. This is the crucial word in mechanism design theory: *incentives*. When Bob cuts the cake, he has a strong motivation—a strong incentive—to divide the cake so that in his eyes, the pieces are equal. Why? Because if one of the pieces is bigger, he knows Alice will take that one. So he will try to cut the cake in such a way that, whichever piece Alice takes, he's happy with the other one. By cutting the cake exactly in half, Bob will be assured of at least half. And Alice is assured of half because she gets to choose the piece she prefers. Thus, the divide and choose procedure—the mechanism from the Bible—solves the mother's problem.

Cutting a cake is a relatively simple problem, but one rich enough to exhibit some of the key features of mechanism design. First, the problem arises because the mechanism designer (the mother, in this case) doesn't have enough information to know which outcomes are best (which outcomes are fair, in this case), so she has to proceed through a mechanism.

In effect, the mechanism (the divide and choose procedure, in this case) has the participants, through their actions, generate the information needed to identify the optimal outcome. But there's a complication: the participants (Alice and Bob) couldn't care less about the mother's goal. *She* wants to achieve a fair division, but Alice and Bob just want more cake. So the mechanism has to take into account that their goals are not the same as the mother's. To use the jargon of the theory, the mechanism must be *incentive compatible*, that is, compatible with Alice's and Bob's objectives.

Before going on to the next example, let's take a quick look at how mechanism design evolved over time. As we've seen, some elements go back thousands of years. But the subject really took off with the writings of the utopian socialists in the United States and, especially, Britain in the nineteenth century. These writers were disturbed by the unpleasant side effects of capitalism, such as income inequality and the destruction of the environment. They thought capitalism could be much improved on, and they tried out various alternatives. The alternatives didn't turn out to work in practice, but they generated some interesting ideas.

A more immediate precursor of the modern theory of mechanism design was a famous debate that took place in the 1930s and 1940s, now called the planning controversy. There were two major figures on each side of it.

On one side were Oskar Lange and Abba Lerner, who argued that, in principle, central planning had to be better than the free market. They reasoned that, at worst, planning could replicate the outcomes of the market, and moreover, it could correct the market's failures. On the other side were Friedrich von Hayek and Ludwig von Mises, who denied that central planning could ever succeed. Indeed, Hayek and Mises held that only a free market could generate prosperity.

This controversy went on for many years. It was important and drew lots of attention, but it had some shortcomings. In particular, none of the crucial terms, such as "central planning" and "free market," were ever defined; they were invoked without being assigned clear-cut meanings. Moreover, the four principals in the debate did not have the technical apparatus we have today, such as game theory and mathematical programming, to express themselves in unambiguous and precise terms. That's where Leo Hurwicz came in.

Leo was inspired by the planning controversy but frustrated by its vagueness. In his two landmark papers (Hurwicz 1960, 1972), he defined all the important terms with formal precision. He also showed how to use modern tools to obtain sharp answers to the questions debated in the controversy.

The follow-up literature to the planning controversy, much of which was inspired by Hurwicz's work, has produced a consensus view that, in some particular circumstances, Hayek and Mises were correct that the market is the best mechanism. But to reach that conclusion, it is essential that those circumstances obtain. In particular, there must be large numbers of buyers and sellers, thus eliminating monopoly power. It is equally important that there be no significant externalities. An *externality* is created whenever I do something that affects your consumption or production and I don't take this effect into account (for example, people don't usually consider the traffic congestion they generate when they drive their cars). When both these circumstances hold, the market mechanism cannot be bettered. But when either circumstance (large numbers or no externalities) is violated, then typically a mechanism that improves on the free market can be found. That is an important lesson of mechanism design theory.

By coincidence, in the same year that Hurwicz produced his first general paper on mechanism design, an equally important paper by William Vickrey appeared (Vickrey 1961). It was on a particular mechanism that has come to be known as the Vickrey mechanism or the Vickrey auction. Vickrey was later recognized for this work with the 1996 Nobel Prize in Economics, which he shared with James A. Mirrlees.

The Vickrey mechanism was one of the first specific mechanisms developed in the modern era using modern tools. It's simple, clever, and practical—it solves some important real-life problems (even more important than cutting a cake fairly!).

My second example of mechanism design uses the Vickrey mechanism in its solution. All of us are beneficiaries of the telecommunications revolution; we communicate now using cell phones or iPads or similar digital devices. This revolution was made possible because governments around the world (starting with the U.S. government) in effect privatized the airwaves. That is, large chunks of radio spectrum that had been in the public domain were transferred to the private sector so that telecom companies could use them more effectively.

Let's look at a simple example of such a privatization. Let's imagine that a government wants to transfer the license to use a particular band of radio frequencies to one of several telecom companies interested in this license. And let's assume that the goal of the government is to put the license into the hands of the company that values it the most. That seems like a natural goal because this company is going to create the most value for society. If the license goes to this company, economists call the outcome *efficient*.

The problem is that the government doesn't *know* which company values the license the most, so it doesn't know the efficient outcome. What can it do? The simplest thing would be to ask each company, how much do you value the license? But if you think about this mechanism—and the companies would certainly think about it—you'll see that it would not work very well: companies will grasp that their chances of getting the license go up when they state higher values, and so they have a strong incentive to exaggerate their values. But if all companies are exaggerating, how is the government to identify which company really does value the license the most? This rather naïve way of proceeding is not likely to work very well.

The government could try something bit more sophisticated: it could ask each company to make a bid for the license. A bid is a statement of how much the company is willing to pay. The government could then award the license to the highest bidder and have the winner pay its bid. That sounds more promising than the first mechanism, but it's not going to work either. The reason is that now companies have exactly the *opposite* incentive. In the first mechanism—whereby the government simply asks companies the value they place on the license—the companies will exaggerate. Now the companies have an incentive to *understate*. Why is that?

Put yourself in the shoes of one of these companies. Say you are Telemax. Suppose the license is worth $10 million to you. Will you bid $10 million? If you *do* bid $10 million and you win, you'll be getting something worth $10 million, but you will be paying $10 million. On net, you will have a profit of zero. There's no point in winning if your resulting profit is zero. This means that Telemax is going to bid *less* than $10 million. It's going to understate. Doing so reduces its chance of winning, but at least if it *does* win, it will get a positive profit. Yet if all bidders understate, then once again there is no guarantee of identifying the company that really values the license the most. So this mechanism doesn't work either, and we face the question, is there a way of reconciling the opposing forces at work in these two mechanisms? That is, can we find a mechanism that achieves the perfect compromise between overstating and understating?

That is where Vickrey came in. The answer is yes, we can, and Vickrey showed how to do it in his 1961 paper. The solution is remarkably simple.

Once again, the government has each company make a bid for the license. Once again, the government awards the license to the company that makes the highest bid. But instead of paying its *own* bid, that company pays the *second* highest bid. For example, if there are three bidders and one bids $10 million, one bids $8 million, and one bids $5 million, then the $10 million bidder will win, but will pay only $8 million, since that's the second highest bid. In this mechanism, I claim that bidders have the incentive neither to overstate nor understate. They will bid *exactly* what the license is worth to them.

Why won't they understate? Well, if Telemax understates, it gains nothing, because it doesn't pay its bid anyway. Suppose the license is worth $10 million to Telemax and it bids $9 million instead. If the second highest bid is $8 million, Telemax will pay $8 million whether it bids $10 million or understates the value. So it doesn't benefit from the understatement. Furthermore, understatement runs the risk of losing the license altogether. Say Telemax bids $7 million but some other company bids $8 million (the bids are sealed, so Telemax doesn't know this). Then Telemax will lose to the other company. Yet if it had bid what the license is actually worth to it ($10 million), it would have won and made a nice $2 million profit ($10 million—$8 million). Telemax never benefits from understating and, worse, it could be harmed by doing so because it might end up losing altogether.

Telemax also doesn't have an incentive to overstate. If it bids $12 million and the second highest bid is $ 8 million, it still pays $ 8 million. So it doesn't gain anything by overstating. Furthermore, it runs the risk of overpaying. If some other company comes in at $11 million, then Telemax may win with a bid of $12 million, but it will regret doing so: it will pay $11 million, more than the $10 million the license is worth to it. So Telemax won't overstate.

The only thing left is for Telemax to bid exactly what the license is worth to it. But if all companies bid exactly what the license is worth to them, then the winner will be the bidder with the highest value, which is what the government wanted to achieve in the first place. So Vickrey's simple but clever mechanism solves the problem, and for that reason it forms the basis of the mechanisms that governments around the world have actually used.

One attractive property of Vickrey's mechanism is that when a company tries to figure out how much to bid, it doesn't have to worry about what other bidders are going to do. Bidding its true value in the mechanism is optimal independent of others' behavior. Unfortunately, there are many settings where the Vickrey mechanism does not apply and this attractive independence property is lost.

So, I have introduced examples, and for each I've produced a mechanism that implements the designer's goals. However, it might plausibly be argued that I have specially constructed these examples so that the goals could be implemented. And so far I have said nothing about how someone could *find* an implementing mechanism other than by making an inspired guess.

These concerns prompt two general questions. First, is there a systematic way to determine whether a goal is implementable or not? (In the examples, the goals were implementable, but I could have introduced other examples in which they are not.) Second, if the goal is implementable, is there a surefire way to find a mechanism that does the implementing?

Those were the questions I struggled with many years ago. I won't say how long it took to find a solution; let's just say it was a long time. But finally, in a 1977 article (published as Maskin 1999), I was able to determine that the answer to both of these general questions is yes. There *is* a way of determining whether goals are implementable, and furthermore, there is a way of constructing mechanisms that do the implementing. I'll forbear from explaining now why the answers are yes. But you can read the paper if you are interested.

Mechanism design theory has been around for a long time; it's been fifty years since Hurwicz's and Vickrey's landmark papers. And the subject remains lively, in part because new potential applications keep coming along and renewing researchers' interest in the field. I'll mention two applications for the future.

One is climate change. This is a global mechanism design problem. We're now in agreement—there is scientific consensus—that not only are temperatures rising but humans are responsible for it by having released greenhouse gases such as carbon dioxide into the atmosphere. The obvious solution to curtailing climate change is to reduce our emissions of these gases.

But there is a conflict between that global goal (which we can agree on) and the individual goals of the countries of the world. Countries are also interested in making sure their economies thrive, and unfortunately, reducing greenhouse gas emissions is economically costly: it requires developing new technologies, or shutting down factories, or reducing output, all of which are expensive. So, each country would like the other countries to reduce emissions, but would prefer not to do so itself. How do we solve this conflict of goals? One way is through an international treaty in which countries pledge to reduce emissions, if other countries do the same. But designing an international treaty on greenhouse gas emissions is a problem in mechanism design. We don't have the solution to that problem; it remains to be found. But one day it will be found.

One last big application for the future: I don't have to remind anyone that we're in the middle of a financial crisis now—I hope it's the middle, rather than the beginning—but I am certain we will be out of it someday (though I'm not making a prediction about when). At that point, we must confront the question of how to prevent such a crisis from happening again. We have a good idea of what went wrong: it was a failure of regulation. Banks had the incentive to take on enormous debt and risk because the possible bad consequences of that debt and risk fell primarily on other people. In such circumstances, it is the job of the regulators to constrain banks, but such constraints were not in place in the years leading up to the crisis. The construction of a regulatory system that actually works is, again, a problem in applied mechanism design. It would be wonderful if some who are economics students today were involved in cracking that one, too.

References

Hurwicz, L. 1960. "Optimality and Informational Efficiency in Resource Allocation Processes." In *Mathematical Methods in Social Sciences*, ed. Kenneth Arrow, S. Karin, and P. Suppes, 27–46. Stanford, CA: Stanford University Press.

Hurwicz, L. 1972. "On Informationally Decentralized Systems." In *Decision and Organization*, ed. C. McGuire and R. Radner, 297–336. Amsterdam: North-Holland.

Maskin, E. 1999. "Nash Equilibrium and Welfare Optimality." *Review of Economic Studies* 66:23–38.

Vickrey, W. 1961. "Counterspeculation, Auctions, and Competitive Sealed Tenders." *Journal of Finance* 16 (1): 8–37.

Eric Maskin

Awarded Nobel Prize in 2007. Lecture presented April 21, 2009.

Date of Birth

December 12, 1950

Academic Degrees

A.B., Mathematics, Harvard University, 1972
A.M., Applied Mathematics, Harvard University, 1974
Ph.D., Applied Mathematics, Harvard University, 1976

Academic Affiliations

Research Fellow, Jesus College, Cambridge University, 1976–77
Assistant Professor of Economics, Massachusetts Institute of Technology, 1977–80
Associate Professor of Economics, MIT, 1980–81
Overseas Fellow, Churchill College, Cambridge University, 1980–82
Professor of Economics, MIT, 1981–84
Professor of Economics, Harvard University, 1985–2000
Visiting Overseas Fellow, St. John's College, Cambridge, 1987–88
Louis Berkman Professor of Economics, Harvard University, 1997–2000
Visiting Professor of Economics, MIT, 1999–2000
SK Professor, Yonsei University, 2009–10
Visiting Fellow, I.A.S., Hong Kong University of Science and Technology, 2010–present
Visiting Lecturer in Economics, Princeton University, 2000
Albert O. Hirschman Professor of Social Science, Institute for Advanced Study, Princeton University, 2000–present

Selected Books

Evolution and Economic Behavior, 2015
The Arrow Impossibility Theorem, 2014 (with Amartya Sen)
Bargaining, Coalition, and Externalities, 2007
Markov Perfect Equilibrium, I: Observable Action, 1997
Recent Developments in Game Theory, Editor, 1999

Joseph E. Stiglitz

We live in an era in which we strive to explain, systematically and scientifically, the world around us. But we also strive to understand the creative process. It is difficult to explain how that process works. How do our ideas come about?

Those of us who are credited with having made advances in understandings, even breakthroughs, do not fully understand how they arise and get developed. So I welcome this long-standing endeavor by Trinity University to expand our understanding of the creative process by sharing some of my own reflections and experiences, joining a long list of distinguished colleagues who have done so.

This is a moment that should give much of the economics profession pause. The world is in the worst economic crisis of the last three-quarters of a century, and our profession bears more than a little responsibility. When medical doctors take up their profession, they sign the Hippocratic Oath, whose clauses include *primum non nocere*, "First, do no harm." We sign no such oath, but had we done so, many within the profession would have found themselves in violation.

Much of the blame lies with market fundamentalism, the belief that markets and market participants are fully rational, that markets are efficient and self-correcting, and quickly so. These beliefs undergirded the deregulatory movement that played such an important role in giving rise to the financial crisis that began in 2007. It is testament both to the power and the inadequacy of these views that, relying on them, so many failed to recognize that a bubble existed, until it burst. Even when they might have admitted that bubbles were possible, market fundamentalists thought it would be easier and less costly to clean up the mess after a bubble broke than to try to prevent one from forming. These kinds of flawed ideas, which economists expressed in both academia and in the public arena, supported the policies that have brought so much suffering to so many.

Ideological wars linked to policy battles have long played an important role in economics. They energized my graduate studies at MIT, which was then engaged in a fierce battle with the Chicago school, headed by Milton Friedman and George Stigler. This was in the early 1960s, a period of real foment in America.[1] It was the Kennedy period—a period when, to paraphrase JFK, people were asking not what the country could do for them but what they could do for their country. That was followed by a period of intense turmoil having to do with the Vietnam War.

I was doing my undergraduate and graduate studies at that time, and within academia, these battles get distilled in a particular way. The Chicago school, politically very conservative, called for a minimal role for government. The Cambridge school in the United Kingdom—people like Joan Robinson and Nicholas Kaldor—carried on the mantle of John Maynard Keynes on the left. Of course, there was a range within each of these institutions—the intellectual battles within Cambridge, UK, were perhaps as intense as any of those between Cambridge and Chicago. These battles played a large role in my intellectual development. But clearly, that can only be part of the explanation of the processes that formed my thinking, since many others were subjected to the same education.

My upbringing and early schooling were also very important. I grew up in the steel town of Gary, Indiana, on the southern shores of Lake Michigan. Gary and the upper Midwest in general were in much better economic shape during my childhood than they are now, but it was still not the kind of background that would normally be thought of as an advantage for a future academic. For my intellectual development, however, it was extremely formative, in several senses. Gary was founded in 1906. A hundred years later it is in deep decline. Its course essentially traced that of the industrial period of America. No one growing up in this town—emblematic of the rise and fall of industrialization in America—could believe that markets were an unmixed blessing. I saw the darker side—and darker not only because of the pollution (which was often invisible) but also because of the obvious economic and social costs: periodic unemployment, labor strife as workers struggled to get a fair share of the benefits that increasing productivity was bringing to the country, rampant discrimination, and urban decay.

I also benefited from a public school system with dedicated teachers working under the educational philosophy of John Dewey. This system helped make America's melting pot work by bringing together disparate groups and teaching them vocational skills (I learned how to be both a printer and an electrician) and life skills (I learned to type as fast as any secretary), as well as the usual academic subjects. Work-study-play was the educational philosophy. I can't fully describe the sense of dedication of my teachers, how they helped shape my thinking and my approach to learning. When I was in sixth grade, a number of them decided there was little point to my studying with the rest of the class, especially mathematics, at which I excelled from a young age. And so until I took advanced calculus in college, what I learned was almost totally self-taught. I suppose this made me not very sympathetic to students who want to be spoon-fed. But more important, it encouraged the habit of mind of figuring things out for myself.

One of my major extracurricular activities was debating. Each year there was a national topic that was debated. The one that sticks in my mind was reforming America's agricultural policies. I found the economics and politics fascinating. I thought what we were doing then was wrong. I formulated what I thought was a set of policies that would be much better at reducing the risk facing farmers, and at lower cost to taxpayers. These were issues I would come back to in my theoretical work,[2] during my years as chairman of the Council of Economic Advisers,[3] and I would write about them in my work on globalization. I am shocked at how little progress we've made in the half century since I debated these issues. It seems as though time has stood still. I still believe my thinking from those high school debates would make sense today.

In the context of my upbringing, I should also mention my parents and the way they conveyed a sense of values. They were very engaged in political discourse, but not in politics. Within our extended family there was a range of views that went from Jeffersonian Democrats who focused on competition policy to New Deal Democrats. They were all within the Democratic family. Even the most economically successful—and there were some that were very well off—believed in the importance of unions and collective bargaining, in fighting for fairness for workers.

My father was born in 1903 and in many ways was a role model for how people can adapt to the quick changes in social mores that America was going through in the 1950s, 1960s, and 1970s. My mother (who had gone to the University of Chicago) did not get the conservative economic disease from going there. She had picked the University of Chicago because during the Great Depression, it was the cheapest place for her to go. She decided later on that she wanted to go to graduate school to get the qualifications that would allow her to teach in elementary school, and my father took up new roles in sharing household duties, which for someone of his generation was quite revolutionary.

I also owe to my parents (my father in particular) my ability to serve in government. A problem for many wanting to serve in the Clinton administration was that, when they were vetted, it would turn out they hadn't paid Social Security taxes on their household help. When I was growing up, my father told me that you should always pay Social Security taxes for anybody who works for you, because many of these people were poor people and particularly in need of help in their retirement. That's why we have the Social Security Administration. So he was one of the generation for whom Social Security (which started in the mid-1930s) was very important. Today, Social Security benefits are too often taken for granted.

My father believed that one should pay the Social Security taxes for one's employees not just because it was the law but also because it was the right thing to do. So I had done so for those who had worked for me—and was able to surmount this hurdle, which had proved an obstacle for so many others.

Like most teenagers, I asked my parents what I should do when I grew up. They said, "Money's not important. You should never do anything for money." (For a future economist, this was a particularly interesting perspective, and especially so since so many of those in the economics profession seem to believe money drives the world.) My parents' view was that one should use one's mind and be of service in one way or another. Their perspective was something I always remembered as I made decisions later in life.

I will skip forward a little to Amherst College, a small college in New England—at the time there were about a thousand male students. One of the reasons I went to Amherst was that my guidance counselor worried that someone coming from Gary, Indiana, would not be adequately equipped to deal with large schools like Harvard, Yale, or Chicago. She thought a small, nurturing community was what I needed, and that Amherst would enable me to live up to my potential.

When I went to Amherst, I was very well prepared. I could give testimony to the quality of America's public education system, at least at that time. Amherst shaped me in more than one way, and I have tried to do what I can to repay it.[4] Amherst, like Trinity University, is a liberal arts school, and I thrived there. At the time, it had what was called the core curriculum. We had almost no choices in the first two years. (One of the few schools that still have a variant of this kind of core curriculum is Columbia.) We could choose which foreign language we would study, and we had also a choice of which "hard" science to study. It was very intense. Everybody had to take calculus, physics, English, history, and humanities.

One of the aspects of that kind of liberal arts education is that it focuses on teaching—very much in a Socratic style, small classes where the teachers would ask questions—which encouraged a questioning spirit, including a questioning of established theories. I think that's one of the most important elements of the creative process, and one of the most important for democratic processes as well. There is no such thing as an established authority. It is really important that our students should question what we say. I try to encourage such questioning in my classes. My teachers at Amherst also stressed that what matters is not so much the answers but how you frame the questions. If you can ask the question—frame the question—in the right way, then it's just a technical matter to figure out the answer. Much of what we did was focused on figuring out what it means to frame the question right—how to frame the questions in ways that give meaningful answers.

What I learned at Amherst stuck with me and affected my thinking and my research years later, as I was doing my work in the economics of information and globalization. For example, my development of the theory of screening was informed by my study of Plato and the notion of Platonic ideals. So, partially obscured by the mathematics, behind the theory of screening were some fairly deep philosophical ideas.

Another example: One of the world history courses I took was concerned with the encounter of civilizations before the expression "clash of civilizations" was fashionable. We studied in particular the encounter between the West and Asia, mainly in the nineteenth century. It was an encounter that was not handled very well. The Western powers engaged in conflicts with China called the Opium Wars. We went to war to make sure that China kept its markets open to our sale of opium. It sounds a little strange now. The problem was that China produced a lot of things that we wanted—like china tableware—and we produced nothing that China wanted. So all we could do was go buy opium in Afghanistan, transport it to China, get them addicted, and make the middle-man profits that made this whole global balance of trade work out. When you try to understand why some people in Asia are less than enthusiastic about what we call market access or opening initiatives, they have memories of what that means, and may not view it as positively as those in the West do. This is an example of some of the understandings I brought to the discussion when I started working at the World Bank that many other people who hadn't had that kind of liberal arts education didn't bring to the subject.

When I was at Amherst, I was very focused on my academic studies, but that was also when I began to be more active in political life. I was elected to the college's Student Council and eventually became its president. But I was always a little bit of an agitator, interested in making changes. At the time, around 93 percent of the students at Amherst belonged to fraternities. But I thought fraternities were a bad idea. I belonged to one, too, but I still thought they were divisive and undermined the sense of community that was so important, especially at a small college like Amherst. And so I began a campaign to abolish fraternities. It succeeded, though only about ten years after I left.

These and other initiatives I undertook were not always popular. There was a recall motion, which I defeated, and a fight with "the press" (the student newspaper). It was certainly not boring.

There were a number of other initiatives we undertook. In the 1960s there was still segregation in the South. I led a small group from Amherst to go down there and engage in pushing the desegregation agenda. We were unaware of the dangers in this kind of endeavor—several people did die, though thankfully, none from Amherst.

I had been a physics major at Amherst. I was attracted to the beauty of mathematics and the way it helped explain reality in some deep and fundamental sense. But I also took a number of courses in economics. We had some fantastic teachers—some of them were analytical, some were very policy-oriented, and all of them were very exciting in their own way.

When I was doing physics, I also got very interested and involved in environmental issues. I was a bit ahead of the time, I suppose. One of the branches of physics I was interested in was oceanography. I spent a summer working at Woods Hole Oceanographic Institute. One of the most exciting and enjoyable parts of that summer was going out on the ocean on a ten-day expedition. In much of my later work I've been involved in work on environmental economics. I was on the IPCC (the Intergovernmental Panel on Climate Change) and one of the lead authors of the 1995 *Report*. (The IPCC shared the Nobel Peace Prize in 2007 with Al Gore.)

There was a moment in the spring of my junior year when—and I can't quite explain why—I decided I wanted to become an economist instead of a physicist. I thought I could make use of the analytical rigor of economics to have some impact on the social problems that were really my passion.

This was still an era of informality, and what happened then likely could not happen today. My professors told me, "If you're going to major in economics, there's no point in staying at Amherst. You might as well just go on and get a Ph.D." One of them got on the phone, called up Paul Samuelson at MIT, and said, "We have somebody that you should take, and can you find some money for him?"

Going to MIT after my junior year meant I would not get a degree. I had this (you might say) risk-taking view. I had the view that degrees were just symbols, and that if you did good work, you didn't need those symbols. Why did I need a B.A. degree anyway? I would just go ahead and become an economist without a degree. So I went to MIT without an undergraduate degree and no understanding that I would ever get one. (Amherst decided to grant me an undergraduate degree after one year at MIT, so I could graduate with my class, and later gave me an honorary doctorate. And a couple of years later, I got a Ph.D., so it all worked out in the end.)

At MIT I again had some absolutely fantastic teachers. Several of them are represented in this lecture series: Franco Modigliani, Ken Arrow, Bob Solow, and Paul Samuelson.

I mentioned earlier the battle MIT had with Chicago, and the Chicago school's view that markets work perfectly, leaving no role for government policy. The problem was the models that we were being taught at MIT actually were consistent with the Chicago school's view. The neoclassical models we were taught (supply = demand, etc.) implied that markets worked perfectly. I knew those models were wrong because I had seen unemployment; I had seen so many things that were inconsistent with the neoclassical model. One thing that really motivated me in my research was my recognition as a first- and second-year graduate student that what my teachers were telling me had to be wrong—even if I didn't yet know what was wrong. Then an active debate began with some of my classmates on what was wrong. Many things were wrong—let me make that clear—but the question was, what was the pivotal thing that was wrong?

For instance, it was assumed there is perfect competition. We all know that's not right, but you could not explain the problems of unemployment with imperfect competition. You could explain some aspects of the distribution of income, you might be able to explain inequality, but you could not explain business cycles. But I was interested in explaining the fluctuations in the economy and the persistence of unemployment. I was trying to figure out which of the assumptions was responsible for these phenomena, and why the models we were being taught could not account for them.

Within the group of people at MIT, I was very much in the center of the political spectrum. There were many classmates who were far to the left of me. There were people who insisted on bringing in Marxian economics, and much more radical departures from the neoclassical models that were at the core of what we were being taught. There was much discussion of "power relationships." At the time I was unconvinced by these approaches.

In the end, the assumption that I became convinced was wrong and that was at the center of the failure of neoclassical economics was that of perfect information. What was interesting about the assumption of perfect information was that if you looked at one of the standard treatises of modern economics, Gerard Debreu's *The Theory of Value* (the analytical workings behind much of what students are taught), he never lists any assumptions about information. And the reason he doesn't is because the assumption of perfect information was so ingrained in his way of thinking he wasn't even aware it was an assumption. I think this is true more generally: Quite often we are not aware of the really important assumptions we make because they are so ingrained in our way of thinking.

The other assumption that was very important is the assumption of rationality—that people are perfectly rational and have well-formed preferences. This is also an ingrained assumption, and it's clearly a bad one. When I look around, it's clear to me that many people are not rational. In fact, when I look at the Chicago economists, they are irrationally committed to the assumption of rationality. So to me it was obvious that those of my colleagues who were wedded to market fundamentalism were so irrationally committed to the hypothesis of rationality that nothing I could say would ever change their minds. It was a religion, not a matter of science. So I focused on those things where I could change their minds, and I thought it was obvious they couldn't really believe everybody has perfect information. I narrowed my research strategy to the simple hypothesis that people have imperfect information but have rational expectations about the world. I assumed all the assumptions of rationality my colleagues had always made but changed one little assumption, and that was the assumption of perfect information. This was a change that nobody, not even they, could disagree with.

This is an idea that has profound consequences. Let me try to briefly describe the evolution of the idea. The first idea was a very simple one—like most ideas, it began very simply and then got elaborated and made more precise. It began with the metaphor of an egg sorter. Some eggs are bigger and some eggs are smaller. If you go to the store and the price is the same for all of them, you want to get the biggest egg for the price you have to pay. It's more efficient (for the farmer or retailer, more profitable) to sort eggs by size, and to sell the larger eggs at a higher price. This provides incentives for farmers to have hens that lay bigger eggs.

I realized that the same principles apply in other markets. When you look at a set of people whom you might hire or a set of products you might buy (such as eggs), you realize there are large differences within the set. At any given wage, you want the most productive worker; at any given price, we want the best product.

The basic idea was that there are very strong incentives on both sides of the market to try to identify who is more able or who has better projects or who is less risky. And this is so on both sides. If I am more able, I have an incentive to convince someone that I am more able because that will drive up my wage. And if I am an employer, I want to try to figure out who the best employees are. This sorting out was a concept that had no role in economics before (even though a lot of the activities of markets are really about sorting) because it was assumed that there was perfect information.

I discussed this basic concept of sorting with my MIT classmate George Akerlof in 1965 (who was to share the Nobel Prize with me thirty-six years later). Two years later, I went to Kenya. I was still quite young—about twenty-six. I was asked a question by the government there: "How much should we invest in education?" And that raised the question, what is education doing? At the time, the standard answer was, "It's improving skills." (This was called human capital.) Another part of the story was, "It's getting credentials." One of my friends in Kenya at the time, Gary Fields, had developed a theory of credentials and how credentialing works. He had made some assumptions that were not consistent with economic equilibrium. Here was a policy question. Fields had provided an analytical framework, but there were some inconsistencies in it, or at least departures from standard equilibrium theory that were unsettling. That led to the development of a number of my ideas that formed the center of my work in the economics of information, in particular the theory of screening.

Another example of how trying to explain or understand what is going on around you can help inspire new theories also occurred while I was in Kenya. In that country (as in the urban areas of so many developing countries) one could observe massive urban unemployment. There was no question of unions, no question of minimum wages, causing the unemployment. Even when there was a minimum wage, it was not enforced. You couldn't blame government or the unions for the unemployment, and the question was, why were wages evidently at levels above market clearing? There had to be an economic explanation, an economic theory. That led to the development of an idea called the efficiency wage hypothesis, which held that the productivity of workers was affected by the wage.

Now, there had been within development economics an analogous idea, based on nutritional concerns: paying workers better led to better nutrition and thus more productive workers. And, thinking about the world of developed countries, I started thinking about how the wage might affect the profitability of firms, as a result of the quality of the labor force firms could hire or the incentives of workers to work or their morale or the turnover rate. Efficiency wage theory helped explain why wages might be above the market clearing level: it paid firms to pay higher wages than they had to in order to get workers.

It also became clear that there was a link between efficiency wage theory and the theory of screening that I was simultaneously developing. One reason that it paid to pay high wages was that higher wages led to an improvement in the quality of the labor force—something that would not have happened if one had perfect information. This is an example of how one theory is linked to the next, and through this linkage each of the theories gets further developed.

It was clear by that point that this approach revolutionized how one thought about labor markets and capital markets, in a quite precise way. I then started thinking about the various mechanisms by which one might sort and screen, such as self-selection mechanisms, examinations, and so forth The mathematics of these theories is extraordinarily complex and—interestingly—not yet sorted out. Many of the problems that I raised forty years ago have still not been fully solved.

The most important idea to come out of this line of research was some work I did about a decade later with my colleague at Columbia, Bruce

Greenwald. One of the principal ideas in economics—certainly one of the most influential—is Adam Smith's invisible hand. That is, individuals in pursuit of their self-interest are led, as if by an invisible hand, to the well-being of society. It's the basic idea behind the belief in a market economy. Adam Smith formulated this idea in 1776. But he didn't prove it; it was just a conjecture, but people took it seriously for a long time.

Arrow and Debreu (who were awarded the Nobel Prize for their work) laid down a specific model, trying to identify a set of assumptions under which the invisible hand hypothesis was true. One of the things that Bruce and I did was to show that the reason the invisible hand often seemed invisible was that it wasn't there. In fact, in general, market economies are not efficient. There are almost always interventions by government that could lead to everybody in society being better off. One of the critical assumptions in Adam Smith was that there was perfect information and a complete set of markets—you could buy insurance against every risk, including the risk, for instance, that your house price might go down. We showed that markets are not efficient whenever these imperfections exist in the markets—and they are pervasive in every economy. They are not caused by government intervention; they are inherent. This was a theoretical result that had very profound policy implications: it was a very strong attack on market fundamentalism, the notion that there was a presumption in favor of unfettered markets because they were necessarily efficient.

I finally achieved what I had set out to do: I had come to understand what was wrong with the models we had been taught. At first this was unsettling to many economists, especially those devoted to "free market" economics. A number of the Chicago school economists tried to refute it. Whenever you have a model like this, you can never be sure you did not make a mistake. All humans are fallible. But in thirty years, no one has found a mistake in the math. Sometimes you make hidden assumptions (such as the hidden information assumptions I mentioned earlier in Debreu's theory of value), but no one has found a hidden assumption that invalidates the results. So it really does provide a very strong counter to the notion that is still very prevalent in American mythology about efficient markets.

Another response to these ideas has been that theoretically it's a nice result, but empirically it is not relevant. That's a hard thing to prove one way or the other, but the recent crisis points to the markets not working very well. That episode of markets not working well is obviously "empirically relevant." Similarly, the episodes of great depressions and great recessions, with the associated episodes of mass unemployment, happen often enough that one has to conclude that "market failures" are empirically relevant.

The final response to this analysis is that yes, markets are inefficient, but government is worse. Now, what's interesting about that response is that it entails economists (in saying that) becoming political scientists. It is a statement not about our economic system but about our political system. Those who make such claims are arguably worse as political scientists than they are as economists. There are subtleties in political analysis that those who make claims about the inevitability of government failure do not go into. They neither establish the result empirically nor show it theoretically. Certainly, at least some governments have historically done a credible job in correcting market failures. Even if government is imperfect, outcomes are better than they would have been in the absence of government intervention.

This brings me to the last topic I want to engage, the evolution of my ideas about another set of issues I have been involved with my whole academic life, namely, macrostability issues, which are very germane to the current crisis. The first question I have already discussed: Is the economy efficient? The results show that in general, the markets are not efficient; there are interventions that can improve the efficiency of the markets. The massive waste of resources in the run-up to the global recession of 2008–2009 and its aftermath (the massive misallocation of resources before the crisis, the massive underutilization of resources after the crisis) should be proof enough of the inefficiency of unfettered markets. The theories that I helped develop provide at least part of the explanation for these failures.

The second question is the following: Are the markets stable? The assertion of people like Alan Greenspan is "Yes, they are stable. We don't have to intervene." If the markets get off course, they are self-correcting—and self-correcting fairly rapidly—so we don't have to steer the economy.

Now, the obvious response to those beliefs is, what about the Great Depression? Didn't that happen? That was a long time ago—certainly before most of us who are writing today were alive—so the assertion is that that was ancient history. We're so much smarter today than those people in the 1920s were; we would never do anything as stupid as they did!

What is remarkable is that historically, people have always thought that way; people have always thought they were smarter than the previous generation and incapable of making the same mistakes. In the history of capitalism there have been bubbles, and the bubbles have inevitably burst. There have been these kinds of booms and busts over and over and over again. Of course, each time those involved in the creation of the bubble believe it is different from the past. Every episode is different—the world is always different—but what is remarkable is how similar they all are. We even had a stock market bubble in 1999, less than a decade before the housing bubble. If you look at bubbles, their structure, and what gives rise to them, they are remarkably similar.

This was a question that was very much on our minds in the 1960s, when I was a graduate student, only thirty years out from the Great Depression. We were still interested then in trying to understand why there were economic downturns. Back then, there were models of business cycles—multiplier = accelerator models—that went out of fashion partly because if these periodicities were detectable, rational behavior would be expected to undermine them—so they weren't sustainable. (I've already expressed my skepticism about economists' excessive focus on rationality.)

One of the worst aspects of these economic fluctuations is the high levels of unemployment associated with the downturns. The actuality runs counter to a major hypothesis of Chicago-style economics and its particular models, that demand equals supply—for everything.

But if demand for labor equals supply of labor, what does that say about unemployment? According to that mode of thinking, there's no such thing as unemployment. What does demand = supply mean when 9.8 percent of Americans are unemployed, as is the case now?[5] How does the Chicago school interpret that stubborn figure? They say that the unemployed are really just enjoying leisure. They're getting a little bit of an early vacation. But when most people go on vacation, they are happy. If you look at most of the people who can't get a job, they're not enjoying a vacation. The Chicago school would say this is not a problem for economists; it's a problem for psychiatrists. The unemployed should all go see a psychiatrist and try to understand why they aren't enjoying their leisure. But my own view is this is really quite an absurd view of economics and what's going on today.

This was not the only unsatisfactory aspect of the standard paradigm. To get equilibrium in these models required a full set of markets extending all the way out to infinity, and a natural question to ask was, what would happen if markets extended out only for a thousand years—or a hundred years, or twenty years? One of the results we showed was that you could have perfect foresight for any arbitrary period into the future and still get bubbles. There is an intrinsic dynamic instability, and to avoid it, markets have to extend out infinitely into the future in economic modeling. That was an insight that somehow got lost in the debate over the subsequent years.

Another question we asked was, what would happen if you don't have instantaneous adjustment of wages? The supply-and-demand model says that wages always adjust right away to get the economy to the point where demand equals supply. Again, that assumption is not credible: adjustments do not happen instantaneously. One of my earliest papers with George Akerlof showed that with reasonable adjustment processes, one can actually get regular, cyclical fluctuations. Another study, with my teacher Robert Solow, showed that with reasonable adjustment processes to wages and prices, one could get longlasting unemployment, as real wages adjust very slowly.

Still another strand of work showed that one could even retain the assumption of rational expectations but change another assumption, that of individuals who are infinitely alive, and get not just cycles but an economy that never settled down to any equilibrium.

The bottom line that I want to convey was that over the past forty years, a wealth of work has rejected the notion of markets as self-regulating, stable systems that converge smoothly to an equilibrium. There were some peculiar models (people infinitely alive, with more than rational expectations, single-individual economics, and so forth), but these were constructed worlds that are not the world any of us live in. And yet these models became the predominant paradigm, rejecting all the theory and empirical work on the other side that questioned both the assumptions and the conclusions of these analyses. That says something about the discipline of economics itself.

There were, of course, strong policy implications of these analyses. Policy became the servant of some special interests, those who benefited from the absence of good regulations (including many in the financial sector.)

In a way, I was lucky to be chief economist of the World Bank when the East Asia crisis struck, because it served to test some of the ideas about macroeconomic stability that I had developed in the preceding twenty years. The disparity between my views, which recognized that market economies could be both inefficient and unstable, and those that were then dominant at the IMF and the U.S. Treasury not surprisingly gave rise to quite a bit of controversy. Those who had advocated the simplistic market fundamentalist models basically said a crisis cannot occur. And responding to a crisis that can't occur obviously poses some problems.

We got into some intense policy debates. I believe that the policies that were foisted on the countries of East Asia by the U.S. Treasury and IMF made the crisis worse; it made the downturns deeper and longer lasting than they otherwise would have been.

The interesting thing is that, on the whole, the economics profession didn't learn the lessons of the East Asian crisis. I wrote about it a great deal, and I continued to do some research on the subject. But because we didn't learn the lessons of that crisis, we've had the crisis that began in 2007.

Let me just conclude with this thought. Economics is a complex and absolutely fascinating subject.

As I think about that spring afternoon when I went for a walk in a New England forest and decided to become an economist rather than a physicist, I am reminded of a Robert Frost poem about two roads that diverged in a yellow wood. I wonder what might have happened had I taken the other road.

Notes

Since the lecture at Trinity, some information has been updated in footnotes, or changed for clarity, but most references to chronological events have been left as is. I have retained the informal tone of the lecture.

1. I graduated from high school in 1960, went to Amherst College from 1960 to 1963, and then attended MIT from 1963 to 1965. I spent a year at Cambridge in 1966, and then I started teaching at MIT and Yale.

2. In 1981 I wrote, with David Newbery, *The Theory of Commodity Price Stabilization* (Oxford: Clarendon Press of Oxford University Press; New York: Oxford University Press).

3. From 1995 to 1997, during the Clinton administration.

4. I served on the Amherst College Board of Trustees for twelve years.

5. The unemployment rate in the United States would peak at 10.0 percent in October 2009.

Joseph E. Stiglitz

Awarded Nobel Prize in 2001. Lecture presented September 30, 2009.

Date of Birth

February 9, 1943

Academic Degrees

B.A., Amherst College, 1964
Ph.D., MIT, 1967

Academic Affiliations

Assistant Professor of Economics, MIT, 1966–67
Visiting Professor, Department of Economics, University of Canterbury,
Tapp Research Fellow, Gonville and Caius College, Cambridge, 1966–70
Christchurch, New Zealand, 1967
Assistant Professor, Cowles Foundation, 1967–68
Associate Professor, Cowles Foundation, 1968–70
Nairobi (under Rockefeller Foundation Grant), 1969–71
Professor of Economics, Cowles Foundation and Department of Econom-
ics, Yale University, 1970–74
Visiting Fellow, St. Catherine's College, Oxford, 1973–74
Professor of Economics, Stanford University, 1974–76
Drummond Professor of Political Economy, Oxford University, 1976–79
Oskar Morgenstern Distinguished Fellow and Visiting Professor, Institute
for Advanced Studies and Mathematica, 1978–79
Professor of Economics, Princeton University, 1979–88
Professor of Economics and Senior Fellow, Hoover Institution, Stanford
University, 1988–2001
Stern Visiting Professor, Columbia University, 2000
Professor Emeritus, Hoover Institution, Stanford University, 2001–
University Professor, Columbia Business School, the Graduate School of
Arts and Sciences (Department of Economics) and the School of Interna-
tional and Public Affairs, Columbia University, present

Selected Books

*An Economic Analysis of the Conservation of Depletable Natural
Resources*, prepared for the Federal Energy Administration, 1977 (with P.
Dasgupta, G. Heal, R. Gilbert, and D. Newbery)
The Theory of Commodity Price Stabilization, 1981 (with D. Newbery)
The Economic Role of the State, 1989

Peasants versus City-Dwellers: Taxation and the Burden of Economic Development, 1992 (with R. Sah)
Whither Socialism?, 1994
Globalization and Its Discontent, 2002
The Roaring Nineties, 2003
Toward a New Paradigm in Monetary Economics, 2003 (with Bruce Greenwald)
An Agenda for the Development Round of Trade Negotiations in the Aftermath of Cancun, prepared for the Commonwealth Secretariat, 2004 (with Andrew Charlton)
Fair Trade for All, 2005 (with Andrew Charlton)
Making Globalization Work, 2006
The Three Trillion Dollar War: The True Cost of the War in Iraq, 2008 (with L. Bilmes)
The Selected Works of Joseph E. Stiglitz, Volume I: Information and Economic Analysis, 2009
Freefall: America, Free Markets, and the Sinking of the World Economy, 2010
Mismeasuring Our Lives: Why GDP Doesn't Add Up, 2010 (with J. Fitoussi and A. Sen)
The Price of Inequality: How Today's Divided Society Endangers Our Future, 2012
The Selected Works of Joseph E. Stiglitz, Volume II: Information and Economic Analysis: Applications to Capital, Labor, and Product Markets, 2013

Paul Krugman

This is actually a very tough assignment. The question is *how do you talk about yourself without coming across as pretentious and full of yourself?*, and the answer is, *There probably isn't any way to do that*. I'll try to mix a bit of personal history with a bit of life philosophy (or, anyway, economics research philosophy) and see if that works.

Back in 1976, when I was in grad school, the grad students at Harvard and MIT in economics combined to put on a special program celebrating the bicentennial of the publication of Adam Smith's *Wealth of Nations*, in which we had Jerry Goodman—who wrote and did TV under the name of Adam Smith—dress up in a frock coat and wig to portray the actual Adam Smith. We also got various people to give humorous speeches about Adam Smith. One of them was Alan Blinder (who is now my colleague at Princeton). He gave a list of reasons why Adam Smith could not have been a great economist. They included things like not knowing a lot of higher math, not growing up in the New York suburbs, not being Jewish, and so forth. The point of this story is that I have a very boring background (the exact standard background for an American economist of my generation). The next generation is very different—it has a lot of Asian Americans, and other non-standard-issue economists.

I grew up on Long Island, in the suburbs, on the Babylon line of the Long Island railroad, went to John F. Kennedy High School—nothing interesting! I spent my time not studying very hard but doing okay, and reading a lot of science fiction novels. In particular, I loved the novels of Isaac Asimov, and especially his classic Foundation novels, which (if you haven't read them, you should) were written around 1940. They are about how at some point in the distant future—when galactic civilization is headed for collapse—the psycho-historians, who are mathematically inclined social scientists, with their theory of society, plan the rescue of galactic civilization and in the end save the day. In my teens I wanted to be one of those guys, and economics is as close as you can get to that in today's world.

At first I didn't know that. I went off to college thinking I wanted to do history. And I still love history—I love to read it—but it turned out I didn't have the temperament. Doing history requires an awful lot of nitty-gritty research, and while economics requires research, nitty-gritty research is not my style. Also, history is primarily about what happened. You can talk in the last chapter of your book about why it happened, but it is mostly about the *what* and not the *why*. I wanted more of the *why*. So I gravitated toward economics and had one of those really lucky breaks—the kind of lucky break you find behind the life story of anyone who has done well in his or her career. In my case, I had a really good instructor who taught a really good course (Bill Nordhaus, at Yale)—a special course on the economics of natural resources. I took it, and stumbled onto a good term paper topic for the course. I found some international data on the price of gasoline and on gasoline consumption, and put it together, and said, "Actually, you know, it looks like gasoline demand *is* affected a lot by the price."

On the strength of that paper, I was hired to work for Bill Nordhaus as a research assistant between my junior and my senior year. I spent most of that summer camped out in the geology library at Yale, doing research on energy for his big paper that year, and discovered that I loved doing it. That is, I discovered that doing research was my thing—that economic research was *really* my thing. So that went well, and I got a recommendation from Bill Nordhaus and went to grad school. The point I'm trying to make is that it was good that there turned out to be something I both enjoyed and was reasonably good at, but it was crucial that I lucked into meeting the right person at the right time.

I went off to MIT and raced through, finishing in three years, because I wanted to get out into the world (although you could argue I never have, given the kind of life I have). At MIT I figured out again what style of research suited me. I again lucked into finding another great mentor, this time the late Rudi Dornbusch, a great international macroeconomist at MIT—some would say the most influential international macroeconomist of the past thirty years or so. He was a great teacher and a great inspiration because of the way he worked.

Rudy had a personal taxonomy of economic researchers. He said that researchers can be divided into pigs and goldsmiths. Pigs are people who jump into a subject and wallow around, and that can constitute good research. Goldsmiths are people who produce very finely crafted little things. Both are good—Rudy described Larry Summers as a fearful pig, which was praise! (Larry is amazing—a kind of juggernaut; I'll come back to that later.) I was a goldsmith, which was a little surprising because I am not an organized, neat person in ordinary life. Should you ever visit my office at Princeton, you'd see it always looks as if a concussion grenade just went off. (I've received a couple of citations from the fire marshal.) I would also like to say there are some people whose office appears to be a total mess, but they can always find just what they need. I am not one of them.

It turned out, however, that I loved and was pretty good at producing little models. What do I mean by model? This is where we get into what research is about. There are various ways to be a good economist. Doing painstaking empirical work (working with, especially uncovering, data, or producing data) is a very important style, and some people are terrific at it. My colleague, Alan Krueger, has done fantastic work on labor markets in part by finding natural experiments you can look at. There are people who do deep theorizing, who work with proofs and theorems and get at very broad principles, and that's important. The style I've always liked, however, is the fairly small conceptual framework that is informed by real-world data and events but that offers a great way to approach the problem, resulting in an "Aha!" moment. It doesn't have to be a mathematical model (though that's by and large what we do); it could be a real-life story with broader implications.

For example, one of the models I've always thought tremendously important is the Capitol Hill Babysitting Co-op. This was a real-life situation, created by about a hundred and fifty couples in the 1970s who had young children and arranged to swap babysitting so as to save money. The co-op operated on a coupon system. Coupons were issued to all the members, each coupon representing a half hour of babysitting time, and when one couple babysat for another, they would exchange the appropriate number of coupons: The couple whose baby was "sat" would give coupons to the couple that was babysitting. (This story, by the way, was published in the *Journal of Money, Credit and Banking*.) It turned out that people wanted to keep some coupons in a drawer, in case they wanted to go out several nights in a row, and the number of coupons people wanted to hold was more than the number of coupons that had been issued. So members of the babysitting co-op were reluctant to go out because they wanted to accumulate more coupons, and that meant there were fewer opportunities to babysit and earn more coupons, which made people even more reluctant to go out. So the babysitting co-op fell into a recession. Obviously, the world is a lot more complicated than that, but this real-life story gets at the fundamental idea of how it is possible to have not enough demand in an economy. That's the kind of issue that opens my mind and gives me a framework for thinking about a problem.

I eventually discovered I was not too bad at doing this myself, and I had another lucky break in 1976. Bob Solow, the great MIT economist, gave a short course just for fun on topics he was interested in, and one was about the new models of monopolistic competition—models of markets that are not like supply and demand, but where everybody is a little monopolist. And there was an outgrowth of new ideas about how to model this that took place in the mid-1970s, with Mike Spence, Joe Stiglitz, and Avinash Dixit all producing little ways to think about this.

I took that course and came back from it; it was fun, but it bounced around in my head a bit. After I had left for my first teaching job, it came together in my head that this was a way to think about international trade. This would be a gadget—a way to think clearly about what happens when countries specialize in different products because there are advantages to producing each product on a large scale. I was at a loss my first year out of grad school—I wasn't sure what I was doing—and I went to talk with my old mentor, Rudi Dornbusch, to try out a few ideas I had. When we got to talking, I described the idea of doing something for international trade. He said, "*That's the one to work on.*" I went back and started working on it some more, and it all fell into place. The more I worked on it, the clearer it got. It was one of those things where the solution was not intuitively obvious until I had done the math. Then it became obvious, and I could figure out a way to do it in plain English afterward. If you're interested, the *American Economic Review* paper that came out of these thoughts—one of their top twenty papers of the past century—was called "Scale Economies, Product Differentiation, and the Power of Trade."

At that point I realized I was developing a style, so I wrote up my rules for research about twenty years ago. Let me give you my four rules for research: listen to the Gentiles; question the question; dare to be silly; and simplify, simplify!

By *listen to the Gentiles,* I mean *listen to people who are not of your tribe.* In economics, there is a lot of work that is not coming from mainstream research; there are a lot of ideas floating around out there. This was especially true in international trade circa 1980. There was a very powerful, standard way to think about international trade, and then there was a counterculture. These counterculture types were saying it is not comparative advantage, there is something else going on. What about imperfect competition? What about the claim that countries export products not for which they have especially favorable supply conditions but for which they have large domestic markets?

All this was floating around, and it was mostly dismissed because people didn't know how to think about it. But once you had some alternative mathematical models—some alternative tools—you could go back and think about these things again, and all of a sudden a lot of that counterculture began to make sense. Ever since, I have said if there are people outside the core—people who are not a part of the standard way of thinking about something—don't assume they're completely wrong. What have they got that we might be missing? That was true for international trade, it was true for economic geography, and it has been true for issues like macroeconomics and financial crises. Just because people are heterodox doesn't mean they're right, either—sometimes someone from mainstream economics comes across as a crank, and he *is* a crank. But you want to listen and think about it. Is there some way in which what these people are saying makes sense?

Question the question: Often, you want to ask whether the question people are asking is the right one to ask. In international trade, a lot of people thought what a model of trade had to do was predict who produces what. That turned out not to be a good question to ask in the context of those models because the models suggested there could be a lot of randomness. The question we *should* be asking is why countries produce different things. Then the model could say it might be a small historical accident that determines what the country produces. But the point was to back up.

The real question is not *why does the United States produce wide-body jet aircraft* but *why is the production of wide-body jet aircraft concentrated in just a few places in the world?* That turned out to be an easier question to answer—and the one that people wanted answered. Today, if you were to ask, *Why did we have a major world financial crisis going nuclear on September 15, 2008?*, I don't know if we would ever be able to answer that question. We ask the question, *Why do modern economies seem to be subject to periodic financial crises?* (as opposed to the specific date and the specific way it happened), and that is a much more answerable question. So see if there is a question that you can answer that is interesting!

Dare to be silly is my third principle. There are always two temptations. One is the temptation to think you always have to be realistic in that what you write has to be a description of the world as it really is (which is impossible because the world is insanely complex, and you have to abstract some things), and the other is the somewhat different temptation to believe that what you are doing has to be technically difficult. In economics there is a strong tendency to believe if the problem does not involve hard math, it can't be real work. That is clearly not right.

Something like the babysitting co-op is a very abstract, stylized, simple story that doesn't use any math at all but tells you something important. In general, finding something that is simple is more important. It doesn't have to be hard. Some of the best economics I have seen is actually very simple, but simple in a way that is sophisticated: *What is it we really need to think about here, and how do we do it?*

In fact, let me use this occasion to put in a good word for Milton Friedman. I don't agree with everything Friedman advocated, but he produced a lot of great economics. His key insight into the value of flexible exchange rates was a spectacular example: he compared flexible rates to daylight saving time. Rather than have everybody change their work schedule, we just move the clocks back. ... That's a comparison that's incredibly simple and yet very powerful.

Last, *simplify*. If you are doing this kind of analysis, you always want to think, "What am I putting into this story that doesn't need to be there?" Always strip it down to as few moving parts as you can.

Those are the four rules, and I have adhered to them throughout my professional life. After the international trade work, which took about six years, I realized I should be talking about economic geography, too. But that was the *listen to the Gentiles* principle. A lot of people compare the way things are within countries—why are some regions more densely populated than others? Why did the fact that in 1817, if you were going to try to build a canal from the East Coast to the Great Lakes you pretty much had to go up the Hudson River, lead to a situation in which New

York is still the largest American city some one hundred sixty years after the canal ceased to be relevant? Very similar underlying economics led me to modeling the geography of economies within countries instead of between countries. I suddenly realized that international economists had been doing economic geography all their lives without realizing it. How do we formalize that?

Now, what you should know about international economics is that it is a very divided field. That is, there are two kinds of international economics. There is real trade (why do countries produce what, where?) and there is international macroeconomics (roughly speaking, what determines the value of the euro?). These two divisions require two quite different sets of tools, and by and large they involve different and often mutually hostile sets of people. Only slightly joking, the real trade people think the international macro people are flaky and ad hoc and often don't make any sense at all, and the international macro people think the real trade people are boring and dull and occupied with minor technical issues of no significant interest. And by and large, both sides are right. Oddly, however, I have always done both, and have felt very comfortable with both sides. A wonderful paper by Rudi Dornbusch, Stanley Fischer, and Paul Samuelson, published in 1977, that redacted one hundred seventy years of economics in one go, bridged the real and the monetary sides. When I saw that, I said, "*Hey, both sides make sense,*" so I've always done that.

In my first couple of decades as an economist I published several papers on currency crises—I actually invented the academic literature of currency crises in grad school—but the real place where that came together and became my big preoccupation was with the Asian financial crisis of 1997–98. If you look at economists focusing on current events, you see a big difference between those of us who were involved in the Asian crisis and those who were not. For many people in the international field, the crises in Indonesia and Thailand and Korea—and also the slide of the Japanese economy into a long stagnation—were a huge wakeup call. The monsters of the Great Depression have not gone away—they're still here! Look at the people who were closest to being right about the current crisis. For example, Nouriel Roubini forecast some aspects of the crisis. He earned his spurs working on the Asian crisis in the late 1990s. And I got very involved with it as well.

The book *The Return of Depression Economics and the Crisis of 2008* is a much revised reissue of a book called *The Return of Depression Economics,* which I published in 1999. The revision was inspired by the

Asian crisis and basically said, *This could happen to us.* When you looked at the problems that had occurred, both the high-speed financial crisis that had happened in places like Indonesia and the prolonged, seemingly intractable slump in Japan, these were not the result of specifically Asian problems. Watching Asia led me to rethink what I thought I knew about macroeconomics. It led me to worry that something like that could happen to us. And then I reissued the book in 2008 when it *did* happen to us. It still remains an important guide.

I've been vocal about the financial crisis and its aftermath partly because I looked at the Asian crisis in 1998, and have worried ever since that we could get caught in something like the kind of trap that Japan was caught in. When it hit, I said, *Here it is. We have to move effectively to deal with this,* and we didn't, and haven't. I think Ben Bernanke is doing the best he can under the circumstances, but my former departmental chairman (now demoted to running the world), is being referred to as "Bernanke-san." It really is amazing how much worse we're doing than the Japanese did.

I wrote a little model in 1998 called "Japan's Trap," which has been my guide to everything. That was one of the best papers I ever wrote. By the standards of economic modeling, it's ridiculous, just a couple of equations and a few diagrams, but it's got the story that you need. There are some elaborations, which I've been working on, that you need, but what I said about Japan turned out to be an alarmingly good guide to the United States over the past five years.

In the last few years I have become known as a public intellectual. I started writing nontechnical economics in 1982, when I was on the staff of the Reagan Council of Economic Advisers, a nonpolitical position. Marty Feldstein, who was the chairman, brought a couple of whiz kids from Cambridge, Massachusetts, to work with him on the staff. Among the junior economists was Greg Mankiw, and he also brought in two people who were senior economists, me and the other guy, Larry Summers.

A funny story: Larry and I were charged with writing the 1983 Economic Report to the President, and Larry's sections were, ah, somewhat lacking in tact. (An old saw says that people grow worse as they grow older because they become more like themselves.) So I ended up taking over the writing—I was good at the euphemisms. You don't say "*Union wages are too high in the steel industry,*" you say "*Prices and wages in some U.S. heavy industries are probably excessive in an integrated world economy,*" or something like that.

After that, I took to writing more popular economics. I wrote a couple of well-received articles for *Foreign Affairs* in the early nineties and then got hired to write for *Slate*, in its early stages, and then got a second gig at *Fortune* (also writing once a month), and I was having a ball doing this stuff. Finally, the *New York Times* approached me in 2000. They said, "*We have all these people writing about the Middle East,* and nobody cares about the Middle East anymore, so we need somebody *to write about the economy.*" They had apparently gone through their list of people who knew economics and were not terrible writers (already a very small set), and there I was.

How do I juggle these roles? First of all, the logistics. It turns out that anybody who does policy-oriented international economics has to be not quite human in some dimension. So Larry Summers is a juggernaut—he gets not just himself but *teams* of people moving in ways I can't imagine. Jeff Sachs is a cyborg. He can take forty-eight hours flying without sleep to get to Outer Mongolia, and this is literal, and step right off the plane into meetings. I don't have any of those things … but I do write faster than anybody. So I can actually handle doing a column for the *Times*.

When I was hired we were in the middle of the dot-com bubble, and I thought I would be writing interesting stories about the new economy. Instead, it turned out to be a pretty bitter political environment. I caught on to that earlier than most people. I'm not a proper journalist (I don't know how to pound the pavement or do interviews with important people), but I do know some things that most of the people in this journalistic venture don't know (arithmetic), and I know how to read statistics, and so sometimes I make the *Times* nervous, but I do get to weigh in on the debate. Surprisingly, a lot of the rules for research actually apply pretty well to writing columns, too. Listen to the Gentiles—don't accept that whatever passes for Washington conventional wisdom is necessarily right. Quite often the crazy people are crazy, but sometimes they are entirely right. There have been some amazing incidents when you could see that a particular line became accepted—nobody who was anybody was going to challenge it—and yet if you took a real look at it, the facts were pointing entirely against that. Just to mention the biggest of those: in 2002, if you asked "*What evidence do we actually have that there are weapons of mass destruction in Iraq? Is there any evidence?,*" it turned out there wasn't. So I was one of those people who said, "*There is not a case for this war,*" which wasn't economics, but it was the same style of thought that lay behind the economics.

Now we are in the crisis, and it is still going on, and we are *not* responding to it effectively. It's terrible, but it's actually good for column writing—and also for economics. I'm coming up on fifty-eight years old, and people at my age do not do a lot of fundamental research anymore. Even Paul Samuelson had slowed down a lot by the time he was my age. But I have been doing some real modeling work—with Gauti Eggertsson of the New York Fed—because it is interesting. It's horrible, but it's interesting, and there is a lot to be done. I've had a pretty satisfying career, and I'm trying to do what I can to make the world a less bad place. Mostly, I'm just wondering, how does this work out? This is the nightmare that has haunted economists for seventy-five years, and now it's come true. What do we do now? I will keep on trying my best to do something about it.

Paul Krugman

Awarded Nobel Prize in 2008. Lecture presented February 2, 2011.

Date of Birth

February 28, 1953

Academic Degrees

B.A., Yale University, 1974
Ph.D., MIT, 1977

Academic Affiliations

Assistant Professor, Yale University, 1977–80
Visiting Assistant Professor, MIT, 1979–80
Associate Professor, MIT, 1980–84
Professor, MIT, 1984–94
Professor, Stanford University, 1994–96
Professor, MIT, 1996–2000
Professor, Princeton University, 2000–present

Selected Books

Market Structure and Foreign Trade, 1985 (with E. Helpman)
Exchange Rate Instability, Lionel Robbins Memorial Lectures, 1988
Market Structure and Trade Policy, 1989 (with E. Helpman)
The Age of Diminished Expectations, 1990
Geography and Trade, 1991
Currencies and Crises, 1992
Peddling Prosperity, 1994
Development, Geography, and Economic Theory, 1995
The Self-Organizing Economy, 1996
The Accidental Theorist, 1998
The Return of Depression Economics, 1999
The Spatial Economy, 1999 (with M. Fujita and A. Venables)
Fuzzy Math, 2001
The Great Unraveling, 2003

Peter A. Diamond

The title of this lecture series suggests that I try to decipher the process of my change from the time I took my first economics class as an eighteen-year-old math major to my present self as a seventy-two-year-old public policy analyst and public policy–oriented economic theorist. Perhaps a better title would be "My Memory of My Evolution," for I have no diaries, no notes; just working papers and published papers, and memories. I have identified five phases in the evolution of my approach to being an economist: student (first economics class, 1958), applied mathematician (first research, 1960), teacher (first publishable lecture material, 1964), the "what's wrong with economics" phase (first research, 1965), and policy analyst (first detailed analysis, 1974). These were not separate phases but overlapping, as I expanded my repertoire of interests and methods.

My first economics class as that eighteen-year-old math major was a yearlong introductory class at Yale in 1958–59, taught by Charles Berry. It was my first exposure to economics, for I had had no exposure to discussing or analyzing economies or economic policies before that. While my father checked stock prices daily, there was no sign to me that he was interested in the economy that lay behind the stocks, and no discussion of the economy or economic policy at the dinner table. Stocks held no interest for me, apart from a short period between the time I was given shares in a single company for my bar mitzvah and the time that stock became worthless. The gift came from a neighbor who was a stockbroker, making the experience particularly salient.

I didn't look closely at stock prices again until nearly 2000, when asked to do so by the Office of the Actuary of Social Security, at a time when I was much involved in the policy process around Social Security. Starting in the mid-1990s there were lots of proposals with a similar theme of investing in stocks, through a trust fund or through individual accounts. The Office of the Actuary had the problem of projecting stock returns as part of projecting Social Security finances. I was commissioned to write an essay addressing the question of what stock market rate of return they should use in the projection, given their projection of the workings of the economy. The essay appeared in the *Social Security Bulletin* (2000). It turned out to be a very lucrative assignment. As I studied the determinants of stock prices in general, not just of individual stocks, and looked at the bubble happening at the time, I kept adjusting my retirement portfolio. When my study started, my 401k was 95 percent stocks. By the time I completed the report, it was down to 35 percent stocks, somewhat before the bubble broke.

Phase 1: Student

I want to begin a year before that first economics class, with the start of my college education. I was obliged to name a major. I chose to name electrical engineering. I had no idea what the major really was, or what a career in the field entailed. I was required to name a major. I thought that engineering paid well, that I had been good at math and science in high school, and that I needed a subject that did not require being able to work with my hands. Partway through my freshman year, I learned a little about what the subject entailed, and promptly thought to change my major. Stepping back from my first decision, starting over in choosing a major, I chose the subject I liked best and did my best in—mathematics. Not that I had any idea of what a career as a mathematician might entail, either. This choice surprised the graduate student who had shown me a graduate electrical engineering text with its unattractive (to both him and me) mathematics. Choose what you like and do well still seems a good rule of thumb for an undergraduate.

In my second year at Yale, I took a yearlong class in real analysis from Shizuo Kakutani in which I learned how to do a rigorous mathematical proof. I took one-semester classes in probability and number theory, both taught by Øystein Ore, and I took the yearlong introductory economics class from Charles Berry as a seminar, not as part of a large introductory class. I have no memory of how I chose that class; I suspect I needed to fulfill a social science requirement, but that would not be a full explanation. While I enjoyed the class and was good at it, at its completion, I had no intention of taking any more classes in economics. The following summer I was an actuarial trainee at Metropolitan Life, which did not catch my interest and did not add much to my understanding of what a mathematician might do for a living.

For my third (and last) year at Yale, I planned to take three yearlong math classes in order to complete the major—the senior seminar, which was devoted to game theory (yes, I did read every word of von Neumann and Morgenstern)—and two graduate classes, in topology and abstract algebra. And I planned to take a second year of French. Beyond those four classes, I was shopping for something interesting. Several famous possibilities were being offered by visiting professors instead of the usual faculty members, which left me at loose ends. For advice, I turned to Charles Berry, the faculty member I had become most friendly with. He suggested that I take the yearlong intermediate theory class for economics honors majors, taught by Edward Budd. Not knowing how academe worked, I was a little surprised to be let in, as I was not an economics major. My pleasure in the fall microeconomics class started my serious consideration of economics versus mathematics—not that I knew what economists did for a living, either.

This class increased my interest in economics enough that I ended my study of French and registered for the graduate mathematical economics course taught by Gerard Debreu. The class was based on his newly published *Theory of Value* (1959). Debreu was an outstanding teacher, *Theory of Value* was an outstanding text, and I remained unsure in what direction to go for graduate work. I remain grateful to Debreu for this early and thorough grounding in general equilibrium theory, which has stood me in good stead, shaping my thinking about economics. The class was also taken by several of my math major classmates. Although I have no idea of the source, something was pushing us math majors collectively away from math. This push affected my friends Dick Beals, who tried economics and then returned to math, and Dave Krantz, who became a psychologist. (I have wondered whether Dick's outcome might have been different had he tried economics at MIT instead of Harvard.) I applied to graduate school in both economics and mathematics while trying to make up my mind.

Phase 2: Applied Mathematician

I do not know which teacher (or teachers) provided the information that led to an offer of a job as a summer research assistant for Tjalling Koopmans in 1960. I was hired to help with the mathematics as he continued to work on infinite horizon preferences. When Koopmans asked me to produce an example of a function satisfying certain conditions, I thought it might be a lot easier to consider a whole set of functions—a class of functions—that would satisfy these conditions rather than cranking one out. The class of functions I provided led Koopmans to reorient his research plan, giving this class of functions a central role. And he promoted me to co-author for my first publication (Koopmans, Diamond, and Williamson 1964). I have always viewed Koopmans as a splendid economist and a splendid person, and so as a role model for doing economics and relating to people.

I had no idea when doing the analysis that the class of functions would make for interesting economics. I was just avoiding what I thought would be tedious calculations. It has been interesting to be on the other side of a similar experience. At one point I gave a graduate student RA a math assignment—something to crank out—and he came back with an answer that was so interesting it became a short paper in the *American Economic Review* (Aura, Diamond, and Geanakoplos 2002). As when I was the RA, Saku did not realize how interesting his calculation was. An important part of maturing as a researcher is figuring out what is interesting in what you have stumbled across. In general, it is important to figure out what problems have stronger possibilities of turning up something interesting. I do it as a theorist, but of course, the same thing is true with empirical work. One needs to ask whether the answer to the question being researched is likely to be interesting. If you just come up with an answer nobody's interested in, it may not have been a good use of your time.

I applied to graduate schools in both math and economics, and then settled on the MIT math department. My initial plan was to take micro- and macroeconomics and complex and real variables, and to decide at the end of the year which subject was better for me. A beauty of the American educational system is its enormous flexibility. But the complex variables class conflicted with both micro and macro, and I needed a different plan. I dropped complex variables, planning to make it up in the summer if economics didn't hold me. Given the imbalance in classes, the math graduate registration office (GRO), represented by George Thomas (author of the best-selling calculus book I had studied), thought I should be advised by the economics department. Thomas straightforwardly transferred me (along with my fellowship) to the economics department. I enjoyed the economic theory classes and didn't enjoy the real variables class (and I was better at the economics). My reaction to the real variables class was that it was about proving the same theorem about integration and differentiation again and again, in steadily more general settings. I had no interest in the generalizations, perhaps because I was ignorant of what could be done with greater generality that couldn't be done otherwise. On the other hand, for me, economics was all about new models for different phenomena. That is indeed what I've been devoting my career to—trying to focus on how to capture insights into the complex things that are happening—so it was an easy decision. After the fall semester, I was committed to economics; my experimentation had ended after one semester. The Math Department still had to pay the second semester of my fellowship.

I was still approaching economics research as an applied mathematician, as I had as Koopmans's RA. That is, my focus was on finding math to use on well-defined economics questions. Browsing in a pamphlet of theorems about matrices, I saw one that would provide a result on *tâtonnement* convergence to general equilibrium, a theorem that I had not seen in the literature. I took it to Frank Fisher, who was giving a reading class to Steve Goldfeld and me at the time—basically an exploration of potential thesis topics. Frank hadn't seen the theorem either, and we immediately headed for Paul Samuelson's office. Paul went straight to his bookcase, pulled down a conference volume, and opened it to a chapter by Lionel McKenzie. It had exactly the theorem I had in mind. While I had lost a potential thesis chapter, I felt that I was in very good company.

As I finished my classwork and started working on my thesis, I continued working in the applied mathematician mode. Over the summer (1962, spent at RAND Corporation), I looked at the same problem I had worked on with Koopmans, examining properties of infinite horizon preferences, but using a different mathematical structure. The resulting analysis became my job market paper and landed me a job at Berkeley. With that paper done, I read the Yale thesis of T. N. Srinivasan, with whom I had driven around the country after we had shared an office at the Cowles Foundation while I was working for Koopmans. I had an idea for solving a problem he didn't get to in his analysis of growth theory. So this was his problem and my answer—I was still an applied mathematician at work.

These first two thesis chapters were finished before September was over. I cockily asked my thesis supervisor, Bob Solow, how many theorems it took to complete a thesis. He said a year's worth. But I promptly hit a wall and had no ideas for the compulsory third essay. Early in the spring semester, Solow gave me a book to read by W. E. G. Salter (1960), *Productivity and Technical Change,* which analyzed the falling costs of production for a firm as a result of technical progress. I recognized that the structure could be inverted and turned into a growth model, and I was off and running on my third essay, including an extension of the one-sector model to two sectors. I finished just in time for a June degree. Again, I was reacting to something I had read, finding a way to use math on well-structured questions.

Phase 3: Teaching

Following a summer at the Council of Economic Advisers, working for George Perry, I became one of the four new assistant professors at Berkeley who started in September 1963. Hiring was organized by Andy Papandreou, shortly before he left for a political career in Greece. There are three Nobel Prizes among the four of us. In 1963–64, Berkeley was a perfect place to be a young theorist. The junior faculty interacted all the time, and became close friends. Dan McFadden, Bernie Saffran, and Sid Winter were particularly important for me, both personally and professionally. For part of the fall I shared an office with Olly Williamson, and we played handball each week. And the senior faculty were supportive of us.

I didn't know it at the time, but I was about to start phase three of my evolution—with research driven by the process of teaching. I taught the graduate micro-macro sequence (one semester of each) jointly with Tibor Scitovsky. But key for me was a yearlong undergraduate public finance class for majors, which had a prerequisite of intermediate theory. Since the students had had intermediate theory and we had all year for the class, I could develop the material systematically and thoroughly, with enough time to start with foundations.

Of course, I drew on the public finance class I had taken at MIT, taught by E. Cary Brown. We had worked all the way through the recently published *The Theory of Public Finance* by Richard Musgrave (1959). It is an outstanding book, written by an outstanding scholar. Musgrave's approach was to put public finance on a general equilibrium footing (as had happened to international trade theory). This was important for my intellectual development and complemented the general equilibrium orientation I had learned from Debreu. This background played a central role in my later work on optimal taxation.

As I read about different topics for class, I did not want just to teach the articles or book chapters; I wanted to figure out my take on the topics. This started a phase transition as material prepared for class evolved into a good paper. I attribute this success to the circumstance of preparing carefully for a class of sharp, attentive students. And it meant I was thinking about the economics, not just applying math. In the spring, preparing to lecture on the public debt, I read the relevant writings of James Buchanan (*Public Principles of Public Debt: A Defense and Restatement*, 1958) and Modigliani ("Long-Run Implications of Alternative Fiscal Policies and the Burden of the National Debt," 1961). These were very different in both focus and modeling style. I realized I could construct a model that addressed the distributional issues central to Buchanan's analysis and the economic growth issues central to that of Modigliani. The model started as a handout to the students in this undergraduate class, and then became my 1965 paper on the public debt. I have continued to prefer developing my own materials rather than teaching the contents of existing papers. While many people worry about the time needed for teaching taking away from the time for research, my experience was that they reinforced each other. Indeed, the times when my research went most slowly occurred when I did little teaching.[1]

Berkeley was great for me for more reasons than just good teaching and research opportunities. First on the list was meeting my wife, Kate (real name Priscilla Myrick), who was a student at Berkeley law school when I started teaching economics. I was teaching public finance, and she found taxation to be her least favorite class. Nevertheless, we married in 1966. In Berkeley I witnessed the 1964 start of the student uprisings with the Free Speech Movement. I saw repeated mistakes made by the Berkeley administration, and watched the same mistakes repeated by university administrations across the country. I was part of a faculty that was trying to help, but not succeeding much.

The teaching phase of my research continued until I stopped teaching in 2010. Before turning to the start of phase four in the summer of 1965, let me mention two later examples of research coming from lecture preparation. My return to MIT in 1966 meant teaching graduate public finance for the first time. The standard analysis of the deadweight burden of taxation was the model of Al Harberger ("The Measurement of Waste," 1964). But I didn't like it; thinking that it didn't show consistent underpinnings. So I worked up a different approach using the expenditure function, which was a hot new tool at the time. While this eventually became part of a joint paper with Dan McFadden (Diamond and McFadden 1974) combining my analysis of the burden of taxation with his analysis of the evaluation of lumpy investments, both using the expenditure function, the impact for me came much sooner.

As I was teaching this topic to graduate students at MIT in 1966–67, having put the analysis on the blackboard, I had the thought that it might be interesting to see what kind of tax structure would give the least possible deadweight burden in the economy, while raising the amount of revenue needed, using only linear taxes on transactions. I walked out of the classroom, down to my office, and immediately started writing down the calculation. And I was launched onto optimal taxation and the aggregate efficiency theorem. Shortly after arriving at Churchill College, Cambridge, for the next summer, I presented the optimal taxation results I had developed. That the expenditure function is defined in terms of prices, not the quantities consumed, was critical for the next step. Jim Mirrlees came up after the seminar and pointed out that by being in price space, my model of a one-consumer economy could be used as a start on analyzing a many-person economy. That is, with prices the same for all households, the welfare, demand, and supply functions were interpretable as coming from a many-person economy. We started working together on optimal taxation that summer and had essentially finished our first paper by the end of the summer, which we then presented at Econometric Society meetings that fall. The paper was not published until 1971 for a variety of reasons, including the absence of the Internet. Collaboration at a distance was slow, with the compensation of the value of spending time together, which we did repeatedly.

Jim and I have completed a dozen papers together and have had something in progress (sometimes very slowly) ever since, even today. The success of this collaboration reflects a number of factors, including our having perhaps the ideal distance between the ways our minds work. Our thinking has been similar enough that communication has been quick and thorough, but our different approaches to things make me suspect that much of this would not have happened had we been working separately. (One of our rare miscommunications opened up an issue neither of us had recognized.) This collaboration has been a joy.

When trying to work out something new for class, I'm showing students the research process as it is happening. This approach is exciting, but it is very hard on the students. Some of them love it; some of them hate it. But it works for my getting into new research. In time, having thought a lot about a subject and found a way of teaching it that I like, I am no longer exposed to many new issues. That doesn't stimulate my thinking, and it also results in a tendency to get rather boring in class.

After hitting diminishing returns from teaching taxation, and having trouble making it exciting for students, that topic was passed to my public finance colleagues, and I returned to teaching pensions. Years later I was asked to cover optimal taxation again, because of the department's teaching needs that year. The mathematics used to analyze the optimal income tax, following Mirrlees, was very complex. I thought to give the students a simple example and looked for an assumption about the economy that would make the calculation simple enough to make it easy to see some of what was involved in the optimization. The assumption I chose to explore was that there were no income effects in labor supply, which followed from having preferences linear in the single consumption good in the model. While not fully realistic, as people do change in response to some income changes, it is also not too far off because those changes are often small and slow (apart from triggering earlier retirement for some). I set to work cranking out the optimum in this case, and found that it greatly simplified the problem. That simplification allowed a lot of insight into some of what matters when trying to decide on marginal income tax rates.

The results were so interesting, and so suggestive of insights that would be relatively robust, that I assumed I was merely rediscovering what must have already been in the literature. I was surprised to discover that was not the case, and the result was that the handout I had made for the students became the basis for another paper in the *American Economic Review* (1998), which ignited a literature drawing inferences, particularly on how high the marginal tax rates should be on the very top earners. It is something that I continue to write about, and, by the way, the number is a lot higher than what we have now.

Phase 4: What's Wrong with Economics

Now I jump back to 1965. Among the pleasures of an academic career are the visits to other places, for short times and, especially valuable, for long ones. My first year of leave was 1965–66. Frank Hahn organized the opportunity for me to be an Overseas Fellow at Churchill College, Cambridge. Talking economics with Frank lived up to expectations. At Cambridge, I gave a series of four lectures on the economics of uncertainty (my first venture into teaching that subject) and had the experience of tutoring outstanding undergraduates—you can imagine the pleasure of meeting weekly with Tony Atkinson and Geoff Heal. But I no longer had my usual teaching load.

The summer of 1965, just before leaving for England, was the beginning of phase four, of my doing research built around what struck me as inadequacies in economics. From Debreu I had acquired a thorough understanding of a model in which the present and the future are treated exactly the same, as comes with the assumption that markets are complete. With no costs to creating or using markets and a complete list of the states of nature, all plans for the future are made and coordinated before anything actually happens in the economy. I thought the range of insights one could gain were limited because markets are incomplete and because we deal with the future very differently from the way we deal with the present. I have thought of the complexities of what happens over time as the source of one of the real holes in a lot of economics. What particularly interested me was creating models that avoided the completeness of the coordination of agents that happens with complete competitive markets.

I set up a model of price adjustment in which each firm sets prices each period, and consumers don't know all the prices that are out there. To find out a price in this simple model, you visit a store, and that uses some resources. You can think of it as time; you can think of it as utility or money. If you want to see whether a different store has a better price, you've got to pay—excuse the expression—a "search cost" to go to another store. It turned out this process had a rather stunning result. Not only did it not go to a competitive equilibrium, it went to what would be a monopoly price if all the firms colluded and worked together. It did that because, if I have a customer in my store and I know there's a cost to checking the price elsewhere, then my price can be a little bit higher than elsewhere by less than that cost, without triggering a departure to shop elsewhere. So I have a little bit of market power, but that's true of every store. Each store, taking advantage of that little bit of market power, contributes to a dynamic process that results in stability only when at the monopoly point. At that point, nobody wants to raise the price, even though they can. They just don't want to.

What I wanted to do next was to push into other settings, and eventually to get a model of the economy as a whole in order to consider Keynesian issues. The desire for a microeconomic foundation for macroeconomic analyses was shared by a number of economists at the time, although the thinking varied considerably as to what they thought it might lead to. What would it take to have a model of the economy as a whole, in which all transactions involved some of these costs? There are costs to trying to sell things, as well as costs to trying to buy them. But only after a decade of working on the same thing again and again did I get to the point of modeling the whole economy (1982).

I took to thinking in terms of a process in real time (and using a Poisson process, as I had seen Dale Mortensen do). Ironically, this resulted in a law-and-economics-related question, the effects on overall efficiency of alternative rules for breach of contract (jointly published with Eric Maskin, 1979, 1981). But, as I recall, the question fit the modeling approach, rather than vice versa. Then I moved on to modeling the labor market (1981, 1982a), and then the entire economy (1982b). And in work with Olivier Blanchard, I went from examining steady states to looking at the cycle, particularly the Beveridge curve, on which I am still working.

Phase V: Policy Analyst

My activity as a policy analyst started in 1974. While continuing to do basic research, I have been involved in policy discussions and analyses, primarily about public pensions. Pensions have been the subject of a series of enjoyable collaborations, with Bill Hsiao, Peter Orszag, and Nick Barr. In 1972, the Social Security benefits schedules were overhauled to include automatic adjustments for inflation, but they were not indexed properly. The Social Security Administration was aware of this but did not consider it important. The year 1972 was a bad time to have indexing that would rely on continuing mild inflation not to explode in cost. With Social Security costs projected to explode, Congress was told of a need for reform. First, Congress wanted to check whether it would have to do something about it. Bill Hsiao was asked to form a panel to answer whether the expenditures were growing too rapidly, as the Office of the Actuary had said. At the recommendation of Paul Samuelson, Bill approached me, and I joined the Panel on Social Security Financing, consulting to the U.S. Senate Finance Committee.

Our answer to whether there was a need to change the indexing was yes. Then came a request to Bill to form a panel to lay out the issues that lay ahead in accomplishing reform, because this called for a significant, fundamental change in the way benefits were constructed in the system. This wasn't just tinkering with the parameters. And I joined that panel and became part of the debate that led to the 1977 Social Security reform.

Our consultant panel prepared a report that both Ways and Means and the Senate Finance Committee wanted (*Report of the Consultant Panel on Social Security to the Congressional Research Service*, August 1976). Now I was involved in recommending policy, involved in exploring the multiple aspects that matter for putting together a policy analysis that reflected many issues that seemed important.

I got caught up in Social Security for two reasons. First, it matters: the Social Security Administration and its programs matter a great deal for a lot of people, and trying to get them to function well is important. And second, as with teaching, thinking about policy has fed my basic research. The prime example was addressing the question of what should determine how much bigger monthly benefits should be after a delay in the start of benefits. I was aware of no theory beyond using the actuarial equivalent for the average person. Jim Mirrlees and I set to work to develop a theory of what ought to be done, drawing on the role of insurance with asymmetric information about job opportunities (our first paper was published in 1978, and work is ongoing). The dynamic nature of choosing a time to retire led us to find (but not name) the inverse Euler condition.

In addition to a focus on Social Security in the United States (which led to a series of articles and a book with Peter Orszag in response to seeing the report of the commission appointed by President Bush), I have studied and written about public pensions in a sizable number of countries, including Australia, Chile, China, France, Germany, Italy, the Netherlands, New Zealand, Spain, Sweden, and the UK. The work on China led to two books with Nick Barr (and another one in process). Both collaborations have been a source of great pleasure from the writings and real satisfaction from the outputs.

I am not sure Nick and I would have launched into the first book had we seen this passage from Honoré de Balzac, "It is as easy to dream a book as it is hard to write one." On the other hand, we have not learned to stop, even as we had this experience.

Pensions have been a perfect topic for me. They fit well with my public finance theory interests and with my social concerns. I have given many talks on economics, particularly on Social Security, which has remained a hot topic in the United States for a long time. I have ended some of those talks with a quotation from Franklin Roosevelt's second Inaugural Address, January 20, 1937, which I saw carved on a wall at his memorial in Washington, D.C.: "The test of our progress is not whether we add more to the abundance of those who have much; it is whether we provide enough for those who have too little."

Note

1. For more on how valuable teaching has been for my research, and for the diverse ways I approached finding and choosing topics to work on, see Giuseppe Moscarini and Randall Wright, "An Interview with Peter Diamond," *Macroeconomic Dynamics* 11 (2007): 543–565 (doi:10.1017/S1365100507060403), and my "My Research Strategy," in *Eminent Economists II: Their Work and Life Philosophies*, ed. Michael Szenberg and Lall Ramrattan (New York: Cambridge University Press, 2013).

References

Aura, Saku, Peter Diamond, and John Geanakoplos. 2002. "Savings and Portfolio Choice in a Two-Period Two-Asset Model." *American Economic Review* 92 (4): 1185–1191.

Buchanan, James. 1958. *Public Principles of Public Debt: A Defense and Restatement*. Homewood, IL: R. D. Irwin.

Burdett, Kenneth, and Kenneth L. Judd. 1983. "Equilibrium Price Dispersion." *Econometria* 51 (4): 955–970.

Butters, Gerard R. 1977. "Equilibrium Distributions of Sales and Advertising Prices." *Review of Economic Studies* 44:465–491.

Debreu, Gerard. 1959. *Theory of Value: An Axiomatic Analysis of Economic Equilibrium*. New Haven, CT: Yale University Press.

Diamond, Peter A. 1965. "National Debt in a Neoclassical Growth Model." *American Economic Review* 55 (5): 1126–1150.

Diamond, Peter A. 1967. "The Role of a Stock Market in a General Equilibrium Model with Technological Uncertainty." *American Economic Review* 57:759–776.

Diamond, Peter A. 1978. "Welfare Analysis of Imperfect Information Equilibria." *Bell Journal of Economics* 9 (1): 82–105.

Diamond, Peter A. 1981. "Mobility Costs, Frictional Unemployment, and Efficiency." *Journal of Political Economy* 89:798–813.

Diamond, Peter A. 1982a. "Wage Determination and Efficiency in Search Equilibrium." *Review of Economic Studies* 49:217–227.

Diamond, Peter A. 1982b. "Aggregate Demand Management in Search Equilibrium." *Journal of Political Economy* 90 (5): 881–894.

Diamond, Peter A. 1998. "Optimal Income Taxation: An Example of a U-Shaped Pattern with Optimal Marginal Tax Rates." *American Economic Review* 88 (1): 83–95.

Diamond, Peter A. 2000. "What Stock Market Returns to Expect for the Future?" *Social Security Bulletin* 63 (2):3 8.

Diamond, Peter A., and Eric S. Maskin. 1979. "An Equilibrium Analysis of Search and Breach of Contract: I. Steady States." *Bell Journal of Economics* 10:282–316.

Diamond, Peter A., and Eric S. Maskin. 1981. "An Equilibrium Analysis of Search and Breach of Contract: II. A Son-Steady-State Example." *Journal of Economic Theory* 25:165–195.

Diamond, P. A., and D. L. McFadden. 1974. "Some Uses of the Expenditure Function in Public Finance." *Journal of Public Economics* 3 (1): 3–21.

Harberger, Al. 1964. "The Measurement of Waste." *American Economic Review* 54 (3): 58–76.

Koopmans, Tjalling C., Peter A. Diamond, and Richard E. Williamson. 1964. "Stationary Utility and Time Perspective." *Econometrica* 32 (112): 82–100.

Marshall, Alfred. 1948. *Principles of Economics.* 8th ed. New York: Macmillan.

Modigliani, Franco. 1961. "Long-Run Implications of Alternative Fiscal Policies and the Burden of the National Debt." *Economic Journal* 71:730–755.

Musgrave, Richard. 1959. *The Theory of Public Finance.* New York: McGraw-Hill.

Report of the Consultant Panel on Social Security to the Congressional Research Service. 1976. 94th Congress, 2d Session. Washington, DC: U.S. Government Printing Office, August. http://www.ssa.gov/history/reports/hsiao/hsiaoIntro.PDF.

Salter, W. E. G. 1960. *Productivity and Technical Change.* Cambridge University, Department of Applied Economics, Monograph No. 6. New York: Cambridge University Press.

Peter A. Diamond

Awarded Nobel Prize in 2010. Lecture presented April 17, 2013.

Date of Birth

April 29, 1940

Academic Degrees

B.A., Mathematics, summa cum laude, Yale University, 1960
Ph.D., Economics, MIT, 1963

Academic Affiliations

Assistant Professor, University of California, Berkeley, 1963–65
Acting Associate Professor, University of California, Berkeley, 1965–66
Overseas Fellow, Churchill College, Cambridge, 1965–66
Associate Professor, MIT, 1966–70
Professor, MIT, 1970–88
John and Jennie S. MacDonald Professor, MIT, 1989–91
Paul A. Samuelson Professor, MIT, 1992–97
Institute Professor, MIT, 1997–2011
Department Chairman, MIT, 1985–86
Visiting Professor, University College, Nairobi, 1968
Visiting Professor, Hebrew University, Jerusalem, 1969
Visiting Professor, Nuffield College, Oxford, 1969
Visiting Professor, Balliol College, Oxford, 1973–74
Visiting Professor, Harvard University, Various years
Visiting Professor, European University Institute, 1992
Visiting Professor, University of Siena, 2000

Selected Books

A Search Equilibrium Approach to the Micro Foundations of Macroeconomics, 1984
On Time: Lectures on Models of Equilibrium, Churchill Lectures, 1994
Social Security Reform, the 1999 Lindahl Lectures, Oxford, 2002
Taxation, Incomplete Markets and Social Security, the 2000 Munich Lectures, 2002
Saving Social Security: A Balanced Approach, 2004 (with Peter R. Orszag)
Reforming Pensions: Principles and Policy Choices, 2008 (with Nicholas Barr)
Pension Reform: A Short Guide, 2010 (with Nicholas Barr)

Roger B. Myerson

Deciding What to Study

My great-grandfather was a poor immigrant in America, but he brought from Europe a deep appreciation of scholarship. He liked to say that a scholar needed to be like a pin, with a sharp end for finding new insights and a dull end for the long work of studying and writing between flashes of insight.[1] I would suggest that the scholar's sharp end itself depends on two elements: a mastery of the analytical methods of one's academic discipline and a passionate desire to understand something better with the help of these tools. The mastery of analytical tools comes from long study (where the dull end helps). But the ultimate source of the vital curiosity that drives our desire to study and learn remains somewhat mysterious to me. Let me illustrate with a personal story.

In a press conference at the 2007 Nobel awards celebration in Stockholm, a reporter asked the new Nobel laureates how we could encourage more children to become interested in science. As my good fortune that day included not only being a new laureate but also having my parents there with me for the celebration, I took the question as a welcome opportunity to express my gratitude to them for years of encouragement and support. So I described to the reporter how my mother had actively encouraged me to develop an early interest in science by reading to me a wonderful Disney book about atomic physics when I was in first grade. True, I did not become a physicist (though my brother did), but I wanted to honor my mother's decision to introduce science to me at such a young age. After the press conference, my mother thanked me for the nice words but admitted that she actually preferred reading fiction to children, and she included this science book in our bedtime reading only because I had insisted on it, bringing it from my big brother's bookshelf. This revelation was very surprising to me at the time, but I should have known from my own experiences as a parent that children's interests and passions must develop from within according to their own mysterious internal logic. Parents and teachers can encourage this development but cannot direct it.

When I talk to prospective doctoral students, I regularly ask them about what they might want to study in their thesis research, but many students hesitate to respond because they feel that they do not know enough yet to identify a good research questions in economics. I then try to explain that any scholar's most precious asset is his or her sense of what is a good question that could be worth months or years of careful study. Students should expect that their teachers in graduate school will introduce them to new areas of research that may cause their interests to grow and change, but their potential to make unique contributions in science will ultimately depend on their personal interests and curiosity that guide their choice of research questions.

Starting with a passion to better understand some big questions about the world, scholars use the analytical tools of their discipline to rigorously study some small parts of these big questions, and in this way we take small careful steps toward the better understanding that we need. A researcher's passionate curiosity about a big question and mastery of the analytical tools of a discipline are both essential for the hard task of finding a small part of an important question that is ready for new analysis and understanding.

A scholar's motivation can be applied or theoretical. Indeed, an alternation between methodological interests and applied substantive interests is common in many academic careers. A concern for applied problems in the real world can lead one to develop new tools of theoretical analysis, and a sense of the untapped power of new analytical tools can lead one to explore other applied problems for which these tools seem potentially useful.

Since I was a student, I have always felt that questions of social science are important, because the peace and prosperity of our world may depend on a deeper understanding of how our societies function. When I learned in college that there were gaps in economists' basic ability to analyze interactions between rational decision-makers who have different information, I very much wanted to be part of filling those gaps. So my early research as a graduate student and as a young professor was motivated largely by methodological concerns, as I worked along with many others to develop fundamental methods of analysis in game theory and information economics. But in later decades, when these methodological gaps had been somewhat reduced, my research became more motivated by applied problems for which the methods of game theory seemed potentially useful, such as the comparison of political incentives under different electoral systems, or the problems of democratic state-building. The subsequent sections of this essay summarize the broad themes of this progression: from finding my way into the methodological questions of game theory to developing a framework for the analysis of incentive constraints in games with communication, and then exploring new research directions with more applied motivations from political science and even macroeconomics.

Finding My Way into Game Theory

I grew up in a comfortable suburb of Boston with a fine public school system, in a family that greatly valued reading and scientific learning. My father did research and engineering for a family business of manufacturing artificial teeth, and each of my parents returned to school to earn advanced degrees at different times in my youth. But concern about the new risk of nuclear war was widespread in the 1950s, and, like many of my generation, I was aware of this terrible threat from a young age. I have early memories of telling my father that I was worried by political cartoons that depicted global dangers of the 1956 Suez Crisis, when I was five years old. My father reassured me that the leaders of the world were bringing all their wisdom and understanding to the task of managing the crisis peacefully. This perspective suggested, however, that perhaps it might be better if our leaders could have even more wisdom and understanding, to provide guidance for a safer and more peaceful world in the future.

When I was twelve, I read a classic science fiction novel that depicted a future in which advanced mathematical social science provided the guidance for a new utopian civilization. Ideas from this and other readings grew in long discussions with my friends. It was natural, perhaps, to hope that fundamental advances in the social sciences might help find better ways of managing the world's problems, as fundamental advances in the physical sciences had so dangerously raised the stakes of social conflict in our time.

I have always loved to read about history and found a fascinating beauty in historical maps. But I hoped for something more analytical, and so I was naturally intrigued when I first heard about economics. I began reading Paul Samuelson's basic economics textbook on a high school vacation. When I got to college, I chose to concentrate in economics and applied mathematics, but my high school chemistry teacher predicted that I would switch to physical science before the end. I was not sure whether he might have been right until I discovered game theory in 1972.

In the spring of 1972, as a third-year student in Harvard College, I took a beautiful course on decision analysis from Howard Raiffa. He taught us to see personal utility functions and subjective probability distributions as measurable aspects of real decision-making that are expressed, however imperfectly, in our daily lives. At the end of the course, he told us that the analysis of interactions among two or more rational utility-maximizing decision-makers is called game theory, and he described game theory as a field in which only limited progress had been made. This negative assessment provided a positive focus for my studies thereafter. I felt that, if we do not know how to analyze such obviously fundamental models of social decision-making, then how could one pretend to understand anything in social science? I started reading a book on game theory that summer.

There were no regular courses on game theory then at Harvard, so I began to do independent reading on the subject, searching through the libraries for books and articles about game theory. My primary form of intellectual dialogue was scribbling notes into the margins of photocopied journal articles written by the distant leaders of the field: Robert Aumann, John Harsanyi, John Nash, Thomas Schelling, Reinhard Selten, Lloyd Shapley, and others. Their published writings gave me good guidance into the field. In particular, when I discovered the work of John Harsanyi sometime in the fall of 1972, I knew that I had found a part of the research frontier that I wanted to help advance.

I was first attracted to Harsanyi's work by his 1963 paper defining a general cooperative solution concept that included both the two-player Nash bargaining solution and the multiplayer Shapley value as special cases. These two solution concepts had elegant axiomatic derivations, and their single-point predictions were much more appealing to me than the multiple sets of solutions that other cooperative theories identified. I worked for three days in the library to understand and reconstruct the derivation of Harsanyi's cooperative theory, simplifying it until I found that everything could be reduced to a simple balanced-contributions assumption. This was my first result in game theory.

But Harsanyi also wrote a series of papers in 1967–68 about how to model games with *incomplete information,* in which the players have different information at the beginning of the game. Harsanyi called these models *Bayesian games,* and the different possible states of each player's private information were called the player's possible *types.* In 1972, Harsanyi and Selten published a new paper that suggested a generalized Nash bargaining solution for two-person games with incomplete information. This Harsanyi–Selten solution maximized a particular social welfare function (computed from the expected gains from cooperation for every possible type of each player) over a rather complicated feasible set, but it was defined only for games with two players. So I saw an important question about game theory that had not yet been addressed in the literature: How can we extend these cooperative solution concepts to games with more than two players who have incomplete information about each other? Nobody had any general theory for predicting what might happen when cooperative agreements are negotiated among three or more rational individuals who have different information. This was the problem that I set out to solve in my dissertation research.

I did not solve this problem in college or in graduate school, but it was a very good problem to work on. To try to build a theory of cooperation under uncertainty, I first needed to rethink many of the fundamental ideas of cooperative game theory and noncooperative game theory, and along the way I got a reasonable dissertation's-worth of results. My adviser, Kenneth Arrow, patiently read and critiqued a series of drafts that gradually lurched toward readability.

In 1976, I had the good fortune to be hired as an assistant professor by the Managerial Economics and Decision Sciences (MEDS) department in the (soon to be Kellogg) School of Management at Northwestern University. In the 1970s, game theory was a small field, and few schools would consider having more than one game theorist on their faculty, but Northwestern was actively building on strength in mathematical economic theory. The MEDS department was probably the only academic department in the world where game theory and information economics were not viewed as peripheral topics but as central strengths of the department. I had great colleagues, and every year we went out to hire more.

Everything that I did in game theory was ultimately motivated by the long-run goal of developing a coherent general methodology for game-theoretic analysis. What kinds of game models should we use to describe situations of conflict and cooperation among rational decision-makers, and what solution concepts should we use to predict rational behavior in these game models? In this quest, I was greatly influenced by three classic ideas of game theory: von Neumann's principle of strategic normalization for reducing dynamic games, Nash's program for subsuming cooperative games into noncooperative game theory, and Schelling's focal-point effect for understanding games with multiple equilibria. These ideas are so important that I cannot describe my work on game theory without explaining something about them.

Game theory could not have developed without a basic understanding that some conceptually simple class of models could be general enough to describe all the complicated game situations that we would want to study. John von Neumann ("Zur Theorie der Gesellschaftsspiele," 1928) argued that one-stage games in which players choose their strategies independently can be recognized as such a general class of models, even if we want to study dynamic games where the play may extend over time through many stages. The key to this argument is to define a *strategy* for a player to be a complete plan that specifies what the player should do at each stage in every possible contingency, so that each player could choose his or her strategy independently before the game begins. By this principle of strategic normalization, for any dynamic extensive game, we can construct an equivalent one-stage game in *strategic form,* where the players choose strategies independently, and these strategy choices then determine everyone's expected payoffs.

After presenting this argument for the generality of the strategic form, however, von Neumann actually studied cooperative games in a different nonstrategic *coalitional-form* model of games. In response, John Nash ("Non-Cooperative Games," 1951) argued that the process of bargaining should itself be recognized as a dynamic game in which players make bargaining moves at different stages of time, and so it should be similarly reducible to a game in strategic form. To analyze games in strategic form, Nash defined a general concept of equilibrium. In a *Nash equilibrium,* the predicted behavior of each player must be his or her best response to the predicted behavior of all other players.

When we follow this Nash program and write down simple models of bargaining games, however, we regularly find that these games can have many equilibria, and so a predictive theory cannot be determined without some principles for selecting among all these equilibria. Thomas Schelling (*The Strategy of Conflict*, 1960) argued that, in a game that has multiple equilibria, anything that focuses the players' attention jointly on one equilibrium can cause them to expect it and thus rationally to act according to it, as a self-fulfilling prophecy. The focal factors that steer the players to one particular equilibrium can be derived from the players' shared cultural traditions, or from the coordinating recommendations of a recognized social leader or arbitrator, or from any salient properties that distinguish one equilibrium as the focal equilibrium that everybody expects to play. In my view, the cooperative solutions which I was studying in my early papers were theories about how welfare properties of equity and efficiency can identify a focal equilibrium, which an impartial arbitrator could reasonably recommend, and which may be implemented by the players as a self-fulfilling prophecy.

I understood, however, that some general principles for eliminating some Nash equilibria might be also be appropriate. In particular, I knew that the theory of Nash equilibria for strategic-form games could yield predictions that seemed irrational when interpreted back to the framework of dynamic extensive games with two or more stages. The problem is that, if an event was assigned zero probability in an equilibrium, then the question of what a player should do in this event would seem irrelevant when the player plans his strategy in advance, and so a Nash equilibrium could specify strategic behavior that would actually become irrational for the player if this event occurred. In graduate school, I recognized that such irrational equilibria could be eliminated by admitting the possibility that players might make mistakes with some infinitesimally small probability. Reinhard Selten ("A Reexamination of the Perfectness Concept for Equilibrium Points in Extensive Games," 1975) was also developing similar ideas about refinements of Nash equilibrium. When I read his important paper on perfect equilibria in the *International Journal of Game Theory*, I sent my paper on proper equilibria to be published there also. The motivation for these refinements of Nash equilibrium was developed more formally a few years later by David Kreps and Robert Wilson when they defined *sequential equilibria* of dynamic extensive-form games (1982). From this perspective, perfect and proper equilibria may be seen as attempts to recognize in strategic form the equilibria that would be sequentially rational in the underlying dynamic game. But Kreps and Wilson cogently argued for dropping our reliance on strategic normalization and instead analyzing sequential equilibria of games in the dynamic extensive form.

Learning to Analyze Incentive Constraints in Games with Communication

Basic questions about information and incentives in economic systems were frequent topics of discussion at Northwestern in the late 1970s and early 1980s. There was great interest in Leonid Hurwicz's ideas of incentive compatibility, and these ideas influenced my search for a cooperative theory of games with incomplete information. But from my student days, I had learned to see games with incomplete information in the general framework of Harsanyi's Bayesian model. After I heard Alan Gibbard's early version of the revelation principle for dominant-strategy implementation, I became one of several researchers to see that it could be naturally extended to implementation with Bayesian equilibria in Harsanyi's framework. The revelation principle basically says that, for any equilibrium of any communication system, a trustworthy mediator can create an equivalent communication system in which honesty is a rational equilibrium for all individuals. With the revelation principle, we can generally formulate some mathematically simple constraints that summarize the problems of giving people appropriate incentives to share their private information. So I wrote a paper showing how these incentive constraints could extend and simplify the feasible set for Harsanyi and Selten's (1972) bargaining solution for two-person games with incomplete information. This idea was the basis of my first article on the revelation principle, which was published in *Econometrica* in 1979.

In the Harsanyi–Selten bargaining solution, however, the objective is to maximize a littleunderstood multiplicative product of the players' expected utility gains over the feasible set. In discussions with Robert Wilson and Paul Milgrom about auctions, I began to see that there might be more interesting economic applications where other objective functions are maximized over the same feasible set. I realized that the revelation principle could become a general tool for optimizing any measure of welfare in any situation where there is a problem of getting information from different individuals. During a visit to the University of Bielefeld in Germany (1978–79), I wrote a paper that applied these ideas to the problem of designing an auction where the objective is to maximize the seller's expected revenue, subject to the incentive constraints of getting potential buyers to reveal information about their willingness to pay. When I returned to Northwestern, I worked with colleagues on other important applications and extensions of these ideas. David Baron and I worked on optimal regulation of a monopolist with private information about costs. Mark Satterthwaite and I analyzed efficient mechanisms for mediation of bilateral trading problems involving one seller and one potential buyer for a single indivisible good.

With some simple but natural technical assumptions, we were able to derive powerful *revenue-equivalence* theorems that show how the expected profit for any type of individual with private information can be computed from the expected net trades for other possible types of the same individual. In this calculation, an individual's profit is seen to depend on the way that his private information could affect the ultimate allocation of valuable assets, but not on the details of how asset prices are determined in the market. Thus, people who have private information may be able to earn informational rents under any system of market organization in which the allocation of assets depends on their information.

The problem of providing incentives for people to share private information honestly, which has been called the problem of *adverse selection,* was not the only incentive problem that economists were learning to analyze in the 1970s. There was also a growing literature on the problem of providing incentives for individuals to choose hidden actions appropriately, which has been called the problem of *moral hazard.* Robert Aumann ("Subjectivity and Correlation in Randomized Strategies," 1974), in his definition of correlated equilibria for games with communication, formulated a version of the revelation principle that applied to moral hazard problems. In 1982, I published a paper to extend the revelation principle in a unified way to problems with both moral hazard and adverse selection, yielding a general theory of incentive-compatible coordination systems for Bayesian games with incomplete information. Later, in 1986, I showed how to extend the revelation principle to dynamic multistage games where sequential rationality is required in all events.

Bengt Holmström and I published a paper in 1983 on how economic concepts of efficiency should be extended to situations where people have private information. According to Pareto's basic concept of efficiency, the functioning of the economy is efficient when there is no feasible way to make everyone better off. But we must rethink many parts of this definition when we admit that each individual may have different private information, which is represented in our Bayesian games by a random, privately known *type* for each player. An economist's evaluation of efficiency or inefficiency cannot depend on information that is not publicly available, and a realistic concept of feasibility must take into account incentive constraints as well as resource constraints. Thus the concept of incentive efficiency should be applied to the entire mechanism or rule for determining economic allocations as a function of individuals' privately known types, not just to the final allocation itself. Holmström and I suggested that an incentivecompatible mechanism should be considered *incentive-efficient* when there is no other incentivecompatible mechanism that would increase the expected utility payoff for every possible type of every individual. If a change would make even one possible type of one individual worse off, then an economist cannot say for sure that the change would be preferred by everyone, when each individual privately knows his or her own type. This recommended efficiency criterion considers each individual's welfare at the *interim* stage, after he has learned his own type but before he can learn anyone else's type. Holmström and I also discussed other alternative criteria that consider individuals' *ex ante* expected welfare before learning anyone's type, or *ex post* welfare after learning everyone's types.

Among the areas in which I had the privilege of contributing to information economics, I see a uniquely central importance of this paper with Holmström, even though it was not actually mentioned in the citation for the Nobel Prize in 2007. Pareto's concept of efficiency is the most important normative criterion for economic analysis, and our paper was the first to carefully consider how this fundamental concept should be extended to economic situations where people have different information. It was published in the prestigious journal *Econometrica* after the usual scrutiny by anonymous referees, and I still remember their reports on this paper. One referee said that the first half of the paper (which surveyed six alternative definitions for extending Pareto efficiency as a normative concept) was a fundamental publishable contribution but then said that the second half (which proposed a complicated extension of Pareto efficiency as a positive predictive concept) should be cut, as it was speculative and unconvincing. The other referee said that the first half should be cut, as it was obvious and trivial, but then said that the second half should be published, as it was a subtle and interesting new idea. Fortunately, the editor chose to publish the union of the sections that referees liked, rather than their empty intersection.

In the early 1980s, I returned to the problem of defining general cooperative bargaining solutions for Bayesian games in which players have different information. To identify one bargaining solution among the many mechanisms on the interim incentive-efficient frontier, we need to define some principles for equitable compromise not just among the different individuals but also among the different possible types of any one individual. In particular, to avoid leaking private information, a player's bargaining strategy may need to be an inscrutable compromise between the payoff-maximizing goals of his actual type and the goals of the other possible types that other players think he might be. Such an inscrutable intertype compromise must be defined by some principles for measuring how much credit each possible type can claim for the fruits of cooperation. For example, when a player could be a good type or bad type and would prefer to be perceived as the good type, so that the incentive constraint that bad types should not gain by imitating good types is binding and costly in incentive-efficient mechanisms, then an inscrutable intertype compromise should put more weight on the goals of his good type than his bad type. In the early 1980s, I began to see that this idea could be mathematically formalized and measured by using the Lagrange multipliers of the informational incentive constraints in the mechanism design problem. Economists have long recognized the importance of Lagrange multipliers of resource constraints, which correspond to the prices of these resources, but economists had not previously done much with Lagrange multipliers of incentive constraints. With this mathematical insight, I was at last able to solve the problem of extending the Nash bargaining solution and the Shapley value to Bayesian games with incomplete information, which I published in *Econometrica* and the *International Journal of Game Theory* in 1984.

In the years since then, my two papers on cooperative games with incomplete information have not attracted much interest, and probably very few people have ever read them. But my interest in these questions, even if it was not shared by many others, led me to approach other questions of information economics from a different perspective, which was essential for my other contributions in mechanism design and auction theory ,which have been more widely valued.

New Directions

In 1980, I met Gina Weber, and we married in 1982. Our children, Daniel and Rebecca, were born in 1983 and 1985. Everything in my life since then has been a joint venture shared with them.

The biggest focus of my work in the later 1980s was on the writing of a general textbook on game theory, which was published in 1991. In this book I presented, as coherently as I could, the general methodology for game-theoretic analysis that so many of us had been working to develop. Other textbooks on game theory were also published in the early 1990s, and general textbooks on economic theory also began to treat game theory, information economics, and mechanism design as essential parts of microeconomic analysis. When the importance of game theory in economics was recognized by the Nobel Committee in October 1994 by its award to John Nash, John Harsanyi, and Reinhard Selten, I opened bottles of champagne to celebrate with my colleagues at Northwestern. These were bottles that I had been saving, in eager anticipation of such an event, for so long that the champagne had gone flat, but it still tasted good that day.

The last section of my game theory book considered markets with adverse selection, for which theorists since Michael Rothschild and Joseph Stiglitz (1976) have found that simple concepts of competitive equilibrium may be impossible to satisfy in simple examples. I suggested that equilibria for such markets may be sustained by a version of *Gresham's law*, that bad types would circulate in the market more than good types. I formalized this argument in a paper in 1995 which showed that such sustainable equilibria exist for general markets with adverse selection.

In the late 1980s, I began to work on game-theoretic models of politics. I had always felt that game theory's applications should go beyond the traditional scope of economics. In constitutional democracies, political constitutions and electoral systems define the rules of the game by which politicians compete for power. So game-theoretic analysis should be particularly valuable for understanding how changes in such constitutional structures may affect the conduct of politicians and the welfare-relevant performance of the government. I saw some analogy here with well-known ideas from the economic theory of industrial organization. In particular, the ability of political organizations to extract profits of power (corruption) should be expected to depend on barriers against the entry of new competitors into the political arena.

My first paper on comparison of electoral systems with Robert Weber was followed by several more papers in which I explored various models for evaluating the competitive implications of electoral reforms. For example, a politician could try to appeal broadly to all voters or could try to concentrate narrowly on appealing to small subgroups of the voting population; and I developed game models to show how different electoral rules can systematically affect politicians' competitive incentives to appeal more broadly or narrowly. In other papers, I showed how some electoral rules can yield a wider multiplicity of equilibria, including discriminatory equilibria in which some good candidates might not be taken seriously by the voters. I argued that such discriminatory equilibria can become barriers to entry against new politicians, thus allowing established political leaders to profit more from their political power. Democratic competition is intended to reduce such corrupt profit-taking by political leaders, but my analysis suggested that the effectiveness of democracy against such corruption can depend on the specific structure of the electoral system. In several models, I found that approval voting could induce stronger incentives for politicians to compete vigorously at the center of the political spectrum.

The constitutional distribution of power among different elected officials can also affect political incentives. Daniel Diermeier and I wrote a paper to show how presidential veto powers and bicameral subdivision of the legislature can decrease legislators' incentives to maintain coherent discipline in political parties or legislative coalitions.

The analysis of games with incomplete information has shown economists how probabilistic analysis of decision-makers' uncertainties can offer practical insights into competitive strategies, but my MBA students at Kellogg did not seem well prepared to apply such analysis. So I felt that it was important to seek new ways of teaching that could make practical probability models accessible to them. After trying many different approaches throughout the 1980s and 1990s, I found that the best pedagogical solution was to use simulation modeling in spreadsheets. Models and techniques that seemed too difficult for students when I wrote on the blackboard became intuitively clear to them when we worked together in electronic spreadsheets. So I wrote an MBA-level textbook on probability models for economic decisions, which was published in 2005.

Since 1996, I have written several papers on the history of game theory itself. I had the privilege of speaking about the importance of John Nash's contributions to economic theory at the American Economic Association's luncheon in honor of his Nobel Prize in January 1996. This presentation developed into a longer paper that was published in the *Journal of Economic Literature* in 1999, for the fiftieth anniversary of the day Nash submitted his first paper on non-cooperative equilibrium.

As the end of the twentieth century approached, I began to ask whether the advances in competitive analysis that meant so much to me might actually offer hope for a better twenty-first century. So I wrote a theoretical retrospective on the history of Germany's Weimar Republic, the failure of which was so central to the disasters of the twentieth century. The establishment of the Weimar Republic was framed by the Treaty of Versailles and the Weimar constitution, which were written in 1919 with expert advice from leading social scientists, including John

Maynard Keynes and Max Weber. I wanted to ask whether any recent advances in political or economic theory might offer a better framework for understanding such practical problems of institutional design, so that mistakes like those of 1919 should be less likely in the future. In this retrospective, I found that the advances that seemed to offer the most valuable insights for improving international relations were based largely on the ideas of Thomas Schelling and Reinhard Selten, in particular, the focal-point effect and the analysis of strategic credibility.

So, when America set out to invade Iraq in 2003, I applied Schelling's ideas about credible deterrence to show how America's rejection of multinational military restraint could exacerbate threats against America. When a powerful nation uses military force without clear limits, instead of deterring potential adversaries, it can actually motivate potential adversaries to invest more in militant counterforces. Thus, I argued, the greatest superpower in the world may have the greatest need to articulate clear and credible limits on its use of military force, according to rules and principles whose worth the rest of the world can judge.

In recent years, my research agenda has been increasingly shaped by a broad study of political history. To understand the great problems of political change and economic development, we need new theoretical models that can help us better understand the functional logic of the traditional systems from which many nations are now evolving. To have any hope of finding such broader models, however, a theorist needs the broadest possible understanding of different economic and political institutions of different societies throughout the world, from ancient times until today. For such a program of study, I found Samuel Finer's *The History of Government from the Earliest Time* (1997) to be a particularly valuable introduction to the global history of political institutions, but it needs to be followed by much more reading. From this historical perspective, I have come to believe that new theoretical models of oligarchy or feudalism or tribalism could become as important for political analysis as the Arrow–Debreu general equilibrium model for analysis of competitive markets.

In searching for universal principles that underlie all kinds of institutional structures, I have come to see agency incentive problems and the reputations of political leaders as critical factors that are fundamental to the establishment of any political institution. The rules of any political system must be enforced by government officials, and getting these officials to act according to these rules is a moral hazard problem. The incentives for lower government officials depend on rewards and punishments that are controlled by higher political leaders. So we find, at the heart of the state, a problem of moral hazard for which the solution depends on the individual reputations of political leaders. As I argued in a paper in 2008 in the *American Political Science Review,* the institutions of any political system must be organized by political leaders whose first imperative is to maintain their reputation for rewarding loyal supporters. I suggested that constitutional constraints on powerful leaders may be naturally derived from their fundamental need to maintain the long-term trust of their active supporters.

The problem of cultivating a democracy can then be recognized as a problem of creating opportunities for more politicians to begin cultivating good democratic reputations for serving the voters at large, even while rewarding active supporters with patronage benefits. In 2006 in the *Quarterly Journal of Political Science,* I published a formal model to show how the federal division of powers across national and local governments can increase such opportunities for promoting new leaders with good democratic reputations.

As an application of these ideas, I have written critically about American policies to establish democracy in Iraq and Afghanistan. I have argued that, in 2003, the first priority of the occupation authority in Iraq should have been to create elected and well-funded local councils, in which local leaders throughout the country could begin building independent reputations for responsible democratic governance. The centralized constitutional structure of the government in Afghanistan after 2003 may have similarly frustrated democratic state-building efforts there.

After the financial crisis of 2008, I began to think more about the great questions of macroeconomic stabilization, the importance of which had unfortunately become much more evident to people everywhere. My guiding intuition was that, just as the problems of moral hazard in government should be fundamental to our understanding of politics, so the problems of moral hazard in finance should be fundamental to our understanding of macroeconomics. Moral hazard arises in finance because agents who are entrusted with responsibility for prudently investing other people's savings may be tempted to profit inappropriately by abusing their power over other's money. Problems of moral hazard in financial institutions were widely evident in the financial crisis, but such problems were often ignored in traditional macroeconomic theory, because the basic economic principles for analyzing moral hazard agency problems were developed as part of information economics only in the 1970s.

More recently, in a paper on moral hazard credit cycles ("A Model of Moral-Hazard Credit Cycles," 2012), I have shown that a simple standard model of repeated moral hazard problems can offer a fundamental explanation of macroeconomic instability. The key point is that efficient incentive plans involve large latecareer rewards, to motivate an agent to maintain a record of good service throughout his or her career. The promise of a late-career reward for a good performance record may be seen as an investment in a relationship of trust, which is in many ways analogous to investments in capital that economists have traditionally studied. In each case, a large expense at one point in time can buy productive services that yield returns over a long interval of time. But whereas the greatest expense in a capital investment normally comes before the returns are realized, the largest moral hazard incentive payments come late in the agent's career, after investors have earned returns from the agent's service. More important, whereas capital investments are normally assumed to depreciate over time, the motivational value of late-career incentive payments increases during an agent's career, as normal time discounting causes the agent to value the prospective late-career rewards more as the time of their realization draws nearer. Changing depreciation to appreciation is mathematically like changing the direction of time, which can change a dynamically stable system to an unstable system. Thus, where simple economic models with capital investment tend to be dynamically stable, I found that equally simple economic models with moral hazard agency problems tend to be dynamically unstable, falling into boom-bust cycles that can go on forever.

I have had other big changes late in my own career. In 2001 I accepted a job in the Department of Economics at the University of Chicago. This was only my second academic position. Northwestern University's long tradition of great strength in economic theory made it an ideal home for me to work with great colleagues in game theory and political economics. But after twenty-five years at one school, it seemed time for a change, especially when the alternative on the other side of town was a university with another outstanding tradition of scholarship in economics.

In 2007, the Sveriges Riksbank Prize in Economic Sciences in Memory of Alfred Nobel was awarded to Leonid Hurwicz, Eric Maskin, and me. I am very proud to have my name so prominently linked with Leo's and Eric's, and with the advances in analysis of coordination mechanisms and incentive constraints to which we contributed, along with many other great economists. The opportunity to share this honor with my wife and my family and to celebrate with so many friends and colleagues has been a wonderful experience for me. But I understand that the true laureates are the ideas of incentive analysis and mechanism design, the importance of which seemed compelling to me long before they became the subject of a Nobel Prize.

Thus I have had the privilege of exploring some new ideas that were eventually recognized as worthy of study by students of subsequent generations. This is ultimately greatest honor that any scholar can hope for, of which Nobel Prizes can highlight only a small part. I have also worked on many other ideas and questions that excited me equally but that have not attracted much subsequent attention or interest from others. I have regularly shared ideas and questions that intrigue me with colleagues and students, but I do not try to steer students toward these questions, because good research takes a long time and nobody can know what will prove fruitful in research until it is done. Any scholar must make his or her own choices about what questions to study. For me, the greatest prize has been to work in a long career as a professor with opportunities to explore so many ideas, in search of the better understanding that we need.

Note

1. See Abraham Myerson, *Speaking of Man* (New York: Alfred A. Knopf, 1950), 7.

Roger Myerson

Awarded Nobel Prize in 2007. Lecture presented February 27, 2014

Date of Birth

March 29, 1951

Academic Degrees

B.A., Harvard University, 1973
M.A., Harvard University, 1973
Ph.D., Harvard University, 1976

Academic Affiliations

Visiting Researcher, Universität Bielefeld: Z.i.F. 1978–79
Assistant Professor of Managerial Economics and Decision Sciences,
Northwestern University, 1976–79
Associate Professor, Northwestern University, 1979–82
Professor, Northwestern University, 1982–2001
Visiting Professor of Economics, University of Chicago, 1985–86, 2000–01
Professor of Economics, University of Chicago, 2001
Glen A. Lloyd Distinguished Service Professor, University of Chicago,
2007–present

Selected Books

Game Theory: Analysis of Conflict, 1991
Probability Models for Economic Decisions, 2005

Thomas J. Sargent

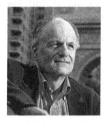

Introduction

Macroeconomics and econometrics are tools for recognizing patterns in data and interpreting them in ways that distinguish cause from coincidence. What attracted me to macroeconomics were its noble goals of identifying the causes of economic depressions and of inventing government policies to promote prosperity. In school, I learned that modern macroeconomics required more math than I knew. Therefore, for years at Minnesota I audited math classes. It was easy to select classes. If I sought to understand economics papers about X, then I wanted math Z. During math classes, I would get ideas for papers and recognize how to solve economic problems that had stumped me.

Macroeconomics from 1930 to 1968

Macroeconomics began in the 1930s with a catastrophic depression, the construction of national income accounts by Colin Clark, Simon Kuznets, and Richard Stone, and John Maynard Keynes's 1936 *General Theory of Employment, Interest and Money.* Keynes combined assumptions about the proximate determinants of the main national product components and their interactions into a theory of the level of national output. Depression data had convinced Keynes that drops in demand, not supply, had driven output down and unemployment up. Intuition led Keynes to postulate demand functions for consumption and investment. He guessed a demand for aggregate consumption that is an affine function of aggregate income. He posited that the aggregate demand for investment is a decreasing function of an interest rate. An interest rate was also a key variable in Keynes's demand function for money.

For many years, people debated "what Keynes meant." (No one asked, "What did Robert Lucas or David Kreps mean?") Its mostly nonmathematical style is one feature that made the *General Theory* difficult to understand, but not the only one. Keynes could write clearly (read his *Tract on Monetary Reform* or *Indian Currency and Finance*), but he did not in much of the *General Theory*. A list of insights and conjectures does not add up to a coherent model. Labels like "fundamental psychological law of consumption" are bluffs that do not describe what motivates people. Keynes's *General Theory* is confusing because Keynes was probably confused.

Keynes's literary style reflected his limited equipment. Important tools that now serve modern macroeconomics had not been invented. Keynes stressed people's expectations about future outcomes as volatile determinants of aggregate investment, but because he had no theory of expectations, he treated them as exogenous variables. Norbert Wiener and Andrei Kolmogorov created a statistical theory of prediction during World War II. Rudolf E. Kálmán invented a recursive version of that theory in 1960. Abraham Wald and Richard Bellman invented dynamic programming in the 1940s and 1950s. John von Neumann, Oskar Morgenstern, and Leonard Savage completed their theories of expected utility only in the 1940s and 1950s.

Keynes meant his *theory* to be *general* in the sense that it explained big transient declines in output and employment that could not be accounted for by the classical economics that Keynes said continued to be relevant near full employment.[1] Keynes was both conservative and optimistic in advocating that aggregate demand be manipulated to put the economy in full-employment positions where classical principles apply. Faith in that "neoclassical synthesis" continues to influence macroeconomics today.

Because Keynes's *General Theory* was obscure, John R. Hicks in 1937, Trygve Haavelmo in 1939, and Franco Modigliani in 1944 wrote down what they inferred was Keynes's theory as sets of simultaneous equations (n unknowns in n equations) that constituted a static macroeconomic model. These equations became the foundations of a three-front research program called Keynesian economics that dominated scientific macroeconomics until the early 1970s. First, adding explicit sources of dynamics and random errors created stochastic models that could be compared with time series data. Properly formulating and estimating Keynesian econometric models were the principal goals of the research of Jacob Marschak, Tjalling Koopmans, Leo Hurwicz, and others at the Cowles Commission. Second, deeper and more realistic foundations were sought for each of the demand functions making up a Keynesian model: deeper by providing an explicit theory of the motives and constraints underlying them, and better in fitting both aggregate time series and cross-section microdata. Finding micro foundations meant using a constrained optimization problem to deduce a decision rule for a component of aggregate demand or for the demand for money. A third research line opened by the Haavelmo–Hicks–Modigliani contributions and their econometrics-ready successors was the Tinbergen–Theil research program of computing optimal government policies for an analogue economy.

Using the notion of econometric identification to disentangle cause from effect was an essential part of this three-front program. Key discoveries about identification were made by researchers at the Cowles Commission, who married econometrics to policy analysis by distinguishing structural parameters from reduced form parameters. Structural parameters are objects that an economic theory asserts remain fixed when government polices change. Reduced form parameters characterize population regressions of endogenous variables on exogenous and lagged endogenous variables. Reduced form parameters are tangles of structural parameters and government policy parameters. An economic theory asserts how reduced form parameters change when government policies change. An economic model's structural parameters are said to be identified if they can be uniquely disentangled from reduced form parameters.[2] Identification requires that a theory assert that some things remain constant while others vary. To get identification, the Cowles Commission extended the idea that forces affecting quantities and prices can be sorted into two disjoint categories, one operating exclusively through demand, another exclusively through supply. Supply curves are supposed to remain fixed when demand shocks arrive; demand curves are supposed to remain fixed when supply shocks arrive. Such "exclusion conditions" for identification were immediately and widely applied to Keynesian macroeconometric models.

In addition to its stress on identifying structural parameters, Keynesian econometrics made two enduring practical contributions. One is the idea that a model is a joint probability distribution over a sequence indexed by pertinent free parameters. The second is a scientific rule that it takes a model to beat a model.

Now on to micro foundations. Friedman, Modigliani, and Tobin improved the statistical fits of aggregate consumption functions by adding dynamics. Baumol and Tobin derived demand functions for money from constrained optimization problems. But identifying the microeconomic underpinnings of a Keynesian investment function proved elusive. Reflecting that, in 1955 Tobin published a "dynamic aggregative model" that differed significantly from Hicks's 1937 IS-LM model because Tobin's model has no demand function for investment and no IS curve. Instead, it has a demand function for capital.[3] Haavelmo's 1960 *Study in the Theory of Investment* elaborates the failure of a Keynesian investment function to emerge from an intertemporal optimization problem for a representative firm. Haavelmo showed how that theory implies a demand function for capital like the one Tobin used in his dynamic aggregative model, not a demand curve for investment. Finding the micro foundations for a Keynesian investment function was at the top of the agenda of 1960s macro, one that attracted the best talent. Accepting Haavelmo's challenge, Dale Jorgenson created a widely admired theory of investment by augmenting Haavelmo's theory of a demand for capital with a distributed lag delaying responses. Complete success occurred only in the late 1960s when Treadway, Gould, and Lucas added adjustment costs to Haavelmo's specification of the firm's problem and thereby derived a Keynesian demand function for investment—that is, a decision rule for investment rates driven by expectations of future interest rates.

Early static Keynesian models took the aggregate money wage as exogenous. A time series econometric incarnation of a Keynesian model required a dynamic statistical model of the money wage. Keynes had offered fruitful hints about this important missing component when he said that the fall in the wage rate that classical economics had relied on would occur too slowly to arrest unemployment. Inspired by a 1958 paper using UK data by A. W. Phillips, in 1960 Paul Samuelson and Robert Solow published a scatter plot of a rate of change of an aggregate wage index against the U.S. unemployment rate. The scatter plot traced a negatively sloped Phillips curve that confirmed Keynes's hunch. Samuelson and Solow gave no formal micro foundations for that negative slope, but they offered insightful remarks about possible sources of such a slope, together with important caveats, including guesses about how expectations about future inflation might position that scatter graph.

In addition to its stress on econometric identification of structural parameters, the Tinbergen–Theil program of using econometric models to make quantitative statements about optimal government policies brought optimal control theory and dynamic programming into macroeconomics. Early applications recommended that a government apply dynamic programming to an econometric model that had not in any consistent way imputed dynamic programming to the agents living inside it. The "Lucas critique" asserted that models with good micro foundations would let private agents apply dynamic programming too. Early responses to the Lucas critique reversed the situation by constructing economies in which private agents use dynamic programming but governments do not. Eventually macroeconomists would construct structures in which private and government agents both use dynamic programming. But in the late 1960s, those advances lay in the future. Accomplishing them required a new way of thinking about peoples' expectations and a new equilibrium concept for macroeconomics.

Microeconomics-founded theories of the dynamics of consumption, investment, and the demand for money assigned important roles to decision-makers' expectations about future outcomes. Incorporating expectations in a workable macroeconometric model requires either measuring them or treating them as hidden variables whose laws of motion can be estimated. Researchers at the Carnegie Institute of Technology and elsewhere had tried to measure them and study their properties before modeling them. But data on expectations were scarce, so econometricians, including Marc Nerlove, Jorgenson, and Zvi Griliches, modeled expectations as hidden variables governed by distributed lags. The most popular theory was the "adaptive expectations" model that Milton Friedman had applied in the 1950s. It assumed that expectations about a future value of a scalar variable x are a geometric sum of past values of x. Imposing that the weights on lagged x's sum to one makes this a one-parameter model of expectations formation.

Edmund Phelps's 1967 model of the dynamics of inflation and unemployment imposes adaptive expectations and has people's expectations about inflation position the Phillips curve. With a particular definition of "long run," Phelps's model implies that there is no long-run trade-off between inflation and unemployment. But there is a temporary trade-off whose duration depends on the rate at which adaptive expectations discount past data. Phelps solved a Tinbergen-style optimal control problem for a best inflation-stabilization policy. Starting from initial conditions of sustained inflation, the best thing to do is to lower inflation gradually.

The rate at which inflation should be reduced depends sensitively on the geometric rate at which adaptive expectations discount past data.

In addition to Phelps's Phillips curve analysis, other fruitful uses of adaptive expectations in macroeconomics included Milton Friedman's application to an aggregate consumption function and Philip Cagan's to the monetary dynamics of hyperinflation.

But what about micro foundations? Why should people form expectations about a variable by exponentially smoothing past values of the same variable? Why use exponential smoothing and why not consult other variables, too? John F. Muth asked and answered these two questions in ways that would revolutionize applied economics. For Muth, finding micro foundations for expectations meant interpreting them as outcomes of least squares problems. Least squares forecasts are conditional mathematical expectations. Muth advocated assuming that the artificial people inside a model have personal subjective expectations that equal the objective conditional mathematical expectations implied by the model.

In his 1960 "Optimal Properties of Exponentially Weighted Forecasts," Muth posed an "inverse optimal prediction problem" having the form "I tell Muth an arbitrary formula for forming expectations about future outcomes of a random variable x; then Muth's job is to find a joint probability distribution for sequences of x that make my formula optimal in the linear least squares sense." This is an inverse problem because it takes the form "I tell you the answer, you tell me the question." Muth posed and solved this problem when Friedman's adaptive expectations scheme is the answer. Muth proved that if the first difference of x is a first-order moving average of a serially uncorrelated mean zero shock, then the optimal predictor of x over any horizon is a geometric average of current and lagged x's, and the decay parameter in the geometric sum equals the coefficient defining the moving average component of x. Muth's answer showed that optimal forecasting functions have no free parameters: all parameters of an optimal forecast function are exact functions of parameters describing the stochastic process being forecast.

The message of Muth's 1961 "Rational Expectations and the Theory of Price Movements" is that when expectations are about endogenous variables, "rational expectations" is a "fixed point" property. In a typical macroeconomic model, how people inside a model forecast future x's influences how future x's should be forecast. For my purposes here, Phelps's model is a good macroeconomic laboratory for illustrating the rational expectations equilibrium concept of Muth's 1961 paper.[4] A conditional expectation of future wage inflation implied by Phelps's model differs from the exponentially smoothing expectations rule that Phelps imputed to the people inside his model. Phelps's model makes better forecasts than do the people inside his model. As an equilibrium condition, rational expectations eradicates any such systematic gaps between the personal expectations of agents inside a model and the best forecasts implied by the model. Phelps's model induces a mapping from an arbitrary sequence of expectations about wage growth to a sequence of best forecasts of wage growth. Phelps had evaluated this mapping only at the one point associated with adaptive expectations. A rational expectations equilibrium is a fixed point of the mapping. Imposing the rational expectations equilibrium concept on Phelps's 1967 model would substantially alter the model's policy implications in ways that I describe below.

Rational Expectations Econometrics

My work in the 1970s sought to put rational expectations to work on each of the three fronts of the post–World War II Keynesian program of (1) constructing an econometric theory appropriate for macroeconomics, (2) providing micro foundations that would improve econometric fit and stability, and (3) using macroeconometric models to make quantitative statements about good government policies. We had to rethink sources of parameter identification in econometrics, rework the micro foundations of virtually every component of the Keynesian structure, and reformulate quantitative optimal policy analysis. Their internal logic tied the three problems together, so I worked on all three.

A stroke of good luck was my learning Clive Granger's definition of causality for a covariance stationary vector time series stochastic process. Granger's definition is about properties of optimal forecasts of one variable as a function of the history of all other variables. Consequently, Granger's causality criterion shapes answers to the two questions about the micro foundations of expectations that we met earlier when we discussed Muth's "inverse optimal prediction" problem: What current and past variables should a decision-maker use to forecast? And what function of those past data should be used?

It helped me to read Christopher Sims's papers connecting Granger causality to an econometrically useful definition of exogeneity. I was fortunate to be with Chris at Minnesota. Sims's papers clarified Granger's work by deepening its mathematical foundations.

Granger and Sims adopted the same mathematical setting that Muth had used in his 1960 and 1961 papers about rational expectations. This framework naturally accepts economic models in which decision-makers have quadratic objective functions and random disturbances have finite second moments. This neatly separates the problem of forecasting from the problem of making the best decisions given a set of forecasts, a special "certainty equivalence" property that substantially simplifies economic models. It was widely used in early rational expectations models.

In these ways, many people's hard work had determined for me a tightly focused research agenda: (1) put decision-makers in a setting in which uncertain exogenous variables are described by linear stochastic processes in the style of Granger and Sims, make assumptions that validate that "certainty equivalence" applies, then find a rational expectations equilibrium random process for prices and quantities; (2) extract econometric implications of that rational expectations equilibrium; (3) estimate that econometric model and then use it to find consequences of alternative government policies. My early papers applied parts of this program to study the natural unemployment rate hypothesis, the term structure of interest rates, the monetary dynamics of hyperinflation, the Gibson paradox, and the coordination of monetary and fiscal policies.

An early application was my 1971 "Note on the Accelerationist Controversy," which criticized Solow and Tobin's then popular test of the Phelps–Friedman natural unemployment rate hypothesis for not properly imposing rational expectations, and then suggested a test consistent with rational expectations. The test that I criticized had used adaptive expectations in the form of exponential smoothing of past inflation rates. Relying on Friedman's one-parameter adaptive expectations model, Solow and Tobin had imposed a unit sum on the exponential coefficients describing how people forecast inflation. I pointed out that for a unit sum to be a property of optimal univariate forecasts of inflation, inflation itself would have to be a very persistent process (today we would say that it has a "unit root"). But until 1970, post–World War II inflation had been only weakly serially correlated. This simple application of univariate optimal prediction theory let me conclude that Solow and Tobin's test could give false rejections of the natural unemployment rate hypothesis and indicated a more appropriate test of cross-equation restrictions. After I had written my paper, I discovered that Bob Lucas had written a paper that also described how to test the natural unemployment rate hypothesis in a rational expectations equilibrium.

Hicks's 1937 *Value and Capital* had set forth an "expectations theory" of the term structure of interest rates according to which the yield on a risk-free zero-coupon n-period bond should be a geometric average of one-period yields expected to prevail over the next n periods. I had read a number of good papers that supplemented Hicks's expectations theory with something like Friedman's adaptive expectations model for the one-period rate to construct an econometric model of the term structure. I responded to the challenge of formulating and estimating a rational expectations version of the expectations theory of the term structure by writing three papers, each a little better than its predecessor. The challenge was to use optimal prediction theory to construct a theory of expectations about the short rate and then to deduce what that implied for the evolution of the long rate. My first attempt, published in the *Journal of Money Credit and Banking* in 1972, followed my procedure in a "Note on the Accelerationist Controversy" and simply posited that the short rate followed a univariate linear stochastic process, that traders used this process to forecast short rates, and then applied Hicks's geometric averaging formula to get long rates. In this way, I deduced from the dependence of short rates on lagged values of the short rate how longer rates should also depend on lagged values of the short rate. This yielded a cross-equation restriction: a long rate equation inherited all of its parameters from the short rate equation.

Thanks to Sims, vector autoregressions were in the air at Minnesota in the mid-1970s. The term structure of interest rates is a vector. What restrictions does a rational expectations version of the expectations theory of the term structure put on a vector autoregression? My 1972 paper did not answer that question because it assumed that traders forecast the short rate by using only the history of the short rate. If they observe the entire term structure, shouldn't they use the entire vector of interest rates (the term structure) to forecast all rates? My 1979 "Note on Maximum Likelihood Estimation of the Rational Expectations Model of The Term Structure" used all rates and deduced a subset of the restrictions that the rational expectations theory imposes on a vector autoregression for the term structure. That subset heavily overidentifies the free parameters of the model and opens a maximum likelihood estimation strategy.

Angelo Melino's 1981 Harvard Ph.D. thesis succeeded in imposing all the restrictions that the theory imposes on a vector autoregression. I admired Melino's work but wanted to approach the problem from a different angle. To do that, technical reinforcements arrived in the form of a research assistant at Minnesota, Lars Peter Hansen. We reformulated the problem by building on Sims's extensions of Granger's paper on causality. Sims had used vector Wold moving average representations to study implications of the causality structure Granger had originally defined in terms of restrictions on a vector autoregression. Lars and I reformulated the rational expectations version of the expectations theory of the term structure as a set of restrictions on a vector moving average. To preserve covariance stationary and ergodicity of the key objects to be estimated,[5] we imposed a restriction that Engle and Granger subsequently called "cointegration." In addition to letting us completely characterize the restrictions, we recognized that our model belonged to a broader class that proved to contain good laboratories for discovering useful econometric properties of linear rational expectations models. Key issues involve possible differences in the information contained in histories of moving average errors and innovations to a vector autoregression.

Phillip Cagan's 1956 "Monetary Dynamics of Hyperinflation" had posited that the demand for money is a semilogarithmic function of the expected rate of inflation, modeled via a single-parameter Friedman-style adaptive expectations scheme. Cagan's model presented the following multivariate counterpart of the question that Muth had posed in his 1960 paper: for what bivariate inflation–money creation process would Cagan's adaptive expectations scheme for forecasting inflation be an implication of rational expectations? In my 1977 "Demand for Money during Hyperinflation under Rational Expectations," I constructed that bivariate model and applied a maximum likelihood estimation strategy. The resulting rational expectations model has the sharp implication that money creation fails to help predict inflation, an implication that is broadly confirmed in Cagan's data. This finding provokes one to think about relationships between Granger causality and other senses of causality. The economic sense of the model is that sustained high rates of money creation are responsible for high inflation outcomes.

Common to those early papers were sources of econometric identification coming from rational expectations. These differ in their mathematical form and economic content from the "exclusion restrictions" that had been employed in most earlier macroeconometric work. Exclusion restrictions identify parameters by assuming that sources of variation that affect some decisions (e.g., demand) do not affect others (e.g., supply). That they move demand and not supply is what generates variation along a fixed supply curve.

The logic of rational expectations pulls the rug out from under exclusion restrictions because dynamic demand and supply functions depend on expectations of future paths of many of the same variables. The rational expectations equilibrium concept implies that decision-makers use the histories of all variables to forecast those paths. Instead of exclusion restrictions, rational expectations brings cross-equation restrictions that recognize that demand and supply decisions depend in different ways on the same forecast paths. That in turn makes these decisions depend on histories in different ways. By disentangling these dependencies, the theory identifies structural parameters describing preferences, technologies, and information sets. In applications, these cross-equation restrictions have substantial bite and become tighter when more variables appear in decision-makers' information sets.

My 1978 *JPE* paper exploited such restrictions in the context of a dynamic model of the demand for labor in the presence of adjustment costs. Two joint 1980 papers with Lars Peter Hansen substantially generalized that work. In these papers, we derived a set of formulas expressing the cross-equation restrictions associated with a class of linear rational expectations models of interrelated factor demand.

Neil Wallace and I studied identification in a model of inflation whose structural equations consist of a Cagan-style demand for money and a government budget constraint determining the growth rate of money. The model has a continuum of rational expectations equilibria, some of them being driven by "sunspots," and many of them displaying "rational bubbles." Nevertheless, data on money creation and inflation together with the rational expectations cross-equation restrictions strongly identify parameters and uniquely pin down a single equilibrium. This paper tells a useful story about a logically distinct pair of possible multiplicities, one pertaining to the number of equilibria consistent with a given vector of parameters and the other pertaining to uniqueness of parameters characterizing bivariate observations.

In 1978, I published a note answering no to the question, should you use seasonally adjusted data to estimate rational expectations models? Seasonally adjusted data are long symmetric two-sided filters of the original data, meaning that seasonally adjusted data at t are functions of data at *future* dates. For that reason, seasonal adjustment alters the information in a history of a series by letting the filtered data peek at the future.[6] Imposing the cross-equation rational expectations restrictions on the seasonally adjusted data leads to false restrictions if decision-makers are actually using seasonally unadjusted data. My dynamic demand for labor model was a good laboratory for illustrating these claims.

Chris Sims told me that my conclusion would be modified if the rational expectations model being estimated was misspecified more along some dimensions than others. Sims conjectured that by distorting the cross-equation restrictions implied by a false rational expectations model, seasonal filtering could improve maximum likelihood estimates of a subset of parameters capturing more trusted parts of the model. To investigate that idea, Lars Hansen and I constructed examples in which an econometrician estimated parameters of one rational expectations model while the data were actually governed by another. Some of our examples confirmed Sims's conjecture. While doing that research, we investigated several alternative ways of modeling seasonality in rational expectations models, building on earlier work by G. C. Tiao and M. R. Grupe and by M. F. M. Osborne about models with hidden periodicity. (I view Lars and my work on seasonality as an early part of our current research program on robustness to model misspecification.)

Suppose that a theoretical model is formulated at a fine time interval, such as weekly or in continuous time, while data are available only at coarser time intervals. What restrictions does a continuous time model impose on the available discrete time data? What features of the continuous time model can be identified from the discrete time data? Sims had analyzed these questions in the context of distributed lag models. But he had not posed them for rational expectations models. Lars Hansen and I wrote several papers showing how the hallmark rational expectations cross-equations restrictions are especially powerful in identifying continuous time models from discrete time data.

Bob Lucas presented a problem to me at a conference at the Minneapolis Fed in the mid-1980s when sustained U.S. federal deficits were being widely discussed. Bob asked what restrictions the assumption of a present value budget balance would impose on a vector autoregression for total tax collections and total government expenditures. I produced a preliminary answer describing a sense in which the observable implications are very weak and published it in the second edition of *Macroeconomic Theory*. The weakness of the restriction ultimately comes from the freedom to promise big surpluses in the distant future. Subsequently Lars Hansen, William Roberds, and I studied the problem in greater depth. We discovered that even with a constant risk-free interest rate, a present value budget balance imposes no restrictions on a bivariate vector autoregression for government expenditures and tax collections. The present value budget balance hypothesis acquires empirical bite only when supplemented by additional principles guiding either tax collections or expenditures. We used a class of permanent income models to illustrate the role of such restrictions in rescuing identification. Since the 1980s, macroeconomists have routinely estimated vector autoregressions, computed impulse response functions, and then applied procedures to associate rotated VAR innovations with shocks purportedly impinging on some incompletely specified deeper economic model. Lars and I analyzed the problem in "Two Difficulties in Interpreting Vector Autoregressions." The first difficulty arises in situations in which VAR innovations contain less information than the shocks hitting agents' information and budget sets. The second arises when aggregation over time conceals agents' information from the econometrician. Lars and I used the rational expectations equilibrium concept to extend Chris Sims's earlier work on related time-aggregation issues. We showed how exploiting the cross-equations restrictions of rational expectations econometrics overcomes both kinds of difficulties and also identifies shocks hitting a decision-maker's information set.

To reform the third branch of the Keynesian quantitative research program, we sought optimal government policies in settings that impose the rational expectations equilibrium concept. Since expectations of endogenous variables depend on government decision rules, there is a distinct rational expectations equilibrium for each government policy. The optimal policy problem is to find the best rational expectations equilibrium. One of my first efforts along these lines involved finding optimal policy in a rational expectations version of a Phelps–Friedman natural unemployment rate model. In a 1973 paper, "Rational Expectations, the Real Rate of Interest, and the Natural Rate of Unemployment," I cast an econometric version of what I had decoded from Milton Friedman's 1968 AEA presidential address. Imposing a rational expectations equilibrium on that structure produced some striking results. Friedman's original model with adaptive expectations had contained a transient trade-off between inflation and unemployment that could be optimally exploited along the lines that Phelps had analyzed in his 1967 paper. That exploitable trade-off evaporates under rational expectations. There still exists a Phillips curve, but it cannot be exploited by any systematic government policy. Using rational expectations also changed the relevant analytical concepts from "long-run versus short-run" to "systematic versus random."

My 1973 Brookings paper originally had used the systematic-versus-random policy classification to obtain a stronger irrelevance result for systematic monetary policy. The editors of the *Brookings Papers* declined to publish that result. So Neil Wallace and I refined and published it as "Rational Expectations, the Optimal Monetary Instrument, and the Optimal Money Supply Rule" in the *JPE* in 1976. The point of our irrelevance examples was not that monetary policy is irrelevant in all imaginable rational expectations models. It was that to make monetary policy matter requires more frictions than were present in the particular models on which Neil and I had imposed rational expectations.

In terms of the evolution of twentieth-century macroeconomics, my two papers about a natural unemployment rate theory were transitional creatures because they retained many features of earlier Keynesian models, including IS-LM curves. Their micro foundations were not coherent. Neil and my papers didn't close what Kenneth Arrow in 1967 had called a "scandalous" gap between macroeconomics and general equilibrium theory. But a paper by Bob Lucas had. In his 1972 "Expectations and the Neutrality of Money," Bob completed a general equilibrium investigation of how to interpret and exploit the Phillips curve. Bob's paper stated a sharp policy ineffectiveness result that, like a similar one in Neil and my papers, hinged sensitively on rational expectations.

After the mid-1970s, Neil and I emerged from the Keynesian waters in which we had evolved and thereafter mostly used general equilibrium models that incorporated the rational expectations assumption. The rational expectations assumption had not been a necessary piece of earlier general equilibrium theories. The general equilibrium models that have come to dominate applied work in finance, macroeconomics, and public finance are special instances of Arrow–Debreu models. That is because Arrow–Debreu models assume general representations of preferences that allow agents to have diverse beliefs about the future. The special general equilibrium models used today in macroeconomics typically (1) restrict the preferences of each agent to be some version of discounted expected utility and (2) impose an extensive "communism" that precludes any heterogeneity of beliefs across agents inside a model, as well as any differences between these and either nature's probability distribution or the econometrician's. This communism of beliefs is heavily exploited in the rational expectations fixed-point equilibrium concept and also in all empirical implementations that rely on a law of large numbers. A compelling scientific justification for assuming rational expectations is that it drastically reduces the number of objects and parameters constituting an econometric model. Pure general equilibrium theorists do not have to be in the "dimension reduction" business, but econometricians do.

In the same ways that it made us rethink econometric identification, the dimension reduction brought by rational expectations reshaped our understanding about the channels through which fundamental economic forces operate. An irony is that while the rational expectations equilibrium concept emphasizes people's expectations, it makes those expectations disappear as exogenous variables. They are outcomes.

Economic forces that shape equilibrium expectations are today a focus of applied analysis throughout economics. The hallmark cross-equation identifying restrictions brought by rational expectations are routinely used to study runs on banks and sovereign bonds, the effects of employment protection and social safety nets on labor supply decisions, enforcement and information constraints in incentive-compatible social insurance and financial arrangements, how deposit insurance and lender-of-last-resort facilities alter equilibrium prices and risk-taking and, through them, taxpayers' implicit insurance obligations, and alternative arrangements for coordinating monetary and fiscal policies.[7]

Concluding Remarks

I have followed instructions to write about my education as an economist and the scientific challenges it presented. I am indebted to the giant macroeconomists from my youth for their idealism and purpose, the high scientific standards they set, and the scientific challenges they presented to my generation. Rational expectations econometrics has refined old problems and opened new ones. Lars Hansen's Nobel lecture describes how studying these improves our understanding of equilibrium expectations and macroeconomic outcomes.

Notes

1. Read his *Tract on Monetary Reform.*

2. Or equivalently, they can be uniquely recovered from a likelihood function.

3. Significantly, the interest rate in Tobin's demand function for capital is a real interest rate, while the interest rate in his portfolio balance equation is a nominal interest rate. Tobin's instantaneous nominal interest rate equals his real interest rate plus an exogenous expected rate of inflation. Similarly, Hicks wanted a real interest rate in his IS curve and a nominal rate in his LM curve.

4. In his 1961 *Econometrica* paper, Muth illustrated his equilibrium concept by applying it to a model of prices and quantities in what, with adaptive expectations, was called a cobweb model.

5. Stationarity and ergodicity are technical conditions that make it possible to learn from large samples of time series data.

6. Technically, the data are smoothed, not filtered.

7. The high rates of money creation in the hyperinflations studied by Cagan had fiscal origins. Thinking about the economic forces that shape equilibrium inflation led Neil Wallace and me to our 1981 "Unpleasant Monetarist Arithmetic" in the *Quarterly Review of the Federal Reserve Bank of Minneapolis*. We combined a rational expectations version of Cagan's demand for money with a specification of the money supply process that depends on how "fiscal" and "monetary" policies are coordinated. Fiscal policy partly determines the rate at which total government debt grows, while monetary (a.k.a. debt management) policies use "open market operations" to determine what fractions of the public's holdings of government debt do and don't bear interest, fractions that also influence the rate at which government debt grows. The arithmetic of a consolidated government budget constraint entangles monetary and fiscal policies. The equilibrium paths of the price level depend on how monetary and fiscal policies are coordinated. Our 1981 paper is sometimes accurately called a fiscal theory of equilibrium price paths.

Thomas J. Sargent

Awarded Nobel Prize in 2011. Lecture presented April 21, 2015.

Date of Birth

July 19, 1943

Academic Degrees

B.A., University of California, Berkeley, 1964
Ph.D., Harvard University, 1968

Academic Affiliations

Research Associate, Carnegie Institute of Technology, 1967–68
First Lieutenant and Captain, U.S. Army. Served as Staff Member and Acting Director, Economics Division, Office of the Assistant Secretary of Defense (Systems Analysis), 1968–69
Associate Professor of Economics, University of Pennsylvania, 1970–71
Associate Professor of Economics, University of Minnesota; 1971–75
Professor of Economics, University of Minnesota; 1975–87
Research Associate, National Bureau of Economic Research, 1970–73, 1979–present
Member, Brookings Panel on Economic Activity, 1973
Ford Foundation Visiting Research Professor of Economics, University of Chicago, 1976–77
Adviser, Federal Reserve Bank of Minneapolis, 1971–87
Visiting Professor of Economics, Harvard University, and Research Associate, National Bureau of Economic Research, 1981–82
Visiting Scholar, Hoover Institution, Stanford University, 1985–87
Senior Fellow, Hoover Institution, Stanford University, 1987–present
David Rockefeller Professor of Economics, University of Chicago, 1991–98
Donald Lucas Professor of Economics, Stanford University, 1998–2002
William Berkley Professor of Economics, New York University, 2002–present
Distinguished Term Professor, Singapore Management University, 2015–present

Selected Books

Uncertainty Within Macroeconomic Models, 2014 (with Lars Peter Hansen)
Rational Expectations and Inflation, 3rd edition, 2013
Robustness, 2008 (with Lars Peter Hansen)
Recursive Models of Dynamic Linear Economics, 2013 (with Lars Peter Hansen)
Rational Expectations Econometrics, 1991 (with Lars Peter Hansen)

Amartya Sen

1

If it is hard to be sure whether one is leading a troubled life, it is harder to have a clear idea of what kind of trouble one may be going through. But why ask about troubles when the wonderfully kind Trinity University wants me to talk about a much pleasanter subject—my evolution as an economist? I think there is a clear connection. To be moved by an intellectual challenge enough to want to work hard to address that challenge tends to be closely related to being troubled by the existence of—and the importance of—a challenge. To follow one's intellectual evolution, it is, I think, very important to understand what had looked troublesome enough at some stage or other in one's life to lead one to put in serious efforts at providing a response.

An intellectual determination to meet a challenge—to learn what one does not yet know—cannot but be central to one's intellectual evolution. And this is, of course, the very opposite of what J. Alfred Prufrock portrayed in his love song, narrated by T. S. Eliot:

> For I have known them all already, known them all:
> Have known the evenings, mornings, afternoons,
> I have measured out my life with coffee spoons.

An intellectual challenge, in contrast, is an invitation to the unknown—however overpowering the challenge might be.

I have to confess that I have been troubled—indeed, deeply troubled—by problems of many different kinds. Some of them have fairly obvious social relevance (such as analyzing the causes of famines and identifying ways and means of preventing starvation and hunger); others may well have some political use (such as finding out the conditions under which majority decisions tend to be consistent); and others may demand a critical examination of social institutions and economic policies. But there are still others that are definitely captivating as scrutiny of foundational ideas, such as equity, justice, and efficiency. The domain of theory can proceed hand in hand with attempts to reduce poverty, curb deprivation, and defend liberty and freedom.

2

As I look back on the little work I have been able to do over my long life, it seems to be broadly divided into quite abstract reasoning (for example, in pursuing the idea of justice and in exploring various avenues in social choice theory, with axioms, theorems, and proofs) and rather practical problems (famines, hunger, economic deprivations, inequalities of class, gender, and caste, and others).

I was forced to reflect on all that when the Nobel Foundation asked me to give them, on long-term loan, two objects that had been closely associated with my work, to be displayed in the Nobel Museum, which would start in Stockholm and tour the world. I believe the roving museum has by now gone around the world, and is back in Stockholm. The generous—and overly kind—citation with which the Swedish Academy had announced my award was heavily inclined in the direction of my analytical work in social choice theory, quoting chapters and verses (in fact, theorems and proofs), but it also briefly mentioned, at the end of the statement, my work on famines, inequality, and gender disparity. After some dithering on which object to choose, I gave the Nobel Museum (1) a copy of *Aryabhata* (one of the great Sanskrit classics on mathematics and astronomy from A.D. 499), from which I had benefited so much, and (2) my old bicycle, which had been with me from my school days and which I used a great deal in parts of my empirical research.

I had used the bike, first, in famine studies, to collect data on wages and prices from fairly inaccessible places, like old farm sheds and warehouses. I was then studying how the Bengal famine of 1943, which killed nearly three million people, made it so hard for some occupation groups (for example, rural wages laborers) to buy enough food to meet their families' survival needs. Later I used the same bike for studying gender inequality. In particular it was an essential means for me to move from one village to another to weigh boys and girls up to the age of five. It gave me first-hand data on gender discrimination and the emergence of the relative deprivation of girls over their early years.

I should say here that I was also tempted to consider giving the Nobel Museum a weighing machine rather than my bike. This was the weighing machine my co-workers and I had used to measure the weights of young children to make cross-gender comparisons. Some of the observations on the relative weights of boys and girls, including how they diverged as social care replaced the natural equity in the womb, that I used in my publications—and that, I am happy to say, have been widely used by others as well—came from that rickety old weighing machine. I have to confess that I was very proud of taking over the task of weighing whenever my research assistants were deterred by being bitten by toothy children. I became the local expert on weighing without being bitten. They may not give you a prize for that, but it certainly made me feel quite accomplished!

As the Nobel Museum, starting in Stockholm, went around the world, I often received questions about what a bike had to do with Aryabhata's mathematics. I had to explain why the answer was "a great deal." Aryabhata was an astronomer as well as a mathematician, and second to none in his attempt to understand the world as it was, rather than as it had been portrayed. Among other claims, Aryabhata insisted on a rotating Earth (a thousand years before Galileo Galilei) and on the existence of gravitational pull (he used it explain why things are not hurled out from a rotating Earth). He had to stand up to the orthodoxy surrounding him, and if there was great intellectual encouragement in his work, there was also a strong invitation not to be cowed by the forceful certitude of authority and power. These qualities are inspirationally as important in studies of poverty, inequality, and gender discrimination as they are in understanding how economic relations work through markets and state interventions.

3

If there is one field of study that has been particularly central to my interests and pursuits, it is what is called social choice theory. When I had to give a Nobel Lecture in Stockholm, I chose social choice theory as the subject of my talk. This is partly because the subject is of great intellectual interest to me, but also because it is also of considerable social use.

What is social choice theory? Human beings have always lived in groups, and the lives of individuals have invariably been dependent on group decisions. However, the challenges of group choice can be extensive and exacting, particularly because of the divergent interests and concerns of its members. Even though an absolute dictator, who wants to control every aspect of people's lives, may wish to ignore the preferences of every-one else, that level of total control is hard to achieve. More important, dictatorship of any kind is a terrible way of governing a society. Social scientists have investigated, for a very long time, how the concerns of the members of a society can be reflected in one way or another in the deci-sions made in a responsive society, even if it is not fully democratic. For example, Aristotle in ancient Greece and Kautilya in ancient India, both of whom lived in the fourth century B.C., explored various different pos-sibilities in social choice in their classic books respectively called *Politics* and *Economics*.[1]

Social choice theory is a very broad discipline, covering a variety of distinct questions, and it may be useful to mention a few of the prob-lems as illustrations of its subject matter. When would *majority rule* yield unambiguous and consistent decisions? How can we judge how well a *society as a whole* is doing in the light of the disparate interests of its different members? How can we accommodate the *rights and liberties* of persons while giving adequate recognition to the preferences of all? How do we measure *aggregate poverty* in view of the varying predicaments and miseries of the diverse people that make up the society? How do we evaluate public goods such as the natural environment, or epidemiolog-ical security? These are all practical questions of importance, and there is nothing contradictory in the fact that social choice theory, which has intrinsic intellectual excitement, actually helps us to think clearly about these real-world issues.

Indeed, some investigations, which are not directly parts of social choice theory, have been helped by the understanding generated by the study of group decisions—such as the causation and prevention of famines and hunger, or the forms and consequences of gender inequality. Going much beyond that, a theory of justice can substantially draw on insights as well as analytical results from social choice theory (as I have discussed in my 2009 book, *The Idea of Justice*).

4

How did formal social choice theory originate? It emerged as a formal discipline in the eighteenth century, in the works of French mathematicians, particularly the Marquis de Condorcet and Jean-Charles de Borda. So it is very much a product of the Enlightenment. It happened in a world in which the need for treating human beings in an equal way was gathering momentum. This would be most sharply reflected in the French Revolution, which erupted even as the early social choice theorists—Condorcet, Borda, and others—were presenting their mathematical theorems that shared the general framework of treating people as equals.

In its modern form, social choice theory was constructed as an integrated discipline by Kenneth Arrow at the middle of the last century. Arrow is also an heir of the egalitarian tradition of the Enlightenment, and this is well reflected by him in the framework of modern social choice theory, in not discriminating between the attention that should be paid to different individuals involved. The implications of that normative commitment are indeed enormous, as the development of the discipline of social choice theory has brought out—beginning with Arrow's impossibility theorem, but also with various extensions and diverse constructive moves that Arrow's subversive challenge has dialectically generated.

Arrow's attempt at giving social choice a democratic foundation is entirely in line with what the other pioneer, the Marquis de Condorcet, wanted to do in his theories about the future of France after the revolution—a revolution that was very much on the horizon as Condorcet was establishing his mathematical results in the 1780s, and later pursuing his less formal investigations in *Esquisse*. In the world of the European Enlightenment, there were also other, less mathematical explorations of systematic social assessment, presented by Adam Smith (1759, 1790), Tom Paine (1776, 1791), Immanuel Kant (1788), Jeremy Bentham (1789), Mary Wollstonecraft (1790, 1792), and others, and many of their ideas are also relevant to the discipline of social choice.

5

The year 1950, in which Arrow published his pioneering paper on social choice theory, which made him, as a young graduate student, a new leader of innovative social thought, also saw quite a few developments of interest to practical social choice. Communist China received widespread diplomatic recognition, the United Nations dispatched troops to Korea, the

Republic of India was established, with its new democratic constitution, and Senator Joseph McCarthy went on a political rampage in his campaign to find "un-Americanism" among Americans. Social choice theory is relevant—in different ways—to all these highly practical matters. And so it is also to academic intrigues related to group decisions, well portrayed, for example, in C. P. Snow's popular novel, *The Masters*, which too was published in the same year, 1950, as Arrow's pioneering essay.

Despite the relevance of social choice theory to all these practical matters, it would be rather eccentric to think of *formal* social choice theory as being immediately applicable to these practical "social choice events." The development of mathematical social choice theory has, in fact, tended to concentrate on theoretical analyses at some distance from instant application, even though (as many of us have tried to show in our works) they are ultimately relevant to practical concerns. That apparent remoteness has its advantages, not least in allowing the development of sophisticated techniques of analysis that need formal reasoning and the use of mathematical methods, which would have been hard to sustain if every analytical departure had to be justified in terms of instant relevance to day-to-day matters.

The conceptual generality of axiomatic methods has also allowed applications of similar analytical results in widely different fields. For example, while Arrow's immediate concern was with welfare economics, and in particular with the attempts (especially by Abram Bergson (1938) and Paul Samuelson (1947)) to reconstruct "social welfare functions" on what were seen as the ruins of utilitarian welfare economics, his results were equally relevant to political issues of democracy and participatory governance. As Samuelson (1967) rightly noted, Arrow's "mathematical politics" does throw "new light on age-old conundrums of democracy" (p. viii).

6

Almost certainly the most important result associated with social choice theory is Arrow's "impossibility theorem." In 1948, when Arrow was a graduate student, Olaf Helmer, a philosopher at the RAND Corporation whom Arrow had met through Tarski, the great logician, wondered about the legitimacy of applying game theory to international relations ("the 'players' were countries, not individuals," he worried). Helmer asked young Arrow, a Ph.D. student, "in what sense could collectivities be said to have utility functions?" Arrow replied (I suspect with some disciplinary pride) that "economists have thought about that question and it has been answered by Abram Bergson's notion of the social welfare function" (referring to Bergson 1938). As Arrow settled down to writing an exposition for Helmer (paying particular attention to putting together a collection of individual preferences into a social ordering), he soon became convinced that no satisfactory method of aggregating a set of orderings—the preferences of the people—into one coherent ordering would, in general, exist.

The impossibility theorem and related mathematical results and their proofs came, as Arrow recollects, within "about three weeks." There was huge interest in the academic circles about this newly identified result. Arrow himself became fascinated by the challenge his result posed to reasoned social decisions, and he changed his dissertation topic—abandoning his already advanced research on mathematical statistics—to present and discuss the new finding. He also sent off a brief exposition of the result ("A Difficulty in the Concept of Social Welfare") to the *Journal of Political Economy*, at the request of the editor, which was promptly published (Arrow 1950).

Arrow's impossibility result is often seen as a generalization of the old paradox of voting. Arrow himself encourages this view, and motivates the presentation of his impossibility result by referring to the voting paradox. Consider a case in which person 1 prefers x to y and y to z; person 2 prefers y to z and z to x; person 3 prefers z to x and x to y. The result is that in majority voting, x defeats y, y defeats z, and z defeats x. This is certainly a convincing enough demonstration that majority voting may not yield a consistent ordering, and also that there may be no majority winner at all. There is no doubt also that this voting paradox played a part in making Arrow think along the lines that he did. In describing his response to Olaf Helmer's request for a note on the social welfare function, Arrow mentions that he "already knew that majority voting, a plausible way of aggregating preferences, was unsatisfactory; a little experimentation suggested that no other method would work in the sense of defining an ordering" (Arrow 1950; reprinted in his *Collected Papers*, vol. 1, pp. 3–4).

However, the analogy with voting has some important limitations when it comes to social choice theory as applied in economics. In making distributional decisions we cannot just go by people's ranking of social alternatives. If we did, we could end up with absurd judgments. For example, in dividing a cake among three persons, if each person prefers to have a larger rather than a smaller slice, then taking away all the cake from the person who has got the *least* amount of cake and dividing it between the two others would generate a majority improvement. But it would be odd to claim that destituting the poorest person for fattening the richer also must be seen as a social improvement. We need more informational inputs for social judgments in general and for social choice theory in particular. We have to make judgments that involve interpersonal comparisons of well-being and freedom, and when that is done, the impossibility theorem tend to retreat. Ultimately we are left with an embarrassment of riches; we can have various positive possibility results, and the real question becomes one of choosing between alternative sets of axioms that best reflect the demands of justice. This is of course a problem of considerable complexity and one that calls for widespread public reasoning, but it is a problem very different from that of an impasse of impossibility. I have discussed these issues in my Nobel Lecture, "The Possibility of Social Choice" (Sen 1999), and will not try to repeat that discussion.

7

As an analytical discipline, social choice theory got the kind of systematic formulation it needed with the work of Kenneth Arrow, and even the departures from his work, in which I have been particularly involved, draw heavily on the structure he built for us. Arrow's book *Social Choice and Individual Values*, published in 1951, revolutionalized the formal analysis of social decisions, and led to the birth of modern social choice theory. That was the year I entered Presidency College in Calcutta as an undergraduate. I was fortunate to encounter Arrow's book only a few months after the book was published. My attention was drawn to it by my brilliant classmate, Sukhamoy Chakravarty (I remember his showing me the book, which he had borrowed from a local bookshop, and telling me, "This will interest you very much, given your concerns!"). Sukhamoy and I discussed the formal results and informal insights in the book, particularly the significance of Arrow's "impossibility theorem," in long sessions, sitting in the Coffee House on College Street, across the road from our college.

After a two-year degree in Calcutta, studying economics and a bit of mathematics, when I went to Trinity College in Cambridge, my attempt to get my fellow students—or teachers—interested in social choice theory was a dismal failure. The small exceptions were all in my college, Trinity, rather than anywhere else in the large university, and they included Michael Nicholson among the students, and Maurice Dobb and Piero

Sraffa—two Marxist economists—among my teachers. When I became a lecturer at Cambridge, my renewed efforts were no more successful, but I was allowed to teach a devised course in "welfare economics," which included some airing of social choice theory. I was told by the Economics Faculty Board in no uncertain terms that this was a very special concession to me, which they hoped I would appreciate (I did). It was only after I was "through Cambridge" that I could get others around me—students and colleagues—to take some interest in social choice theory. This happened wonderfully at the Delhi School of Economics, where I began teaching in 1963.

8

Arrow's impossibility theorem had presented a startling—and profound—formal result showing that some apparently undemanding conditions, in relating social decisions to individual preferences in a democratic way, cannot be simultaneously satisfied through any procedure. Since I was convinced that Arrow's impossibility result was ultimately a constructive beginning of a systematic subject rather than the demolition of cherished human desires (in this case, of the aspiration to have reasonable democratic politics), I was eager to devise a new course and try it out on my students. The course fitted well with my other teaching programs at the Delhi School of Economics (which the students called the "D-School"), namely, the principles of microeconomics and elementary game theory. My first book on social choice theory (Sen 1970) emerged mainly from the lectures I gave at the D-School. The time was ripe for an ambitious book covering much of the large subject of social choice theory, and I was lucky with the reception the book received. When I produced an expanded edition of the book nearly half a century later (Sen 2017), I was happy to see how widely that product of the D-School had penetrated the new work being done in different areas of the large subject of social choice theory.[2]

The inspiration for teaching that course, in an evolving form (I taught at the D-School for eight years), came partly from my attempts to discuss aggregate assessments of India in terms of the social lives of people (including the miserable lives that most of my fellow Indians lived). But it also came from my growing involvement with the mathematical results on the subject, going back to the pioneers such as Condorcet, Borda, and of course Arrow, but also with the sizable literature the subject had generated over the centuries (Lewis Carroll, writing under his real name,

Dodgson (1876, 1884), provided some much-needed amusement, along with important formal results).

However, what really consolidated my commitment to teach—and to pursue further my research on—social choice theory was the big response I got from my students, whose enthusiasm and encouragement made me feel vindicated in having initiated lectures and classes on the new subject of social choice theory. We "talked" social choice often enough, and new results in formal social choice theory kept being established by the more adventurous of my students. To take a particular example, the skill and originality of a new student from Orissa, Prasanta Pattanaik, took my breath away, as he showed his ability to solve new analytical problems, however difficult, as fast as I could formulate them. Pattanaik also wrote his Ph.D. thesis in less than a year, and, on the recommendation of his examiners (Frank Hahn and Kenneth Arrow), Cambridge University Press published it as a book immediately, making an impact on the subject.[3]

During my years at the D-School, I also visited Berkeley, in 1964–65, and Harvard, in 1968–69, and at both places I tried out the new things I was working on in social choice and inflicted them mercilessly on my colleagues and students. I benefited immensely from the fact that my students and colleagues at both Berkeley and Harvard took an interest in what I was trying to do. While at Berkeley, I also benefited from regular participation in the joint Berkeley–Stanford seminars in mathematical economics (I presented a few of my ideas there). At Harvard I taught a course on social choice and justice jointly with Ken Arrow and John Rawls. It generated hugely interesting discussions among our students (they included Allan Gibbard, who would soon become a great social choice theorist in addition to a leading philosopher) and a galaxy of auditors (including Howard Raiffa, Robert Dorfman, Thomas Schelling, Franklin Fisher, Jerome Rothenberg, and many others). Another course, one I taught jointly with Stephen Marglin and Prasanta Pattanaik (who was also visiting Harvard along with me), on cost-benefit analysis produced excellent discussions on the relation between the theory and practice of social choice.

My interest in social choice was also intensified and sharpened by the ideas that the students' agitations were generating at Berkeley and Harvard exactly when I was teaching there, with the Free Speech Movement at Berkeley in 1964–65 and the antiwar demonstrations and occupations at Harvard in 1968–69. I could spend a lot of time listening to—and learning from—the students at Berkeley and Harvard, just as I was doing at the D-School.

The original 1970 book was to a great extent an attempt to expand Arrow's reasoning—extending some results, consolidating some insights, questioning some imposed restrictions, and proposing some modifications of the Arrow framework, while being guided by Arrow's own motivations and concerns. In some of the departures I made use of the original insights of the early pioneers of social choice theory, particularly in trying to integrate welfare economics with political and social philosophy.

After I moved to the London School of Economics in 1971, I also had the wonderful opportunity of working with Kotaro Suzumura, Peter Hammond, Charles Blackorby, Wulf Gaertner, and others. I was also hugely privileged to have new research students at the LSE and at Oxford who helped me advance my own ideas as I tried to help them in their doctoral work. One of the wonders of the academic world is how easily we can draw on the ideas of each other.

9

I will take the liberty of ending this lecture with comments on one particular departure that I think is both underdiscussed and actually very important. This concerns the use of *partial ordering* as the basic relation of social ranking, rather than demanding, as the Arrovian framework does, the *completeness* of admissible social rankings. A complete ranking demands that every pair of alternatives can be ranked firmly against each other—either x is better than y, or worse than y, or exactly as good. A partial ranking—indeed, even a partial ordering (satisfying the demands of transitivity)—can leave some pairs unranked.

The departure has large implications. The classical framework of optimization used in standard choice theory can be expressed as choosing, among the feasible options, a "best" alternative, that is, an alternative that is at least as good as every other alternative. In contrast, a "maximal" alternative—formally defined—is one that is not worse than (or at least not known to be worse than) any other alternative. If we cannot rank x and y against each other for whatever reason, whether because of unbridged epistemic gaps, or unintegrated ethical plurality, then there is no best—or optimal—alternative in this pair (x,y) but both are maximal.[4]

The mathematical distinction between "best" and "maximal" is of critical importance in the theory of sets and relations (well emphasized in the classic mathematical treatise of Bourbaki (1939, 1966, 1968), *Éléments de Mathématique*). The general discipline of maximization differs from the special case of optimization in taking an alternative to be a reasoned choice when it is not known to be worse than any other (whether or not it is also seen to be as good as all the others). For an element x of S to qualify as maximal, we have to make sure that it is *not worse than* any other alternative; it is not necessary to show that it is *better than*, or *as good as*, all other alternatives.

The basic contrast between maximization and optimization arises from the possibility that the preference ranking R may be incomplete; that is, there may be a pair of alternatives x and y such that x is not seen (at least, not *yet* seen) as being at least as good as y, and further, y is not seen (at least, not yet seen) as being at least as good as x. In the famous story of Buridan's ass, the ass died of starvation because it could not choose between two haystacks, neither of which it could identify as better than (or even as good as) the other. It overlooked the existence of a maximal choice—either haystack would have been a reasoned *maximal* choice, and either would have been definitely better than starving to death. It is easy to see that when a maximal choice exists, to decide to do nothing because no optimal alternative has emerged is not particularly smart.

An alternative interpretation of the problem of Buridan's ass is to assume that the ass was *indifferent* between the two haystacks, which led to its dithering. This interpretation—though often invoked—makes the famous donkey much more asinine than we need to assume (even an ass should be able to figure out that if it were really indifferent between the two haystacks, it could not lose anything by choosing either). I would much prefer to think that Buridan's ass died for the cause of "optimal choice," leaving us an important lesson in favor of "maximal choice" over a set with an unranked pair.

The admission of partial orderings vastly expands the applicability of social choice theory. It can be shown that nearly all the social changes that have made the world a better place have drawn on an emergent agreement on a partial rather than a complete ordering. Those who worked against slavery did not have a unified view of a perfect world. The abolition of slavery went hand in hand with many different preferences for a slavery-free world. It was a partial ordering that ultimately came to rule the roost. Similarly today, people can have very different ideas of a perfect world and yet can agree on the importance of people having enough to eat, enjoying freedom of speech, having arrangements for medical care, and priorities of that kind. There may not be an agreement on the kind of partial ordering we should fight for, but the debates have to be engaged there—about our priorities—and not only about distant visions of perfect justice. That understanding may well be one of the main contributions of contemporary social choice theory.

Notes

1. The Sanskrit word *"Arthashastra"* (the title of Kautilya's book) is best translated literally as "Economics," even though he devoted much space to analyzing political conflicts and the demands of statecraft. English translations of Aristotle's *Politics* and Kautilya's *Arthashastra* can be found respectively in Barker (1958) and Rangarajan (1987).

2. See also Arrow, Sen, and Suzumura (2002, 2011) [*Handbook of Social Choice and Welfare*, vols. 1 and 2].

3. Pattanaik (1967, 1971).

4. See also Suzumura (1983, 2016) and Hammond (1985).

References

Arrow, Kenneth J. 1950. "A Difficulty in the Concept of Social Welfare." *Journal of Political Economy* 58 (4): 328–346.

Arrow, Kenneth J. 1951. *Social Choice and Individual Values*. New York: Wiley (republished New Haven, CT: Yale University Press, 1963).

Arrow, Kenneth J. 1983. *Collected Papers of Kenneth J. Arrow, Vol. 1: Social Choice and Justice*. 6 vols. Cambridge, MA: Harvard University Press.

Arrow, Kenneth J., Amartya K. Sen, and Kotaro Suzumura. 2002. *Handbook of Social Choice and Welfare, Vol. 1*. Amsterdam: Elsevier.

Arrow, Kenneth J., Amartya K. Sen, and Kotaro Suzumura. 2011. *Handbook of Social Choice & Welfare, Vol. 2*. Amsterdam: Elsevier.

Bentham, Jeremy. 1789. *An Introduction to the Principles of Morals and Legislation*. Boston: Payne.

Bergson, Abram. 1938. "A Reformulation of Certain Aspects of Welfare Economics." *Quarterly Journal of Economics* 52 (2): 310–334.

Bourbaki, Nicolas. 1939. *Éléments de Mathématique: Théorie Des Ensembles*. Paris: Éditions Hermann.

Bourbaki, Nicolas. 1966. *Éléments de Mathématique*. Paris: Éditions Hermann.

Bourbaki, Nicolas. 1968. *Éléments de Mathématique*. Paris: Éditions Hermann.

Dodgson, Charles. 1876. *A Method of Taking Votes on More than Two Issues*. Oxford: Clarendon Press of Oxford University Press.

Dodgson, Charles. 1884. *The Principles of Parliamentary Representation*. London: Harrison and Sons.

Eliot, T. S. 1915. "The Love Song of J. Alfred Prufrock." In *Poetry: A Magazine of Verse*, edited by Harriet Monroe, 130–135.

Hammond, Peter J., and George R. Feiwel. 1985. "Welfare Economics." In *Issues in Contemporary Microeconomics and Welfare,* ed. George R. Feiwel. Albany: SUNY Press.

Kant, Immanuel. 1788. *Kritik Der Praktischen Vernunft.* Leipzig: Philipp Reclam jun.

Paine, Thomas. 1776. *Common Sense; Addressed to the Inhabitants of America, on the Following Interesting Subjects.* Philadelphia: W. and T. Bradford (republished New York: Penguin, 1982).

Paine, Thomas. 1791. *Rights of Man: Being an Answer to Mr. Burke's Attach on the French Revolution.* London: J. S. Jordan (republished London: Dent, New York: Dutton, 1906; London: Dent, 1930).

Pattanaik, Prasanta K. 1967. "Aspects of Welfare Economics." Ph.D. diss., Delhi University.

Pattanaik, Prasanta K. 1971. *Voting and Collective Choice.* Cambridge: Cambridge University Press.

Rangarajan, L.N., trans. 1987. *The Arthasastra of Kautilya.* London: Penguin.

Samuelson, Paul A. 1947. *Foundations of Economic Analysis.* Cambridge, MA: Harvard University Press.

Samuelson, Paul A. 1967. "Foreword." In *Theoretical Welfare Economics,* by Jan de Van Graaff, 2nd ed. Cambridge: Cambridge University Press.

Sen, Amartya K. 1970. *Collective Choice and Social Welfare.* San Francisco: Holden Day (republished Amsterdam: Elsevier North-Holland, 1979).

Sen, Amartya K. 1999. "The Possibility of Social Choice." *American Economic Review* 89 (3): 349–378.

Sen, Amartya K. 2009. *The Idea of Justice.* Cambridge, MA: Harvard University Press.

Sen, Amartya K. 2017. *Collectives Choice and Social Welfare: An Expanded Edition.* Cambridge, MA: Harvard University Press.

Smith, Adam. 1759. *The Theory of Moral Sentiments.* London: A. Millar, Edinburgh: A. Kincaid and J. Bell (republished London: A. Millar, 1790; New York: Penguin, 2009, with an introduction by Amartya K. Sen).

Smith, Adam. n.d. *The Theory of Moral Sentiments.* 6th ed. London: A. Millar.

Snow, C. P. 1950. *The Masters* (Strangers and Brothers No. 5). London: Macmillan.

Suzumura, Kotaro. 1983. *Rational Choice, Collective Decisions, and Social Welfare.* Cambridge: Cambridge University Press.

Suzumura, Kotaro. 2016. *Choice, Preferences, and Procedures: A Rational Choice Theoretic Approach.* Cambridge, MA: Harvard University Press.

Wollstonecraft, Mary. 1790. *A Vindication of the Rights of Men, in a Letter to the Right Honourable Edmund Burke; Occasioned by His Reflections on the Revolution in France.* London: J. Johnson.

Wollstonecraft, Mary. 1792. *A Vindication of the Rights of Woman: With Strictures on Political and Moral Subjects.* Dublin: James Moore.

Amartya Sen

Awarded Nobel Prize in 1998. Lecture presented April 7, 2016.

Date of Birth

November 3, 1933

Academic Degrees

B.A., Presidency College, Calcutta 1953
B.A., Trinity College, Cambridge, 1955
M.A., Trinity College, Cambridge, 1959
Ph.D., Trinity College, Cambridge, 1959

Academic Affiliations

Professor of Economics, Jadavpur University, Calcutta, 1956–58
Fellow of Trinity College, Cambridge, 1957–63
Professor of Economics, Delhi School of Economics, University of Delhi, 1963–71
Professor of Economics, London School of Economics, University of London, 1971–77
Professor of Economics, Oxford University, and Fellow of Nuffield College, 1977–80
Drummond Professor of Political Economy, Oxford University, and Fellow of All Souls College, 1980–88
Thomas W. Lamont University Professor and Professor of Economics and Philosophy, Harvard University, 1987–98, Senior Fellow, Harvard Society of Fellows, 1989–98
Master of Trinity College, Cambridge, 1998–2004
Thomas W. Lamont University Professor and Professor of Economics and Philosophy, Harvard University, 2004–present

Selected Books

Collective Choice and Social Welfare, 2017
On Ethics and Economics, 1999
Development as Freedom, 2000
The Idea of Justice, 2010
Inequality Reexamined, 1997
Poverty and Famines: As Essay on Entitlement and Deprivation, 1998

A. Michael Spence

I was born in New Jersey during World War II in 1943. I stayed two days, and then we (my mother and I) went back to Ottawa, where my family resided during the war. My father was working on price controls during the war on the Canadian side. Price controls were required during the war effort because of shortages from the diversion of resources of all kinds.

The Canadians and Americans had to coordinate because the economies were so closely linked. My father was going back and forth to and from Washington. My mother came from Minnesota, from a tiny town called Minnieska on the Mississippi River, and if you can find it on the map, you get ten points. It took me about two years to locate it. Fortunately, I remembered the name. The family moved to Canada (Winnipeg), where my grandfather drove a train.

In Canada, there are two big transcontinental railways, created largely to prevent the United States from annexing a large chunk of the Canadian west. You may remember the slogan, "54 40 or fight," referring to moving the boundary with Canada from the 49th parallel, where it is now, to the 54.4th parallel. That would shift most of the farmable land in the Canadian prairies to the United States. It did not happen. In moving to Winnipeg, where my father was, my mother was moving out of the refrigerator into the freezer. It is one of the coldest places on Earth where people actually live.

I still have an accent because I grew up in Canada, and I remained there until college. After the war we moved from Ottawa back to Winnipeg, which was a kind of hometown for both my parents. Around 1950 we moved to Toronto, where I more or less grew up, on a farm at first, and then in the city. And what I remember about my young life, other than it was very pleasant, was that my family was an upper-middle-class family. The most important thing they gave to me was to tell me a lie, which was that I could do anything I wanted. The bad thing about that is it was not true. The good thing was I did not have much fear about trying new things. I did not really think it was necessary to plan my future, at least not in any detail. Perhaps through luck, I guess, I got away with that strategy, although I would not recommend it to everybody.

Hockey Background

My early life was focused on athletics, and if you live in Canada that tends to include ice hockey. I played hockey from the time I was three years old. By the way, we did not have climate change then. (I know some think we do not have it now, but that is okay; we will just let that go.) We had natural ice (that is, ice that froze because the air was cold, without refrigerating units underneath) for four months out of the year. We all learned to skate and play hockey because every schoolyard had a rink. It was an important part of my life, and when I was thirteen and in a school called University of Toronto Schools, which is like the Lab School at the University of Chicago, attached to the University of Toronto, I played for a team called Ted's Pals, which was partially sponsored by the Chicago Black Hawks. Ted's father also sponsored the team and owned a chain of drugstores.

This system was like baseball used to be in the United States. The feeder system for professional baseball was a set of teams that were not built into the educational institutions. The same was true of hockey. It's not fatal to your education, so I played for Ted's Pals. Ted was a dreadful hockey player, but his father was a sponsor of the team. I covered for Ted as a defenseman.

We practiced and played all over southern Ontario. I'm surprised my parents survived this. We played seventy-five games that year. A normal high school or college year would be twenty-five games. We won the championship for our age group in Canada. My academic performance suffered. There was this little guy at UTS, Jack Life, who was the athletic director. At age thirteen I was taller than he. He called me into his office and he said, "You got to stop doing this. In fact, if you keep doing it I'll get you kicked out of the school, if you don't flunk out first." I looked skeptical, since I was looking down at him. He looked up at me and he said, "You know what, young man?" Then he said something I will never forget, because it does not make any sense. He said, "This is a democracy and I run it." I thought, what does that mean? So I went off and thought about it and I decided he was probably right, whatever it meant, and I quit playing that kind of hockey and I gave up my goal of being a professional hockey player. These days you can play college hockey and make it to the NHL This is a big and beneficial change, because in the old days, if you tried and did not make it, you were handicapped with a poor education.

I continued to play hockey in school, all the way through high school, and I played for Princeton. When I went to Princeton I thought I was going because I was a pretty good student, having quit playing seventy-five games a year. I was a University Scholar, and then I went out for freshmen football. I got all the equipment and went out there, and the coach pulled me over about halfway through the first practice after he figured out who I was, and he said, You should hand in the equipment; we don't want you here. And I said, Well, why? I mean, I have not competed yet. And he said, You are here to play hockey. And then I realized I was at Princeton to play hockey. And the scholarship part came later. We were not very good as a hockey team. In fact, we were routinely described by the *Daily Princetonian*, the college student newspaper, as a comedy act snatching defeat from the jaws of victory. The usual reason was that we had a somewhat erratic goalie, whom one of my teammates described as a cross between a sieve and a funnel, depending on whether the puck was heading for the net or was going to miss it. Anyway, we had a lot of fun. We were very entertaining. We filled the stadium every Saturday night and I received, I have to say, a superb education, majoring in philosophy eventually.

Choosing Academia

My parents were a strong influence. My Dad was close to being an academic. His career was in and out of business and in and out of teaching, a kind of mix. He held a Ph.D. in commerce and finance from Northwestern University. Mom and Dad loved Chicago. If the war had not intervened, I think they would have stayed. My Mother had a master's degree in biology, molecular biology in those days, from the University of Iowa, which was a center of excellence at that time, and probably still is. For me, they were extremely supportive. I think they did not provide much direction but secretly hoped (and I probably picked it up) that I should take a running shot at research and higher education. I had that in mind, but I did not have that as a commitment. I just thought it was one of those possibilities. So off I went. By the time I finished Princeton, I had reached the following conclusions:

1. I did want to take a running shot at being an academic.
2. I did not know what field it was in but it probably was not philosophy, which was my major.

I had decided that sitting by myself thinking deep thoughts was not going to work for me. In the end, I picked economics, in part because it is a field with a wide range of subdisciplines. We have colleagues who are essentially mathematicians or statisticians, we have colleagues who are policymakers, and we have colleagues who are applied micro theorists and others who are specialists in various fields. Some of us are even employed outside academia in financial institutions, in the government, and in companies and nonprofits. I thought this was the closest I could come to hedging my bets, so economics seemed pretty safe, provided I liked it.

I went off to Oxford, and somebody advised me to enroll in Philosophy, Politics and Economics, which is the standard kind of Rhodes undergraduate thing. I did that, but quickly switched to a graduate program in economics, a kind of high-level master's program that resulted in a B.Phil. I thought I had better learn some more mathematics and statistics first, so I switched again, this time to mathematics, and for reasons you will understand shortly, that was a pretty important and lucky decision. It was a wonderful education, I have to say. I was extraordinarily lucky. Wonderful teachers, wonderful colleagues and students. Hard to complain about any of this. Great opportunities.

With math and philosophy undergraduate degrees under my belt, I went to Harvard as a Ph.D. student in economics, but I almost quit in the second year. By then I had been in high school through grade thirteen in Canada. Then I had been at Princeton as a hard-working student, when I was not playing hockey, for four years, and then I had gone to Oxford, where you spend a lot of time doing your own thing and talking with your tutor. Then I went to Harvard and did two years of intense course work. I was sitting in the library getting ready for general exams, and I got up one morning and said, I do not want to do this anymore.

I thought I would try to get a job at McKinsey in Cleveland because it was an excellent place to work at that time. What saved me, though maybe not the economics profession, was that I went to talk to Dick Zeckhauser, a good friend then and now; he is still with the Kennedy School of Government, and he was one of my thesis advisers. I said to Dick, I have had it; I just cannot do this anymore, and he said, You need to teach. You need more human contact. Then I said all right, I will give it a try before I quit. He was teaching an undergraduate class on such topics as social choice theory, risk and insurance, moral hazard, and adverse selection. Dick said, Why don't you come and teach one of the classes in my course, just to see if you like it. I said okay, and he gave me a subject in insurance and risk where I had a chance of doing reasonably well, because we had written a little paper that everybody has mercifully forgotten that was in the *American Economic Association Papers and Proceedings* from some distant past year.

I thought, I am going to do this well. I prepared for about a week, wrote out about thirty to forty pages of single-spaced notes for an hour-long undergraduate class. And I started out. I was doing pretty well, not going too fast, and after forty-five minutes of a fifty-minute class, I noticed I was on page 3. Then I did what many young teachers do. I thought if I am going to get through this, I had better speed up. I did, and it was incomprehensible. Dick Z. described it as the closest thing he had seen in academia to whiplash, and that was my introduction to teaching.

I became better after that. I slowed down, became more interactive, and even learned to listen fairly carefully. I learned to love teaching and I still do. It is because of the interactive part. I know we now have flip classrooms and videos to take care of some of the lecturing. But I loved the interactive part. For me, it still works now in groups as large as sixty, provided the students are engaged and feel entitled to ask questions and to comment and introduce their own thinking. I think that is probably an important part of the education here at Trinity, because with this size, you can teach and learn in a way that in much larger environments you can't.

Researching Asymmetric Information

We all know research is an important part of what academics do. At Harvard, I had three thesis advisers: Kenneth Arrow, Thomas C. Schelling, and Richard Zeckhauser. I do not think many people get to have a group like that on their thesis committee. Two of them are Nobel Prize winners. Ken Arrow was one of the first, when the Nobel Prize in Economics was created back in the 1960s. He was not the first to receive the award, but he did so before Milton Friedman, and that pissed some people off—that is a technical term. Tom Schelling received the Nobel Prize after me, and I actually went back to Stockholm when Tom and Alice went there to receive the Nobel Prize. It was fun to be there as a guest observer. The Nobel Prize people say you can always come back and we will look after you, and you are welcome just as when you receive the prize. I thought it was probably not true but I would try it. It was true. They were extraordinary.

These advisers did something for me that I still treasure. I was the kind of person who liked to go and think about things that was just a fog, phenomena where our conceptual frameworks did not shed much light. That is a high-risk strategy because there is not much to build on. Many thesis advisers will tell you not to do it. Alternatively, if you want to do that, then do it later. Do something safer now. Risk aversion is an important part of this, and I am not saying that people who give that advice are wrong, or wrong in particular cases, but I would not have done what I did if any one of the three of them had said it is too risky. I told them I would like to think about the informational structure of markets and about market performance in the presence of informational gaps and asymmetries. These informational gaps are ubiquitous in markets and in other contexts, we now know. But I probably sounded a bit more muddled back then, when I made the proposal. They could have said do not do it, but they did not. They instead said try it. I think that was probably on the advisers' side the greatest gift I was given.

I always had an experimental attitude toward all of this. It started with a Ph.D., I thought I am going to try this ... maybe I will hate it; then I will quit, and do something else. If it works, fine, and if it does not, then I will do something else or I will move on. Again, I am not recommending this, but it is not a bad way to approach things. I gave it a shot and then I started thinking about the specific subject, which is asymmetrical informational structures and markets. What happens in markets when those gaps either persist or get closed somehow? It turned out there were three of us, at least, working on the same thing; actually four. There were George Akerlof and Joe Stiglitz, with whom I received the Nobel Prize, and Mike Rothschild, who was a very important contributor to this literature.

According to the Nobel Prize rules, there cannot be more than three awardees sharing the prize in a given year. There can be fewer than three, but not more. Over time, this rule has produced the occasional injustice, and I think our year was mostly that with respect to Mike Rothschild.

In any case, I was listening to a faculty seminar at the Kennedy School of Government, which was a year old in 1971. By the way, I was the rapporteur for that seminar. Ken Arrow and Frances Bator and Tom Schelling and Dick Zeckhauser and Dick Neustadt, joined by a speakers such as Lester Thurow from MIT, would sit around and have a discussion. As happens with all seminar conversations, the literal transcript was incoherent. I was supposed to produce ten pages that made it sound like a brilliant sequential dialogue, which I did every week. Ken Arrow thought my most distinctive characteristic as an intellect was that I was an excellent rapporteur. Incidentally, both Tom Schelling and Ken Arrow passed away at the age of approximately ninety or ninety-one in the past six months. It is a big loss.

In any case, the late Lester Thurow came and talked about what he called statistical discrimination. By that, he meant you could be discriminated against if you have a visible characteristic that distinguishes you from other people, and the unobserved underlying characteristic is distributed differently in the populations with different visible characteristics. Or, put simply, you could be taken as an average member of the group you visibly belonged to—when in fact almost no one is exactly the average. I started thinking, that cannot be the whole story about asymmetric information but it was an interesting thought. And I walked away and started thinking what about these informational gaps and what happens. It ended up being the subject of my thesis. Much interesting research followed and informational characteristics of markets and incentive structures and agency problems took hold in economics.

In Stockholm, they are patient, and they wait a long time before they decide that something is important. They are interested in not just whether it is a neat idea but whether it takes hold in a discipline.

I should recount one other thing. I wrote the signaling model initially in continuous form. That means with derivatives and other things. I fiddled around with it, and finally I realized that the solution, the equilibrium in the model, was the solution to an ordinary nonlinear difference equation. At this point, I think I might have been slowed down a lot, but I had studied differential equations at Oxford, so I knew the properties. I knew there were multiple equilibria, I knew it was a one-parameter set, I knew they did not cross. All of that had immediate relevance to the economic interpretation. This was just pure luck. But it was extraordinary. I would say this took about twenty minutes.

I then handed it in to Professor Schelling and to Professor Arrow.

Arrow used to inadvertently frighten people. I remember someone who came to the Kennedy School on a junior faculty–recruiting visit and was giving a talk. Ken was sitting at the front of the room reading a newspaper. And what this person did not know was that Ken could multitask. He could read the *Wall Street Journal* and listen to your presentation at the same time. So the recruit became more and more nervous and tongue-tied, but eventually got through it. Then Ken stuck up his hand and asked him a technical question about what he just presented.

He did something similar to me. I handed in a paper on general equilibrium theory in a course and his assistant lost the exam paper. Then I got a call from the secretary saying you have not handed in your exam. Fortunately, I had a copy. Now, that's trivial in this age, but having a copy thirty-five or forty years ago was not automatic. I rushed the copy over, hitting a deadline, and Professor Arrow said come in. This paper was about fifteen pages long. It was on the general equilibrium model where you had to work through the whole thing. I sat down in front of his desk and he read, flipping pages at about once every three seconds. I thought, I am really pissed off, because he is not reading it. He got to the end, and said that is an excellent piece of work, earning you an A. Then he asked me a question about what was on page 7. I realized he actually read it. Amazing! Anyway, that was fun, and it got me launched. My thesis became a book, slightly cleaned up and written in length.

I handed my signaling research to Schelling, and Tom looked at it and said I think it is interesting, but write down the simplest model that does not get rid of the structure that gives rise to signaling. It was an interesting exercise, when you think about it. Remove all the continuous stuff. I sat and wrote something with two groups and a potential signal, an equation that had requisite characteristics for a signal. It is important to remember that signals that survive in the marketplace are actions or characteristics or investments that are visible and negatively correlated with the thing that you want to see that is valuable but you cannot see.

One example I developed of signaling to overcome the asymmetric information problem is the signal sent to potential employers by talented individuals who are willing to incur the costs of a good college education. If you want to know how good somebody is at something, then the only thing that will provide that signal is something that has a lower cost for people who are better at it than people who are not. It is just that simple. Everything else self-destructs in the marketplace because essentially everything else has the property that if it has signaling value and either it is equally costly or that cost relationship I described is inverted, then everybody will do it. That means that on the next round it has no informational content and it has been destroyed as a carrier of information in the marketplace. It goes well beyond economics. Actually, I have had many emails from sociologists over the years who have discovered this kind of thing in social interactions.

Administration and the Tech Bubble

I had a period in academic administration that I loved. I learned a lot. I spent a lot of time with colleagues. At Harvard, as dean of the Faculty of Arts and Sciences, I had the chance to listen to my colleagues tell me what molecular biology was all about, and condensed matter physics, and biochemistry. Field after field after field; it was a high-speed education, like drinking from a fire hose. Then at Stanford's Graduate School of Business, which was a lot smaller and where I actually knew what most of my colleagues were doing, I found administration an expanding experience, and I do not regret it.

There are the two stories I remember from that period. Academic administration is a little weird in that you do not have much power. You try to collect people together, which sometimes has been described as herding cats. Sometimes they go after you because they do not like what is going on. I remember Derek Bok, who was president of Harvard, telling me in a relaxed moment, "Just remember that famous expression attributed to a psychologist: just because you're paranoid, it doesn't mean they aren't out to get you."

In 1999, I stepped down as dean of the Stanford's business school. My timing was good because the internet bubble crashed about a year and half later, with particular reference to Silicon Valley. Things got a little rough on the fundraising front for a while. Many people think the internet bubble was just nuts and in many dimensions, like valuations, it was nuts. Actually, there were many people, entrepreneurs and investors, who saw the potential of the digital technologies and internet and were reasonably accurate. The problem was that they misjudged by several standard deviations the speed with which it would happen. The valuations were just crazy and had to be dispensed with using an efficient mechanism for conducting experiments and getting rid of the worst ones, called company formation and failure, but some of it was just misguessing how soon all this was going to come to pass.

A great deal of what you see around you now is what was in the minds of people at the time. The internet bubble crashed, people said it was all nonsense, and then the real power of digital technology started to kick in, affecting the global economy, global supply chains, automation, and other things that are constant subjects of discussion now. I thought at the time of the flowering of the internet in the early years (a particular academic point of view that relates to my past), because this is really about information and its availability and cost. This will transform the informational structure of markets. And it looks like it has, or at least is in the process.

Much of the current concern about automation, robotics, and AI is serious, but I suspect that, as in the past, we tend to overestimate how fast it will happen. And that means we underestimate the length of time we have to adapt, individually and as a society.

Economic Development

My first idea in returning to academic research was to go back and try to figure out whether we were in the early stages of transforming aspects of the informational structural markets. Largely, I am still interested in that, but I got sidetracked. A very good friend of mine now, who was at the World Bank then, phoned me and asked me if I would deliver a lecture on investment to the WB/IMF major spring conference in the Poverty Reduction and Economic Management Program (PREM). This had to do with developing countries. I asked why he had picked me. I have never studied development. The answer was, You are a micro economist, you know something about investment and information, and you may have some insights. I thought that with my screening and signaling background, I am going to do this, and here is the model. There's about 10,000 people trained in development economics, and I am going to go give this lecture. The probability is at least 70 percent that it will be a disaster, and then I will know something important, which is I should not do that. Or there is a 30 percent chance that I have something useful to say, in which case in both scenarios I will have learned something important. The lecture could be considered a screening mechanism.

As it turned out, I got interested in the subject of developing country growth, and they did not find it completely uninteresting, and this resulted in my appointment to the Commission of Growth and Development. It was an attempt in the 2006–10 period to assemble what we had learned from research and experience about sustained high growth in developing countries. This was a period in which China had grown a great deal; India had also taken off and its economy had started a slower but significant acceleration. Many countries were starting to perform well. It was a significant period from, say, 1989, when John Williamson coined the term " Washington Consensus," to 2005–06. We thought, Let's listen to our colleagues, look at the experiences of a variety of countries, and see if we can, in a very simple way, write down what we learned in a form that is useful not only to academics but to policymakers and to the next generation of leaders in these countries. That is what we set out to do.

It was fun, and I think we made a useful contribution. It is obvious that any effort like that will always be dated because there is always new research, and there is always new learning from experience. You have to do it every now and then, and you cannot say that is a definitive treatment. It never is. We were talking about what worked, and we looked at countries that had grown at 7 percent or more a year for twenty-five years or more. That is a high standard. Very few have lived in that kind of environment, ever. Developed countries never grew that fast. If you are any good at economic history, you know the maximum sustained growth rates since the Industrial Revolution in countries that we now call advanced or developed was probably 2½ percent in real terms. In the postwar period, we have countries that have grown at much faster rates. It is called catch-up growth because what they are doing is relying on all that technology and expertise that were accumulated over two hundred years since the Industrial Revolution.

We went to work on this, and at some point my Indian colleague, who was a good friend at Oxford, said, this is boring. And I said, what do you mean, this is boring? He said, people would understand this better if they see lousy approaches to growth. He said we should have a section called "bad ideas." And everybody on the commission should be responsible for submitting two of the worst ideas they've ever heard with respect to how you go about growing in a developing economy. Everybody thought that was a terrific idea. We all submitted ideas and ended up with twenty, with some duplication. Two pages in the report (it is called *The Growth Report*) consist only of our bad ideas. They are stunningly bad ideas but surprisingly common. But they are interesting; subsidized energy was one. It was the best part of the report. After it was published, I started getting emails from all over the world. The typical email read like this: I liked your report, but by far the best part was the two pages on bad ideas, and I have checked—our government is doing seventeen of the twenty.

After that, I wrote a book, which leads me to the last part of this presentation. What this book is about is a little bit of what I just said. We did not really have growth in the sense we know it in the modern era up until about 1750. It started in the United Kingdom as the British Industrial Revolution. When I say growth, I do not mean just growth, but growth in per capita incomes and wealth. It was technologically and scientifically driven; I think we know that now. Why the Malthus effect did not happen and population growth did not expand and use up all the growth, we do not know. Historians have written serious pieces of work on that, and I would not pretend to be an expert. But that growth went on for two hundred years. That was 15 percent of the world's population. The other 85 percent, who live in what we now call developing countries, stayed more or less where they were. And after two hundred years, even with modest growth rates, the difference between the industrialized countries and the rest was enormous.

Most of the countries that were not in the 15 percent group were called backward, third world, underdeveloped. Now we simply use the word "developing," acknowledging that the situation might change. When I was young, in the 1950s, most people thought this was a permanent state of the world. There was little evidence of developing country growth and no evidence of convergence. This 85 percent had per capita incomes of about $400 per person and their economies were not growing. Then something quite amazing happened: those economies started to grow. The postwar architecture that was put together with leadership from the United States was designed to facilitate war recovery. The General Agreement on Trade and Tariffs, which was the mechanism for opening the global economy, was put in place and eventually turned into the WTO. Colonial empires were abandoned, and with them the economic asymmetries that had been built into that set of relationships.

There were many problems. Africa consisted of a bunch of countries that were former colonies that were not countries at all unless you think a country is a thing with a line drawn around it on a map, as opposed to a group of people who think they are in it together. The second part was not true. And a good deal of postwar development in Africa has entailed building a sense of national identity and building it together, which is what you need before you get on with the hard part of actually making the economy grow sufficiently to turn into a modern economy. The growth was halting at first, and was hard to see at the start; it was essentially an unanticipated spillover effect from developed countries trying to create a benign postwar international environment. Then, of course, technology started to turbo-charge economic development. It always has. There were jet airplanes, declining transportation costs, the invention of containerized shipping, the internet, telecommunications technology, all of which turbo-charged the trend that was under way.

Current Economic Challenges

Now, the way I characterize it in this lecture, we are more than halfway through a century-long process of having the 85 percent become economically and in terms of well-being and opportunity more like us and less like the way they were at the start. It takes decades. China has been growing at 10 percent for thirty years. Nobody has ever done that before. At 10 percent, you double every seven years. At 7 percent, you double every ten years. If you start at $400 per capita income, then you can do the math. How many times do you have to double before you get to $5,000? Something like five times and five decades. The notion that this happens quickly is just not true. In the book, I wanted to expose this rather benign sort of trend. I also wanted people to be aware that something fundamentally different was happening that people were only vaguely aware of. Finally, to the extent this is successful, we are in the process of making the global economy huge relative to what it would have been if this growth hadn't occurred. There is a very big difference between 15 percent and 85–98 percent. Even if it isn't completely successful, if you just freeze-frame the thing and say we'll take 15 percent and add another 60 percent, and there you have the same per capita incomes as the 15 percent at the start, you've got a global economy that's bigger by, I don't know, a factor of four.

That is where sustainability problems come in. There is no sustainability problem with no developing country growth. If 15 percent of the people live well and consume energy the way we do, and you multiply times four, there is a huge problem. That is the real issue. We cannot deny the opportunities that go with that growth. So we have to solve the problem by changing the growth model, to reduce its energy and carbon intensity and its impact on water and a host of other natural resources.

Another thing that concerns me is the relationship between automation and jobs, particularly in the United States. If you look at growth globally since World War II, up until about the late 1970s, everything looked good. We were growing well; war recovery went well, thanks to enlightened policies; developing countries started to grow; and our income distribution was going well, too. The middle class was getting richer, the rate of measured income inequality wasn't rising, and the fraction of income going to labor as opposed to capital or the government was rising. Then that pattern changed in every one of those dimensions. Gradually at first, right around the late '70s and early '80s, you started to get a shift in the opposite direction. You find rising inequality and a decline in the labor share of national income.

In every data series I look at there is a big inflection point in the year 2000. I was puzzled about it until I started to think about what happened around the year 2000. There are at least three or four major developments: First, we had a huge financial crisis in Asia in 1997–98. We learned what the word *contagion* meant. I will never forget friends in Brazil phoning me and saying, "There is an assault on our currency and our assets." What does this have to do with us? Do we have investments in Malaysia? Indonesia? The answer, of course, was people—investors—could not distinguish, so they got scared about everything in the developing world. This is what contagion was really all about. Second, China entered the WTO; third, the euro was created, completely changing the way Europe is organized; and fourth, the digital technology that I described earlier, the digital technologies that are operating on the structure of pretty much everything—job markets, economies, global supply chains—started to kick in. I think a combination of those developments with a couple of other factors thrown in produced these turbo-charged effects, not all of which are positive.

Jobs can be classified in different ways. For example, routine or not routine, blue or white collar, or what MIT researchers call cognitive or manual or noncognitive. Nonroutine jobs have grown in our economy, but routine jobs have been drifting downward since the year 2000. What is a routine job? The best description of a routine job is that there are rules that govern the performance of it. We know those rules, we can codify them, we can write them in software and at some point a machine can do the job or can do part of it. This gives you a hint that something important, perhaps not directly related to globalization, is going on in the economy. Many important jobs do not exist now or have been substantially reduced in number. Secretaries in economics departments; we do not need them anymore. There is only one department administrator. By the way, this is not just manufacturing robotics, although that is part of it. It is information systems in companies, it is bank tellers; it is disintermediation of labor all over the place.

In general, the old model captured by the word *codifiable* meant that we if we understood precisely how we did something, we could have a machine do it. The limits are if we can do something but we do not know how we do it, and we can't describe it precisely, in that model a machine can't do it. For example, there is an uncountable number of variants of chairs. Can you write down code that tells a machine how to identify all of them precisely? No! Recognizing a chair is simple for humans, as is building a robot that can see and respond to its environment. But with data, pattern recognition capabilities, and deep learning algorithms, machines can recognize images. They can lip-read, diagnose skin cancers, understand language spoken with an accent, and translate reasonably well.

Machines have the ability to win games where you cannot codify the results. The Google Deep Mind group won three out of four games of GO against the world's expert. The number of configurations, I am told, of the game of GO is larger than the number of atoms in the known universe. It is difficult to exhaustibly catalogue that. But the machines behave more intuitively. So this is a real breakthrough. If you look at manufacturing jobs, which is front and center in the discussion, we have lost about five to six million routine jobs. It has happened in almost every manufacturing sector, and it is a result of some unknown combination of globalization and digital technology. By unknown, I mean weighting, despite assertions by economists.

I did some research with Sandy Lake, a young South African who grew up in Illinois. He was at NYU at the time and was interested in the tradable side of the American economy, which is essentially the part that produces goods and services that trade internationally. Although that area grew quite nicely in the American economy in the last two decades, it generated no net employment. Zero. All of the employment creation in the U.S. economy is on the nontradable side, which is about two-third of the American economy. It is huge: it is government, education, construction, health care, retail, hotels, food, restaurants, and big labor-intensive sectors. It is a very large part of the American economy. But the middle-income jobs in the tradable sector were lost. Those people found employment, but they found employment mostly in lower-value-added jobs on the nontradable side of the economy.

Putting it slightly crudely, if you were an employer, it was a buyer's market. And there has been very little wage and income growth on that side of the economy, which is part of the story of rising inequality. These trends have been going on for at least a couple of decades and it appears that with digital technology, they will continue or even accelerate. Middle-income people were adversely affected by a combination of technological and global trends. However, the system did not respond. In fact, it did not even notice for a while, and when it did notice, it just talked about it. While I do not have an easy answer, just ignoring the problem probably is not the way to go. When—and now I go back to my experience in developing countries—something like that happens, at least in a democratic structure, if there is no policy or economic response or corrective mechanism, then the response is political. I call them political circuit-breakers. Somebody representing a large enough group says that is enough. My interpretation of much of what is going on around us now is exactly this. It is complicated, and there is a different story in every country, but we now have a rising tide of populism in the world.

The referendum on Brexit was the declaration of a desire for sovereignty, along with a statement that the growth patterns were increasingly noninclusive. The trends that I just described appear in one form or another in virtually every developed country. It is called job and income polarization, that is, a loss of middle-income jobs and a decline in the size of middle-income groups. The distribution of income is getting flat in the middle and fatter in the tails. Now, an expanding right tail is good. Getting a fatter left tail is not so good. In Britain, because of the combination of those two things and frustration with Brussels, they voted themselves, unfortunately, out of the EU. We have a similar problem in the United States with Brussels to complain about. Somebody was going to walk through that open door politically. It turned out it was the current administration. A very substantial fraction of the support for President Trump is people who felt like they had been sideswiped by these growth patterns.

That is not a bad thing. That is what is supposed to happen in a democracy. If you get elites that don't respond to the experiences of average people, the political system is supposed to give you an avenue for doing something about it, and that's what we got. Now that we have it, the question is, what are we going to do with it? I am not going there because there is so much uncertainty that we really do not know at this point. There is part of the economic policy program of the current administration that makes good sense: tax reform, heightened public and private investment, some review of regulations.

I live in Milan, in northern Italy. My wife is Italian, and we have similar things going on. We just had a populist candidate lose in the Netherlands, so everybody is breathing a sigh of relief because that was really an anti-immigrant and anti-Muslim candidate. There is an anti-euro candidate who is very powerful in France named Madame Le Pen. She is likely to win the first round of voting in France. If she gets 50 percent, she is in and, at least according to her, France is leaving the euro, which destroys the euro zone. It is the second biggest economy after Germany. We have an anti-euro populist movement in Italy. Even the Germans, surprisingly, have a nationalist party that is somewhat anti-immigrant and right wing and kind of anti-Europe and against the European project. The single most important thing that happened in the postwar period was that sixty years ago, we had the Treaty of Rome, and that started the project of building Europe into a unified entity. For a long time, it was a stunning success.

It has gone badly since the euro came into existence. In Europe, it is not so much the distributional issues narrowly defined; it is growth and unemployment in my country of Italy. It is a happy lot here for many, but it's challenging. The GDP this year is the same as it was in the year 2000. That is seventeen years of no growth. The youth unemployment rate is 45 percent and the overall unemployment rate is 12 percent. The sovereign rate to GDP ratio, which is the amount of government debt in relation to the size of the economy, is 135 percent. That is too high. In southern Europe, we are 20 percent out of bounds in terms of competitiveness relative to Germany with the same currency, so we cannot devalue and get back in the game. We have a very difficult situation that either is going to change economically in a positive direction through aggressive action at both the national level and the European level or the populace is going to keep getting stronger because the system is not working. So hold on to your chairs or your hats.

A. Michael Spence

Awarded Nobel Prize in 2001. Lecture presented March 29, 2017.

Date of Birth

November 7, 1943

Academic Degrees

B.A., Yale University, 1966
M.A., University of Oxford, 1968
Ph.D., Harvard University, 1972

Academic Affiliations

Associate Professor of Economics, Stanford University, 1973–75
Professor of Economics and Business Administration, Harvard University, 1975–90
Dean of the Faculty of Arts and Sciences, Harvard University, 1984–90
Philip H. Knight Professor and Dean of Stanford Graduate School of Business, Stanford University, 1990–present (emeritus since 2000)

Selected Books

The Next Convergence: The Future of Economic Growth in a Multispeed World, 2011
In the Wake of the Crisis: Leading Economists Reassess Economic Policy, Editor, 2012 (with Oliver Blanchard)
Equity and Growth in a Globalizing World, 2010 (with Ravi Kanbur)
After Capitalism, 2014
Intellectual Property, 1997
Leadership and Growth, Editor, 2010 (with David Brady)

Christopher A. Sims

The Nobel Prize Foundation asks prize winners to present a lecture on their work related to the prize and to write an autobiographical essay. Both of these are freely available on the internet. Rather than rehash that material, this essay adds to what I wrote for the Nobel website, in three ways. Since I wrote the Nobel essay, I have learned more about the family background of my economist grandfather, so I begin by discussing his life in more detail than appears in the Nobel essay. Then I discuss two of my main research areas outside the area for which the Nobel was awarded. In each case I try to explain where the research ideas came from and which scholars influenced my thinking. Along the way, the essay provides nontechnical explanations of the research ideas.

My mother's father was an immigrant from Estonia. He arrived in the United States when he was about eight years old with his two older brothers and his mother. I knew that. I knew that he had written an essay in which he described himself as having been born in what he called Revel, which is now Tallinn, the capital of Estonia. He characterized himself as a Russian Jew. Estonia now is a separate country, but at that time it was part of Russia.

My mother tried to find evidence of him in public records in Tallinn many years ago and did not succeed. This was not surprising since she knew only his American name and had to guess what its original form might have been. I visited Estonia just a couple of years ago to talk to the Nordic Econometric Society. My visit, and my Estonian ancestry, were publicized, and Mark Ryback, who runs the Estonian Jewish Archive, contacted me. He was able to locate a record of my grandfather's *bris*, or circumcision ceremony, as Movsha Wulf, with father Mendel Leiser and mother Sore (Sarah in Yiddish). The corresponding record for one of my grandfather's brothers was also in the archive.

My grandfather's name in the United States was William Morris Leiserson. What led him (and his brothers) to add the "son" is unclear. "William Morris" preserved his original initials, and perhaps reflected young Leiserson's political orientation; William Morris was a well-known British socialist politician and artist at the time, whom young Leiserson may have admired.

How did the family come to emigrate to the United States? Estonia at that time was part of Russia. The year before my grandfather was born, Czar Alexander II, who had liberated the serfs and was slowly liberalizing Russia, was assassinated by anarchists. Jews had for a long time been confined to a particular region of Russia called the Pale. Under Alexander II, it had become more and more possible for Jews to go to other parts of the country. While they were limited in what occupations they could undertake, those limitations were being relaxed. Alexander III started reversing these reforms.

As my grandfather recounted it in an autobiographical essay, his mother Sarah was taking care of her boys alone in the period before they emigrated. (Possibly Mendel was elsewhere trying to make a living, or possibly he was a political dissident hiding from police.) While they were registered as Revel residents, Sarah believed that to survive, they needed to be in the larger city Riga (now part of Latvia). The move was illegal. They lived with relatives, changing locations often, and Sarah had to bribe police to stay in Riga. The bribes did not always work, and when they did not, the family was marched for many days, along with other lawbreakers, back to Revel on foot. Sarah was determined to leave Russia. They fled by night through woods across the German border and boarded a ship to New York. The plan was that they would meet Mendel in the United States, but they did not see him again.

This was a group—a mother who had no particular education, who ended up working as a washerwoman, and three children—that I think would be denied entry into the United States today. They were not "high-quality" immigrants. They were refugees, but probably more economic than political.

My grandfather's two brothers eventually owned and ran garment factories. They were among the targets of the first large strike by the International Ladies Garment Workers Union. My grandfather worked in those factories. He never graduated from high school, but he went to free night classes and speeches at Cooper Union, a privately funded college. With no high school education, having had to work for a while, when he was twenty-one he went to Wisconsin and tried to get entry into the University of Wisconsin, where he was told he could not be admitted without a high school diploma. In response, he submitted an essay about why he wanted to study with John R. Commons, who was at that time famous as an institutional economist. His essay gained Billy (as my grandfather was by then known) admission to the University of Wisconsin. He went on to earn a Ph.D. from Columbia University, was a member of the first National Labor Relations Board under FDR, and then worked with the National Mediation Service, helping settle strikes and avert strikes in cooling-off periods.

He had seven children with his wife, Emily, who was not an immigrant. Her ancestry went back to the *Mayflower*. They were a lively and challenging bunch of uncles and aunts. One became president of the American Political Science Association; one was an economist, my Uncle Mark, who was one of the main intellectual influences on me as a teenager; one was an uncle whom I never knew and who died in training with the Naval Air Corps during World War II; and one was my mother, Ruth. Perhaps her most prominent public achievement was being elected first selectman of Greenwich, Connecticut, the first Democrat in many years and the first woman ever to hold that position.

It seems to me this family history holds some lessons for thinking about our country today. We are a country of immigrants, and it is one of our great strengths. We should expect that the immigrants who are coming to us today, even the ones who do not seem "high quality," are likely over time to make great contributions.

As I mentioned above, the Nobel Committee awarded the prize for my work on methods of statistical inference and their application to monetary economics. The development of my ideas in that area is covered in what I have posted on the Nobel website.

Another area that eventually became a research focus for me grew out of a course I took and a book I read as an undergraduate. The book was *The Mathematical Foundation of Information Theory* by A. I. Khinchin. About the same time I encountered this book as an undergraduate, I took a course on the psychology of language taught by Eric Lenneberg, and there were guest lectures by David A. Huffman, who was one of the early leaders in information theory. He gave his lectures on Huffman codes, which was a type of coding for efficient information transmission that he invented. It may be because I had had that exposure that I decided to buy the book.

I read the book as a reading course. My adviser, Andy Gleason, was a well-known mathematician. I was a math major. I knew from talking to other students that he graded reading courses by asking the student to prove a theorem from the material read for the course. I memorized the proof of the coding theorem of information theory and reproduced it for him.

Then I asked whether I could write my senior thesis extending the coding theorem that Khinchin gave in that book from finite memory channels to infinite memory channels. It really was a technical modification, but it was something I found challenging, interesting, and fun.

Gleason did not know how to evaluate it, so he passed it on to electrical engineering faculty. After they gave me the grade, they called me in for an interview, during which they tried to convince me to become an electrical engineer, which I did not really want to do. By that time I had decided I wanted to be an econometrician rather than a mathematician. I probably would not have been a good mathematician. I might have been a good electrical engineer, but I am glad I became an economist. Economics is more interesting, really.

The psychology of language course was a great course, if sort of disorganized. It was not just a series of lectures. Lenneberg was extremely enthusiastic, and he had us all divide into teams.

Besides listening to coding theory, which is math, we were sent out into the field to visit families who had two-year-old children and take notes on how they interacted. We were supposed to be learning about how children acquire language. At the time, and I think it's still true, there was a lot of debate over how much of our ability to learn language is hard-wired into us as children and is purely genetic and how much is simply reinforcement, and what it is about how parents and children interact vocally that leads people eventually to learn language. I am not sure we made great scientific contributions, but it was fun to visit these families and very stimulating to have these two different ways of thinking about communication in the same course.

I put that aside when I went into economics. My thesis was a technical proof. I never did anything in economics that drew on information theory until after I had gone to Princeton in 1999. However, before that I was bothered by what I saw as a pattern in macroeconomics as people began building larger macroeconomic models with more variables that were serious about fitting data. If you set up a model populated by optimizing agents who are continually monitoring everything the policymakers do, and optimizing at every instant, it will imply that when the Federal Reserve changes the federal funds rate from 3 percent to 3.25 percent, boom, everybody should react the next morning, if not sooner. Of course, most people do not even know it has happened by the next morning, and even if they read it in the newspaper, most people do not take any action in response. People do not react as fast or as reliably as the models of fully informed, optimizing agents suggest they should.

The models people knew how to deal with, models that could match the degree of inertia and randomness in people's behavior, had to introduce adjustment costs. They had to introduce the notion that the reason why people did not move fast when the interest rate changed or when the tax rate changed was that they had to pay some kind of penalty for moving quickly. These costs were accumulating all over these big models, and nobody could really point to what resources get used up when people change fast. What are the costs people face for changing fast? Why should we think that there really is a cost, a physical cost of any kind, for buying a more expensive brand of cereal because you are richer? Why should there be any adjustment cost there? Most economists are still using that kind of model and are still uncomfortable with the way adjustment costs appear in them to make them fit realistically the way people behave.

I wrote a paper, "Stickiness," whose theme was that you could explain almost any kind of inertia with a flexible enough model of adjustment costs. But the form of the costs needed to match data seemed complex and not well founded in observation of individuals' behavior. I added an appendix, though, because it had occurred to me that it might be possible to eliminate most of these adjustment costs by instead saying people had a cost to processing information, with the information being measured the way it is in Shannon's information theory and the way electrical engineers measure it. The basic insight is that perhaps we can explain the sluggish, erratic behavior of people not by assuming they face costs or are not optimizing, but by assuming that they are optimizing subject to an additional constraint.

The paper I wrote in this area that has had the most impact, "Implications of Rational Inattention," came about because Bob King, who is now at Boston University, saw the appendix I wrote to the adjustment cost paper and asked me to write a new paper, expanding that appendix, for a conference he was organizing. I might not have pursued these ideas were it not for his encouragement.

Claude Shannon's great contribution was an abstraction that characterizes information transmission that can be applied in many different fields. A channel is defined by what it takes as input, and by what comes from the channel as output for any given input. The output may or may not have an error attached to it. One example of a channel is a telegraph key. Telegraph keys hardly exist anymore, but people who used telegraph keys would transmit using Morse code, for example. That is dits and dahs. They would do that with a key. Every time they entered a dit signal, somebody at the other end would see a dit, and every time they entered a dah signal, or hit the key a different way, for a longer duration, the person at the other end would get a dah. To a first approximation, there were no errors in that. You might ask, suppose people are able to transmit a dit or a dah every tenth of a second, say, or every half second, in Morse code. How long would it take to send the words of "The Star-Spangled Banner" over this connection? That is one kind of channel.

Another kind of channel is a telephone wire, which takes what you say at one end, turns it into an electrical signal, and produces output at the other end that is not exactly the same as what you said. There is some noise in it. Some frequencies are lost. Suppose instead of a telegraph key to send "The Star-Spangled Banner," we have a phone. How long does it take to send "The Star-Spangled Banner" over the phone? There is a naïve way to estimate it. If you say, "I'm going to recite it to you over the phone. You time me, and then you get a good Morse code person to send it using a telegraph key, and you find out how long it takes. That is the rate of transmission in those two channels."

The Morse code transmission will proceed letter by letter. Morse code has a distinct pattern of dits and dahs for each letter. If I recite the words to "The Star-Spangled Banner" on the phone, that is much more efficient than spelling them out. But if I'm sending you a French translation of "The Star-Spangled Banner" and you don't speak French, I will have to spell it out. And why stop at words we know in common? Maybe I know you know the words to many songs, including "The Star-Spangled Banner," so that after the first few words you know the whole message.

Shannon's insight was that the rate at which something can be sent over a channel depends on the initial uncertainty about what is to be sent. If you know that I will be sending the words to some familiar song, it will be inefficient to send all the words—you will know the rest of the words after the first few. But if you think the message will be in some random language using the Roman alphabet, you will need to have it spelled out. Shannon showed that given the channel's characteristics and the probability distribution of what is to be sent through it, there is a maximal rate, called channel capacity, at which the message can be sent with minimal error.

This means that we don't need to know whether the channel is in fact a telegraph key, a telephone line, or a satellite dish. If we know its capacity and what we want to send through it, we can calculate the speed at which it can be sent.

You know Shannon's measure. It is bits per second, or bytes per second. You all have internet connections. You know you pay extra to get higher rates. What you pay for is Shannon capacity. With Shannon's measure, you do not have to know whether your internet connection is over a telephone line, or over fiber, or over a wireless connection. Its capacity is bits per second. We do not worry when we talk about the speed of the channel, whether there is a different speed for music, images, or text, because each of those kinds of information can be sent efficiently, using Shannon's ideas, at the same rate through different channels with the same capacity.

The idea of rational inattention is to suppose that people are rational agents who are also finite-capacity channels. Without rational inattention, people who optimize should change their behavior minute by minute with every change in the stock market valuation of their retirement account. Every change should make at least a small impact on how much they spend on lunch, but actually, nobody pays that kind of detailed attention to their retirement portfolio minute by minute or day by day. One way to explain that is to say that people have finite capacity, and most of the time it's much more important to monitor other things, such as information about interactions with other people, information about whether there's been a menu change at your favorite place for lunch, and lots of day-to-day things that are much more important to us than reacting perfectly and instantly to fluctuations in our retirement portfolio or to the federal funds rate.

It turns out that this kind of model of behavior can explain many of the broad empirical regularities we see in the data about people. Shannon's theory implies both a delay in response to information and that the processing of information will introduce an element of noise or randomness into people's behavior. We see both those things when we look at a list of macroeconomic variables in the usual national accounts. We see consumption and investment. People at the national accounts try to divide spending in the economy into categories, often related to who is doing the spending. Consumers are doing the consumption spending. People who are making decisions in firms are doing the investing. Bureaucrats in the government are making decisions about government expenditure.

When we estimate statistical models of business fluctuations with many variables, we see that changes in consumption, or government spending, or investment, or the federal funds rate are erratic, hard to predict. But the responses of other components; say, the response of consumption to a change in government spending, is not fast. Government spending itself will jump to a new level, and it will take a while for the reactions of other components of the national accounts to move with it. You can explain that by assuming adjustment costs everywhere, but it is difficult to explain this pattern just with adjustment costs, because if it is costly to change, then consumption or investment changes themselves should not be hard to predict over short spans of time. They should change smoothly. That is hard to explain with adjustment costs but follows easily from costly Shannon capacity.

I think this is an idea with lots of promise. There are people working on it. It is hard to use in a fully formal model. There is no example of a central bank policy model now that incorporates this formally. Economic theorists who build abstract, small, easily interpreted though mathematically difficult models have found this idea stimulating. There is quite a large literature now in economic theory that uses rational inattention ideas, and it may be that in another decade or two we will actually reach the point where we can make it manageable to use in policy models.

This all came out of a psychology course I took as an undergraduate and a book I found in a bookstore. The ideas had lain dormant for decades, and suddenly reemerged as research topics in economics.

Another "non-Nobel" area of my research is the fiscal theory of the price level. My Uncle Mark, who was a labor economist, used to harass me. He wanted me to become an economist. He gave me von Neumann and Morgenstern's *Theory of Games* when I was about eleven and kept telling me that I was going to become an economist. Of course, I found this annoying and thought it was having the opposite effect of what he intended, that it was just making me decide I was never going to be an economist. Though Mark was annoying, he was also interesting. He used to ask thought-provoking questions. I might run inside in the rain, and he would say, "Well, do you think that running inside lets you avoid getting wet, or would you be drier if you just walked?" I would think for a minute and give an answer: "I think the answer is you do stay drier if you run if the rate of rainfall stays the same." He would then argue against me and force me to try to give a detailed counterargument.

One of his questions came when I was an undergraduate and had just taken a couple of economics courses: "If you just keep the money supply fixed, will prices necessarily stay stable?" I said, "Sure." I had not yet seen any model where that was not true. As usual, he took the opposite side and said, "How do you know that? Give me an argument," and I tried. He did not think I had any good arguments, which was true. In fact, it is not true that just holding the money supply fixed will necessarily stabilize the price level. Now I do have a good argument for its not being true. This is the fiscal theory of the price level.

In developing this theory, the main influence on me, besides the subconscious conditioning by Mark Leiserson, was Michael Woodford. Mike was my colleague for several years at Princeton, and he is now at Columbia. The first time I encountered the basic idea in the fiscal theory of the price level was in a lecture he gave when I was at the University of Minnesota. He is not now identified as one of the main promoters of the fiscal theory of the price level because he has not pushed its implications for policy in recent years. Yet his early papers on this topic are really the definitive work on the theory.

At an early stage of my thinking about this area I supervised the Ph.D. work of Eric Leeper, now at the University of Virginia, who came up with a way of classifying monetary and fiscal policy regimes as "active" or "passive," and showed how pairings of fiscal and monetary policy rules of these types affected the economy. This was a major step forward in making the implications of the theory for policy understandable.

John Cochrane at Stanford is a public and passionate advocate of fiscal theory. I would say he goes a little overboard, but sometimes going overboard and getting attention is what you have to do to get people to wake up. We rarely agree on policy implications, even though we exchange criticism of our theoretical work. I am very appreciative of feedback he gave me on one of my papers. It is called "Stepping on a Rake" and is about how the central bank can cause recessions by raising interest rates, yet still lose control of the price level. He was impressed with that conclusion—so impressed that he tried to reproduce all the detailed math in my paper, which I had not laid out very well. I had laid out the conclusions in graphs of how the models worked, but I had not actually given systematic code for it. He reproduced everything, in the process rooting out errors in what I'd written in the paper. This kind of critical interaction is a central part of progress in economics, or any discipline.

What is this fiscal theory? To understand it, and understand why it is still thought of as controversial, you have to understand what went before it, monetarism. Actually, Keynesian models retained most of the core of monetarism. They certainly were not fiscal theory models.

The simple version of monetary theory is an oversimplification of it. You may have seen it in Econ 101 classes in the form $MV = PT$. The money stock times velocity, which is really defined by this equation, is the price level P times some measure of transactions volume, which is usually taken to be something like the GDP. The theory postulates that V, which is the rate of turnover of the money supply, is stable. It does respond somewhat to the interest rate. Milton Friedman and his followers, who were the main monetarists in the '70s, did admit V could change, but the intuition is V does not move very much. And in the long run, T does not change very much. When M goes up, P goes up. When M goes down, P goes down. That is the monetarist theory. If you want to control inflation, you keep M stable. At least in the long run, you will keep prices stable.

There are problems with monetarism, though, and the most obvious one is that nowadays most government liabilities are bonds, not non-interest-bearing currency. Both currency and a mature government bond trade for goods at the same rate. The intuition behind $MV = PT$ as a theory of inflation is that when there is too much money chasing goods, prices start going up. If you expand the money supply when output is not growing very fast, you are bound to cause inflation. But if you are thinking that way, why focus on non-interest-bearing currency, since people can also purchase real goods by trading bonds for them? Bonds also are government paper, and the ratio at which they trade for goods is P.

Yet the idea behind the fiscal theory of the price level it is not just replacing $MV = PT$ with $(B + M)V = PT$. While money is held for its transactions value, bonds are held for the investment return they provide. The total net payments to bondholders in a given period are the sum of interest payments and net bond redemptions (or minus net bond sales). This is called the *primary surplus*. It differs from the conventional measure of government surplus in that it adds in "interest expense," so it is usually larger than the conventional surplus and often positive when the conventional budget is shown as in deficit. If the primary surplus is stable over time and the market-determined real rate of return is also stable, the real value of the government debt has to match the discounted present value of the primary surplus:

$$\frac{B}{P} = \frac{\tau}{\rho}$$

where τ is the primary surplus and ρ is the real rate of return. This is the same formula, derived by the same principles, as the one we use to determine a stock price as the present value of future dividends. This formula is overly simple. The primary surplus and the discount rate are not constant, and the government can raise revenues through seigniorage (printing money), which the formula ignores. Nonetheless, it captures the fact that it is not just current deficits, that is, B in the formula, that the government controls. It also controls τ, the level of future primary surpluses. B depends on current fiscal policy, while τ depends on both future fiscal policy and future monetary policy. Any actual policy change, for example tax reform legislation, is likely to affect both sides of the equation. Thus even in this simplified form, the fiscal theory approach to understanding inflation is more demanding than the one-dimensional monetarist approach. But this makes it more realistic and allows it to address situations where monetarist theory comes up with a blank.

In Japan and the United States, people are very aware that there's a fiscal problem coming up as the population gets older, as retirement benefits and health care become more expensive, and as the working population becomes smaller relative to the retired population. It is not just economists. There are results from a Gallup poll where they ask Americans who are not retired if they believe that Social Security will be there for them when they retire. The majority of people say no, they do not believe Social Security will still be available when they retire. People are if anything overly pessimistic about future fiscal problems. If that is the case, and if the government runs a big deficit, it may not make people feel that they have got more to spend. It may make them think, "I'm now holding more government bonds, but my taxes are going to be higher," or more likely just "I have no idea of what this is going to do to my future taxes," and become more scared than before about their future fiscal situation. This may help explain why large deficits combined with near-zero interest rates in the United States, Japan, and the EU had disappointingly weak stimulative effects.

The common theme through this article has been that the ideas and people that eventually turn out to make contributions to us all often have disparate or obscure origins. Progress depends on ourselves retaining wide interests and open minds, and on our country retaining open borders.

Christopher A. Sims

Awarded Nobel Prize in 2011. Lecture presented April 4, 2018.

Date of Birth

October 21, 1942

Academic Degrees

B.A., Harvard University, 1963
M.A., University of California–Berkeley, 1964
Ph.D., Harvard University, 1968

Academic Affiliations

Instructor in Economics, Harvard University, 1967–68
Assistant Professor of Economics, Harvard University, 1968–70
Associate Professor of Economics, University of Minnesota, 1970–74
Professor of Economics, University of Minnesota, 1974–90
Henry Ford II Professor of Economics, Yale University, 1990–99
Professor of Economics, Princeton University, 1999–present
Harold H. Helm '20 Professor of Economics and Banking, Princeton University, 2004–12
Associate, Department of Operations Research and Financial Engineering, Princeton University, 2012–present
John J. F. Sherrerd '52 University Professor of Economics, Princeton University, 2012–present

Selected Books

Editor, Advances in Econometrics: Sixth World Congress, Volume 1, 1994
Editor, Advances in Econometrics: Sixth World Congress, Volume 2, 1994

Alvin E. Roth

I. Prologue

My evolution as an economist has been shaped by the fact that I've had
the privilege of witnessing, and participating in, three insurrections in
what is included in "mainstream" economics. The first brought game theory and mechanism design into the fold, the second brought in experimental and behavioral economics, and the third, still under way, brought
in market design. I'll tell this story chronologically, focusing mostly on
my work in market design, and aided by the half dozen overviews of
market design I have published over the latter part of my career, as my
experience has grown and my perspective has changed.

Telling a largely chronological story of an intellectual journey runs the
risk of making it appear that each event followed predictably from those
before. So I'll come back at the end and suggest some pointers that would
have made the path smoother had I been able to send them back in time
to my younger self.

II. Early Life and Education

I was born, prematurely, on December 18, 1951, and grew up in a New
York City neighborhood of garden apartments, built shortly after the

end of World War II to help fill the demand for affordable housing for returning veterans and their young families. There were many children of around my age in the neighborhood, who often had an older sibling, as I did.

The Russian Sputnik satellite was launched in 1957, so science was in the air as I started school. Largely influenced by my older brother, I happily joined the ranks of aspiring child scientists, complete with chemistry sets and microscopes and a variety of out-of-school activities. The most important of these for me was Columbia University's Science Honors Program, which offered weekend classes that I attended when I was a rather disaffected high school student. In the fall of 1968, I enrolled as a freshman at Columbia's engineering school.

I settled on studying operations research, which, among the engineering disciplines, seemed to offer the shortest path between thinking analytically and helping improve the working of the world. I surely didn't think of it that clearly then—OR offered a connection between math and engineering without the intermediate steps of manufacturing, which would have appealed to me as an engineer who could barely pass the then still mandatory first-year class in drafting. Back then (when computers were programmed via punch cards), drafting involved pencils and T-squares, those ancient instruments of torture.

Studying OR was a satisfying distraction from the pleasures of college life, and I decided to pursue it in graduate school. I entered the Ph.D. program in what was then the Department of Operations Research at Stanford, also in the School of Engineering, in the fall of 1971. I found it much more demanding than my undergraduate studies and flunked the comprehensive exams at the end of my first year, but managed to pass on a second attempt.

There was no game theory in the regular curriculum, but Michael Maschler, visiting from the Hebrew University of Jerusalem, offered a course. I was entranced, and prevailed on Bob Wilson in Stanford's Graduate School of Business—the only regular faculty member at Stanford then working on game theory—to supervise my dissertation. In those days, game theory was thought of as having two quite distinct parts, cooperative and noncooperative game theory, intended to apply to different economic environments. Cooperative game theory was directed at studying what kinds of agreements rational agents might reach, in an environment that allowed them to make binding agreements. Noncooperative game theory was directed at finding strategic (Nash) equilibria that were mostly interpreted either as self-enforcing agreements that could be reached in the absence of any technology to make agreements binding or as fixed points of a process of strategic calculations or adjustments that resulted in each participant choosing a strategy that was a best response to the choices of all the others.

Breaking down this apparent barrier between cooperative and noncooperative game theory, and some others as well, turned out to be important in the development of market design.

My dissertation focused on cooperative games, exploring the "solution" of a cooperative game originally proposed by von Neumann and Morgenstern. That whole line of research didn't flourish, and it isn't even taught in most game theory classes today. Nevertheless, research makes valuable progress by studying dead ends and blind alleys, because until an attractive idea has been explored from many angles, it's hard to tell whether it will lead to new discoveries and unexpected directions.

III. Illinois, 1974–82

After I finished my Ph.D. I started teaching at the University of Illinois in 1974. I offered a course in game theory and realized I had a very incomplete understanding of some of the things I had been taught. I addressed that by writing a series of papers (and books) about other ideas in cooperative game theory, including Nash's model of bargaining and the Shapley value. Both of those ideas generated substantial literatures, but neither is thriving today. However, three things that I started to do at Illinois (although I wasn't the first to work on any of them) have proved to be productive, ongoing avenues of research that continue today to open windows on new questions and doors to new opportunities.

The first of these was to start testing game theoretic predictions experimentally, in the laboratory. My first partner in this was my late colleague, Keith Murnighan, whose Ph.D. in social psychology was as new as mine was in OR when we both arrived in Illinois as assistant professors. Experimental economics was also new in those days, and there hadn't been many experiments motivated by game theory, so he and I had to teach each other how to design experiments that would be persuasive both to economists and psychologists. For example, I think we may have been the first to design a repeated-game experiment in which there was a fixed probability that each period of play would be the last. This helps avoid altered behavior in a known last period of play, and helps to control for unobservable beliefs that participants in the experiment might form about when the game might end if no ending rule is announced in advance.

Of my Ph.D. students at Illinois, one who stands out was my very first. Just as Keith Murnighan and I had to teach each other to do experiments, Mike Malouf and I had to teach each other to be student and adviser together. He and I also implemented novel experimental designs, which had participants bargain over lotteries with only two outcomes, in a way that allowed the behavior observed in the experiment to be analyzed in comparison to what particular theories (such as Nash's model of bargaining) predicted should be the behavior of expected utility maximizers.

I also began (with my colleague Andy Postlewaite) what I then imagined would be an entirely theoretical line of research, following up on a 1974 paper by Lloyd Shapley and Herb Scarf in the very first issue of the new *Journal of Mathematical Economics*. They formulated a model in which each agent possessed a unit of an indivisible good, which they called "houses," and had preferences over the houses, which could be traded. But there was no money in the model: houses had to be traded without using money. The question they asked was: Must there always exist a matching of people to houses that was in the core of the game that arose when people had property rights over their own house, but could trade? The core is an idea from cooperative game theory: a given allocation x is in the core if no coalition of traders could, by trading among themselves, receive a house that they prefer to the one they would have gotten at x. Shapley and Scarf showed that indeed, no matter what preferences the participants might have, there would always be an allocation of houses to people that was in the core. And they demonstrated an algorithm they called top trading cycles (TTC), and attributed to David Gale, that would produce an outcome in the core, for any preferences. Andy and I showed that when no agent was indifferent between any two houses, the core consisted of a unique outcome.

I subsequently wondered whether the TTC algorithm could be used as the basis for a clearinghouse to organize the otherwise cumbersome barter that would be needed to identify and accomplish all the necessary trades. An obvious obstacle is that the algorithm requires as input the preferences of each participant, and preferences are private information. If we were to ask each participant to reveal his or her preferences, would it be safe for them to do so, or could they do better by giving us some strategic answer? In a 1982 paper I showed that, when TTC is the engine of the clearinghouse, it would be a dominant strategy for each participant to reveal his or her true preferences: that is, no participant could obtain a preferred outcome by stating preferences falsely, and so the clearinghouse would be "strategy-proof."

I also began a different but ultimately related line of research of a much more obviously applied sort. I started to study the problems faced by the clearinghouse through which medical school graduates in the United States get their first jobs. It arose after a history of previous market designs had failed, and it was a kind of clearinghouse in which all participants were asked to state their preferences. I wondered whether it could be strategy-proof. In my first paper on the subject, also published in 1982, I showed that it couldn't be both strategy-proof and in the core. To do this, I piggybacked on the wonderful 1962 paper by David Gale and Lloyd Shapley, which formulated and studied a two-sided matching model, which in its simplest form they called the marriage model. This model was "two-sided" in the sense that people on one side had preferences over being matched to agents on the other side, and could only be matched to those on the other side (which made it very different from the "one-sided" model of trading houses, in which anyone can transact with anyone else—that is, in which everyone is on the same side.) Gale and Shapley formulated what they called the deferred acceptance (DA) algorithm, which for any stated preferences produced an outcome in the core of the game whose rules were that any two people on opposite sides of the market could be matched if they both agreed, and anyone could choose to remain unmatched if they preferred. In my 1982 paper I showed that no such algorithm could be strategy-proof for all participants, but that it was possible to make it strategy-proof for the participants on one side of the market, provided they wanted no more than one job (i.e., to be matched to no more than one person on the other side), which was the assumption that gave the marriage model its name. (Dubins and Freedman also proved that second result, and Bergstrom and Manning also proved the first result, so some questions seem to become ripe to be asked and answered. ...)

Notice that I've just told you about both the core of two matching games, and about the strategic incentives that participants in clearinghouses for these kinds of games would have. The first kind of result, about the core of the game, is in the tradition of cooperative game theory, while the second, about strategies, is in the tradition of noncooperative game theory. But each pair of results is about a single game, not two games, one "cooperative" and the other "noncooperative." This turns out to be a first step in understanding how to proceed with the practical design of marketplaces. But that was still far in my future in 1982.

IV. Pittsburgh, 1982–98

While at Illinois, I met and married my wife Emilie, and not long after she finished her Ph.D. in cognitive psychology, we moved to Pittsburgh, in 1982, to better pursue our dual careers. She went to work at Westinghouse, where she helped found the branch of human-factors engineering that is now known as cognitive engineering. I taught economics at the University of Pittsburgh, where I developed courses on experimental economics and on game theory.

In my game theory class, when I taught the work on TTC, my students sensibly objected that a model of trading houses without money was not very realistic. The medical school at Pitt is a big center of organ transplantation, and so, instead of houses, I eventually started pointing out that if we thought of each participant in the market as an incompatible patient-donor pair,[1] we could talk about "kidneys," since (after 1984) U.S. law criminalized the sale of organs for transplantation, so the assumption that money could not be used to reduce the obstacles to barter was realistic. I still had no idea that kidney exchange might become a real thing.

My research on two-sided matching, on the other hand, quickly turned toward empirical work as I studied the history of the medical match, and the kind of marketplace failures, related to the timing of transactions, that had led to the creation of a centralized clearinghouse. I found that, by trial and error in the early 1950s, the medical labor market had settled on an algorithm essentially equivalent to the DA algorithm. My 1984 paper also noted that the algorithm that had successfully produced a stable matching in the days when almost all American medical graduates were men might fail to produce stable matchings in the modern environment, in which substantial numbers of medical graduates were married to each other and were seeking two jobs, not just one. I followed this with studies of related medical labor clearinghouses in Britain, and of other markets that had suffered coordination failures related to issues of market timing, and found that producing a stable matching was an important ingredient in the success of these kinds of clearinghouses. Together with Marilda Sotomayor, who had come to Pittsburgh as a postdoc and become a close collaborator, I wrote a 1990 book on stable matching.

In 1991, I also published what I now think of as the first in a series of overviews about my evolving views on market design. This first one was something of a manifesto, calling for economists to become market designers. In the paper, titled "Game Theory as a Part of Empirical

Economics," I argued that economists would eventually encounter diminishing returns from merely explaining the features of markets and marketplaces that we observed in the world, and that game theory would thrive in the longer term only when it started to contribute to the design process in a practical way.

Motivated by the history of the markets for new doctors, I also became interested more generally in understanding the timing of transactions, and the strategic incentives involving timing in decentralized markets. With my student Xiaolin Xing, I eventually wrote two papers about market timing. The first was about markets that "unravel" in time, with offers each year becoming earlier (further in advance of employment) and more diffuse in time. This is what had happened in the market for new doctors, and it turned out to be a surprisingly common development in a variety of labor markets in which workers were sometimes hired years in advance of the start of employment. The second paper focused on the fact that transactions take time to evaluate and complete, and so markets can become congested, with more transactions needing to be considered than there is time to do in an orderly way. It seemed to me then (and still seems now) that we know much more about the prices of transactions than their other properties, and that a big factor in determining the success of marketplaces is whether they are well designed to help manage congestion.

By 1995, I thought I knew something about the market for new doctors, but when my phone rang one day and I was asked whether I would direct a redesign of the American medical match, I realized that I still had a lot to learn. It was no longer going to be enough to point out difficult problems faced by the organizers of the match—I would now have to propose workable solutions. If there was a single moment when I ceased being merely a scholarly observer of the economy and started being a market designer, it was during that phone call.

Working with Elliott Peranson (who founded a company called National Matching Services, which organizes matches, and provided software for the residency match), I helped formulate a new algorithm that was adopted by the residency match in 1998, and subsequently by many similar clearinghouses. The empirical study of these marketplaces raised questions that continue today to motivate advances in the theory of stable matchings.

Several more things about my many happy years at Pitt are worth mentioning. Together with my colleagues John Kagel and Jack Ochs, I helped organize a thriving experimental laboratory, and a lot of my work in those years was experimental (including an experiment with John on the importance of stability in contributing to the success of a clearinghouse, one with Jack on bargaining, and an early cross-cultural experiment run in Pittsburgh, Ljubljana, Jerusalem, and Tokyo). Two students who were particularly attracted to experiments were Gary Bolton (who actually got his Ph.D. from the neighboring Carnegie Mellon University but who worked with me and Jack), and Nick Feltovich, and as usual, I learned as much from them as they learned from me.

John Kagel and I edited the first *Handbook of Experimental Economics,* which came out in 1995 and I like to think contributed to establishing experimental and behavioral economics as a regular part of academic economics. The introduction to the volume, and some earlier surveys I had written, spoke about my evolving understanding of the uses of experimentation in economics, which I characterized as "Speaking to Theorists, Searching for Facts, and Whispering in the Ears of Princes." (John and I edited a second volume of the *Handbook,* which came out in 2016).

I also started offering postdoctoral positions both to new Ph.D.s and to people who would take a leave from their current position to spend a year largely free of responsibilities with me at Pitt. There was neither a requirement nor a promise that we would collaborate in our research, but some of them in fact became long-term collaborators and co-authors. I've already mentioned Marilda Sotomayor in this connection, and I would be remiss if I didn't mention Ido Erev and Bob Slonim, with both of whom I explored, in experiments, how participants learn over time about the strategic environments in which they are interacting with one another. (Learning about the environment is something that has to concern market designers who are contemplating introducing any new marketplace mechanism into practice. If there is any situation in which economists' traditional assumption that participants are all playing some particular equilibrium is likely to be wrong, it is when the game being played is a new one that none of the participants have experienced before.)

Even those postdocs with whom I did no joint research provided lots of positive externalities—it's a great benefit to a department to have energetic people around who aren't weighed down by teaching and administrative assignments and so have time to chat about research. I think that academic economics may have underinvested in postdoc appointments (or junior faculty leaves), and I'm glad to see some growth in those kinds of positions today, often in which a new Ph.D. who has succeeded on the job market will defer his or her job for a year to spend a year somewhere else as a postdoc.

V. Harvard, 1998–2012

Emilie and I and our two children (both born in Pittsburgh) moved back East in 1998, where I took a job at Harvard, half in economics and half at the Harvard Business School. My first years were invigorating but hectic as I met new colleagues and students, helped organize an experimental lab, and developed new graduate courses in experimental economics and (together with Paul Milgrom, who visited) in market design. As far as I know, Paul and I may have taught the first-ever course in market design. Our most practical examples concerned his work with Bob Wilson on spectrum auctions and my work on medical residency matching.[2]

Those were also the two main examples in my second market design overview in 2002. Based on those two design efforts, which had moved from theory to adoption to implementation, I felt I could say something about the progress we'd made since I had written about game theory as a part of empirical economics. The new paper was "The Economist as Engineer: Game Theory, Experimental Economics and Computation as Tools of Design Economics." As the title makes clear, I wanted to emphasize that our experience strongly suggested that market design (although I hadn't yet given up on a broader name for the field) wasn't going to be a subset of game theory but rather a collection of tools that we would wield as engineers.

At Harvard I also started studying in more detail the designs of other markets that had experienced problems with the timing of transactions. The American market for new lawyers had perennial problems coordinating the timing of transactions, like the market for doctors before 1950. One part of this market is the market for new law grads who wish to start their careers by clerking for an appellate judge. With my Harvard colleagues Chris Avery and Christine Joles, and with Judge Richard Posner, we eventually wrote two papers describing in detail the operation of this market, and how its rules and customs left it open to coordination problems, which often had law students being hired right after their first year of law school for positions that they would take up only after graduation, two years later. We did not succeed in redesigning this market, nor has anyone yet done so. (The judges prefer to be their own market designers, and have made half a dozen attempts in the last thirty years.)

While judges and hospitals often hire new graduates early, in some markets the strategic use of time causes transactions to happen late. Axel Ockenfels and I studied such a case in the online marketplace eBay when it was still quite new. In those days, most eBay sales were by auction, and a very high percentage of bids were submitted in the last minutes or seconds of the auction. We were able to show, by comparison with other auctions, how eBay's auction design, which included a fixed ending time, gave bidders incentives to delay placing their bids. (Axel came to Harvard as one of my first postdocs there and is today a leading market designer, who lives and works in Cologne.)

I also had the opportunity of helping develop new designs that were adopted and implemented in marketplaces for gastroenterologists, for school choice, for the labor market for new Ph.D. economists, and (the most unusual of the markets I have helped design for) for kidney exchange.

The market for gastroenterology fellows in the early 2000s was suffering from an unraveling of appointment dates. Gastroenterologists were all familiar with centralized matching (not least because medical fellowships are preceded by residencies). But there was a lot of concern among fellowship programs that if they agreed to delay hiring until information about candidates was available and they could participate in a match, their competitors would continue to hire early. Muriel Niederle and I proposed an intervention in the design of the decentralized market that might operate ahead of when a centralized clearinghouse was scheduled. We helped Debbie Proctor, a Yale gastroenterologist, persuade the relevant professional organizations to empower applicants who accepted early "exploding" offers before the match to later change their mind and participate in the match. This effectively abolished the "early offer" equilibrium in the decentralized market and allowed the centralized clearinghouse to successfully organize the market at a more efficient time.

Another decentralized labor market I had an opportunity to consider was the labor market for new Ph.D. economists. Starting in 2005, I chaired a committee of the American Economic Association charged with developing ways to facilitate the annual market for new Ph.D. economists. The early part of that market involves employers interviewing candidates at the annual meeting of the AEA, and that part of the market is congested, since employers receive very many applications from candidates they might like to interview, but they can interview only relatively few applicants in the available time. To help better coordinate the choice of whom to interview, the AEA introduced a signaling mechanism in 2006, which allowed each candidate to send up to two signals of particular interest, to help guide interviewing decisions. (In a congested market in which not all attractive candidates can be interviewed, it is helpful for employers to be able to judge not only how much they are interested in a candidate but how interested a candidate is in them.) We also introduced a "scramble" website, to help employers and candidates who are still available late in the market to contact one another.

Regarding centralized marketplaces, in the early 2000s my then student Parag Pathak and I accepted an invitation from the New York City Department of Education to try to redesign the school choice system by which students were assigned to high schools. The invitation arose because the NYCDOE recognized that their problems were related to those facing medical residency programs. We were quickly joined by Atila Abdulkadiroğlu, who had written specifically about matching for school choice (in a paper with Tayfun Sönmez that has since become influential). Not all our suggestions were accepted, but the system we helped put in place, based on a deferred acceptance algorithm, remains in use today. The three of us also subsequently teamed with Sönmez to design a similar school choice system in Boston, and with Neil Dorosin to design systems now used in Denver and New Orleans and a few other cities. (Neil had been the director of high school operations in NYC when we worked on the school choice system there, and Atila and Parag and I assisted him in forming the nonprofit Institute for Innovation in Public School Choice, which was the vehicle through which for many years we interacted with school districts on market design issues.)

In the years since, Parag and Attila have developed new statistical techniques to understand not only the impact on school assignments that these new designs have had but to use the data to understand the effect that school assignments have on student outcomes. I think of their work as the beginnings of a third generation of market design. In the first generation we were game theorists, turning our attention to theoretical "mechanism design." Those of us who pursued design into practical implementation had to become economic engineers. Parag and Atila and some of their colleagues are now bringing a distinctly new, third-generation level of sophistication to the empirical study of these markets. (In 2018 Parag was awarded the AEA's Clark Medal, a high honor given each year to an economist under age forty.)

Around the same time as the school choice work was producing practical results, we also started to see the first fruits of a very different kind of matching, to increase the number of kidney transplants. Shortly after I moved to Harvard, the first kidney exchange in the United States was performed at Rhode Island Hospital, between two incompatible patient-donor pairs. Over the next several years three more such exchanges were accomplished among the fourteen transplant centers in New England, as well as a small number elsewhere in the country. I realized that my notes on the Shapley–Scarf housing model might be helpful in thinking about how to organize kidney exchange on a larger scale, and I asked Utku Ünver, who was visiting me at Harvard for the year from Koç University in Turkey (and who had been my Ph.D. student at Pitt), to join me in giving a market design class lecture, based on my earlier work, and on extensions to the housing model that had been made by Abdulkadiroğlu and Sönmez. We were joined shortly after in this effort by Sönmez, who was Ünver's colleague at Koç and who later also came to visit me at Harvard for a year. That work led to a collaboration with Frank Delmonico, my Harvard Medical School colleague who was also the medical director of the New England Organ Bank, the organization responsible for procuring deceased donor organs for transplants. We helped him to found the New England Program for Kidney Exchange (NEPKE), the first interhospital kidney exchange. The initial design focused not on TTC but on organizing two-way exchanges because of the logistical complications involved in larger exchanges.

The relatively complicated logistics of kidney exchange involving transplants from living donors, together with the very long waiting list for deceased-donor kidneys, brings to the fore a natural question: Why is there a shortage of transplantable kidneys? (Gary Becker used to say that there shouldn't be a shortage, there should be a surplus, because healthy people have two kidneys and can remain healthy with one.) A proximate answer is that the law forbids donors to be compensated, so that the only legal price is zero—kidneys must be gifts. This is the law virtually everywhere in the world—the market for kidneys is banned, not regulated—with the single notable exception of the Islamic Republic of Iran, which has a legal monetary market for living-donor kidneys. And when you see that something is against the law almost everywhere, you can't expect that the shortest path to relieve the shortage will be to explain, ever more clearly, that voluntary transactions between well-informed adults can be expected to raise welfare if they don't have negative externalities that harm people not party to the transaction. The concerns that lead to these legal bans have to do with fears that vulnerable people will be exploited and harmed.

To understand this better, I began to study what I call *repugnant transactions*, which are transactions that some people would like to engage in but others don't think they should be allowed to, even though the transaction may not even be apparent to third parties unless they are told about it, so there don't appear to be any easily measurable negative externalities affecting those others. An important class of repugnant transactions are those that aren't repugnant in themselves but become repugnant when money is added (which is the case with kidney donations versus kidney sales). In medieval Europe, charging interest on loans was repugnant, although making interest-free loans was not. Repugnant transactions—and the bans that they sometimes engender—can have large scale consequences.

This was the background to my third market design overview, published in 2008 and titled "What Have We Learned from Market Design?"

That paper noted that the markets I've just talked about are quite different from one another—gastroenterologists have different careers than economists, and matching them to jobs is different from matching children to schools, and even more different from matching kidneys for exchange. But while the design of each marketplace depends on the details of each market, there are things common to all of them. I argued that across a wide range of markets, successful marketplaces share some common characteristics, namely, that marketplaces have to help the market become thick by attracting many participants; that they have to help those participants deal with the congestion that a thick market can cause; and that they have to make transactions safe and simple and reliable. And markets need social support, which markets in repugnant transactions may lack.

Before I left Harvard, four years later, it had already become clear that designing kidney exchange—which involves the day-to-day operations of transplant centers and health care providers and payers—is quite a bit more complicated than designing marketplaces that operate only on an annual basis. By September 2011, after performing fewer than one hundred kidney exchange transplants, NEPKE ended its operations because of problems with its financial design, which involved being an integral part of the New England Organ Bank.[3] It was replaced by other interhospital kidney exchanges, and, as kidney exchange became a standard part of American transplantation, also by many exchanges conducted internally within a single transplant center. My closest colleagues in this ongoing work of design include Mike Rees, the intrepid surgeon who founded the Alliance for Paired Donation, which is the most innovative of the inter-hospital kidney exchange organizations I have worked with, and Itai Ashlagi, who came to Harvard as a postdoc, and is now my colleague at Stanford.

VI. Stanford, 2012–Present

We moved to Stanford in 2012, so it is still too early for me to think of that historically. I'm in the economics department now, with just a courtesy appointment at my old home in the engineering school. But this move had a "homecoming" feel in another way because several of my colleagues at Stanford had been my students at Harvard.

While there are lots of similarities between the economics departments at Stanford and Harvard, one of the big differences is in who drops in to visit from off-campus. At Harvard, visitors are often from Wall Street or Washington; at Stanford they come from the tech firms of Silicon Valley. Many of those are engaged in market design via computer-assisted markets (think Google, eBay, Airbnb, Uber …).

In October 2012, about two months after we arrived at Stanford, the Nobel Prize that I shared with Lloyd Shapley was announced, and I suddenly found myself talking to a wider variety of audiences than I had been accustomed to. After taking some time to get used to this, I wrote a new kind of overview of market design, in the form of a general-interest book called *Who Gets What and Why*. It emphasizes that markets and marketplaces are human artifacts, and that market design by economists is part of an ancient and very human activity. But though markets are an ancient human technology, changes in other technologies change the possibilities for marketplaces, as we are seeing with modern computation and communication. For example, eBay and Amazon became possible after the invention of the internet, when individuals, or an individual bookstore, suddenly had inexpensive access to a wide market. But internet technology wasn't sufficient for the marketplaces created by Uber and Lyft and similar ride-hailing services. They had to wait for GPS-equipped smart phones, which know where you are and where the available cars are, so that you can call a car from wherever you are, and riders can be matched to cars that are near them.

Even computerized marketplaces have to create thickness, deal with congestion, and be safe and reliable. Some of these ancient challenges take new form—for example, internet markets have had to create new tools to let reliable parties establish a good reputation, even though they may not be located near any of their customers. Safety and security, particularly of payments, also need new designs (e.g., when credit cards must be communicated securely). And because computerized markets generate and record lots of data, we're still struggling with what that should mean for privacy—who owns your data and who may access it, for what purposes? Silicon Valley is a good place to think about these things.

By the time I arrived at Stanford, kidney exchange had already started to be a standard mode of transplantation in the United States, and today about 15 percent of U.S. living donor transplants are accomplished through exchange, as we've learned to overcome financial as well as logistical barriers. But new design issues still keep me busy, especially since the demand for transplantable kidneys has grown faster than the supply, and thousands of people still die from kidney failure each year in the United States. In fact, kidney failure is one of the top ten causes of death around the world, so there's a pressing need to increase access to transplantation everywhere. Part of that growth can come by making kidney exchange an international option: disease doesn't respect political boundaries. But further design innovations will be needed to overcome both the logistical and financial barriers to exchange internationally, especially since the financial design of health care and the customary ways of organizing transplants are different in different places.

Kidney exchange is not even legal everywhere. For example, in Germany, only in exceptional cases (involving the intervention of a judge) can a patient receive a kidney from someone not in his or her immediate family. So repugnance is still a barrier as well, but I predict that it will be overcome in Germany, as kidney exchange thrives in the UK and the Netherlands, and is making a beginning in many other EU countries. As the world becomes more connected, it becomes ever clearer that marketplaces are embedded in a larger economic environment.

This was a point I emphasized in my 2018 overview, "Marketplaces, Markets, and Market Design." The object of design is often a market-*place*, which can be a relatively small institution operating in a large economic environment. Because they are in a large environment, potential participants in a marketplace may have many other choices, and part of the job of designing a new marketplace is to make it enticing to participate in. And markets need social support, so designing a marketplace for a new market may involve dealing with issues of repugnance; that is, it may involve taking into account the views of people who don't themselves plan to participate in the market but whose support might be needed to establish it.

The same can be said for efforts to ban certain kinds of marketplaces, in an effort to abolish or prevent some kinds of transactions. Bans also need widespread social support to be effective, since otherwise they will give rise to active black markets that may be worse in some respects than a regulated legal market. Consider the market for heroin and related opioids, which remains active in the United States even though a high percentage of federal prison inmates are serving sentences for drug convictions. We have tens of thousands of deaths from opioid overdoses each year, in a black market whose design is largely determined by the laws banning heroin and related drugs. So we can't escape the responsibility for design even for a market that is generally agreed to be harmful to all who participate in it. It may thus be time to consider whether we should modify our laws—as we have already begun to do by allowing clean needle exchanges to reduce the spread of disease among intravenous drug users—to let addicts be treated more like patients than like criminals.

Another sense in which marketplaces are small parts of large economies is that it is hard to maintain a ban on things that neighboring jurisdictions allow. Thus in the last few years marijuana has become legal in many American states, and I anticipate that neighboring states will have increasing difficulty maintaining their own bans. And because much that people find repugnant is variable and history-dependent, this is going to be commonplace in global markets. For example, in California, where I live, commercial surrogacy is legal and reliable—a couple can pay someone to bear a baby, and have their names as the parents on the California birth certificate. But in some places, including many American states, and Canada and England, commercial surrogacy is illegal (a surrogate can't be paid), and in other places surrogacy itself is illegal (the legal mother is the person who bears the child, even if she and the child are not genetically related). But you won't be surprised to learn that there is fertility tourism to California and other jurisdictions where markets for surrogacy exist. So just as repugnance can constrain what markets exist, markets can constrain what can effectively be banned.

The fact that a marketplace operates within a large environment has an effect on how we use and interpret mathematical models in market design. This is the subject I address, with Bob Wilson, in my most recent overview, "How Market Design Emerged from Game Theory: A Mutual Interview." We discuss how we often use strategic models—the kinds that used to be called noncooperative game theory—to model the choices that participants must make within a marketplace. And we use coalitional models—the kinds that used to be called cooperative game theory—to model the kinds of outcomes a marketplace must produce to entice participants away from their opportunities to transact outside the marketplace. And just as market design has been shaped by game theory, it has also started to shape it—we understand our relationship to our subject matter better than we used to.

VII. Looking Back on a Changing Perspective

One way to summarize the things I think I've learned so far would be in a message to my younger self, that could have provided signposts and encouragement. Maybe that reverse time capsule could have contained the following points:

1. There are lots of markets other than commodity markets in which prices do all the work. Many markets are matching markets, in which you care whom you're dealing with and you can't just choose what you want (even if you can afford it), you also have to be chosen.
2. Marketplaces are small parts of large environments.
   a. Successful marketplaces help make the market thick; they overcome the resulting potential for congestion, and they are safe and reliable venues.
3. Markets need social support.
   a. Novel market designs need internal champions. An important step in creating a new design and getting it adopted and implemented is to find an internal champion (who can explain to you what you've missed, and explain the new design to his or her colleagues as an insider).
   b. Some transactions are repugnant (even if there aren't any easily measurable negative externalities). This is too important an issue to be left to philosophers.
   c. Bans on markets also require social support to be effective; otherwise they may simply create black markets or drive participants to other venues.
4. Postdocs and research visitors are good to have in a department. They help break through the congestion caused by a department's day-to-day responsibilities.

I've also learned something about the culture of economists. Although it isn't always readily apparent in the short term, economics has very open borders. During my career so far I've seen economics incorporate ideas from math, OR, computer science, psychology, and sociology, and some cross fertilization with biology. I am far from the only intellectual immigrant who has come to economics from another discipline, and of course my colleagues come from all over the world. This openness is something to be grateful for (I certainly am), and to guard vigilantly. It is what will keep economics thriving.

Notes

1. By an incompatible patient-donor pair I mean a patient with kidney failure and a healthy person who loves that patient and wants to give him or her one of the healthy person's kidneys but cannot because the kidney and the patient aren't compatible. So the pair has a kidney, which they cannot actually use themselves to save the life of the patient but which they can trade with one or more other pairs, so that each patient gets a compatible kidney from another patient's donor.

2. I recall wondering if years later those would still be our main two examples, or if new opportunities to study markets' designs and to design new markets would give us a ready way of keeping the course current. I needn't have worried, as things turned out.

3. See the website https://web.archive.org/web/20110920202506/http://www .nepke.org.

References

Roth, A. E. 1991. "Game Theory as a Part of Empirical Economics." *Economic Journal* 101 (January): 107–114.

Roth, Alvin E. 2002. "The Economist as Engineer: Game Theory, Experimental Economics and Computation as Tools of Design Economics." *Econometrica* 70 (4): 1341–1378.

Roth, Alvin E. 2008. "What Have We Learned from Market Design?" Hahn Lecture. *Economic Journal* 118 (March): 285–310.

Roth, A. E. 2015. *Who Gets What—and Why: The New Economics of Match-making and Market Design.* Boston: Houghton Mifflin Harcourt.

Roth, Alvin E. 2018. "Marketplaces, Markets, and Market Design." *American Economic Review* 108 (7): 1609–1658.

Roth, Alvin E., and Robert J. Wilson. 2019. "How Market Design Emerged from Game Theory: A Mutual Interview." *Journal of Economic Perspectives* 33 (3): 118–143.

Alvin E. Roth

Awarded Nobel Prize in 2012. Lecture presented March 28, 2019.

Date of Birth

December 18, 1951

Academic Degrees

B.S., Columbia University, 1971
M.A., Stanford University, 1973
Ph.D., Stanford University, 1974

Academic Affiliations

Assistant Professor and (from 8/77) Associate Professor, Department of Business Administration and Department of Economics, University of Illinois, 1974–79

Professor, Department of Business Administration and Department of Economics, and (from 8/81) Beckman Associate, Center for Advanced Study, University of Illinois, 1979–82

A. W. Mellon Professor of Economics, University of Pittsburgh. Also; Fellow, Center for Philosophy of Science (from 1983); and (from 1985) Professor of Business Administration, Graduate School of Business, University of Pittsburgh, 1982–98

George Gund Professor of Economics and Business Administration, Department of Economics, Harvard University, and Harvard Business School, 1998–2012 (emeritus since 2012)

McCaw Senior Visiting Professor of Economics, Department of Economics, Stanford University, 2012

Craig and Susan McCaw Professor of Economics, Department of Economics, Stanford University, Senior Fellow, Stanford Institute for Economic Policy Research; Professor, by courtesy, Management Science and Engineering, 2013–present

Other Appointments Include:

Institute Associate, Institute for Mathematical Studies in the Social Sciences, Stanford University, January–June 1978

Mendes-France Visiting Professor of Economics, The Technion, Haifa, Israel, 1986

Bogen Visiting Professor, Department of Economics, Hebrew University of Jerusalem, Israel, June 1995

Visiting Professor, Department of Economics, University of Tel Aviv, Israel, July 1995
Research Associate, National Bureau of Economic Research, 1998–present
Senior Fellow, Stanford Institute for Economic Policy Research, 2013–present

Selected Books

The Shapley Value: Essays in Honor of Lloyd S. Shapley, Editor, 1988
Two-Sided Matching: A Study in Game-Theoretic Modeling and Analysis, 1990 (with M. Sotomayor).
Handbook of Experimental Economics, Editor, 1995, 2016 (with J. H. Kagel)
The Handbook of Market Design, Editor, 2013 (with Nir Vulkan and Zvika Neman)
Who Gets What—and Why: The New Economics of Matchmaking and Market Design, 2015

Lessons from the Laureates: An Afterword

A goal of the Nobel Economists Lecture Series at Trinity University has been to enhance our understanding of the link between biography, especially autobiography, and the development of modern economic thought. Each of the thirty-two lectures, organized around the theme "my evolution as an economist," provides source material for this endeavor.

The purpose of this afterword is twofold. The first section identifies common themes as well as some disparate views expressed by the laureates in describing their development as economists. Among these are the importance of real-world events, coupled with a desire for rigor and relevance; the critical influence of teachers and scholars during the laureates' formative years; the need for scholarly interaction and a lively intellectual environment; and the role of luck or happenstance in their lives. Most, but not all, of the laureates view their research program as having been largely unplanned, evolving through the marketplace for ideas and taking form as a coherent body of thought only after the fact. There are exceptions, however. In summarizing these themes, we rely heavily on the words of the laureates, taken from their Trinity University lectures.

The second section assesses the difficult question of whether or not biography is important for understanding the development of modern economic thought. Ultimately, we cannot provide a definite answer to this question. One can neither observe nor simulate in any methodical fashion the appropriate counterfactual—how economic thought would have developed absent these individuals and their particular life histories. The inability to answer this question in a definitive way, though, does not imply that it should be ignored. These thirty-two essays provide ample source material for reasoned speculation on the significance of biography in the evolution of economic thought.

Common Themes and Disparate Voices

Few individuals begin life expecting or desiring to be an economist. This same generalization holds true among Nobel economists. The laureates came to economics through the influence of particular teachers or scholars, because of the intellectual challenge and rigor of economics, or because economics was perceived as relevant for addressing real-world issues. Several of the laureates cite factors that drew them to economics. Five examples follow:

> Rare is the child, I suspect, who wants to grow up to be an economist, or a professor. ... Like many other economists of my vintage, I was attracted to the field for two reasons. One was that economic theory is a fascinating intellectual challenge, on the order of mathematics or chess. I liked analytics and logical argument. ... The other reason was the obvious relevance of economics to understanding and perhaps overcoming the Great Depression and all the frightening political developments associated with it throughout the world. ... Thanks to Keynes, economics offered me the best of both worlds. (James Tobin)

> In the first semester of my sophomore year I took required courses in accounting and microeconomics. The former was, in reality, bookkeeping—and mindless bookkeeping at that. I loathed it. But microeconomics had everything: rigor, relevance, structure, and logic. I found its allure irresistible. The next semester I changed my major to economics and never turned back.
>   Thus my first stroke of luck. I sometimes break out in a cold sweat thinking about what might have happened had I taken a modern accounting course and an institutional economics course. (William Sharpe)

> I've also learned something about the culture of economists. Although it isn't always readily apparent in the short term, economics has very open borders. During my career so far I've seen economics incorporate ideas from math, OR, computer science, psychology, and sociology, and some cross-fertilization with biology. I am far from the only intellectual immigrant who has come to economics from another discipline, and of course my colleagues come from all over the world. This openness is something to be grateful for (I certainly am), and to guard vigilantly. It is what will keep economics thriving. (Alvin E. Roth)

> I had decided that sitting by myself thinking deep thoughts was not going to work for me. In the end, I picked economics in part because it is a field with a wide range of subdisciplines. We have colleagues who are essentially mathematicians or statisticians, we have colleagues who are policymakers, and we have colleagues who are applied micro theorists and others who are specialists in various fields. Some of us are even employed outside academia in financial institutions, in the government, and in companies and nonprofits. I thought this was the closest I could come to hedging my bets, so economics seemed pretty safe, provided I liked it. (A. Michael Spence)

I relished the unbending rigor of mathematics, physics, and engineering, but then, as a senior, I took an economics course and found it very intriguing—you could actually learn something about the economic principles underlying the claims of socialism, capitalism, and other such "isms." I knew little, but I was intrigued. Curious about professional economics, I went to the Caltech library, stumbled on Samuelson's *Foundations of Economic Analysis* and, later that year, von Mises's *Human Action*. From the former, it was clear that economics could be done like physics, but from the latter there seemed to be much in the way of reasoning that was not like physics. I also subscribed to the *Quarterly Journal of Economics*, and one of the first issues had a paper by Hollis Chenery on engineering production functions. So economics was also like engineering. I had not a hint then as to how much those first impressions would be changed in my thinking over the decades to follow. (Vernon L. Smith)

The desire for relevance is an important theme in the lectures. As indicated in the earlier quotation from James Tobin, for the older generation of Nobel laureates it was the Great Depression that triggered an interest in economics. Tobin, as well as other laureates, makes this point forcefully:

Keynes's uprising against encrusted error was an appealing crusade for youth. The truth would make us free, and fully employed too. ... Economic knowledge advances when striking real-world events and issues pose puzzles we have to try to understand and resolve. (James Tobin)

Yes, 1932 was a great time to be born as an economist. The Sleeping Beauty of political economy was waiting for the enlivening kiss of new methods, new paradigms, new hired hands, and new problems. Science is a parasite: the greater the patient population, the better the advance in physiology and pathology; and out of pathology arises therapy. The year 1932 was the trough of the Great Depression, and from its rotten soil was belatedly begot the new subject that today we call macroeconomics. (Paul A. Samuelson)

Soon there will be no more active economists who remember the 1930s clearly. The generation of economists that was moved to study economics by the feeling that we desperately needed to understand the Great Depression will soon have retired. Most of today's younger and middle-aged macroeconomists think of "the business cycle" as a low-variance, moderately autocorrelated, stationary, stochastic process taking place around a generally satisfactory trend. That is an altogether different frame of mind from the one with which I grew up in the profession. (Robert M. Solow)

Although the Great Depression is long past, the desire for relevance remains crucial among Nobel laureates. Edmund S. Phelps characterizes his research as a response to a prevailing orthodoxy that lacked relevance, leaving too little room for realistic human behavior and uncertainty. For example:

Having read Hayek's *Prices and Production* (2nd ed., 1935) and Keynes's *General Theory*, I could sense that the neo-Keynesian research, though intriguing and possibly useful in some ways, had utterly abandoned the modernist emphasis on incomplete information and imperfect knowledge in favor of some new method or methodology with which I was not at all comfortable. Instinctively, as Keynes would have said, I understand that the neo-Keynesian models, in abstracting from these things, inadvertently left no role for humans to play. There could be no beliefs as distinct from what is true, no expectations as distinct from what is or will be, no mental stimulation and challenge, no problem solving, no creativity, and no discovery. (Edmund S. Phelps)

Roger B. Myerson is one of several laureates who looked for relevance with respect to social issues:

But concern about the new risk of nuclear war was widespread in the 1950s, and, like many of my generation, I was aware of this terrible threat from a young age. I have early memories of telling my father that I was worried by political cartoons that depicted global dangers of the 1956 Suez Crisis, when I was five years old. My father reassured me that the leaders of the world were bringing all their wisdom and understanding to the task of managing the crisis peacefully. This perspective suggested, however, that perhaps it might be better if our leaders could have even more wisdom and understanding, to provide guidance for a safer and more peaceful world in the future.

When I was twelve, I read a classic science fiction novel that depicted a future in which advanced mathematical social science provided the guidance for a new utopian civilization. Ideas from this and other readings grew in long discussions with my friends. It was natural, perhaps, to hope that fundamental advances in the social sciences might help find better ways of managing the world's problems, as fundamental advances in the physical sciences had so dangerously raised the stakes of social conflict in our time.

I have always loved to read about history and found a fascinating beauty in historical maps. But I hoped for something more analytical, and so I was naturally intrigued when I first heard about economics. (Roger B. Myerson)

I have to confess that I have been troubled—indeed, deeply troubled—by problems of many different kinds. Some of them have fairly obvious social relevance (such as analyzing the causes of famines and identifying ways and means of preventing starvation and hunger); others may well have some political use (such as finding out the conditions under which majority decisions tend to be consistent); and others may demand a critical examination of social institutions and economic policies. But there are still others that are definitely captivating as scrutiny of foundational ideas, such as equity, justice, and efficiency. The domain of theory can proceed hand in hand with attempts to reduce poverty, curb deprivation, and defend liberty and freedom. (Amartya Sen)

During my senior year at Princeton, however, I was losing interest in economics and began to think that I should go into something else. Economics seemed

excessively formal to me. ... Economics appeared incapable of helping me
understand the issues in which I had an interest: inequality, class, race, prestige,
and similar issues that were important for society. ... I remained unhappy—
unhappy by what seemed to me a disconnect between what economists would
talk about in textbooks and elsewhere and what I wanted to talk about. ...

[At Chicago,] Milton Friedman became the greatest influence of any individual on my development as an economist. Attending his graduate course
in price theory was just exciting, and I would eagerly wait for that course
to come twice a week. ... Here I saw economics as a tool and not simply as
a game played by clever academics. ... [Friedman's course in price theory]
showed me what I thought was not possible. You can do economics and do
it in a rigorous way and nevertheless talk about important problems. (Gary
S. Becker)

The above quotation from Becker shows how Milton Friedman opened
his eyes to the relevance of economics. Most who were students at the
University of Chicago mention the charismatic importance of Friedman
in their lives. Personality matters. But none of the Nobel laureates, even
Friedman, is more renowned for his personality than for his scientific
work. Becker is far from alone in recognizing the influence of a great
teacher or a particular individual. Myron S. Scholes, James M. Buchanan,
Edward C. Prescott, and Eric S. Maskin are among the others:

McMaster turned out to be a fortuitous choice. Because it was such a small
school, Professor McIver, a University of Chicago graduate in economics,
worked closely with me in my studies. He directed me to read and understand
the work of many classical economists, including the more contemporary
teachings of Milton Friedman and George Stigler. ...

Because of my enjoyment of economics and my planned return to business,
I decided on business school, not law school. Although my family wanted me
to apply to other schools, such as Harvard, I wanted to go only to the University of Chicago, where Stigler and Friedman were teaching and conducting
research. (Myron S. Scholes)

I am not a "natural economist" as some of my colleagues are, and I did not
"evolve" into an economist. Instead I sprang full blown upon intellectual conversion, after I "saw the light." ... I was indeed converted by Frank Knight, but
he almost single-mindedly conveyed the message that there exists no god whose
pronouncements deserve elevation to the sacrosanct, whether god within or
god without the scientific academy. Everything, everyone, anywhere, anytime—
all is open to challenge and criticism. There is a moral obligation to reach one's
own conclusions, even if this sometimes means exposing the prophet whom
you have elevated to intellectual guruship. (James M. Buchanan)

With this collaboration, I understood the comment he [Lucas] made after
I defended my dissertation. He was telling me to use dynamic economic
theory to model aggregate phenomena. I became a Bob Lucas student and

an economist. To return to the theme of this lecture, Bob Lucas is the most important person in my development as an economist. Having been at the right place at the right time was another stroke of luck.

The principle guiding my research is the importance of theory interacting with measurement. I came to the conclusion that there was no hope for the approach being used in macroeconomics of empirically searching for the policy-invariant laws of motion of the economy. I had read the Lucas critique. Something else was needed. Given this, I stopped teaching what was then called macroeconomics and began using dynamic equilibrium models to study aggregate economics as practiced by Bob Lucas. (Edward C. Prescott)

Notwithstanding such odd episodes, I found mathematics a very attractive subject, and I might well have stayed a mathematician had I not wandered almost by accident into a course in economics that the great economist Kenneth Arrow was offering on the economics of information. I didn't know who Arrow was at the time, and I certainly didn't know what the economics of information was, but I thought that the class should at least be informative. Arrow's lectures were improvisational. He appeared to have thought up what he was going to talk about on the way over to the lecture room from his office, and sometimes not even then. But in addition to being improvisational, they were inspirational. The list of topics was a bit of a hodgepodge. There was some information economics, as the name of the course suggested. There was some team theory, there was a unit on planning procedures, there was a discussion of moral hazard and adverse selection. But the highlight of the course, and the part that changed my life, was Leonid Hurwicz's work on mechanism design theory. (Eric S. Maskin)

Nearly all the laureates identify a particular work environment, usually but not always a university economics department, as a critical factor in their evolution as an economist. Lawrence R. Klein and William F. Sharpe are particularly emphatic on this point:

A truly exceptional group of people was assembled in Chicago during the late 1940s. I doubt that such a group could ever be put together again in economics. From our closely knit group, four Nobel laureates have emerged, and two others came from the next bunching of Cowles researchers—partly at Chicago and partly at Yale. We worked as a team and focused on a single problem—to put together an econometric model of the American economy (a second attempt after Tinbergen's of the 1930s)—using the best of statistical theory, economic theory, and available data. After about four or five years of intensive research built up around this theme, the team dispersed to new openings in academic life. (Lawrence R. Klein)

The RAND [Corporation] of 1956 was a truly unique organization. ... Employees were free to work any hours they chose, within wide limits. Office doors were open, intellectual discussions on the most wide-ranging topics were de rigueur, and everyone was expected to spend one day per week on research of strictly personal interest.

Those were heady days. Some of the key work in systems analysis, operations research, computer science, and applied economics was being done at RAND. One of our first computers was designed by John von Neumann. George Dantzig was working on linear programming. Some of the most illustrious academics served as consultants. Everyone was on a first-name basis. If ever there was a place for one interested in practical theory, the RAND Corporation in the 1950s was it. (William F. Sharpe)

A common theme in the laureates' lectures is the role of luck. The emphasis on the role of luck no doubt stems in part from the general tone of humility expressed in many of the lectures. Obviously, a combination of brilliance and hard work is a necessary, though not sufficient, condition for being awarded a Nobel Prize. The laureates often use the term "luck" to mean the unpredictability or unplanned path through which their career evolved. Each can readily imagine some alternative turn taken early in life that would have set them on an altogether different path. Friedman, Becker, and Paul Krugman make this fact explicit:

I have been enormously impressed by the role that pure chance plays in determining our life history. ... As I recalled my own experience and development, I was impressed by the series of lucky accidents that determined the road I traveled. (Milton Friedman)

I soon realized that much more was needed. ... There were no foundations for the theory of investment in human capital. ... I set about trying to sketch out a small set of foundations to give the work theoretical content. ... I had no vision at all of what this would lead to. Once again, here is an example of the role of luck. ... I was amazed and then greatly excited when I began to realize that this framework could integrate scores of observations and regularities in individual earnings, occupational differences in earnings, and employment. (Gary S. Becker)

Doing history requires an awful lot of nitty-gritty research, and while economics requires research, nitty-gritty research is not my style. Also, history is primarily about what happened. You can talk in the last chapter of your book about why it happened, but it is mostly about the *what* and not the *why*. I wanted more of the *why*. So I gravitated toward economics and had one of those really lucky breaks—the kind of lucky break you find behind the life story of anyone who has done well in his or her career. In my case, I had a really good instructor who taught a really good course (Bill Nordhaus, at Yale)—a special course on the economics of natural resources. ... So that went well, and I got a recommendation from Bill Nordhaus and went to grad school. The point I'm trying to make is that it was good that there turned out to be something I both enjoyed and was reasonably good at, but it was crucial that I lucked into meeting the right person at the right time. ...

At MIT I figured out again what style of research suited me. I again lucked into finding another great mentor, this time the late Rudi Dornbusch, a great international macroeconomist at MIT—some would say the most influential international macroeconomist of the past thirty years or so. He was a great teacher and a great inspiration because of the way he worked. (Paul Krugman)

One area where there is not a consensus among the laureates is how research programs are developed. The above passage from Becker shows that he had little idea what eventually would develop from his early forays into human capital theory. Many of the laureates likewise insist that their research was not part of any grand design or vision but rather evolved within the highly competitive market for ideas. Buchanan, Samuelson, and Krugman are exemplars:

> I recognize of course that my own research-publication record may be interpreted as the output of a methodological and normative individualist whose underlying purpose has always been to further philosophical support for individual liberty. In subjective recall, however, this motivational thrust has never informed my conscious work effort. I have throughout my career and with only a few exceptions sought to clarify ambiguities and confusions and clear up neglected pockets of analysis in the received arguments of fellow economists, social scientists, and philosophers. To the extent that conscious motivation has entered these efforts, it has always been the sheer enjoyment of working out ideas, of creating the reality that is reflected finally in the finished manuscript. (James M. Buchanan)

> Repeatedly I have denied the great-man or great-work notion of science. Every drop helps, the old farmer said, as he spat into the pond. One does the best one can on the most pressing problem that presents. And, if after you have done so, your next moves are down a trajectory of diminishing returns, then still it is optimal to follow the rule of doing the best that there is to do. Besides, at any time a Schumpeterian innovation or Darwinian mutation may occur to you, plucking the violin string of increasing return. ...
>   Scientists are as avaricious and competitive as Smithian businessmen. The coin they seek is not apples, nuts, and yachts; nor is it the coin itself, or power as that term is ordinarily used. Scholars seek fame. The fame they seek ... is fame with their peers—the other scientists whom they respect and whose respect they strive for. (Paul A. Samuelson)

> At that point I realized I was developing a style, so I wrote up my rules for research about twenty years ago. Let me give you my four rules for research: listen to the Gentiles; question the question; dare to be silly; and simplify, simplify! (Paul Krugman)

Thomas C. Schelling notes that the direction of his research was shaped in no small part by suggestions and requests from others.

> The second, related impression is that nearly everything I've done was stimulated by opportunities I didn't seek but came to me, and many things I've done, including some of the things I'm most satisfied with, I did at the suggestion

of somebody else or as a result of some unsolicited invitation. (Thomas C. Schelling)

Douglass C. North, Franco Modigliani, James Tobin, and Peter A. Diamond are four laureates who describe a more methodical course. One knew where he was headed early on, one attempted to run counter to whatever was currently in fashion, one states that he consciously aimed for the big problem of his day, and one drew his research ideas from teaching.

> I knew where I was going from the day I decided to become an economist. I set out to understand what made economies rich or poor because I viewed that objective as being the essential prerequisite to improving their performance. The search for the Holy Grail of the ultimate source of economic performance has taken me on a long and certainly unanticipated journey, from Marxism to cognitive science, but it has been this persistent objective that has directed and shaped my scholarly career. (Douglass C. North)

> As I contemplate my contributions, I find one unifying thread: a propensity to swim against the current by challenging the self-evident orthodoxies of the moment, be it that the classics are altogether outdated, or that the rich must save a larger fraction of their income than the poor, or that debt financing is cheaper because the interest rate on high-quality debt is lower than the return on equity.
> I would love to be able to continue to play that role. But I don't want to think too much about where I am going. I just like to let things come and be ready to jump in where there is excitement. (Franco Modigliani)

> The most important decisions a scholar makes are what problems to work on. Choosing them just by looking for gaps in the literature is often not very productive and at worst divorces the literature itself from problems that provide more important and productive lines of inquiry. The best economists have taken their subjects from the world around them. (James Tobin)

> As I read about different topics for class, I did not want just to teach the articles or book chapters; I wanted to figure out my take on the topics. This started a phase transition as material prepared for class evolved into a good paper. I attribute this success to the circumstance of preparing carefully for a class of sharp, attentive students. And it meant I was thinking about the economics, not just applying math. ... I have continued to prefer developing my own materials rather than teaching the contents of existing papers. While many people worry about the time needed for teaching taking away from the time for research, my experience was that they reinforced each other. Indeed, the times when my research went most slowly occurred when I did little teaching. (Peter A. Diamond)

Important breakthroughs in economics do not occur in a vacuum. Some of the major developments in economics are likely to have occurred

in much the same fashion absent the contribution of a particular economist. Other contributions are more distinct—very much shaping the
future path of economic literature in that area. For other work, its precise
contribution to economics evolves over time. These alternative possibilities are evident in the following passages:

> Multiple discoveries are in fact very common in science. ... Developments
> in related fields with different motivation help one to understand a difficult
> problem better. Since these developments are public knowledge, many scholars
> can take advantage of them. It is pleasant to the ego to be first or among the
> first with a new discovery. However, in this case at least, the evidence is clear
> that the development of general equilibrium theory would have gone on quite
> as it did without me. (Kenneth J. Arrow)

> But until 1970, post–World War II inflation had been only weakly serially cor-
> related. This simple application of univariate optimal prediction theory let me
> conclude that Solow and Tobin's test could give false rejections of the natural
> unemployment rate hypothesis and also indicated a more appropriate test of
> cross-equation restrictions. After I had written my paper, I discovered that Bob
> Lucas had written a paper that also described how to test the natural unem-
> ployment rate hypothesis in a rational expectations equilibrium. (Thomas J.
> Sargent)

> Further work led to "Expectations and the Neutrality of Money," ... finally
> published in the *Journal of Economic Theory* in 1972. ... The paper contained
> a careful and explicit construction of a theoretical example of an economy in
> which the motives, opportunities, and information of every economic actor
> were unambiguously spelled out. Expectations were rational. In this setting, as
> in Friedman's AEA address, there was no long-run trade-off between employ-
> ment and inflation. Yet the model also implied the kind of correlations between
> employment and inflation that were then widely interpreted as hard evidence
> that such trade-offs did exist. I felt I understood for the first time both why
> Friedman and Phelps were right in arguing there was no long-run trade-off
> between unemployment and inflation and why econometric tests continued to
> reject this "natural rate" view.
>
> Working out this example took me to the limit of my technical skills and
> beyond: it was not easy reading, nor had it been easy writing. ... It is easy for
> me to see the influences of Phelps, Rapping, Prescott, and Cass in this paper,
> but the combination was new and striking: no one else was doing macroeco-
> nomics this way in 1970. The paper made my reputation. (Robert E. Lucas, Jr.)

> The question arises, was that book, *Micromotives and Macrobehavior,* game
> theory? If so, what makes it game theory? ... I didn't think so at the time—
> it just didn't occur to me—but there were hints in the Nobel Committee's
> remarks that the committee thought it was. And I see now that everything
> in that book had to do with individuals' adjustment to or anticipation of the
> choices of others, and with needs and opportunities for coordination, formal
> cooperation, or submission to direction or regulation.

I've now concluded that this is game theory. Game theory, I find (or choose to define), is very much about *situations*. What is prisoner's dilemma but a situation? The logic of choice is central to game theory, but what game theory—again, I'm thinking about the invention of matrices—is often critical for is identifying situations in which choice is somehow puzzling, problematic, or challenging, and in identifying how many distinct situations of a certain kind there may be. (Thomas C. Schelling)

The "lessons from the laureates" identified in this section provide considerable insight into the intellectual process through which ideas in economics, and no doubt other disciplines, develop and evolve. One cannot come away from these lectures without an appreciation for the critical role of teachers, the intellectual environment, the search for rigor and relevance, and the role of happenstance in the evolution of modern economic thought. Contained within these lessons is at least the suggestion that biography matters. It is to this topic that we turn.

Does Biography Matter?

Do the autobiographies presented at Trinity University since 1984 reveal anything of scientific significance? Would our understanding of the laureates' pathbreaking achievements be incomplete without these stories of their intellectual journeys, as told in their own words?

The phrase "as told in their own words" is important. For in the Trinity lecture series each author is the living subject, providing an oral history of his own "evolution as an economist." Of necessity, time constraints force the scholars to present their glimpses into the past in a much abbreviated form. What they choose to reveal or not reveal is of their own election. But in the case of autobiographical data, the voice and image of the living subject are before us in a way not possible in biographies written by others. There is a sense of immediacy in these personal histories that typically is not to be found in more impersonal narratives of their lives. It is likely that the more influential of these economists will inspire biographies written by others long after these subjects have passed from the scene. Absent direct contact with these laureates, the biographers will find it difficult to capture the uniquely idiosyncratic perspective that only autobiography can offer. For that reason, future biographers might find the Trinity lectures providing invaluable insights for their work.

When the lecture series was organized in 1984, it was thought that a larger purpose was to supply crucial source material for a theory of scientific discovery. After thirty years, it is fair to ask whether the rationale has been in any significant sense justified. Do these autobiographical accounts reveal a connection between an economist's life and his or her intellectual achievements?

Certainly the lectures make obvious some links between environment and subsequent intellectual development. The traumatic impact of the Great Depression led several future laureates to identify economics as their intellectual discipline of choice. But this evidence for the role of biography hardly suffices. After all, the most casual observation would lead one to expect that experience affects choices. Does the study of the lives of the laureates do nothing more than confirm what everybody knows? Or can we say something about the extent to which the very substance of their contributions is a reflection of the individual lives they have led?

The last question is complex and can be answered only through the careful study of the autobiographies themselves. In that way, we become observer-participants in the lives of the speakers, focusing not only on what they explicitly reveal but also on any inconsistencies and self-deceptions in their narratives. Yet in doing so, the authors of this afterword must assume the role of biographers themselves, as distinct from the autobiographersubjects of the lecture series. Autobiography is, of course, a subset of biography. Nevertheless, it forms a crucial part of the archive from which biographical data are drawn. The autobiographies provide valuable material from which we, as biographer-editors, try to reach a deeper understanding of the connection between the lives led and the pathbreaking work achieved. If we can accomplish this task, the larger purpose of the lecture series will have been realized.

In the introduction to this volume we asserted that "these autobiographical essays reveal psychological truths—perhaps hidden from the subjects themselves—that an especially perceptive reader will discern." The autobiographical elements give us some tantalizing glimpses into the imaginative and creative minds of these scholars, insights that only autobiography could provide. Below we offer some examples.

A link between autobiography and subsequent intellectual development is implicit in Christopher A. Sims's essay.

> My grandfather's two brothers eventually owned and ran garment factories. They were among the targets of the first large strike by the International Ladies Garment Workers Union. My grandfather worked in those factories. He never graduated from high school, but he went to free night classes and speeches at Cooper Union, a privately funded college. With no high school education, having had to work for a while, when he was twenty-one he went to Wisconsin and tried to get entry into the University of Wisconsin, where he

was told he could not be admitted without a high school diploma. In response, he submitted an essay about why he wanted to study with John R. Commons, who was at that time famous as an institutional economist. His essay gained Billy (as my grandfather was by then known) admission to the University of Wisconsin. He went on to earn a Ph.D. from Columbia University, was a member of the first National Labor Relations Board under FDR, and then worked with the National Mediation Service, helping settle strikes and avert strikes in cooling-off periods.

He had seven children with his wife, Emily, who was not an immigrant. Her ancestry went back to the *Mayflower*. They were a lively and challenging bunch of uncles and aunts. One became president of the American Political Science Association; one was an economist, my Uncle Mark, who was one of the main intellectual influences on me as a teenager; one was an uncle whom I never knew and who died during training with the Naval Air Corps in World War II, and one was my mother, Ruth. Perhaps her most prominent public achievement was being elected first selectman of Greenwich, Connecticut, the first Democrat in many years and the first woman ever to hold that position.

It seems to me this family history holds some lessons for thinking about our country today. We are a country of immigrants, and it is one of our great strengths. We should expect that the immigrants who are coming to us today, even the ones who do not seem "high quality," are likely over time to make great contributions. (Christopher A. Sims)

Joseph Stiglitz observes the impact on his thinking of the midwestern locale of his childhood and the guiding principles learned from his parents.

My upbringing and early schooling were also very important. I grew up in the steel town of Gary, Indiana, on the southern shores of Lake Michigan. Gary and the upper Midwest in general were in much better economic shape during my childhood than they are now, but it was still not the kind of background that would normally be thought of as an advantage for a future academic. For my intellectual development, however, it was extremely formative, in several senses. Gary was founded in 1906. A hundred years later it is in deep decline. Its course essentially traced that of the industrial period of America. No one growing up in this town—emblematic of the rise and fall of industrialization in America—could believe that markets were an unmixed blessing. I saw the darker side—and darker not only because of the pollution (which was often invisible) but also because of the obvious economic and social costs: periodic unemployment, labor strife as workers struggled to get a fair share of the benefits that increasing productivity was bringing to the country, rampant discrimination, and urban decay. ...

I also owe to my parents (my father in particular) my ability to serve in government. A problem for many wanting to serve in the Clinton administration was that, when they were vetted, it would turn out they hadn't paid Social Security taxes on their household help. When I was growing up, my father told me that you should always pay Social Security taxes for anybody who works for you, because many of these people were poor people and particularly in need of help in their retirement. That's why we have the Social Security Administration. So he was one of the generation for whom Social Security (which started in the mid-1930s) was very important. Today, Social Security benefits are too often taken for granted.

My father believed that one should pay the Social Security taxes for one's employees not just because it was the law but also because it was the right thing to do. So I had done so for those who had worked for me—and was able to surmount this hurdle, which had proved an obstacle for so many others. (Joseph E. Stiglitz)

Thomas Schelling is widely recognized for developing the idea of a focal point (sometimes called a Schelling point). Kenneth Boulding inspired the development of the concept.

Again, I happened to run into Kenneth Boulding outside the Yale Cooperative Store in New Haven one afternoon. ... I told Ken that there was one topic I'd wanted to include in the article that I couldn't get a grip on, and I tried to express what it was. I couldn't be explicit or else I'd have been able to deal with it in the article. Boulding said something to me—I've never been able to reconstruct what it was—that clicked in my brain and revealed what it was I was trying to formulate. Just one sentence on a sidewalk in New Haven and I had the grasp I needed. His suggestion—actually it wasn't a suggestion, just a hint of some kind—led me to the idea of a "focal point," and the concept of tacit bargaining and its influence on explicit bargaining. (Thomas C. Schelling)

Vernon L. Smith's essay focuses on the lessons learned from his childhood experiences in Kansas. In this passage, he contrasts the vibrancy of city life, characterized by impersonal exchange, with an earlier farm life and personal exchange.

In 1934, my father returned to the Bridgeport Machine Company [in Wichita] for alternate-week half-time work and subsequently full-time work. This was fortuitous, as we lost "ownership" of the farm to the mortgage bank. ... We were returning from the farm world of personal exchange through the trading of favors to a world of impersonal exchange through markets. More, but far from all, of our needs would be met by store-bought goods, and that world would gradually be emerging, reinvigorated, from the Great Depression. (Vernon L. Smith)

Another example linking autobiography and one's intellectual approach is that of Milton Friedman. Yet here we attempt to draw a perhaps unconscious link that the author has not drawn. Friedman made it respectable for economists to question the efficacy of Keynesian policy; he resurrected the quantity theory of money and placed in on a secure footing; and he championed the private market economy at a time when intellectuals who did so were often subjected to ostracism in respectable academic circles. Few would doubt that we are all richer for his having become an economist. But why did he enter graduate school in economics? Initially, Friedman had planned to choose mathematics because he liked the subject. The Great Depression was under way, though, and Friedman was intrigued by what he called "the paradox of great need on the one hand and unused resources on the other." Moreover, making the decision process more difficult, he had offers of financial aid from two universities—one for the study of mathematics at Brown, and the other to study economics at Chicago. The final decision came down almost to the toss of a coin. Economics and the puzzle of the Great Depression won out. In his autobiographical lecture he attempts to explain his choice. To do so he quotes Robert Frost's famous poem, "The Road Less Traveled":

> Two roads diverged in a yellow wood,
> And sorry I could not travel both
> I took the one less traveled by.
> And that has made all the difference. (1–2, 19–20)

And yet reference to the Frost poem does not seem appropriate in his case. During the Great Depression, when Friedman entered college, economics was not the road "less traveled by." To the contrary, it was among the most popular of majors. He said he chose economics because of its relevance to the issues of the day, as did so many others of his generation. But this leaves us with a mystery. What is the relevance of Frost's poem? Why did he quote it?

Perhaps the choice of the poem reveals something about Friedman that was hidden from him when he quoted its words. Even if entering economics during the Great Depression was not really taking the road less traveled, nevertheless Friedman's subsequent career persistently took him along untrampled pathways *within economics*. Was this a conscious decision? For in his attempt to answer questions posed by the Great Depression, Friedman stood apart and almost alone. He rejected the Keynesian solutions that the overwhelming majority of the profession had come to accept. Friedman lived long enough to see many of his ideas become the consensus view of a younger generation of economists. Because he was different, he attracted attention: his persuasive powers, style, and charisma did the rest. For Friedman, the road less traveled indeed "made all the difference."

From the other side of the spectrum of political economy, another economist, Joseph E. Stiglitz, also draws inspiration from the same Robert Frost poem in pondering his choice of a career in economics:

As I think about that spring afternoon when I went for a walk in a New England forest and decided to become an economist rather than a physicist, I am reminded of a Robert Frost poem about two roads that diverged in a yellow wood. I wonder what might have happened had I taken the other road. (Joseph E. Stiglitz)

In the end, the case for biography generally, and autobiography in particular, is a strong one. To believe that biography is *essential* for understanding economics and the evolution of economic ideas admittedly requires a leap of faith. We simply are unable to meaningfully compare the current state of economic science to what might have existed under some reasonable counterfactual. That being said, the thirty-two lectures in this volume provide strong evidence that biography matters. We have seen how the most important developments in modern economics did not spring out of the air randomly but were intimately related to the laureates' backgrounds, intellectual environments, interactions with teachers and colleagues, desire for relevance and rigor, and competition in the marketplace for ideas. For individual laureates, the road traveled was sometimes the result of happenstance and sometimes not. Following the laureates on their intellectual journeys not only makes for fascinating reading but also enriches our understanding of the development of contemporary economic thought.

Printed in the United States
by Baker & Taylor Publisher Services